GREATER TUNIS
AND CAP BON
PENINSULA

TUNIS

Sousse

Cairouan

El-Jem

THE
SAHEL

Sfax

Gabes

JERBA AND THE
MEDENINE AREA

• Medenine

**GREATER TUNIS AND
CAP BON PENINSULA**
Pages 90–121

THE SAHEL
Pages 144–173

**JERBA AND THE
MEDENINE
AREA**
Pages 174–189

EYEWITNESS TRAVEL

TUNISIA

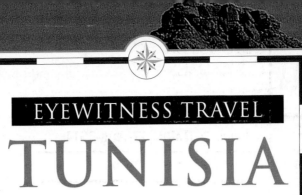

EYEWITNESS TRAVEL
TUNISIA

ELŻBIETA AND ANDRZEJ LISOWSCY

DK

LONDON, NEW YORK,
MELBOURNE, MUNICH AND DELHI
www.dk.com

PRODUCED BY Wydawnictwo Wiedza i Życie, Warsaw

SENIOR GRAPHIC DESIGNER Paweł Pasternak
EDITORS Robert G. Pasieczny,
Joanna Egert-Romanowska, Agnieszka Majle
AUTHORS Andrzej and Elżbieta Lisowscy
GRAPHIC DESIGN Paweł Kamiński, Piotr Kiedrowski

CARTOGRAPHERS Magdalena Polak, Olaf Rodowald
PHOTOGRAPHERS Artur Pawłowski,
Nicolas Fauque, Krzysztof Kur
ILLUSTRATORS Bohdan Wróblewski,
Michał Burkiewicz, Paweł Marczak
CONTRIBUTORS MaDar sc
and Sabina Kocieszczenko

For Dorling Kindersley

TRANSLATOR Magda Hannay
EDITOR Matthew Tanner
SENIOR DTP DESIGNER Jason Little
PRODUCTION CONTROLLER Rita Sinha

Reproduced by Colourscan, Singapore
Printed and bound in by L-Rex Printing Company Ltd., China

First published in Great Britain in 2005
by Dorling Kindersley Limited, 80 Strand, London, WC2R 0RL

11 12 13 14 10 9 8 7 6 5 4 3 2 1

Reprinted with revisions 2008, 2011

Copyright © 2005, 2011 Dorling Kindersley, London
A Penguin Company

ISBN: 978-1-40536-075-3

FLOORS ARE REFERRED TO THROUGHOUT IN ACCORDANCE WITH BRITISH
USAGE; IE THE "FIRST FLOOR" IS THE FLOOR ABOVE GROUND LEVEL.

Front cover image: Bourguiba Mausoleum, Monastir

MIX
Paper from
responsible sources
FSC   FSC™ C018179
www.fsc.org

◁ **Mosque in Chenini – a town built on rocky terraces**

CONTENTS

**Ruins of a Roman temple on the
capitol hill in Dougga**

INTRODUCING
TUNISIA

**Comfortable tents for visitors in
Ksar Ghilane**

Tourist centre in Port el-Kantaoui

Vegetable stall at Menzel
Temime market

Fresh figs, grown in Tunisia since
ancient times *(see p268–9)*

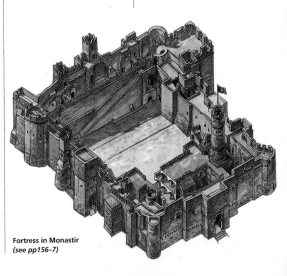
Fortress in Monastir
(see pp156–7)

HOW TO USE THIS GUIDE

This guide will help you to make the most of your visit to Tunisia. The first section, *Introducing Tunisia*, locates the country geographically and gives an outline of its history and culture. The following sections are devoted to the country's capital and various regions, and include the major towns, sights and attractions. Information on accommodation, restaurants, shopping, entertainment and activities can be found in the *Travellers' Needs* section, while the *Survival Guide* provides practical tips on everything you need to know, from money and language to getting around and seeking medical care.

TUNIS

The country's capital has its own section. All the sights are located and numbered on the area map. The main streets, post offices, hospitals and tourist information offices are also shown.

Sights at a Glance lists the sights by category.

A locator map shows the area of the Street-by-Street map in red.

1 Town Map
For easy reference the major sights are numbered and located on the town map.

A suggested route for a walk is marked with a red dotted line.

2 Street-by-Street Map
This shows the location of the main museums and sights within the town centre, including mosques and historic buildings.

3 Detailed Information
All the major sights in Tunis have a separate entry that includes details of addresses, opening hours and any admission charges.

1 Introduction
This section provides a brief overview of each region, describing its history, geographical features and cultural characteristics as well as its main attractions.

TUNISIA REGION BY REGION
In this guide Tunisia is divided into six regions, each of which has its own section. The most important cities, towns and villages, as well as other major attractions, are marked on the Regional Map.

2 Regional Map
The map shows the main road network and the overall topography of the region. All sights are numbered, and there is also information on public transport.

Colour coding, explained on the inside front cover, makes it easy to locate each region.

3 Regional Information
Towns, villages and tourist attractions are listed in numerical order, corresponding with the Regional Map. Each entry contains information on important sights. Major towns are given at least two pages.

The town map shows the main roads, stations, car parking areas and tourist offices.

4 Tunisia's Top Sights
At least two pages are devoted to each major sight. Historic buildings are dissected to reveal their interiors.

Stars indicate the main points of interest that no visitor should miss.

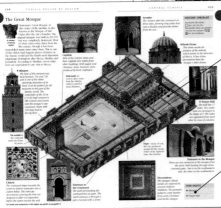

INTRODUCING
TUNISIA

DISCOVERING TUNISIA

People who arrive in Tunisia expecting only beach resorts may be surprised by the astonishing wealth of ancient remains in this relatively small North African nation. The landscape is also full of pleasant surprises with lush date gardens, vast olive groves and forest-covered

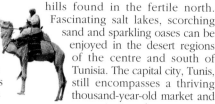
Camel-trekking in the Sahara

hills found in the fertile north. Fascinating salt lakes, scorching sand and sparkling oases can be enjoyed in the desert regions of the centre and south of Tunisia. The capital city, Tunis, still encompasses a thriving thousand-year-old market and an ancient medina as well as high-tech, luxury hotels.

Local goods for sale at a busy souk in Tunis's medina

TUNIS

- Ancient medina
- Monumental Great Mosque
- World-class Bardo Museum

Tunis is a captivating city. For over 1,000 years life in the capital has centred around the **medina** *(see pp68–9)*, with its maze of winding streets and the sights, sounds and smells of the vibrant souks (markets). Towering over its markets are the vast marble walls of the **Great Mosque** *(see pp70–71)*, which has been calling the Muslim community to prayer here since the 8th century.

Beyond the medina, the city's more cosmopolitan Ville Nouvelle reveals itself, especially along **Avenue Habib Bourguiba** *(see p86)* where French-style cafés and Art Nouveau architecture serve as a reminder of Tunisia's colonial past. The **Bardo Museum** *(see pp88–9)*, housed in an impressive 17th-century Husseinite palace,

holds a priceless collection of Roman mosaics, Greek statuary and Islamic art.

GREATER TUNIS AND CAP BON PENINSULA

- Sparkling Sidi Bou Saïd
- Historic majesty of Carthage
- Beaches at Hammamet

Some of the country's best attractions are within easy reach of Tunis. The smart coastal village of **Sidi Bou Saïd** *(see pp96–8)*, with its dazzling whitewashed houses and vivid blue doors and shutters, has long attracted artists. Today many visitors come to explore its shops, galleries and cafés.

The extensive ruins at Carthage *(see pp102–6)*, including the 2nd-century Antonine Baths, highlight Tunisia's role as a Phoenician, then Roman, outpost, while the country's biggest beach resort, **Hammamet** *(see pp118–20)*, is more representative of its modern appeal. Here, restaurants, bars

and hotels cluster around the wide, well-groomed beaches. Nearby at **Nabeul** *(see pp112–17)*, today's visitors ensure that centuries-old ceramic traditions survive.

Exploring the Cap Bon Peninsula reveals not only the archaeological remains of the Punic settlement at **Kerkouane** *(see pp110–11)* but also fertile vineyards and olive groves.

NORTHERN TUNISIA

- Wildlife at Ichkeul National Park
- Charming harbour towns
- Exquisite Roman mosaics

From the rugged shores of the Mediterranean to the forested **Khroumirie Mountains** *(see p130)*, the landscape of Northern Tunisia is surprisingly varied. The freshwater lake at the UNESCO World Heritage Site, **Ichkeul National Park** *(see pp136–7)*, offers sanctuary to flocks of migrating birds such as geese and flamingoes, while the marshes around it provide a

The crisp colours of Sidi Bou Saïd

◁ Decorative Tunisian tiles

permanent home for a diversity of wildlife.

The natural harbour of **Tabarka** *(see p126)* is flanked by a coral reef teeming with marine life, while the pretty town is backed by pine and cork oak forests. Straddling the entrance to its lake, the picturesque coastal town and port of **Bizerte** *(see pp140–41)* lies on the northern tip of Africa. Inland at **Bulla Regia** *(see pp132–3)*, Roman life is made vivid by the intricate mosaics which are still *in situ* in subterranean villas here.

Island beach life on the northeast coast of Jerba

Cave dwellings in the Berber village of Matmata in the Sahel

THE SAHEL

- **Classic resort towns**
- **The ancient amphitheatre at El-Jem**
- **Mahdia's unspoilt port**

Tunisia's eastern coastline is blessed with unhurried resorts such as **Sfax** *(see pp164–9)*, **Sousse** *(see pp150–53)* and **Monastir** *(see pp154–9)*, where it's possible to combine a hedonistic beach life with an appreciation of Tunisia's traditions by way of ancient mosques and defensive ribats (fortresses).

Film buffs flock to the troglodyte town of **Matmata** *(see p172)* which appeared in the film *Star Wars*, while the magnificent Roman amphitheatre at **El-Jem** *(see p163)* and the medieval town and unspoiled port of **Mahdia** *(see pp160–62)* bear testament to Tunisia's illustrious heritage.

JERBA AND THE MEDENINE AREA

- **Jerba's golden beaches**
- **Bustling Houmt-Souk**
- **Berber villages around Medenine**

A patchwork of citrus, palm and olive groves makes Jerba, the largest island off the North African coast, a green jewel in an azure sea. The island's northeastern fringe of wide, sandy beaches extends from **Ras Remel** *(see p181)*, where pink flamingoes bask in the mild climate all year round.

Jerba's capital and ancient trading post, **Houmt Souk** *(see pp178–9)*, is now largely focused on tourism but still enjoys a brisk trade in the island's produce, including ceramics from **Guellala** *(see p182)*. On the mainland, ancient Berber villages can be visited around the **Medenine** *(see p186)* area.

SOUTHERN TUNISIA

- **Camel trekking in the Sahara**
- **Shimmering salt lake**
- **Lush mountain oases**

The true sands of the **Sahara** *(see pp200–201)* start to emerge at **Douz** *(see p198)*, which is the best starting point for camel-trekking trips across the dunes. Close by, the vast salt lake known as **Chott el-Jerid** *(see p208)* is a dream-like landscape of sparkling salt crystals and shimmering mirages. At its northern end stands the oasis of **Tozeur** *(see p208)* with its 3,000 palm

trees producing the country's finest dates. Another notable oasis is the rocky **Midès** *(see p211)*, which sustains lush green fruit trees.

CENTRAL TUNISIA

- **Impressive Roman cities**
- **Holy city of Kairouan**
- **Striking Jugartha's Table**

The central region of Tunisia holds some of its most impressive sights. Prime among these are the evocative remains of the preserved cities of Roman **Dougga** *(see pp228–9)* and **Sbeïtla** *(see pp218–19)*.

The ancient medina of **Kairouan** *(see pp234–41)* is the fourth-holiest city in Islam. First among its many attractions is the **Great Mosque** *(see pp238–9)*, a revered place of pilgrimage.

Further west lie the stark, flat-topped rock formation known as **Jugurtha's Table** *(see p221)*, and the thickly-forested slopes of **Chambi National Park** *(see p227)*.

Upright columns and tiered seating at Dougga's Roman theatre

Putting Tunisia on the Map

Mediterranean Sea

The northernmost point of the African continent, Tunisia is sandwiched between Algeria to the west and Libya to the east. Some 1,300 km (800 miles) of Mediterranean coastline mark the country's eastern and northern boundaries. Covering an area of 163,610 sq km (63,170 sq miles), Tunisia measures 150 km (93 miles) from east to west. It has a wide diversity of landscapes, ranging from its northern mountainous region to the fertile Medjerda Valley and, in the south, a region of desert.

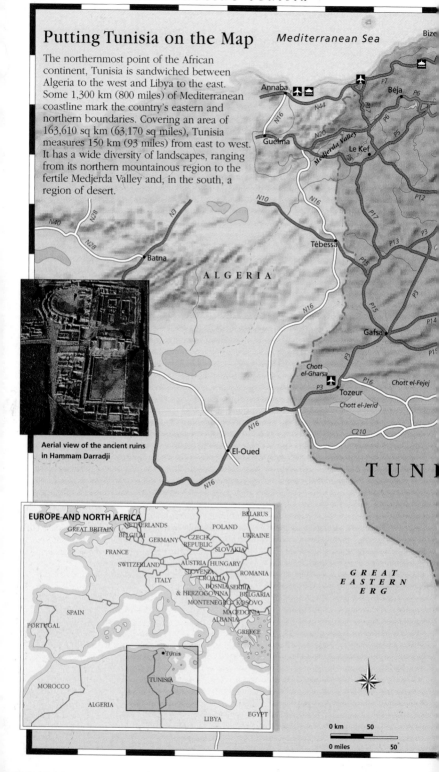

Aerial view of the ancient ruins in Hammam Darradji

Bize

Annaba

Béja

P7

P6

N16

N44

Guelma

N20

Le Kef

Medjerda Valley

P5

P17

N10

N16

Tébessa

P12

Batna

ALGERIA

N28

N40

N3

P13

P3

N16

P15

P3

Gafsa

P14

Chott
el-Gharsa

P3

P16

Chott el-Fejej

P15

Tozeur

Chott el-Jerid

N16

C210

El-Oued

N16

TUNI

EUROPE AND NORTH AFRICA

BELARUS

GREAT BRITAIN   NETHERLANDS   POLAND

BELGIUM   GERMANY   UKRAINE

CZECH
REPUBLIC   SLOVAKIA

FRANCE

SWITZERLAND   AUSTRIA   HUNGARY

SLOVENIA   ROMANIA

ITALY   CROATIA

BOSNIA   SERBIA

& HERZOGOVINA   BULGARIA

MONTENEGRO   KOSOVO

MACEDONIA

SPAIN   ALBANIA

PORTUGAL   GREECE

Tunis

MOROCCO   TUNISIA

ALGERIA   EGYPT

LIBYA

GREAT
EASTERN
ERG

| 0 km | 50 |
| 0 miles | 50 |

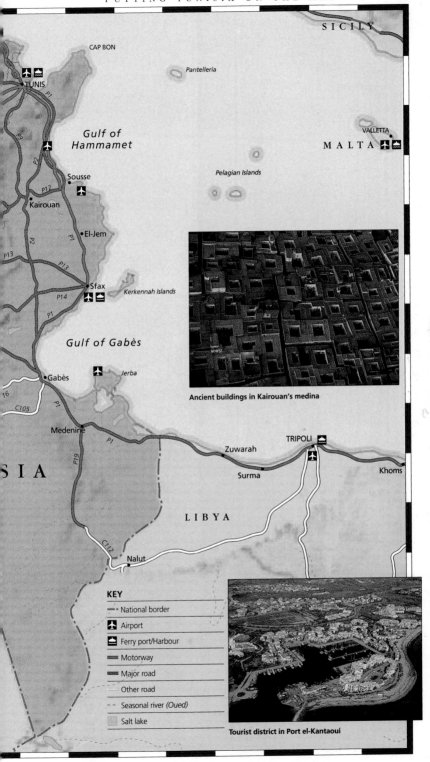

SICILY

CAP BON

Pantelleria

TUNIS

VALLETTA

Gulf of
Hammamet

MALTA

Pelagian Islands

Sousse

Kairouan

•El-Jem

P13

Sfax

Kerkennah Islands

Gulf of Gabès

Ancient buildings in Kairouan's medina

•Gabès

Jerba

C105

Medenine

TRIPOLI

Zuwarah

Khoms

Surma

SIA

LIBYA

Nalut

KEY

— National border

Airport

Ferry port/Harbour

Motorway

Major road

Other road

Seasonal river *(Oued)*

Salt lake

Tourist district in Port el-Kantaoui

A PORTRAIT OF TUNISIA

Tunisia is a visitor-friendly destination with many attractions, including the walled medinas of Tunis and Sousse, historic remains at Bulla Regia and Dougga, and Jerba's glorious beaches. For the more adventurous, there is much to explore including ancient troglodyte villages, the glimmering Chott el-Jerid salt flats and the vast expanse of the Sahara Desert.

The history of Tunisia has been shaped by the Phoenicians, Romans, Turks, Berbers and – above all – the Arabs. The mountainous north acts as the country's garden, providing cereals, vegetables and fruit. This area has many Phoenician and Roman remains, and includes the once-mighty Carthage. In contrast to the fertile north, the yellow-red desert in the south is almost completely deprived of rain. Here, Tozeur and Nefta are fascinating towns that have grown up around desert oases. Nefta, surrounded by desert sands, once provided a refuge for Muslim mystics, and now produces the best dates in

A tombstone from Carthage

Tunisia. Even further south there is nothing but desert – an endless sea of hot sand. Many visitors flock to "blue" Tunisia, to enjoy the warm waters and beaches of Hammamet, Sousse and Jerba, but the country has much more to offer.

Tunisia's colourful past has left it rich in historical remains. These include the sites of Phoenician and Roman Carthage, the ruins of the Punic town of Kerkouane, the Roman remains at Dougga, the amphitheatre at El-Jem, the holy city of Kairouan and the magnificent medinas of Tunis and Sousse where Islamic architecture dating back more than 1,000 years can be seen.

Green fields and olive groves around Testour

◁ **Women walking by the medina wall in Kairouan**

Cobbler in a souk in Tozeur

SOCIETY

Tunisia has a population of more than 10 million and the vast majority of the country's inhabitants, some 98 per cent, is of Arab stock. Nearly all are Muslim, though there is a tiny percentage of Jews and Christians. The original Berbers make up a small part of the population and are found mainly in the south of the country.

Tunisian society is young; the average age is 26 and slightly over one quarter of the population is under the age of 15. A family planning policy introduced in the 1960s has brought about a steady fall in the birth rate and the model of the Tunisian family has gradually changed since independence. It is now becoming common for Tunisian

Berber dressed in traditional *djellaba* and turban

An indoor vegetable stall

women to go out to work. As a result of factors such as these, families living in the major towns and cities are generally smaller in size than those in the villages.

Tunisia has a modern and well-developed education system; primary education is compulsory and a great deal of importance is attached to learning foreign languages in school. Nearly three-quarters of the population is literate.

CULTURE AND TRADITIONS

Tunisia's busy tourist areas show many signs of western influence, including fast food, modern pop music and the latest fashions. Elsewhere, traditional life has developed at a gentler pace and the mosque and bathhouse (hammam) are still important parts of everyday life. Tunisian culture has evolved over the generations through an intermingling of strands from both European and Arab traditions. Successive cultures, rather than simply supplanting their predecessors, blended with them to produce a wonderfully diverse social and cultural melting pot. This blend is most clearly manifested in Tunisian music, which displays Berber and Andalusian influences (these also have echoes in modern Tunisian pop music).

Tunisian literature is mainly associated with Arabic writing. In its early days, it consisted primarily of theological and historic works. In the 20th century, however, there was an increase in the popularity of Tunisian writers who expressed themselves in French. The most famous modern Tunisian writer is Abu el-Kacem el-Chabbi (1909–34), a native of Tozeur, whose poem "Will to Live" is taught to schoolchildren throughout the Arab world.

Though open to foreign ideas, Tunisian society is very protective of its traditions. The *hijab* (veil or headscarf) is often seen on the streets of Tunisia, though it is more common in rural areas. Muslim festivals are celebrated with due ceremony in Tunisia, particularly two feasts known as Aïd el-Adha and Aïd el-Fitr *(see p39)*. Ramadan – the month of fasting from sunrise to sunset – is strictly observed. As with most Islamic countries, family is particularly important in Tunisian society and relatives are expected to celebrate festivities together, as well as help one another.

Modern Tunisian painting by Ali ben Salem

An Early Christian relief

THE ARTS

Pottery and ceramic arts have flourished since Roman times and have been enriched by Andalusian and Italian influences. Ancient Tunisian mosaics are justly famous and a great many have been found, some of which date back to the 2nd century AD. Most places of any size in 3rd-century Tunisia had a mosaic workshop which produced wonderfully colourful designs with a distinctive African influence including scenes of hunting and wildlife, which were used mainly as floor decorations. From these early beginnings, mosaics have become one of the main decorative elements of Tunisian architecture.

Many public buildings, including hammams, kasbahs and, above all, mosques, are works of art in their own right. All are based on Islamic styles and motifs and generally include elaborately decorated doorways, bright colours and striking minarets.

Influenced by the French and Italians, painting has become a popular art form in Tunisia. The year 1949 marked the birth of the most famous Tunisian school of painting – the École de Tunis. Its pioneers combined new trends in art with scenes from everyday life, and introduced modern art to Tunisia. Yahia Turki, an early member of this school, is considered by

Stonemason at work

many to be the father of modern Tunisian painting. The traditional Arab-style music that visitors are likely to hear is *malouf* (which means "normal"). It was first introduced in the 15th century by refugees from Andalusia. Using a mixture of western and Arab instruments, it is a lively blend of Hispanic and Arabic folk music.

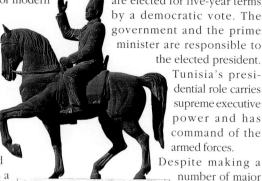

Equestrian statue of Bourguiba

are elected for five-year terms by a democratic vote. The government and the prime minister are responsible to the elected president. Tunisia's presidential role carries supreme executive power and has command of the armed forces.

Despite making a number of major reforms, Habib Bourguiba eventually lost touch with his people and the Arab world in general and in 1987 he was replaced by his Interior Minister Zine el-Abidine Ben Ali. This change marked a turning point in the history of modern Tunisia. Ben Ali abolished life presidencies and introduced a multi-party system. At the time of going to press, there have been major political changes in Tunisia. Weeks of public protest against government corruption and autocracy led to Ben Ali dissolving the government and fleeing the country in January 2011. This resulted in a new president and an interim government that has pledged to rid the country of corrup-

MODERN-DAY POLITICS

Tunisia is a constitutional republic and won its independence from France on 20 March 1956 with Habib Bourguiba, a French-educated lawyer, as its first prime minister and then its president. Three years later, Tunisia's assembly passed a constitution that put a lot of power in the hands of the president and gave the country a legal system based on a mixture of French civil law and Islamic law. Under this constitution, which has undergone a series of reforms over the years, the members of the National Assembly

Posters of President Ben Ali, once seen on the streets of Nabeul

Women on the beach in La Goulette

WOMEN IN TUNISIA

Thanks in large part to the influence of Tunisia's former president, Habib Bourguiba, the freedom allowed to Tunisian women is greater than in most Muslim countries. In 1956 he outlawed such practices as polygamy and divorce by renunciation and banned the *hijab* (veil) from schools as part of an (unsuccessful) campaign to phase it out altogether.

Women in Tunisia have far more opportunities to work than in many Muslim countries and these days it is not unusual for women to be doctors, lawyers and airline pilots. Since 1961, as a result of the family planning policy, pharmacies have begun to sell methods of contraception. The signing of further conventions during the 1980s ensured women's rights to education, and to equal pay. What this adds up to is that the problems faced by Tunisian women are not so different from those faced by women in the West.

In the villages, however, where many traditional norms still apply, the situation can be somewhat different. If in work, it is not unusual for women to

Berber woman in traditional attire

tion. The process is very slow, but democratic elections are scheduled to take place before the end of 2011. Political parties will be able to stand in opposition to the government and many people in exile overseas have returned to take part in the formation of a new political system.

During the 1990 Gulf War public opinion in Tunisia was strongly behind the former Iraqi leader Saddam Hussein. Ben Ali condemned Iraq for its invasion of Kuwait but felt unable to fully support the United States' action. Tunisia also withheld its support during the Iraq conflict that began in 2003.

Tunisia has played an important role in North African affairs, as well as mediating in the Israeli-Palestinian conflict. It exerted a major influence in promoting regional economic co-operation. Tunisia's influence in the region is indicated by the fact that the protests through December 2010 and into the new year sparked similar unrest in Egypt, Jordan, Algeria Yemen and Libya.

hand over all of their pay directly to their husbands or (if unmarried) save their wages towards a dowry. And even though many women can be seen socializing in some of the European-style cafés, they are a less common sight in traditional

The old and new: women in the street in Bizerte

Tunisian cafés, which are normally occupied by pipe-smoking, card-playing men. But overall, the situation of women has improved vastly since the country gained independence.

ECONOMY

Tunisia's economy is based on agriculture, power generation, tourism and the service industry. Tunisia is the world's largest producer of dates (a fact not reflected in its export figures) and the fourth largest producer of olive oil. Mining also plays an important part in the country's economy and Tunisia is among the world's leading producers of phosphates.

Tunisian craftsmen, important contributors to the economy

Agricultural land occupies nearly half of the country's total area. The main crops include cereals, olives, tomatoes, oranges, dates, pomegranates, grapes and sugar cane. The agricultural sector has declined in the last few years, however, and Tunisia now imports 40 per cent of its food.

The country's natural resources include phosphate rock, oil and natural gas (in the south), as well as iron, lead and zinc ores.

The processing of olive oil, petro-chemicals and ceramics account for a significant portion of the country's economy, as does the production of handicrafts (including carpets, jewellery and tourist souvenirs). Fishing brings in additional income and is based mainly on tuna, sardines and mackerel.

By far the largest share of Tunisia's national revenue comes from the textile industry with most exports going to France, the USA, Italy and Germany. In 1995 Tunisia signed an agreement with the EU that opened up new markets. Under this agreement, trade tariffs should one day be dropped, leading to free trade between Tunisia and the EU. Following Ben Ali's departure, and with the promise of a new democratic government from the end of 2011, it is possible that foreign investment and private enterprise could now flourish within Tunisia.

An oil well, producing one of Tunisia's natural resources

TOURISM

Tourism is a major source of the country's income. Since 1998, Tunisia has allocated over 300 million dinars a year to developing its tourism infrastructure. The country now attracts some five million visitors annually, generating nearly $2 billion a year for the economy. During the political protests at the end of 2010 and into 2011, many governments advised against travel to Tunisia. However, as the situation stabilises, the tourist industry is expected to make a good recovery.

A covered souk in Tunis – popular with both locals and tourists

The country's 1,300 km (800 miles) of coastline and the coral reef around Tabarka makes Tunisia a good destination for those who want a beach holiday. The many historic sites are also a big draw, of course, especially for holidaymakers interested in ancient history. For sports lovers, there are the championship-quality golf courses, and the many opportunities for hiking, horse riding, camel-trekking, fishing and diving.

A decorated jar from Nabeul

To cope with the demand, tourist zones *(zones touristiques)* have been created to give visitors an added feeling of safety and comfort within holiday villages. These offer a high standard of accommodation, lush surroundings, easy access to the beaches, large swimming pool complexes, an easy-going atmosphere and lively entertainment. Their major disadvantage, however, is that they offer little of the culture and everyday life of Tunisia.

Tourism has also been boosted by the many film-makers who have used the country's stunning landscape and architecture in the making of films such as *Star Wars (see pp34–5)*.

A popular beach in the tourist resort of Tabarka

Tunisia's Landscape and Wildlife

Seen from the air, Tunisia appears as a golden-brown land interwoven with green and blue. The mountainous north is overgrown with oak forests and heather. The Medjerda Valley, irrigated by Tunisia's largest permanent river, is used for growing corn and is one of Tunisia's most fertile regions. The craggy northern coast is extraordinarily picturesque, while the eastern shores, with their sandy beaches, are home to most of Tunisia's hotels and coastal resorts. In contrast to the fertile north, Tunisia's flat, southern desert region is almost totally devoid of rain.

Desert area, sparsely covered with palms, at the foot of the mountains near Toujane

SAHARA DESERT

Tunisia's desert covers the southern tip of the country. A sea of sand *(erg)*, it is formed of the eastern extremity of the Great Eastern Erg (or "Grand Erg Oriental") which extends over a large part of eastern Algeria. This inhospitable area is more commonly known as the Sahara Desert. Parts of it can go for years without rain and the rainfall in this region never exceeds 50 mm (1.96 inches) per year.

The fennec, *a desert fox with large ears, is regarded as the most voracious predatory mammal of the Sahara. It hunts at night, feeding on beetles, rodents and birds' eggs. During the day it hides in cool burrows.*

Rocky desert *occupies the large central region of the country. It is overgrown with spiky esparto grass, which is used in the production of high-quality paper.*

Sahara *in the classical Arabic language means "empty area". Later, it also began to mean an area devoid of water – a desert. You can drive for many miles here and not see a single plant.*

Chott el-Jerid – *this dry salty lake bed can turn into a boggy morass covered by shallow pools of water that take on a variety of bright colours.*

OUED

A *oued* (pronouced "wed") is a riverbed. Parched during the dry season, it fills with water with the arrival of the rains. Often with craggy banks, it can run for many miles. The waters may swell suddenly – a single downpour is enough to flood a *oued* in a flash, with the turbulent flow gouging out the valley and altering the shape of the bed. Following rain, the banks of the *oued* burst forth with vegetation.

Roman bridge over a *oued*, near Sbeïtla

THE COAST

Tunisia has two types of coastline: rocky in the north and, in the east, sandy shores that gently descend towards the Mediterranean Sea. The country's long stretch of coast is extended by marshland and seasonal lakes that adjoin the sea. Tunisia has plenty of sandy beaches. These are found mainly on the east coast, in the regions of Hammamet, Gabès, Jerba, and on the Kerkennah Islands, as well as in the northeast – along the Gulf of Tunis and between Bizerte and El-Haouaria. The extraordinarily picturesque north coast, stretching from Bizerte into Algeria, has high rugged cliffs. Coral reefs, rich in marine life, can be found here that are unique to this part of the Mediterranean.

Sandy beaches, *used mainly by visitors, are found to the east. Here there are tourist zones (zones touristiques), which have facilities and entertainment laid on. The beaches on Tunisia's north coast around Tabarka are far less frequently visited.*

The craggy coastline *around El-Haouaria dropping steeply into the sea creates small picturesque coves.*

Oyster-catchers *are one of many species of wading bird found along the sandy regions of the coast.*

Rocks *in Tabarka display some of the most striking geological formations found along the north coast.*

CENTRAL REGIONS

The landscape of the interior is somewhat harsh, its colours faded. To the north is the Tell region, separated from the Tunisian Atlas range of mountains by the Medjerda River. Tell forms the western end of the Atlas range that runs east from Morocco. Its western section comprises agricultural land. The southern part of the central region has two salt lakes – Chott el-Jerid and Chott el-Gharsa – which are dry for much of the year.

Mountain oases *and palm oases are features of the Tunisian landscape. The roads leading to them are often extremely picturesque and wind among volcanic rocks.*

The northwestern *and western regions are among the greenest corners of Tunisia, with extensive fields and wooded hills.*

Prickly pear *(called* hindi *in Arabic), cultivated in the western region of Tunisia, is also a popular hedge plant. It grows to a height of 7 m (23 ft), forming an impenetrable barrier.*

Olive groves *are found everywhere in Tunisia. Olives, planted here in even rows, are an important part of Tunisia's economy.*

Tunisian Architecture

Alongside the obvious presence of Islam, Tunisian architecture includes a variety of influences. The earliest of these can be seen in the Roman and Punic remains that are scattered throughout the northern regions and along the coast. Much later, the colonial era brought with it new civic styles including the French Ville Nouvelle with wide streets, public parks and houses with elaborate street-facing façades. Ancient Berber architecture is most common in the south of the country where the troglodyte pit houses and *ksour* (fortified granaries) reveal a way of life that has changed little over the centuries.

Makthar – the remains of one of many Roman towns in Tunisia

SOUTHERN ARCHITECTURE

Some Berbers of southern Tunisia lived partly underground. Their ancient homes, dug down into circular pits, maintained the same temperature of about 17° C (63° F) throughout the year. This building tradition goes back many hundreds of years, but the most famous homes of this type, found in Matmata, date from the 19th century. A "pit house" was inhabited by just one family, with the number of rooms being appropriate to the family's size and wealth.

The courtyard (houch) *in the shape of a giant well is accessed through a descending tunnel. The living quarters, well away from the sun's rays, are dug into its walls, on one or two levels.*

The entrance *and inner walls are white. Simple rooms have recesses and dug-out shelves for storing everyday items.*

PUNIC ARCHITECTURE

Punic architecture is associated mainly with Carthage, which was founded in 813 BC. Its most obvious feature is a distinct town layout, with houses built on slopes around a square. Another hallmark of this style is the horizontal and vertical arrangement of building stones, known as *opus africanum*. Coastal towns often had two harbours, northern and southern, which were used depending on the wind direction. The temples were built in the mountains, close to springs, trees and stones, which were seen as sacred.

Carthage *has many remains of Punic architecture, although they can be hard to spot amid the Roman ruins.*

Capitals *and other architectural details bear witness to the architectural skills of the Carthaginians.*

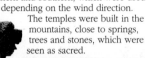

The Antonine Baths *is one of Carthage's most important Roman sites. What little remains gives visitors some idea of their sheer scale.*

ROMAN ARCHITECTURE

A typical Roman town was constructed on a chequered layout. At its heart was the forum, which was dominated by a temple (capitol) devoted to various deities. Everyday life concentrated around the market square. Entertainment was provided by the theatre, and the baths were used for relaxation and hygiene.

The Capitol *in Dougga was built to stand on the town's highest point.*

The theatre *was of equal importance as the capitol. Some could accommodate an audience of several thousand people.*

THE COLONIAL ERA

With the advent of the French protectorate in 1881, Tunisian towns acquired straight avenues, flanked by public buildings. The style of the day combined European and Islamic elements. European design incorporated arcades and horseshoe arches and the façades of elegant villas were further embellished with loggias and balconies adorned with beautiful wrought-iron grilles.

Tunis's Cathedral, *with its eclectic mix of forms and styles, is one of the few remaining churches from the colonial era.*

Buildings *in towns such as Tunis and Bizerte were designed in contemporary styles. Multi-storey hotels and apartment blocks often bore the signs of Modernism and Art Nouveau.*

Villa in Hammamet, *an early 20th-century Modernist house owned by George Sebastian.*

MODERN ARCHITECTURE

Initially, 20th-century Tunisian architecture was under the influence of Art Nouveau. The Art Deco style arrived during the 1920s and 30s, bringing with it more geometric ornamental patterns. The late 1990s marked a return to simpler, traditional forms.

Contemporary offices *in Tunisia can be an interesting blend of modern materials, such as smoked glass, and Islamic influences.*

The Hotel du Lac *in Tunis, built in the shape of an upturned pyramid, is one of the most interesting examples of modern architecture.*

Tourist zones, *seeking to amuse, often feature fairytale designs. Some hotels are built to resemble ancient palaces or Tunisian ksour (age-old Berber strongholds).*

Islamic Architecture

Tunisia has been under the influence of Islam since the 7th century and this is apparent in its architecture. The most striking example of this influence is the large number of mosques, with their distinctive minarets. Other Islamic buildings include medersas, *zaouias* (tombs) and the humble hammam or bathhouse. Islamic architecture is the result of many cultures and includes Roman, Moorish and Persian elements. However, from grand Aghlabid buildings to domestic courtyards, a number of common features run through it. These include the horseshoe arch, richly-coloured tiles forming swirling arabesques and the frequent use of carved plaster as a decorative element.

Elaborate doorways, a typical feature of Islamic architecture

MINARETS

Minarets (from the Arabic for lighthouse) are found at one corner of a mosque. According to tradition, the Prophet Mohammed intended to use a trumpet (as did the Jews) or a rattle to call the faithful to prayer but one of his disciples saw a mysterious apparition that revealed to him the words of a prayer. Mohammed instructed Bilal (the first muezzin), endowed with a powerful voice, to learn the words. Since then, five times a day, the muezzin's chant cuts through the daily bustle of Muslim towns and villages. There are two main styles of minarets found in Tunisia; the older one has a rectangular base, while the ones built on an octagonal plan were popularized by the Turks.

Dome on top of the minaret

Gallery, from which the muezzin calls the faithful to prayer

The minaret *in Kairouan dates from AD 730, and is older than most of the mosque it serves.*

The decorations *of some Tunisian mosques are very ornate; others are more austere.*

Octagonal minarets *are based on Turkish towers. Many Tunisian minarets are square all the way up.*

MOSQUES

The mosque or *masjid* ("a place of worship") is one of the main forms of Islamic architecture. The basic elements include a courtyard surrounded by columns, and a prayer hall. The design is thought to be based on the house that belonged to Mohammed in Medina which had an oblong courtyard with huts. This courtyard has become the prayer hall which faces toward Mecca. The hall is separated from the rest of the mosque by a step or balustrade.

Bourguiba Mosque *in Monastir is a modern building but has some traditional features.*

Mosques *were often surrounded by zaouias (tombs). These were used as burial grounds for Islamic holy men (marabouts) and serve as destinations for pilgrimages. One such complex can be found in Le Kef.*

ZAOUIAS

Zaouias are humble resting places for people who have dedicated their lives to Islam. Simple in design, they are usually whitewashed and less grand than mausoleums, and can be found dotted around the towns and villages of Tunisia. Initially the name was given to an isolated part of a mosque that was used as a gathering place for Muslim mystics, mainly ascetic Sufis. Following the death of its master, a *zaouia* often became a sanctuary that attracted pilgrims.

Zaouia *in Mahdia, situated outside the town beside a cemetery. The site is conducive to meditation. Zaouias are not only used as places of pilgrimage but often have a social function as well. They may be used to hold a weekly market, for instance.*

MEDERSAS

In the Middle Ages, a medersa was a law school, a type of Muslim university, and the main centre for promoting Sunni orthodoxy, Muslim law and theology. They generally included lecture halls and, as students traditionally lived there, boarding rooms. Designed along the same lines as a mosque, merdersas have an inner courtyard beyond the main entrance and also a prayer hall. The classrooms are generally located to the side of the courtyard. Most often found in the medina of large towns and cities, medersas can have incredibly elaborate decoration.

The courtyard of a medersa *is surrounded by arcades, much like a mosque. The shaded arcades sheltered visitors and provided a place for quiet contemplation.*

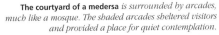

BAB

A *bab* is a door or gate that not only leads into a town but is also used to divide a town's areas into smaller quarters, creating a feeling of security, and guarding against unwelcome visitors. In the 20th century many of the gates disappeared, turning the private areas into public ones. But even now in Tunis or Kairouan, there are still gates that are centuries-old leading to private homes.

Bab Diwan *is one of the gates leading to the medina in Sfax.*

Medinas *were always surrounded by high walls. Entry was through a number of gates guarded by fortified towers or bastions.*

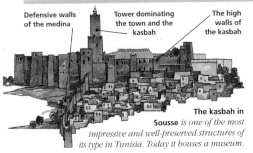

Defensive walls of the medina

Tower dominating the town and the kasbah

The high walls of the kasbah

The kasbah in Sousse *is one of the most impressive and well-preserved structures of its type in Tunisia. Today it houses a museum.*

KASBAH

The kasbah is a specific type of fortress palace. It was normally the residence of the local ruler but it also provided shelter for the local population. Kasbahs (or citadels) were generally built on hilltops, mountain slopes or near harbours. Their distinctive features include high walls and small windows. Some of the most beautiful examples have survived in Sousse, Le Kef and Tunis.

Islam in Tunisia

Islam reached Tunisia in the wake of the Arab conquest and began to spread as early as the second half of the 7th century. It rapidly became the dominant religion and, despite a period of colonial rule, remains so today. Islam is the state religion, though Tunisia's system of government is largely secular.

Decorative minaret

Islamic customs play a major role in people's lives and over 98 per cent of Tunisians profess adherence to the practices of Sunni Islam.

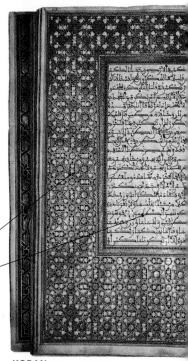

Wells *are used for ritual ablutions and are found in many mosques. For Muslims, prayers should be said in a state of cleanliness achieved through ritual cleansing.*

Before entering *the prayer hall it is obligatory for the faithful to remove their shoes. Similar to the practice of ritual washing, the aim is to ensure spiritual cleanliness.*

Pages of the religious books produced for many wealthy Muslims were often richly ornamented.

Koranic verses are written in a decorative script and are believed to be the literal word of God.

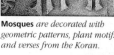

Mosques *are decorated with geometric patterns, plant motifs and verses from the Koran.*

Ceramic tiles *are a popular decorative element and often adorn mosques or other religious buildings such as tombs and medersas. Intricate designs can also often be seen in wealthy Tunisian homes.*

KORAN

The Koran, or Quran, is the holy book of Islam and was revealed by God to Mohammed with the angel Gabriel acting as an intermediary. Mohammed is believed to have been illiterate, and the first written texts of the Koran were compiled after the Prophet's death. The Koran consists of 114 *suras* (chapters), starting with the Fatiha, the longest, and finishing with the shortest. The first *sura* revealed to Mohammed is thought to be number 96. The Koran is in verse and it is not uncommon for Muslims to learn it by heart.

A Muslim *is a person who "submits to the will of God" (Islam means submission). Pious Muslims spend long hours studying the Koran, placing the book on a special folding support.*

Prayer *brings together crowds of the faithful, who gather in the mosque and courtyard. The women are required to stand in an area separated by a screen or curtain.*

The chapters, or *suras*, of the Koran are separated by elaborate circular illuminations.

THE FIVE PILLARS

The Muslim religion rests on five principles – the "Five Pillars" of faith. They are:
1. *shahada* – an avowal of Allah as the only God and Mohammed as his prophet
2. *salat* – the obligation to pray five times a day, facing Mecca
3. *zakat* – the giving of alms to the poor
4. *sawm* – fasting during the month of Ramadan, between sunrise and sunset
5. *hadj* – pilgrimage to Mecca.

A mosque *is a place of communal worship for Muslims. Separated from the outside world by high walls, a mosque's most distinctive feature is its minaret.*

The Kaaba in Mecca is the main destination of Muslim pilgrimages

Tunisian Traditions

Tunisian society attaches great importance to its own traditions. These include religious festivals, rituals associated with religious practices and customs that predate Muslim times including the "night of henna", which takes place before weddings. Circumcision for boys is a requirement. Ramadan (the month in which devout Muslims fast between sunrise and sunset) is celebrated with great ceremony. In the provinces it is customary for people to visit public baths, wear jewellery with magic talismans, and make pilgrimages to the tombs of Muslim holy men. The family is held in high esteem throughout the country, with frequent gatherings of its members and communal meals.

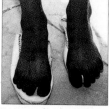

Henna – *a dye obtained from ground privet leaves. The painted patterns are believed to protect and purify.*

Tunisian women *are supposed to cover their heads. The traditional veil* (hijab) *is found in various forms all over the Muslim world. The* sifsari *(above) is mainly worn in Tunis.*

The souk *or market has been the centre of town social life for hundreds of years. They are run according to strict principles, with every product having its own permanently allocated space according to how close it is to the mosque: religious items and books are top of the list while household goods have a low status.*

Wedding jewellery of gold and silver, decorated with precious stones and magic symbols, is intended to bestow beauty, ensure fertility and bring wealth and happiness.

WEDDINGS

During the pre-Islamic era, the Arabs practised polygamy. The Koran maintained this tradition, but limited the number of wives to four. In Tunisia polygamy was outlawed in 1956. A wedding is an important public occasion, attended by the entire family. The bride's feet and palms are covered in henna and nakcha tattoos. Though dancing forms part of the festivity, Western-style discos and mixed dancing are far less common.

The custom of circumcision *involves the removal of a boy's foreskin and is practised by Jews and Muslims. Though the Koran does not pronouce on the subject, the authority for Muslim circumcision probably derives from the example of the Prophet who is believed to be descended from Kedar, a descendant of Abraham's eldest son.*

CHECHIAS

In modern-day Tunisia *chechias* are worn mainly by older men

A red cap with a silk tassel, similar to a fez, was once regarded as a vital element of a man's attire, and during the colonial era it became almost a national symbol. The *chechia* originates from Central Asia. Initially it was taller and took on its present shape around 1850. The tassel has also had many transformations – first changing its colour from blue to black and then, around 1930, vanishing altogether. *Chechias* remain popular to this day and the craftsmen who produce them are held in high regard.

Wedding costumes are rich in adornments. The fabrics and designs are reminiscent of traditional Tunisian costumes.

Games *are popular in Tunisia and men can often be seen in cafés playing dominoes, dice and cards. Dry dates or stones may sometimes serve as pawns in a game of chess.*

Chichas *– hookahs – are popular throughout Tunisia and are used to smoke tobacco in cafés. Solitary smoking is rare; normally one is ordered for a party of people. Many men still smoke* chichas *and the pipes are generally provided free (smokers need pay only for the tobacco).*

The Berbers

Berbers are the indigenous (non-Arab) people of North Africa. Their name probably originates from the Greek word "barbaroi", which was a description attached to anyone who did not speak Greek. The Berbers inhabited the region from around 4000 BC, and survived as nomads. During the 4th and 5th centuries many Berbers converted to Christianity. Until around AD 700 they resisted the Arab invasion. Despite having much in common with the Arabs (their nomadic lifestyle, individualism and tribal solidarity) and despite having quickly embraced Islam, the Berbers have continued to maintain their own ethnic and linguistic identity.

Berber women *decorate their faces and hands with henna patterns in order to protect themselves from evil spirits.*

The International Sahara Festival, *held in November or December, attracts many visitors. The event includes expert displays of horsemanship and recreations of nomadic ceremonies such as weddings and caravan departures.*

BERBER WOMEN

Women are the custodians of the ancient Berber traditions. Their clothes differ considerably from those seen in the towns. Their typical garment – the *hauli* – is a draped piece of material held with a belt and fastened with clasps *(khelalo)* at the shoulders. To this is often added a shawl. Women often weave cloth for their dresses at home. The colours most often worn are deep red, purple and indigo. The designs consist mainly of colourful stripes.

Berber ceramics *are easily recognizable by their pure abstract designs that are reminiscent of tattoos. The most popular colours include beige, red ochre and black. Here, the geometric design is first drawn in raw clay then the grooves are filled with black resin.*

A PORTRAIT OF TUNISIA

A fortified Berber village *is known as a* ksar. Ksour *(the plural of* ksar*) were originally granaries with ghorfas (rooms) situated around an inner courtyard and reached by a concealed entrance. After some time, people began to live in* ksour *and some are still inhabited today.*

The Berber social *system is based on a tribal structure. Berber women perform most of the domestic duties, such as washing, but have maintained an independent status.*

Highly ornamental gold jewellery

Colourful costumes worn all year round

Traditional Berber clasp (khelalo) *combines practicality with decorative and even protective roles. Made of silver, it is often covered with designs that are believed to ensure fertility, guard against the "evil eye" and bestow beauty on the wearer.*

Agriculture and stock keeping *are the main occupations of the Berbers. There are some 50,000–90,000 currently living in Tunisia. Most of them inhabit mountain oases. Some villages are becoming short of men, who move to towns in search of work. It is therefore left to the women to cultivate the land.*

Film-makers in Tunisia

Green hills and palm oases surrounded by a sea of sand; ancient medinas and troglodyte homes; Oriental bazaars and coastal scenery; Roman and Muslim relics – all add up to a fascinating variety of images. For the film director, Tunisia offers rich pickings which is why over 130 world film productions have been carried out under Tunisian skies. It was here that George Lucas shot *Star Wars* and Steven Spielberg filmed *Raiders of the Lost Ark*. The Monty Python group chose it as the location for *Life of Brian*, and Roman Polanski came here to make *Pirates*. *The English Patient* – winner of nine Oscars – was also shot in Tunisia.

Poster for a contemporary Tunisian film, *Une Odyssée*

Rex Ingram, an early film-maker in Tunisia

THE ADVENT OF CINEMA

Local film-makers claim that well-kept roads lead to such romantic places·as the "Jewel of Jerid" – Nefta, the "Garden of Henna" – Gabès, the "Gates of the Desert" – Kebili and Douz and the "Desert Rose" – Gafsa. It was these locations, combined with the great diversity of the landscape and the French cultural influence that brought about the rise of Tunisia's film industry, as early as the 1920s. This coincided with the arrival of foreign film-makers; Rex Ingram was one of the first.

TUNISIAN CINEMA

Tunisia swiftly became a magnet for big-budget film productions (Tozeur in particular), and this soon began to affect the domestic film scene. The epic productions created a group of local, world-class technicians, art directors and extras. Some Tunisian directors achieved a reputation that was not limited to Arab countries. In 1994, Moufida Tlatli's film *The Silences of the Palace* won a prize at the Cannes Film Festival. Tunisians are proud of the fact that the chief art director of *Star Wars* was a fellow countryman – Taieb Jallouli.

Tunisia took advantage not only of its diverse landscape and the enthusiasm of local artists and technicians, but also its natural links – both with the Maghreb countries and with France. Tunisian cinema became a bridge between Arab and European cultures. The attraction of Tunisian locations and the achievements of Tunisian cinema contributed even further to the development of mass tourism.

STAR WARS

You don't have to search for it in a distant galaxy or in Hollywood: Tatooine – the mythical planet of Luke Skywalker, hero of *Star Wars*, can be found in southern Tunisia. Located south of Medenine, Tataouine is full of craters cut into the soft rock. George Lucas also used nearby Ksar Haddada for the filming of the slave quarters in *The Phantom Menace*. However, most of the scenes from *Star Wars* were shot in Matmata, 43 km (27 miles) south of Gabès. The local troglodyte houses are still inhabited; they also house shops, hotels and restaurants. The Sidi Driss hotel was the set for the interior shots of Luke Skywalker's home. There are some 700 of these cave dwellings, half of them inhabited. Some locals earn a living by showing their homes to tourists, many of whom are

Remains of scenery from *Star Wars*, in Matmata

A PORTRAIT OF TUNISIA

fans of the movie. There are even some specialized travel agencies offering overnight accommodation to lovers of the science fiction epic. There is also no shortage of road signs pointing to *Star Wars*.

It is to the creator of *Star Wars* that Tunisia owes its cinematic fame. Lucas arrived here for the first time in the 1970s. He was captivated not only by the scenery and the extraordinary light, but also by the welcome he received. The co-operation brought benefits to both sides and part of the revenue obtained from ticket sales for the original *Star Wars* movie was set aside to help the poorest regions of Tunisia.

The English Patient with Ralph Fiennes and Kristin Scott Thomas

Scene from the epic film *Quo Vadis* shot near El-Haouaria

OSCAR WINNERS

Tunisia also provided about 80 per cent of the locations for *The English Patient*, which scooped an impressive nine Oscars at the 1997 Academy Awards.

The film's director, Anthony Minghella, set up camp on the banks of Chott el-Jerid, a vast dry salt lake about 45 km (28 miles) from Tozeur. Cairo has changed too much over the years for a period drama, so the city scenes set in the 1930s were shot in the medinas of Tunis and Mahdia. In other scenes, Sfax stands in for Tobruk. The most important location of all, however, was the desert. The film's creators decided that the sand in Morocco was too similar to the American desert, and so

Tunisia's Saharan sand proved to be ideal.

Aficionados of the film can follow in the footsteps of *The English Patient's* director by travelling on an early 20th-century train to the Seldja Gorge *(see p216)*, or alternatively by driving a jeep to the mountain oases of Chebika and Tamerza.

TUNISIAN LOCATIONS

Taieb Jallouli, the art director on *Star Wars*, claims that it is the diversity of Tunisia's scenery, within a relatively small area, that attracts film-makers. Northern Tunisia has even stood in for Japan in Frédéric Mitterrand's *Madame Butterfly*, while other regions of the country – squeezed between Libya,

Polanski shooting *Pirates* on Tunisia's coast

Algeria and the Mediterranean Sea, have been used as the Holy Land for Franco Zeffirelli's *Jesus of Nazareth*. In the early 1950s, Tunisia proved the ideal location for the Hollywood adaptations of Nobel Prize winner Henryk Sienkiewicz's novels including *Quo Vadis*. Steven Spielberg also used it to shoot many of the scenes for *Raiders of the Lost Ark*, while the medina in Monastir featured in *Monty Python's Life of Brian*.

It was no accident that the majority of scenes for Roman Polanski's *Pirates* were shot on the Sahel coast, a dozen or so kilometres north of Sousse. Tunisia was once a jumping-off point for Mediterranean corsairs and the base of the famous Red Beard (Barbarossa). Today, Port el-Kantaoui, packed with luxury yachts, is a place where visitors can eat the best fish in Tunisia, and also set sail on board one of the caravels from Polanski's film. Although the original vessels were bought by a Frenchman immediately after filming was completed, their replicas provide an exciting chance to "swashbuckle", particularly for younger would-be pirates!

Handicrafts in Tunisia

Tunisian handicrafts get support from the government and provide employment for over 120,000 people. Each region has its own speciality: Kairouan is famous for its carpets; Nabeul and Jerba for their ceramics; Sidi Bou Saïd for its birdcages; Douz and Tozeur for shoes. It tends to be women who produce the carpets, decorate pottery, and weave baskets and mats while the men attend to carpentry, metalwork and, above all, selling.

Ornate "Hand of Fatima"

Carpet from Kairouan, with traditional Berber patterns

Potter at work at a wheel

CERAMICS

The two main centres of ceramics in Tunisia are Nabeul on the Cap Bon peninsula and Guellala on the island of Jerba. Nabeul is known for its brightly coloured, glazed pottery. Much of this is produced solely for visitors and it can be very good quality. The inhabitants of Guellala cater more for the home market and their workshops offer every type of utility ware – from items used for cooling water and storing food, to enamelled products and "Ali Baba" jars. The northern town of Sejnane and some of the surrounding villages are famous for a primitive Berber pottery that still employs techniques used in Neolithic times. All three styles are available throughout Tunisia.

CARPETS

Tunisian carpets are mainly produced in Kairouan and Jerid. All are handmade but there are two basic types, those that are knotted and those that are woven. The knotted variety cost more and have up to 160,000 knots per square metre. Most of the designs tend to be based on a central diamond shape that is thought to derive from the lamp in the Great Mosque in Kairouan. Knotted carpets come in two main types: *Alloucha* and *Zarbia*. *Zarbia* carpets use reds, greens and blues while the *Alloucha* carpets are produced in beiges, browns and whites. Woven or *Mergoum* carpets are cheaper to buy and have Berber origins.

COPPER AND BRASS PRODUCTS

In small workshops, tucked away in the narrow streets of most medinas, men can be seen bent over hammers and copper sheets, which they shape into bowls, trays and garden ornaments. Bronze is used for making jewellery boxes and jugs with distinctive narrow necks. Intricate birdcages are also plentiful and typically Tunisian; their shapes resemble small mausoleums and their patterns are borrowed from the *moucharabieh* – the lattice-work window or screen seen in traditional Arab houses. Gleaming copper and brass plates are also plentiful and come in a wide variety of sizes – some are bigger than dustbin lids!

Craftsman decorating brass and copper plates in a souk workshop

WOODWORK

Popular wooden items on sale in Tunisia include salad bowls and containers for salad dressing, and wooden dolls dressed in colourful clothes. While strolling through the streets of medinas or exploring a market it is worth stepping into a carpenter's workshop to see how they make cupboards, trunks and traditional Tunisian doors. The material used in the north of the country is mainly olive-tree wood – suitable for making bowls and oil containers. In the south, palm wood is the most popular material.

Traditional fabrics woven on looms in a workshop

Making shoes at a workshop in Kairouan

LEATHER GOODS

Tunisians were once famous for producing saddles though sadly these skills have all but died out. Instead, they produce ottomans and furniture upholstery. Other common products include travel bags, wallets, leather jackets, handbags and a variety of souvenirs. Look out for the *babouche* slippers, with flattened heels, which are worn mainly in the south of the country.

Try to do some shopping in a cooperative craft workshop or a craft village, such as Ken Craft Village near Bou Ficha in the Sahel (*see p292*). These sell quality Islamic art and handicrafts at reasonable prices.

MOSAICS

Mosaic work in Tunisia dates back to Punic times but flourished with the Roman occupation. When artists first began to produce intricate patterns using *tesserae* – finely polished pieces of brick, glass and marble – the workshops could not keep up with demand. Mosaics were used everywhere – from the floors in public baths, to the domes and the walls of public buildings. After the 3rd century, they also began to be used in private homes which led to a distinctive naturalistic Tunisian style.

Modern mosaic from El-Jem

OTHER HANDICRAFT PRODUCTS

Jewellery is popular in Tunisia. It is produced from silver, gold and other metals, with precious and semi-precious stones used in traditional designs. The largest jewellery centres include Tunis, Sfax and Jerba. Tabarka produces lovely coral and amber items. Another typically Tunisian product is the *chechia* – a distinctive red woollen cap. It was originally worn under the turban, but with time it became an item of headgear and a symbol of Tunisian national identity. The production of mats, baskets and fans is also widespread. These are woven using grass and date palm leaves. Increasing numbers of artists are also returning to the tradition of painting on glass, an art form inspired by Egyptian and Syrian examples. Items to look out for include beautiful mirrors and intricately decorated glass perfume jars. The Cap Bon peninsula is known for the production of authentic perfumes and essences; orange blossom, rose and jasmine essences are particularly highly valued in Tunisia.

Making sieves in a souk workshop

TUNISIA THROUGH THE YEAR

One of the most pleasant times to visit Tunisia is in spring when flowers are in full bloom and the temperature has not yet reached its summer peak. During summer, the most comfortable place to be is on the coast where sea breezes cool the air. By autumn the temperature is starting to lower, making the all-important work of harvesting olives a

Desert rose – a symbol of Tunisia

little more bearable. The Tunisian winter can get very cold, especially high up in the mountains, while on the coast the weather can be damp and rather dreary. Public holidays in Tunisia are mostly bound up with Islam and take place according to the Islamic calendar *(see opposite)*. Visitors should get specific details of festivals and events when they are in the country.

A profusion of spring flowers flourish amid olive trees

SPRING

Spring is Tunisia's most colourful season with many flowers in bloom at this time. March and April are ideal for exploring the country. The heat is not oppressive, yet daytime temperatures rise above 20° C (68° F). Rains can be heavy but usually come in the form of brief showers. The first half of March is the final opportunity to embark on a camel trek across the desert; April brings sandstorms; May is filled with the scent of jasmine and the warming seas herald the arrival of summer.

MARCH

Independence Day *(20 Mar)*. National holiday that is celebrated on the anniversary of the country's independence, which was

declared in 1956 by the then president Habib Bourguiba.
Orange Blossom Festival *(late Mar–early Apr)*, celebrated in Menzel Bou Zelfa, Nabeul and Hammamet. A traditional festival with competitions for the best bouquet.
Octopus Festival, Kerkennah Islands. A fisherman's festival that involves locals dressing up in octopus costumes and plenty to eat.
Spring Festival, Sousse. This international arts festival includes traditional concerts, shows and theatre.

APRIL

Festival of the Mountain Oases *(late Apr)*, Midès, Tamezret. A grand display of Berber culture, including a Berber wedding ceremony, body painting with henna, performances of traditional music and horse shows.

Ksour Festival, Tataouine. Celebrates the life and customs of the *ksar* dwellers, including reconstructions of a Berber wedding and scenes from everyday life with music and camel races.
Folk Art Festival, Tataouine. This annual festival includes exhibitions of local handicrafts, folk music, dancing and displays of local costumes.

MAY

Passover Festival *(Apr or May)*, El-Ghriba Synagogue, Jerba. A big event in the Jewish calender, attracting pilgrims from all over North Africa.
The Jerid festival, Nefta and other towns of the region. Festival of traditional art including concerts, music and dance performances.
Music Festival, Sfax. Arab music concerts including both classical and pop.

Independence Day as celebrated in Tataouine

THE ISLAMIC CALENDAR

Muslim religious festivals are celebrated in accordance with the lunar calendar, with each year composed of 12 months and each month of 29 or 30 days. The Muslim year is 11 days shorter than the Gregorian (Western) year. The dates of festivals depend upon the sighting of the new moon for the start of a new month. Ramadan – the month of fasting – is solemnly celebrated. Friday is a holy day; however, unlike the majority of Arab countries, it is not regarded as a public holiday in Tunisia.

Al-Hijra
The first day of the Muslim year, this marks the anniversary of the Hijra (the name given to the Prophet Mohammed's migration from Mecca to Medina).

Aïd el-Adha ("the day of offering")
This is one of the most important dates in the Muslim calendar. It marks the day when, by divine order, Abraham prepared to sacrifice his son before Allah interceded by providing a ram in place of the child.

Aïd el-Fitr ("the small festival")
This festival marks the end of the month of Ramadan, and begins on the evening of the last day of the 30-day fast. Custom decrees that on this day entirely new clothes, from headscarf to socks are put on, and that money is given to children and people in need.

Mouled
This is the anniversary of the Prophet Mohammed's birth and is celebrated on the twelfth day of rabi al-aoual, the third month of the Muslim calendar. For the majority of the population, it is an occasion for family gatherings and festivities.

Ramadan
is the Muslim holy month when the faithful renew their covenant with Allah through fasting during the hours of daylight. It is only after the sun has set, following communal prayers, that Muslims are allowed to eat meals and special sweets.

Wide, sandy beaches attract many visitors during the summer

SUMMER

Summer temperatures on the coast can reach 40° C (104° F) but the sea breezes temper the heat. The south of the country is hotter still, and even the nights don't bring relief. Market stalls fill with every variety of melon and other fruit and vegetables. Summer in Tunisia is the traditional season for weddings; it is also a time when most people visit, filling the hotels and beaches. Many of the concerts and festivals are staged throughout the country at this time of year.

Falcon from El-Haouaria

JUNE

Falconry Festival *(2nd half of Jun)*, El-Haouaria. Flying displays are accompanied by a traditional falcon hunt for partridges.
Jazz Festival *(late Jun)*, Tabarka. One of the most important events in the Tunisian cultural calendar, featuring artistes from all over the world.
Arab Horse Festival, Sidi Bou Saïd. Horse shows, races, displays of riding prowess and music concerts.
International Malouf Music Festival, Testour. Concerts of Arab-Andalusian *malouf* given by artists from Arab countries and Spain.

Kharja Festival, Sidi Bou Saïd. This religious festival is devoted to Sidi Bou Saïd, a 13th-century Islamic Sufi teacher after whom the town is named.

JULY

Ulysses Festival *(1–25 Jul)*, Houmt Souk. Song and dance festival with historic and mythological themes.
International Festival of Classical Theatre, Dougga. Theatre festival held at the site of these monumental Roman excavations.
Plastic Arts Festival *(22 Jul–6 Aug)*, Mahrès (Sfax). Gallery exhibitions of mainly young Tunisian artists.
Mermaid Festival, Kerkennah Islands. Lively concerts and performances by traditional Tunisian and Arab artists.

International Music Festival, Hammamet. Features theatre and world music.
International Festival of Bizerte. Month-long festival of music, art, dance and food.
Nights of La Marsa, La Marsa. Cultural festival with music concerts, live theatre and ballet performances.
International Festival of Symphonic Music, El-Jem. Concerts are held in the amphitheatre, by candlelight.
International Festival, Carthage. A musical high point of the year, also featuring dance, film and theatre.
Republic Day *(25 July)*. The day commemorating the proclamation of the Tunisian Republic in 1957.

AUGUST

Amateur Theatre Festival *(late Jul–early Aug)*, Korba (Cap Bon). Presentation of new works by talented amateur Arab playwrights.
Women's Day *(13 Aug)*. The Citizens' Rights Code was proclaimed on this day in 1956, granting, among other things, equal rights for men and women.
Jasmin Road, Bizerte. Festive end of Toulon-Bizerte yacht race, accompanied by fireworks and lively stage shows.
Sponge Festival, Zarzis. Marine festival, a day of sponge diving, accompanied by folklore shows.
Festival of Diving *(late Aug)*, Tabarka. Diving displays and competitions, music concerts.
Sousse Festival. Celebration of the arts.

Traditional music, a common element of Tunisian festivals

AUTUMN

September can still be baking hot, especially in the south, but by October the coastal temperature is beginning to lower to a comfortable average of around 20° C (68° F). October is a good time to visit Tunisia as the water is still warm enough for swimming and the resorts are far quieter. Autumn is harvest time and the market stalls bend under the weight of fresh fruit and vegetables, while the dates are ripening in Kebili, Tozeur and Nefta.

September, marking the start of the grape harvest

SEPTEMBER

Coralis *(6–9 Sep)*, Tabarka. Festival of diving and underwater photography aimed at promoting the local coral trade.
Wine Festival *(late Sep)*, Grombalia. The end of the grape harvest in the heart of Tunisia's wine growing region gives the locals an opportunity to celebrate.
Wheat Festival *(late Sep)*, Béja. Colourful harvest festival that is celebrated in one of the most fertile regions of the country.

OCTOBER

International Film Festival, Carthage. Tunisia's most important film festival is held every two years. Presented works come from all over the world, but mainly from Arab and African countries.

Theatre performances also feature.
Evacuation Day *(15 Oct)*. Nationwide celebrations are held on the anniversary of the day when the last French troops pulled out of Tunisia in 1963. The celebrations are particularly festive in Bizerte itself, which hosts its own Festival d'Evacuation de Bizerte including street decorations and parades.

NOVEMBER

Festival of Ksour, Ksar Ouled Soltane. One of a handful of festivals held in this region, presenting the culture and traditions of the Berbers. It is accompanied by music, dancing and varied displays of traditional customs.
Date Harvest Festival, Kebili. The end of the date harvest is celebrated with shows, local music and fairs.
International Oases Festival, Tozeur. Celebration devoted to the Saharan way of life that is timed to coincide with the date harvest in this region. The special events include displays of some of the local rituals, traditional dance, storytelling and ceremonies.

The International Festival of the Sahara

International Festival of the Sahara, Douz. This annual event is the most famous of all Tunisian festivals. It provides an opportunity to see many local practices and traditions including the preparation of Bedouin meals, poetry readings, craft and photography exhibitions, camel races and wedding ceremonies. Tents are pitched in the desert and lit by torches at night to create a scene that could have come from the *Arabian Nights*. Other countries participate in the events.

International Festival of Symphonic Music at El-Jem

WINTER

Winter weather is the most unsettled of all. There are days when the midday temperature on the coast and inland rises above 24° C (75° F); but when the winds blow, the chill can be felt not only on Cap Bon, but also way down in the south. These conditions discourage many visitors, and some hotels and restaurants in tourist resorts are closed. The end of winter is usually very sunny, but the winter sun gives little in the way of warmth.

The advent of winter is marked in many regions by festivals celebrating the end of the olive and date harvests. These are fairly low profile events, and apart from the Douz and Dakar Rally, are unlikely to draw large crowds of visitors.

DECEMBER

Olive Festivals, Jerba, Mahdia, Kairouan, Kalaa Kebira. The production of olives is an important part of Tunisia's economy and the end of the olive harvest, also celebrated in other towns, is a big event and always accompanied by a lot of fun.

Camel market during the International Festival of the Sahara

Because of the heavy work involved in the harvest, this is a popular festival.

JANUARY

New Year *(1 Jan)*. The European New Year is celebrated by many Tunisians within their family circle. Celebration of the Muslim New Year is equally quiet and occurs later.
The Dakar Rally. This major endurance race draws many big-name teams and motoring fans every few years when it passes through Tunisia. For a few days off-road cars, motorcycles and trucks pass through local towns. The rally route changes each time so that it can pass through different sections of the Sahara Desert.

FEBRUARY

Aïd el-Adha. This is a major feast in the Tunisian calendar. It takes place 68 days after the end of Ramadan and marks the day when Abraham, under divine orders, prepared to sacrifice his son. The day is celebrated throughout the Arab world and families who can afford it sacrifice an animal as Abraham is believed to have done as a substitute

Harvesting olives in December

for his son. According to tradition, one third of the meat is distributed to the poor while the remainder is consumed within the family circle.
International Instrumental Festival, Tunis. Annual music event emphasizing North African traditions.

ISLAMIC CALENDAR MONTHS

Medina Festival *(Ramadan)*, Tunis. A major festival in the capital that includes numerous pop and traditional music concerts, dance, poetry, Koran-reciting competitions and religious processions.

PUBLIC HOLIDAYS

New Year *(1 Jan)*
Independence Day *(20 Mar)*
Youth Day *(21 Mar)*
Martyrs' Day *(9 Apr)*
Labour Day *(1 May)*
Republic Day *(25 Jul)*
Women's Day *(13 Aug)*, Celebrates the Citizens' Rights Code.
Aïd el-Fitr *(end of Ramadan)*. The changing political situation in 2011 means some events may alter.

The Tunisian Climate

Tunisia lies within the mediterranean subtropical zone. Its hot dry summer lasts from May until October. The southern regions of the country have only two seasons: a long summer and a short, rainy season. The remaining regions also have a spring and autumn – although much shorter than those in Europe. The sweltering summer heat is felt throughout the entire country, but particularly in the mountain valleys, caused by the sirocco wind. The Sahel's climate is tempered by the sea breeze. In late autumn, cold currents from the Atlantic bring wind and rain.

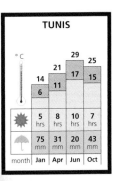

TUNIS

°C			
14	21	29	25
6	11	17	15
5 hrs	8 hrs	10 hrs	7 hrs
75 mm	31 mm	20 mm	43 mm
month	Jan	Apr	Jun	Oct

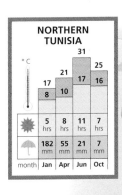

NORTHERN TUNISIA

°C			
17	21	31	25
8	10	17	16
5 hrs	8 hrs	11 hrs	7 hrs
182 mm	55 mm	21 mm	7 mm
month	Jan	Apr	Jun	Oct

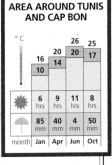

AREA AROUND TUNIS AND CAP BON

°C			
16	20	26	25
10	14	20	17
6 hrs	9 hrs	11 hrs	8 hrs
85 mm	40 mm	4 mm	50 mm
month	Jan	Apr	Jun	Oct

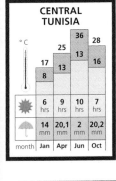

CENTRAL TUNISIA

°C			
17	25	36	28
8	13	13	16
6 hrs	9 hrs	10 hrs	7 hrs
14 mm	20,1 mm	2 mm	20,2 mm
month	Jan	Apr	Jun	Oct

THE SAHEL

°C			
17	23	31	26
9	14	23	20
6 hrs	8 hrs	11 hrs	7 hrs
38 mm	21 mm	3 mm	47 mm
month	Jan	Apr	Jun	Oct

SOUTHERN TUNISIA

°C			
16	28	36	31
8	16	21	17
8 hrs	9 hrs	11 hrs	8 hrs
1 mm	5 mm	0,7 mm	19 mm
month	Jan	Apr	Jun	Oct

0 km 75
0 miles 75

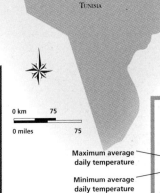

JERBA AND THE MEDENINE AREA

°C			
16	24	32	28
8	18	23	20
7 hrs	10 hrs	12 hrs	8 hrs
29 mm	10,5 mm	1 mm	39 mm
month	Jan	Apr	Jun	Oct

Maximum average daily temperature

Minimum average daily temperature

Average daily hours of sunshine

Average monthly rainfall

THE HISTORY OF TUNISIA

he rich cultural and social heritage that can be found in modern-day Tunisia is largely due to the major powers that have inhabited this area including the Phoenicians, the Romans, the Vandals, the Arabs and the French. Tunisia is one of the oldest countries in Africa and the name given to it by the Romans – Ifriqiyya – came to designate the entire continent.

The earliest prehistoric humans most probably appeared here during the early Palaeolithic era, and primitive stone tools discovered near Kebili in the south date this early activity to about 200,000 years ago. At this time the climate was very different and the area that is now called the Sahara had regular rainfall and may well have been covered in forest. From these early beginnings evolved the Aterians, who were able to make and use specialized tools. The Aterians were followed, about 10,000 years ago, by fair-skinned tribes from western Asia who brought with them the ability to make flint tools. These Capsian people, named after archaeological finds near Gafsa (which was earlier known as Capsa), settled in southern Tunisia and developed a sophisticated culture with a language and early forms of art. They lived here until about 4500 BC and, as well as being hunter-gatherers, began to develop forms of agriculture, domesticating several species of animals. In

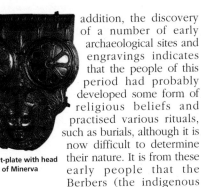

Breast-plate with head of Minerva

addition, the discovery of a number of early archaeological sites and engravings indicates that the people of this period had probably developed some form of religious beliefs and practised various rituals, such as burials, although it is now difficult to determine their nature. It is from these early people that the Berbers (the indigenous non-Arab North Africans) are probably descended.

The information about Berber culture and religious beliefs prior to the arrival of the Phoenicians in 1100 BC is scarce. Their name derives from the Greek word "barbaroi" – meaning anyone who could not speak Greek. The majority of Berbers lived in family-based tribal societies, were nomadic and spoke a language that belongs to the Hamitic group of languages. Roman expansion impinged on their freedom and, because of their intense spirit of independence, the Berbers have often found themselves in conflict with the dominant power throughout Tunisia's history.

TIMELINE

150,000 BC	50,000 BC	10,000 BC	5000 BC	2500 BC	1100 BC

100,000–40,000 BC Neanderthal man appears in Tunisia

9000–4000 BC Capsian civilization arrives in North Africa. Named after implements discovered near Gafsa, Capsian man is distinguished by the use of sophisticated flint tools and early forms of art

10,000–8000 BC *Homo sapiens* appear in the region of Gabès and on the northern edges of the Tell

1100 BC Phoenician sailors establish trading outposts in Tunisia

Flint arrowheads

◁ **Picture of Hannibal fighting a Roman legion in the Alps**

Phoenician traders sailing around the Mediterranean Sea

THE PHOENICIANS

The so-called Punic period (the name given to 128 years of war between the Phoenicians and the emerging Roman empire) began about 814 BC with the founding of Carthage. The Phoenicians were supreme sailors and colonized many islands and coastal regions, which they established as trading posts. They built new towns, mostly on craggy headlands, with two harbours – to the north and south, so that they could be used regardless of the wind direction and the season of the year. As the compass had not yet been invented, they had to navigate by the stars – mainly by *Ursa Minor*, the Little Bear. Their longest sea voyage was the circumnavigation of Africa, which was accomplished on the orders of the Egyptian pharaoh Nechon, in 600 BC. An account of this historic voyage can be found in the writings of Herodotus.

Numidian mausoleum
in Dougga

CARTHAGE

The foundation of Carthage is linked to Dido, Princess of Tyre. Persecuted by her brother, Pygmalion, who murdered her husband, she fled her homeland. Having arrived at what is now Tunisia, she pleaded with the local chieftain, Labus, to give her a piece of land big enough to cover the hide of a bull. Dido cut the hide into narrow strips and used them to encircle the area that later became the site of Carthage's fortress – Byrsa.

Phoenician
terracotta mask

Despite such legends, the history behind this city is more prosaic. The Phoenicians, wanting secure staging posts along the trade route between Tyre (in modern-day Lebanon) and silver mines in southern Spain, needed a presence on the Tunisian coast. The outpost soon grew into a powerful state that took control of the trading posts, which were remote and scattered over a large area. In the 7th century BC, the Carthaginians were strong enough to take control of Tyre in the west and began establishing colonies for themselves. By the 4th century BC, Carthage had become an independent state. Carthage's wealth grew

TIMELINE

814 BC Punic era – founding of Carthage by the Phoenicians. Development of new towns; major centres include Acholla, necropolis in Mahdia, Hadrumètum (Sousse), Kerkouane, Hippo Diarrhytus (Bizerte). Tanit and Baal Hammon are the most popular deities in Carthage

1100 BC	1000 BC	900 BC	800 BC	700 BC

1000–1100 BC Earliest Phoenician settlements

975–942 BC Phoenician economy flourishes under the rule of Hiram I, King of Tyre

1000–900 BC The oldest examples of Phoenician writing

Sphinx-shaped vase

654 BC First Punic colony established on Ibiza (Balearic Islands)

and its culture flourished and at its peak this important Phoenician metropolis had a population of about 500,000.

The Phoenician colonization was purely commercial and did not involve any military conquests but the success of Carthage, which had a strong navy and a firm grip on trade throughout the 5th and 4th century, inevitably threatened to eclipse other powers, especially Rome.

Dido Building Carthage by J.M.W. Turner

The first Punic War began in 263 BC when Rome embarked on a campaign to take control of Sicily, 80 km (50 miles) northeast of Carthage. These two major powers fought each other for the next 20 years until Rome managed to destroy the Carthaginian fleet off Trapani (western Sicily) and forced Carthage to surrender.

The second Punic War began in 218 BC. This time it was Carthage that went on the offensive. With Rome for the time being busy with its new conquests, Carthage had turned its attention to its position in Africa. In an attempt to force Rome's hand, the Carthaginian general Hannibal had earlier captured a region of Spain. Then, in 218, he crossed the Alps with a 90,000-strong army and 37 elephants and launched what would turn out to be an unsuccessful assault on Rome.

The third Punic War began in 149 BC when the Romans landed in Utica and laid siege to Carthage. The mighty city fell three years later and was destroyed. The Romans took possession and the former territory of Carthage became the Roman province of Africa.

Reconstruction of ancient Carthage, from the Phoenician period

THE ROMANS

The destruction of Carthage in 146 BC was followed by the foundation of the Roman province of Africa, with its capital in Utica – a former Punic colony. This was the first Roman colony outside Italy and covered the territory of northeastern Tunisia. The land captured from Carthage became *ager publicus* – state-owned land on which a tribute was levied. Only the towns that had surrendered to the Romans during the war were exempt. In 44 BC, the "infernal land", now dedicated to the goddess Juno, became the site of Julia Carthage. The former city was resurrected and became the capital of this part of the world for several centuries. In 27 BC, a new consular province was created – *Africa Proconsularis* – with a resident proconsul in Carthage. It covered the area from Cyrta in the west to Cyrenaica in the east. After the years of wars, the reign of Octavian Augustus brought with it stability and created a new climate for economic development.

Roman triumph following the defeat of Hannibal

A marble bust from the Roman era

During the period of the Flavian dynasty (AD 69–96), Rome continued with its southerly expansion. The building and maintenance of roads assisted with the development of trade and communication.

Agriculture became increasingly important to the area and the Romans turned the wheat-growing plains of the Medjerda Valley into a "bread-basket" with the region supplying some 60 per cent of the Empire's requirements for grain. This produced a golden age for the African economy. Its wealth was based on the cultivation of corn and olives, and also on its vineyards. Many locals, including the Berbers, prospered under the new regime and a number of colonies sprang up on the Tunisian coastline that provided holiday and retirement homes for wealthy Romans. With so much Roman influence this part of Africa underwent a gradual process of Romanization. Roman towns sprang up everywhere. Religious buildings were erected to honour gods such as Juno and Minerva. Nearly one sixth of Roman senators were of African origin at this time. Africa even provided an Emperor, the Libyan-born Septimius Severus.

The smooth running of the African economy was briefly upset in 238 when Gordian, the proconsul of Africa, proclaimed himself emperor

Roman amphitheatre at El-Jem

TIMELINE

27 BC Founding of *Africa Proconsularis*, covering most of modern day Tunisia, up to Chott el-Jerid (not including the Sahara)

69–96 Flavian dynasty – the country flourishes

238 Revolt in Africa Proconsularis, led by the Gordians (father and son)

100 BC	AD 1	100	200

Relief from Chemtou region

96 Beginning of Antonine dynasty – a golden age for the African economy

193–235 Peak of the territorial expansion under the Severan dynasty. Strengthening of borders and building of defensive walls around many cities

284 Emper Diocletian carri out reform plans Africa becom *Dioecesis Afric*

Ruins of the forum in Sufetula

in a gesture of defiance against the heavy taxes imposed by Rome. Gordian sent his son, Gordian II, into battle against Capellianus, the governor of Numidia, who was loyal to Rome. Gordian II was killed on the battlefield and, on hearing of his death the father killed himself. He had ruled for just 21 days.

THE VANDALS

One of Rome's biggest challenges during the 4th and 5th centuries was the Vandals, a fierce tribe of Aryan barbarians who had been slowly but surely working their way through Spain and into Africa. In AD 429 the Vandals arrived in Africa and began demolishing much of what the Romans had built. In 439, they seized Carthage, which became the capital of a new state that covered the area of present-day Tunisia. Its founder, Genseric, ruled for half a century (428–477) building the Vandal empire and expanding it further into Sicily, Sardinia and Italy. He also had the audacity to

Byzantine-style column decoration

carry out one of the most daring deeds imaginable at that time: the plunder of Rome in 455.

BYZANTIUM

The political makeup of the Roman Empire was changed forever with the adoption of Christianity by Constantine the Great in 312. Much of Rome's power was transferred to Byzantium (Istanbul), which was to control the eastern portion of the Roman Empire.

In 533 the Byzantine Emperor Justinian, who dreamt of reasserting Roman authority, sent his general Belisarius to attack the Vandals at the Battle of Ad Decinum, near present-day Tunis. Belisarius had a swift and decisive victory and on 15 September 533 he entered Carthage.

The next century of Byzantine rule was more troubled. Despite building heavy fortifications, constant Berber resistance and insurrection in the army meant that the Byzantine hold on Tunisia was weak.

A mosaic from the Byzantine period

439 Carthage conquered by the Vandals

Belisarius – commander of Emperor Justinian's army

698 Carthage taken over by Arab forces

300   400   500   600   700

533 Carthage occupied by Byzantine army

647 Beginning of the Muslim era. Byzantine army defeated at Sufetula

670 Founding of Kairouan by Oqba ibn Nafi

A stele with an image of Baal-Saturn

Christian Tunisia

Christianity arrived in Africa from Rome and was taken up by many people in Tunisia, including some of the Berber tribes. Thousands of Christian converts were martyred during the third century, including St Perpetua who was thrown to the animals in Carthage. A split in the church occurred in the 4th century when Donatus, the Bishop of Carthage, refused to recognize the authority of church leaders who had failed to stand up to Rome. These "Donatists" built their own churches and many Roman sites in Tunisia have two churches for this reason.

Christian monogram
This was created by combining the letters X and P. It was used following the Tolerance Edict (4th century).

St Augustine
Augustine (AD 354–430) spent his youth in Carthage and later returned there as a priest and bishop. He also participated in synods.

The apse of a forum basilica was used to seat the officials; the emperor sat in the imperial basilica.

The door of every Christian church has a symbolic meaning.

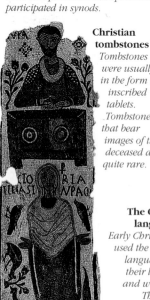

Christian tombstones
Tombstones were usually in the form of inscribed tablets. Tombstones that bear images of the deceased are quite rare.

MOSAICS

This unique mosaic kept in the Bardo Museum, Tunis, shows a Christian church. It gives some idea of the original appearance of the early churches whose ruins can be seen in many of Tunisia's oldest towns.

The Greek language
Early Christians used the Greek language in their liturgy and writing. The first Christian text in Latin was written in AD 180 in Africa.

Ruins of Basilicas
Many Tunisian towns contain the ruins of Christian basilicas that were built in the town centres or on the outskirts, often on the sites of earlier sacred buildings.

Floor mosaics in basilicas included rich animal and floral motifs.

Inscriptions were often incorporated into the mosaics.

Baptistry
Pools decorated with mosaics were used by Christians in their baptisms.

Inscriptions
Many of the surviving Christian inscriptions are on tombstones that bear only the name of the deceased and the simplest of ornamentation.

A peacock featured in Christian tomb mosaics symbolized resurrection.

The Good Shepherd
By the 2nd century AD Christianity was already widespread in North Africa. The image of the Good Shepherd was among the most popular motifs in Christian art.

Catacombs
A well-preserved underground resting-place can be seen in Sousse.

ARAB RULE

One hundred years after the death of Mohammed (632), the Muslim Empire stretched from Spain to India. The first strong resistance encountered by the Muslim army was in the area of present-day Tunisia. The attacks on Ifriqiyya (Tunisia and parts of Libya) started immediately after the conquest of Egypt (640–43); nevertheless it took more than 20 years to win control over it. This was finally achieved by Oqba ibn Nafi after he defeated the Byzantine army in 647. In 670, he founded the city of Kairouan, which became the most important town in North Africa and an excellent base for military operations against the Berber tribes. Oqba, who according to a legend went forward until the Atlantic waves stopped his horse, was killed in 683 near Biskra (eastern Algeria). After his death, the Muslim army was forced to leave Ifriqiyya and it was only during 693–700 that the governor Hassan ibn Nu'man (founder

Muslim cemetery outside the ancient medina walls, Kairouan

A page from the Koran (1202)

of Arab Tunis) quashed the Berbers' resistance and confirmed Arab rule. The work of Ibn Nu'man was continued by Musa ibn Nusair. Under his rule, Kairouan gained independence from Egypt and was controlled directly by Damascus. Having conquered the coast of North Africa, Ibn Nusair opened the gateway to Europe. In 800, power in Ifriqiyya passed to the hands of the independent deputies of the Abassid Caliphs – the Aghlabids. The founder of this dynasty was Ibrahim ibn al-Aghlab who made Kairouan the capital of a region that covered western Algeria, Tunisia and part of Libya. The resulting dynasty proved

Courtyard of the 11th-century Sidi Driss Mosque, Gabès

TIMELINE

800–909 Expansion of Islam. Founding of the Aghlabid dynasty, which rules the country from its capital in Kairouan

921 Founding of Mahdia, which becomes the country's capital

Doorway to the Great Mosque's minaret in Kairouan

700	800	900	1000	1100

Golden coin, from the Aghlabid period

909–972 The Fatimids assume power and rule for a period before moving to Egypt

972–1152 Founding of the Zirid dynasty and their assumption of power. Raid by the Banu Hilal tribe

1056–1147 Period of rule by the Almoravid dynasty

to be successful. This period of Aghlabid rule saw Ifriqiya move away from a Romano-Christian heritage as its Muslim identity developed.

Marble relief from Mahdia depicting a king and a musician

FATIMIDS

Towards the end of the 9th century, the main threat to the Aghlabids came from the increasingly strong opposition movements centring around the Shiite groups. One of the leaders of this movement was Abu Abdullah who claimed descent from the Prophet's daughter, Fatima. Abu Abdullah was a gifted commander and in 909 the Aghlabids were defeated. A little later he conquered Alexandria. The Fatimids constructed a new capital, Mahdia, and set about making plans to capture Egypt.

Abu Abdullah's successors continued this policy of expansion. Having conquered Egypt, they handed control of Ifriqiyya to their Berber nominee. In 972, he founded the Zirid dynasty (972–1152), which withdrew allegiance from the Fatimids in 1041. There followed a period of great instability. The Zirids were overthrown by the Almoravids, who ruled the Maghreb and Spain from 1056 until 1147. They were followed by the Almohads, who in their turn, were replaced by the Hafsid dynasty.

HAFSIDS

The Hafsids (1233–1574) introduced wide-ranging changes beneficial to the economy of present-day Tunisia. Their great political skill enabled them to play the Tunisian tribes off against one another. This, and a reputation for military skill, which was partly earned when they defeated a crusade led by Louis IX of France, led to a time of stability. Tunis was made the capital and did well under the new regime, enjoying a new-found wealth. Separate districts were allocated to Muslim refugees from Spain, European diplomats and merchants. The Great Mosque (Jemaa el-Zitouna) acquired a medersa and a minaret, and a palace was built on the site of the present Bardo Museum. At the same time, the Great Mosque in Kairouan was restored.

OTTOMAN RULE

It was the arrival of the Ottoman Turks that spelt the end for the Hafsid dynasty. The Ottomans had fought wars with Byzantine Rome, which they finally defeated, taking Constantinople in 1453.

Death of Louis IX during a plague epidemic in Tunisia, in 1270, after his unsuccessful crusade

King Louis IX

1159–1230 The Almohads unite the Maghreb countries

1240 The first medersa (Islamic school) established in Tunis

1574 Spanish withdraw from Tunisia. Tunis is partially destroyed in the course of fighting. Tunisia is seized by the Ottoman Turks

1200   **1300**   **1400**   **1500**   **1600**

1233–1574 Tunis is ruled by the Hafsid dynasty. Art and architecture flourish

1270 Crusade by Louis IX

1574 Rise of the corsairs: with the assistance of the Barbary pirates, Aruj and Khair ed-Din Barbarossa, Tunisia falls under the control of the Ottoman Empire. Turkish becomes the official language

Genoese fort guarding the entrance to Tabarka harbour

Turkey. From 1534 to 1574, the Spanish kings tried to establish a protectorate over Tunisia, but were defeated by the Turks, on land and at sea.

Tunisia became a province of the Ottoman Empire and was ruled over by an elaborate hierarchy which included the Pasha (the sultan's representative) and an elite of Ottoman high-ranking army officials including a civil administrator (bey), and a military administrator (dey). Such a complex sharing of power did not result in a stable government and rebellions and struggles for control weakened the state. Central rule was restored by the Muradids (1628–1702), the first line of hereditary beys, who brought about the country's revival. They also enriched its art with Ottoman influences and popularized the habit of coffee drinking.

During the 16th century, the dynasty ruled over a powerful empire that included the Balkans and Arab countries. The golden era of the Ottoman Empire coincided with the rule of Suleyman the Magnificent (1520–66). During that time the Ottomans also took control of Tunisia with the help of mercenaries. In the 16th century the corsairs, sailing under the Ottoman flag, won control of the entire Maghreb coast. Assisted by the Barbary pirates – Aruj and Khair ed-Din Barbarossa – Tunisia was taken. In the later stages of the Hafsids' rule, the country, ruined by numerous dynastic squabbles, had become the object of a dispute between Spain and

Ottoman-style finial of a minaret

HUSAYNIDS

The Muradid line was replaced by the Husaynids in the early part of the 18th century when Husayn bin Ali took control of the country and established a new dynasty that would rule until 1957. Having no sons, Bin Ali at

Ceramic decoration with a plant motif

TIMELINE

first appointed his nephew, Ali, to be his successor in 1709. However, in the same year a son, Mehmed, was born. When he reached maturity, his father made Mehmed his heir and gave him the title of Bey Mahalli. The nephew was given the title of Pasha. This situation led to five years of conflict during which Tunisian society was split into two camps, a division that lasted, in political terms, well into the 18th century. Initially Ali Pasha won the upper hand, but the descendants of Husayn bin Ali regained power with support from Algeria. During the second half of the 18th century, the country was successively ruled by three of his descendants including Husayn's two sons Ali Bey (1759–81) and Hammouda Bey (Pasha) (1781–1813). Under their rule the country prospered for a brief period but in 1819 Tunisia was forced to put an end to piracy, thus depriving it of revenue. The country ran up large debts and taxes on agriculture and trade were increased to make up for the shortfall. The economy suffered and Tunisia was forced to borrow heavily from European (mainly French) banks.

A plate with a stylized image of an antelope

Tunisia's fate was sealed at the Berlin Congress in 1878, which had been called by the Europeans to decide how best to carve up the recently defeated Ottoman Empire. The country was now bankrupt and it was only a matter of time before one power or another stepped in.

In 1881, with the spurious excuse that they were protecting French-occupied Algeria from raids by Khroumirie tribesmen, France sent 30,000 troops across the border into Tunisia from Algeria. The troops swiftly took control first of Le Kef and then of Tunis. The initial opposition was intense but short-lived and the same year the Treaty of the Bardo, signed with Mohammed el-Sadiq Bey, recognized the bey as the nominal ruler with the proviso that France was in ultimate control.

Tunisian section at the 1851 London Exhibition

View of Carthage in the early 19th century

1819 Tunisia outlaws piracy

1836 France becomes the advocate and the guarantor of Tunisia's independence

1750	1775	1800	1825	1850	1875

1814 Death of Hammouda Bey marks the end of the Husaynid's "golden age"

1824–25 Tribal revolts break out in rural regions of Tunisia: trade collapses, peasant poverty increases

1855–56 Tunisian army suffers heavy losses in the Crimean War

THE COLONIAL ERA

The French had always attached great importance to the Maghreb – Tunisia, Algeria and Morocco. The history of their trade links, treaties and agreements made with these countries stretched back over three hundred years prior to taking control.

Tunisia's loss of independence was followed by reform of the central government, which, while preserving the Muslim administration with Sidi Ali Bey at its head, placed it under the control of the French civil service. On assuming the protectorate, the French made a number of key investments. By 1914, they had built olive oil refineries, schools and hospitals and had also embarked on the task of extending the railway network linking Tunis with Algeria, and Sousse with Sfax. In Tunis they extended La Goulette harbour and commenced the rapid development of the Ville Nouvelle (modern town) to which they moved most of the major government offices.

The walls of Tunis as seen in the mid-19th century

Souk in Tunis in the early 19th century

Sidi Ali Bey and his ministers

EARLY INDEPENDENCE MOVEMENT

These blessings of civilization served only the country's elite, however. A negative aspect was the purchase of land by rich Europeans. As a result, many Tunisian peasants were forced out to the poorer areas of the country, and the traditional way of life of stock-keeping shepherds began to disappear. At the same time, some 80,000 Tunisian troops fought in World War I – 10,000 died.

A struggle for independence was linked to growing national awareness, which in turn was brought about by better education within Arab society as a whole. One of the fathers of Arab nationalism was Jemeladdin al-Afghani whose ideology had a great influence on Tunisian activists. Two of the main architects of Tunisia's rebirth were Kheireddine Pasha (*d.*1889) and Sheikh Mohammed Kabadu (*d.*1871), who initiated a number of reforms of the religious tribunal and the Zitouna

TIMELINE

1881 Establishment of the French protectorate (12 May). Resistance movement fights against French rule

1892 One fifth of the area used for cultivation of olives is taken over by French settlers

1880

1890

1900

1910

1890–1914 Building of new schools, hospitals and railway lines (Tunis–Sfax, Tunis–Gabès)

Tunisian Army generals

"Arabic" pavilion in Paris in 1900, promoting the appeal of Tunisia

theological university. Kheiredine also founded the Sadiki College in 1875, an institution that was to play an important role in the cultural and intellectual life of Tunisia.

The college produced many of the later advocates of modernization of the country, as well as members of the "Unbreakable Bonds" society, founded in Tunis in 1885, which co-operated with the Egyptian reform movement. In

Façade of the town hall in Sfax

April 1885, the first public national demonstration took place in Tunis, organized by Mohammed as-Sanusi. At that time the activists demanded not so much independence as permission for Muslims to have their say in the running of the country. The French authorities arrested the leaders. The Tunisians were forced to change their tactics and commenced

French poster advertising Tunisia's attractions

an intensive struggle through the media, aimed in particular at the urban population.

Social unrest continued and the year 1920 saw the foundation of the Tunisian Constitutional Party, commonly known as Destour. It demanded a constitution, and access to all state offices for Tunisians as well as public education. Ten years later, a new generation of activists came to prominence. Among them was a young lawyer, Habib Bourguiba. He founded a newspaper, *L'Action Tunisienne*, and used it to launch a struggle against the authorities.

In March 1934, Bourguiba founded the Neo-Destour Party with the main aim of fighting for the country's independence. He drew massive support and the French, sensing the danger, declared the party illegal and had Bourguiba arrested, though he was later released. By 1938, however, popular resistance to French rule had became widespread. Just before the outbreak of World War II, Bourguiba was arrested again, but by the time the authorities had acted against the nationalists the war had already begun.

1920 Founding of the Destour Party		**1926** French decree puts an end to Tunisian freedom of the press, gatherings and associations	**1932** Habib Bourguiba founds *L'Action Tunisienne* daily newspaper
	1920	**1930**	**1940**

1914–1918
Ten thousand Tunisians are killed in World War I

1934 Founding of the Neo-Destour Party

Cavalry parade during the French Prime Minister's visit to Tunisia in 1939

WORLD WAR II

Tunisia's proximity to Italy suddenly had strategic importance for both sides. Despite aggressive German propaganda and earlier French-Tunisian tensions, the Tunisians came out in support of France and the Allies. The Germans were supporting the colonial ambitions of the Italians in Libya and the Italians, taking advantage of the situation, were also trying to gain control of Tunisia. In June 1940, after declaring war on Britain and France, Italy bombed military targets in Bizerte and around Tunis. German forces landed in Tunisia in 1942 while Rommel's Afrika Korps conducted a military campaign in the south. The German authorities also attempted to win Habib Bourguiba over to their side, but met with his firm refusal to co-operate.

Allied forces, commanded by General Patton (who was soon succeeded by Omar Bradley) and General Montgomery, began their advance into Tunisia in winter 1942. By liberation in 1943, the country had

Allied troops liberate Tunisia in 1943

suffered heavy losses: Sfax and Sousse were heavily damaged, while other towns like Bizerte, Gabès and Tunis suffered various degrees of bombardment. Allied casualties numbered some 15,000.

REGAINING OF INDEPENDENCE AND THE BOURGUIBA REGIME

After the war, France tried to relieve the political tensions persisting in Tunisia. It abolished censorship and installed a new Tunisian government headed by Mustapha Kaak. But the most decisive change in Paris's attitude towards Tunisian independence occurred only in 1954, when the office of French prime minister was taken over by Pierre Mendès-France – an advocate of peaceful solutions to France's colonial conflicts. The French press published an interview with the

Habib Bourguiba after the proclamation of independence

TIMELINE

1942 Germans invade Tunisia	**1943** Allied Forces liberate Tunisia	**1956** Regaining of independence (20 Mar)	**1959** Tunisian Republic gets its constitution (1 Jun)	**1964** Bourguiba nationalizes land of remaining French settlers	**1970s** Growing revenues from tourism stimulate growth of economy
1940	**1950**		**1960**		**1970**
	1957 Proclamation of the Tunisian Republic. Habib Bourguiba becomes the first president of independent Tunisia		**1963** French troops leave Bizerte (15 Oct)	**1967** Bourguiba reforms religious teaching	**1974** Habib Bourguiba is re-elected as president

Bofors gun dating from World War II

imprisoned Habib Bourguiba and the convention on Tunisian autonomy was signed in June 1955. On 20 March 1956 the country regained its independence and a year later the Tunisian Republic was proclaimed. Bourguiba became the country's first president and the leader of the Neo-Destour Party, which later restyled itself and changed its name to Parti Socialiste Destourien (PSD).

Tunisia's golden beaches act as a magnet to visitors

Before this, and immediately after regaining independence, work began on drafting a new constitution, which finally came into force on 1 June 1959. Its preamble affirmed that Tunisia was a free, independent and sovereign state. Its religion was Islam and Arabic was to be given priority in schools and government offices. Its political system was to be a free republic. This same constitution granted far-reaching powers to the new president.

Trade is stimulated by tourist revenue

BEN ALI

Despite a series of reforms and increased prosperity from tourism, there was much social unrest under Bourguiba's rule. A general strike was called in 1984 demanding an end to repression and a revocation of anti-constitutional laws. On 2 October 1987, the Minister of

The exiled President Zine el-Abidine Ben Ali

the Interior, Zine el-Abidine Ben Ali became the country's prime minister. On 7 November he assumed the office of PSD leader and forced President Bourguiba to give up the presidency for life. Bourguiba resigned in view of his advanced years and poor health. Ben Ali became president and promised a series of reforms. In the 1994, 1999, 2004 and 2009 general elections, he was once again elected the country's president, but following extensive protests in 2011 he fled the country. At the time of writing, Tunisia's government is in a state of flux. Elections are expected at the end of 2011.

Monument to Bourguiba in Monastir

1987 Prime Minister Zine el-Abidine Ben Ali becomes the country's president and commander of its armed forces

2002 Terrorist bomb kills 22 people in Djerba

2004 Zine el-Abidine Ben Ali is re-elected for a fourth term as president

2010 Public protests against government corruption begin

1980	1990	2000	2010	2020

1994 Zine el-Abidine Ben Ali is re-elected as the country's president

2002 Rule passed allowing president to rule for five terms

2011 Ben Ali goes into exile. Elections are expected at the end of the year

2009 Zine el-Abidine Ben Ali is re-elected for a fifth term as president

TUNISIA REGION BY REGION

Tunisia at a Glance

Tunisia's regions differ from one another not only in terms of culture, but also in terms of landscape. Travel to the north and northwest and there are forests, mountains and fertile plains. The central region is known for its historic remains dating from the Roman and early Arab eras. Jerba, the Sahel and Cap Bon peninsula, on the east coast, are famous for their magnificent beaches, while the southern section of the country is dominated by great salt flats and the vast expanse of the Sahara Desert.

NORTHERN TUNISIA
See pp122–143

CENTRAL TUNISIA
See pp212–241

Tabarka *is the main seaside resort of north-western Tunisia. It is a picturesque place, nestling beneath mountain slopes. A tourist zone is being developed around the town. This is also a favourite spot for divers who come to explore the offshore rocks and caves.*

Tamerza *is a fairly new village north of Tozeur. Nearby are the ruins of old Tamerza. Set among green palm groves, old Tamerza is a Berber village that was abandoned in 1969 after severe flooding. There are waterfalls and small lakes in which to cool off.*

Chott el-Jerid *is an extraordinary phenomenon. This vast seasonal salt-water lake is dry for much of the year and has salt piles that glitter with a multitude of colours. A trip across it is an unforgettable experience.*

Sbeïtla *lies southwest of Kairouan and is worth visiting for the nearby ruins of Sufetula, an ancient Roman town that has a number of well-preserved ruins including temples and a triumphal arch.*

| 0 km | 75 |
| 0 miles | 75 |

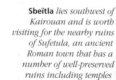
◁ Picturesque ruins of a small town, in the south of Tunisia

GREATER TUNIS AND CAP BON PENINSULA
See pp90–121

TUNIS
See pp64–89

Sidi Bou Saïd *is a charming town just a little way to the northeast of Tunis. The whitewashed houses with their blue doors and shutters create a unique atmosphere and the café-lined cobbled square has a sense of quiet affluence and peace. Set high on a cliff, the village attracted artists and writers such as Paul Klee and André Gide and was for a time the cradle of modern Tunisian painting.*

Bardo Museum *in Tunis is famous for its magnificent collection of Roman artifacts. Among these are some of the finest mosaics in the world, which were found on the sites of ancient towns, including Bulla Regia in northern Tunisia.*

THE SAHEL
See pp144–173

Sfax *is renowned for its medina, one of the most beautiful in the country. The 17th-century Dar Jellouli houses a museum with exhibits relating to the region's culture.*

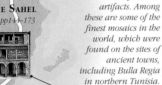

JERBA AND THE MEDININE AREA
See pp174–189

Jerba, *just off Tunisia's southeast coast, attracts large numbers of visitors who come to make the most of the mild climate and glorious beaches. Despite some development, the island has kept its distinctive culture intact, and many locals can be seen in traditional dress.*

SOUTHERN TUNISIA
See pp190–211

The camel *is one of the symbols of Tunisia. It is associated mainly with the Sahara Desert, which was once crossed by caravans. Today, a camel trip in the Sahara, lasting anything from a few hours to a few days, is a popular activity for visitors.*

TUNIS

Tunis has a compact city centre, making it easy to explore on foot. There is plenty to see. The lively medina has fascinating shops and markets as well as Islamic architecture dating back a thousand years. The Bardo Museum contains the world's largest collection of Roman mosaics, while along Avenue Habib Bourguiba there are continental-style cafés and restaurants. Just a little way out of Tunis lies the ancient site of Carthage.

The history of Tunis goes back to the early days of Carthage and it features on Roman maps dating from the first Punic War. Destroyed in 146 BC, it was half-heartedly rebuilt by the Romans but remained a place of little importance until the arrival of the Arabs in the 7th century. Believing it to have a good defensive position, Hassan ibn Nu'man, who had just ousted the Byzantines from Carthage, decided to build here and sited the medina on a bank of high ground next to a salt lake. The most significant work undertaken was the Great Mosque in AD 732 and the city served as the imperial capital during the last years of Aghlabid rule. From then on, Tunis was a major centre of science, culture and religion in North Africa.

During the Hafsid era (1228–1574), with trade flourishing between Europe and the East, it became an Arab metropolis and by the 13th century the Hafsids had made it their capital. The Ottoman Turks (1580–1705) saw no reason to change this and built heavy fortifications round the city as well as a large number of mosques and palaces.

By the 19th century the population was becoming too numerous to remain inside the city walls and the French drained some of the nearby marshland to extend the city. The new part features wide avenues and some distinctly European architecture.

Place de la Kasbah, paved with local stone

◁ Entrance to one of the medina's hammams (Turkish baths)

Tunis Town Centre

Two worlds are side by side in the centre of Tunis. On the one hand, there is the historic district, almost unchanged since medieval times, on the other, a modern metropolis. The western area of the centre is occupied by the medina, full of ancient palaces, mosques, medersas and souks. The eastern part comprises the Ville Nouvelle with the National Theatre, high-rise buildings, Art Deco houses, cinemas, a railway station and busy cafés and bars.

Palm trees and fountain for washing, in the arcaded courtyard of Sidi Mehrez Mosque

Fragment of a mosaic from the Bardo Museum

SIGHTS AT A GLANCE

Areas, Streets and Squares

Avenue Habib Bourguiba **28**
Bab el-Bahr **13**
Belvedere Park **30**
Place du Gouvernement **6**
Rue de la Hafsia **22**
Rue du Pasha **21**
Rue Jemaa Zitouna **12**

Markets

The Great Souk **7**
Main Market **29**
Souk el-Attarine **10**
Souk et-Trouk **3**

Museums & Historic Buildings

Bardo Museum pp88–9 **32**
Dar ben Abdallah **15**
Dar el-Bey **5**

Dar el-Haddad **19**
Dar Hussein **18**
Dar Lasram **23**
Dar Othman **14**
Hôtel Majestic **25**
National Library **11**
Théâtre Municipal **27**
Tourbet el-Bey **16**
Tourbet of Aziza Othmana **9**

Religious Buildings

Cathedral **26**
*The Great Mosque (Zitouna
  Mosque) pp70–71* **1**
Hammouda Pasha Mosque **8**
Jellaz Cemetery **31**
Kasbah Mosque **20**
Medersa Mouradia **17**
Sidi Mehrez Mosque **24**
Sidi Youssef Mosque **4**
The Three Medersas **2**

GETTING AROUND

The most convenient way
of exploring Tunis is on
foot. The buses and trams
can be crowded, but are
useful for reaching sites
further out, such as the
Bardo Museum. The TGM
train's main station is at
the end of Avenue Habib
Bourguiba and links the
centre of Tunis to the
suburbs. See pp326–7 for
more details.

[Map of central Tunis showing streets including Avenue Habib Bourguiba, Avenue de Carthage, Avenue Farhat Hached, and numbered sights; TGM Train Station 500 metres (550 yards); Train Station; Bus Station 1km (1.6 miles)]

0 m   200
0 yards   200

KEY

▨ Street-by-Street: The Medina
  See pp68–9

━ Boundary of old Medina wall

ℹ️ Tourist information

✝ Church

C Mosque

✚ Hospital

⊠ Post office

🚉 Train station

🚈 Light Rail station

🚌 Bus station

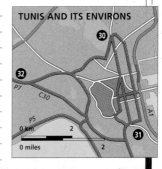

TUNIS AND ITS ENVIRONS

0 km   2
0 miles   2

Street-by-Street: The Medina

Tunis's ancient medina is classed by UNESCO as a World Heritage Site. Bustling with life for over one thousand years, it is full of narrow alleys, mosques, oriental markets and unexpected courtyards. It also has many mysterious and colourful doorways beyond which are ancient palaces and wealthy homes. The medina is centred on an axis formed by the Great Mosque and its many surrounding souks.

The Great Souk
The animated market has kept much of its traditional atmosphere and was used for scenes in the film The English Patient ⑦

Place du Gouvernement is the town's main square. It can be used as the starting point for exploring the medina ⑥

Dar el-Bey is the former beys' palace and is now the prime minister's office ⑤

Sidi Youssef Mosque
This distinctive mosque has the oldest Ottoman-style minaret in the medina (1616) and is crowned with a balustrade and a wooden roof ④

PLACE DU GOUVERNEMENT

RUE DE LA KASBAH

SOUK EL BEY

RUE SIDI BEN ZIAD

SOUK ET-TR

SOUK EL-BERKA

STAR SIGHTS

★ The Great Mosque

★ Souk et-Trouk

★ The Three Medersas

★ Souk et-Trouk
Built in 1630 by Sidi Youssef, this is one of the medina's most colourful rows of shops offering carpets, clothes and souvenirs. One shop has a terrace that provides a view of the medina ③

Hammouda Pasha Mosque

The main feature of this mosque (1665) is the octagonal minaret, which is built in the Turkish style. It is one of the most beautiful mosques in Tunis **8**

LOCATOR MAP
See Tunis map pp66-67

Tourbet of Aziza Othmana is the tomb of Aziza – daughter of Othman, a bey of Tunis **9**

National Library

The National Library contains over two million volumes. It is located at the heart of the medina, in the former military barracks built by Hammouda Pasha **11**

SOUK BLAGHIJA

RUE SIDI BEN AROUS

SOUK EL-ATTARINE (SUK AL-ATTARIN)

SOUK AL TURKI

RUE JAMAA ZITOUNA

Souk el Attarine has traded in perfumes, incense, henna, candles and herbs since the 13th century **10**

RUE DES LIBRAIRES

0 m   50
0 yards   50

★ **The Three Medersas**
These three Muslim schools comprise the Medersa of the Palm Tree, the Bachia and the Slimania **2**

★ **The Great Mosque**
This is the largest mosque in Tunis. Its construction was begun in the 8th century **1**

KEY

– – – Suggested route

The Great Mosque ❶

The Great Mosque has been at the heart of
Tunis since it was begun in the 8th century and
towers over the souks that crowd around it.
Aptly named, its striking east gallery opens up
suddenly when proceeding up the final yards
of Rue Jemaa Zitouna. Though parts of the
mosque have been remodelled many times, its
vast courtyard of polished marble is in its
original form and is surrounded on three sides
by graceful arcades.

★ **Courtyard**
*Shaded by simple arcades,
the courtyard is based
on Kairouan's
Great Mosque.*

The Capitals
*These ornate
decorations can be
seen crowning the many
columns surrounding
the inner courtyard of
the complex.*

★ **Minaret**
*This stands on the site
of a former defensive
tower. It has been
extended to a height
of 44 m (144 ft).*

Minaret Decorations
*These were built to
resemble the decorations
in the Kasbah Mosque.
The upper parts are
lined with ceramic tiles.*

STAR FEATURES

★ Courtyard

★ Minaret

Door to the Prayer Hall
The geometric patterns decorating the entrance to the prayer hall are based on Spanish designs.

VISITORS' CHECKLIST

Rue Jemaa Zitouna. *Tel* (74) 835 844. ◯ 8am–noon Sat–Thu, 8–11:30am Fri (only part of the gallery that overlooks the courtyard and the entrance to the prayer hall). ● Islamic holidays. 📷 📷

Minbar
Standing to the right of the mihrab (indicating the direction of Mecca), this is a pulpit from which the khutba (weekly sermon) is delivered.

Prayer Hall
At the far end of the courtyard, the prayer hall must be kept ritually pure. Non-Muslims are not allowed to enter.

Arcades
The three arcaded galleries in the main courtyard were built during the Husaynid dynasty (18th century).

The Dome
Since AD 864, this dome has topped the vestibule of the prayer hall.

The Three Medersas ❷

Rue des Libraires 11, 19 & Rue de la Medersa 13.

The Great Mosque is adjoined by a group of three medersas. Built by the Husaynids as residential Islamic schools in the 18th century, each of them has a similar layout, with a courtyard flanked on three sides by students' cells. Used by students studying the Koran, the fourth side of the medersas' courtyards adjoin the mosque.

The oldest of them is the **Medersa of the Palm Tree** (1714). Its name derives from the palm tree that stands at the centre of the courtyard surrounded by arcaded galleries. The arcades, with their horseshoe arches, have columns with richly ornamented capitals. The Medersa of the Palm Tree now houses the headquarters of the organization concerned with Koranic law.

Bachia, the second in the group, was built in 1752 by Ali Pasha. Standing next to the entrance is a small fountain with miniature pools that are always full of water. The adjacent *tourbet* (mausoleum) houses the Cultural Society. The third medersa, **Slimania**, also owes its existence to Ali Pasha, who built it in memory of his son Suleyman who had been murdered by his younger brother.

Inside a carpet shop in Souk et-Trouk

Souk et-Trouk ❸

This 17th-century Turkish market is situated between Souk el-Attarine (the scent market) and Souk el-Berka (formerly the site of the old slave market). It contains the north gateway to the Great Mosque and also **Au Palais d'Orient** – one of Tunis's best-known carpet shops and viewing points. Here, visitors will also find **Café M'Rabet** with its miniature garden (a kind of verandah) and a more expensive restaurant on the first floor (overlooking a section of the Great Mosque). This is the place to come to enjoy some traditional Tunisian music, a cup of tea and, for those that want it, a puff of tobacco through a *chicha* (hookah).

Sidi Youssef Mosque ❹

Rue Sidi ben Ziad.

This building is located on the first floor above the shops, which provided Muslim mosques with a revenue during the Turkish era. One of the most interesting Ottoman sacred buildings, the mosque has the the oldest Turkish minaret in the medina (1616). The octagonal minaret is set on a square base and is typical of Ottoman architecture. Most of the 48 columns (eight rows of six columns) in the prayer hall feature antique capitals and are North African in design. Adjacent to the mosque is the mausoleum of its founder – Sidi Youssef – which has a pyramid roof of green tiles. The complex is completed by the medersa, which was built in 1622.

Sidi Youssef Mosque with its 17th-century minaret

Dar el-Bey ❺

Place du Gouvernement.
🚫 to visitors.

The former seat of the bey rulers, and later of the French Protectorate administration, this is now the prime minister's office. Dar el-Bey, with its imposing 18th- and 19th-century façade, is the most important building in Tunis's Place du Gouvernement. Next to the west wing of the government's seat (in Rue Sidi ben Ziad) is the start of a marked walking route that leads towards the Great Mosque and further, to

Arcaded courtyard in the Medersa of the Palm Tree

For hotels and restaurants in this region see pp248–50 and pp272–5

Tourbet el-Bey and Dar ben Abdallah, in the south of the medina. At the start of the route there is a detailed map with the main sights and other points of interest clearly marked on it.

The palace was built as a guest house by a Husaynid monarch in 1795, on the ruins of a royal residence dating from the Muradid period. It was extensively remodelled in 1876 when it was used by the Bey of Tunis as a place to receive important visitors. It was here that he received many heads of state from Germany, England, France and the Ottoman Empire.

The bey himself lived outside Tunis in the Bardo area at this time. Prior to that, until the Husaynid period (18th century), the sultan's main residence was the nearby kasbah. The change was partly brought about by the fashion for building summer residences that prevailed at the beginning of the 19th century.

Place du Gouvernement **6**

This busy square is full of government buildings, fountains, palm trees and flowers. It is also a popular meeting place for young people and serves as a useful starting point for expeditions into the heart of the medina (it is just a short distance from the Great Mosque).

Place du Gouvernement is situated in what would once have been the western limit of the medina. It is flanked on the west by the Boulevard Bab Benat (Tunis's local government building stands on the opposite side of the avenue), and on the east and north by the Government Secretariat and the Ministry of Religious Affairs.

The Dar el-Bey *(see opposite)* stands at its southern end on the side of the Sidi Youssef Mosque. This former bey's residence has been renovated several times and now houses the offices of Tunisia's prime minister.

Busy alley in one of the medina's souks

The Great Souk **7**

The medina in Tunis has more than 20 souks. The major ones are adjacent to the Great Mosque and together form one vast, colourful, animated marketplace. Two terms, both meaning "market", compete with each other in the Muslim world: the bazaar (from the Persian) and the souk (from the Arabic). For centuries a souk had a distinct, cohesive character based on the traditions of the eastern and Mediterranean nations, and featured clearly identified places for various types of goods. From the beginning, this was a venue for trading

in goods and conducting financial transactions, as well as being the centre of social life. Arab souks, as opposed to European markets, were never places of residence for the merchants. The Great Mosque was always the seat of learning and faith, while the souks constituted the town's economic centre. Souks may seem chaotic but actually have a strict hierarchy. The immediate vicinity of the Great Mosque was reserved for the up-market bazaars selling articles such as religious books, perfumes, carpets and jewellery. In Muslim countries, the market was, and continues to be, an important element of Islamic life. The souk is a place where people come to shop, trade and meet friends. According to Muslim tradition, trading is the sweetest occupation. The medieval Arab scholar al-Ghazali, for instance, considered commerce as a form of preparation for the rewards of the next world.

Haggling is a strictly scripted performance: both parties must end up believing that they have struck a good bargain. Any customer who engages in a long bargaining process should not pull out of the deal at the end *(see p291)*.

Fountain in Place du Gouvernement

Hammouda Pasha Mosque ⑧

Corner of Rue Sidi ben Arous and Rue de la Kasbah.

One of the medina's most distinctive buildings, this mosque attracts a large number of the Muslim faithful for the all-important Friday prayers. The entire complex includes the mosque and the *tourbet* (tomb) of its founder, Hammouda Pasha, one of the early Ottoman rulers and the founder of the Muradid dynasty. The mosque was completed in 1665, a year before the monarch's death, and was lavishly decorated by craftsmen from Italy.

Two gates lead to the mosque, which is easily recognisable by its sandstone walls. The main one is the northern gate from Rue de la Kasbah while the side entrance is from Rue Sidi ben Arous. Inside the mosque is a courtyard surrounded with arcades, which are towered over by one of Tunis's most distinctive minarets – an octagonal, Turkish-style structure with black and white arches. The minaret's balcony would originally have been used by the muezzin to call the faithful to prayer, though this role has now been replaced by using loudspeakers.

Interior of the Hammouda Pasha Mosque

◁ **Ceramic and stonemasonry decorations in Dar Lasram**

Tourbet of Aziza Othmana ⑨

Rue Sidi ben Arous 23.

Not far from the Great Mosque stands the mausoleum of Aziza, daughter of Bey Othman, who has been revered by the people of Tunis for over 300 years. It was erected following the princess's death in 1669.

Aziza was renowned for her charity work. Towards the end of her life, she freed her slaves and left her estate to charitable foundations that helped the poor, supported medersas, financed hospitals, and provided dowries for impoverished girls. The entrance leads first to the *zaouia* of Sidi Ben Arous, where a doorman will show visitors the way to the *tourbet* of Aziza Othmana.

Souk el-Attarine ⑩

The scent of perfume and aromatic oils has long hung in the air around this perfume market. The immediate neighbourhood was reserved exclusively for rich souks that did not produce noise or offensive smells (butcher's and blacksmith's souks were always tucked far away from the Great Mosque). The 13th-century Souk el-Attarine owes its existence to the early Hafsid rulers. For centuries it was a venue for trading in perfumes, incense, aromatic essence, henna, candles, wax, as well as a mixture of herbs, flowers and resins. The market no longer specializes in perfume but visitors can still buy scent here and even have a special mixture made up to an individual

A perfume vendor in Souk el-Attarine

recipe. Well-known scents, such as Chanel No. 5, can also be approximately reproduced. For Tunisians, scents have symbolic meanings. To this day, wedding guests are sprinkled with essence of orange, newborn babies with geranium oil, and arriving guests with rose essence. The use of scents is given up only during the month of Ramadan.

Illuminated manuscript from the National Library's collection

National Library ⑪

Souk el-Attarine 20. **Tel** *(71) 325 338.* ⬤ to visitors.

Tunisia's National Library contains over two million volumes and manuscripts. It is at the very heart of the medina and occupies the former army barracks built by Hammouda Pasha. Before becoming a library, the colonial administration had turned the building into the Department of Antiquities and then added a library just for good measure. Following Tunisian independence, in 1956, the Department of Antiquities was moved to Dar Hussein, while the library was reorganized and its collection increased with thousands of Arab manuscripts that were collected together from the medina's many mosques and medersas. Unfortunately, the library is not open to visitors and entry requires permission from the Ministry of Culture.

Bab el-Bahr connecting the medina with the Ville Nouvelle

Rue Jemaa Zitouna ⑫

This is one of the medina's main streets (after Rue de la Kasbah). There are plenty of souvenir shops here but the same souvenirs can be bought much cheaper, and without haggling, in the sidestreets or the souks in the south or north of the medina.

The street runs steeply upwards, from Place de la Victoire and the Bab el-Bahr gate to the Great Mosque where the souks are some of the oldest in Tunis. The place is crowded and noisy from morning until 6pm, except for Ramadan, when it comes alive only at dusk and continues until 1 or 2am. The shops that line the street on both sides offer Nabeul ceramics, "Hand of Fatima"

talismans, birdcages, camel mascots, and hookahs or chicha pipes. The shopkeepers here are a multilingual lot and advertise their wares in most languages – German, English, French, Polish, Czech and Hungarian are all heard.

The top portion of the street has a number of shops selling Tunisian cakes. The **Café Ez-Zitouna** serves coffee and tea and provides the wherewithal for chichas. The end of Rue Jamaa Zitouna provides a view of the east gallery of the Great Mosque, which is illuminated at night. From here, turn right, then left and climb to the viewing roof of the **Au Palais d'Orient** carpet shop from where it is possible to look down on the Great Mosque's courtyard and the medina's roofs and minarets.

Bab el-Bahr ⑬

Place de la Victoire.

The Bab el-Bahr gate marks the symbolic border between the old quarter of Tunis and the Ville Nouvelle that was built by the French during the colonial era. This vast arch standing in Place de la Victoire was once the east gate in the wall that encircled the medina and would have been surrounded by huts and stalls.

Bab el-Bahr is the Arabic for "the Sea Gate" and is so named because of its close proximity to the sea. In the 19th century, the waters of Lake Tunis almost lapped up against the walls of the medina, though today its shores are about 1.5 km (1 mile) away. This is thanks to the French who drained much of the ground in order to lay foundations for the new town. As the Ville Nouvelle prospered, the Bab el-Bahr became a link between two worlds and a symbol of the new era. During the French protectorate, its name changed to the French Gate and only reverted to its old name after Tunisia regained independence. The present gate was built in 1848 on the orders of Ahmed Bey, who was inspired by the Arc de Triomphe and had the old gate demolished. It stands at the end of Avenue de France, which leads to Avenue Habib Bourguiba and the harbour.

HAND OF FATIMA

The "Hand of Fatima", referred to as the *khamsa* meaning "five", is a common talisman thought to ward off bad luck. Many Muslims believe it also protects and bestows blessings. Fatima was the daughter of the Prophet Mohammed and an idealized mother and wife. The Fatimid dynasty claimed descent from her. The five fingers symbolize not only the five pillars of Islam, but also the Muslim prayer that is repeated five times a day.

"Fatima's hand" on a house wall

Garden in the inner courtyard of Dar Othman

Dar Othman ⑭

Rue el-M'Bazza 16. *Tel (71) 321 452.*
☐ *summer: 8am–2pm; winter:
9am–1pm, 3–5pm daily.*

One of the medina's oldest
and most stately palaces, Dar
Othman has a façade of black
and white marble; the interior
has a rich array of mosaics,
wooden ceiling decorations
covered with magnificent
paintings and a small garden
in the inner courtyard. Located in the southern part of the
medina, not far from Dar ben
Abdallah, the palace was built
by Othman Bey who resided
here from 1594 until his death
in 1610. The first owner of
the palace became famous for
his unswerving principle of
separating state affairs from
his private life and this palace
was designed to provide him
with a haven in which he
could take a rest from his
daily work, while separate
sections were allocated for
receiving visitors. Subsequent
inhabitants of the palace
included Bey Hussein and Ibd
Mahmud. Now the restored
palace houses the headquarters of the Medina Conservation Department.

Dar ben
Abdallah ⑮

**Museum of Popular Arts and
Traditions**, entrance from Rue ben
Abdallah. *Tel (71) 256 195.*
☐ *8am–2pm.* ● *Sun.* 📷 📷

This 18th-century palace,
located in the southern part
of the medina, has a fine
courtyard, surrounded by tall
arcaded galleries with walls
that are decorated with
colourful ceramic tiles. One
of the finest palaces in the
medina, it was built by Slimane
Kahia el-Hanafi, a government
official responsible for the
collection of taxes during the
reign of Hammouda Pasha.
The entrance from the courtyard leads to the inner rooms
of the palace, where the
**Museum of Popular Arts and
Traditions** has displays illustrating the lives of the medina's
19th-century inhabitants.

Visitors can still see some
of the rooms that were used
by the owner, his wife and
children, plus additional guest
rooms and the kitchens. The
interior furnishings include
Venetian mirrors, crystal
chandeliers and candelabras.
The palace, originally called
Dar Kahia, got its new name
from its later owner – Ben
Abdallah, a merchant, who
lived here from 1875–99.
The Théâtre d'Art Dar Ben
Abdallah is a theatre and
film venue located opposite
the palace.

Tourbet el-Bey ⑯

Museum–mausoleum, Rue
Tourbet el-Bey 62. ☐ *9am-4:30pm
daily.* ● *Sun.* 📷 📷

This royal mausoleum of the
Husaynids was built by Ali
Pasha II (1758–82). It is not
far from Dar ben Abdallah
and Dar Othman (a marked
trail leads to all three sights,
starting from Place du
Gouvernement). Although
Islam – and particularly the
Malekite school – calls for
simple burials, with the

Mannequins in one of the museum rooms in Dar ben Abdallah

arrival of the Turkish Ottomans the Hanefite school began to gain influence. This allowed for far more fanciful, richly ornamented and opulent mausoleums.

Tourbet el-Bey is an entire architectural complex, covered with several domes of different sizes, and includes two inner courtyards (orange trees grow in the smaller of these), and is reminiscent of palace architecture.

Entrance to Tourbet el-Bey

Medersa Mouradia ⓱

Souk des Etoffes 37.

Just a short distance from the Great Mosque, this 18th-century Muslim residential school is entered through a large and ornately studded wooden door. Its inner courtyard is surrounded by an arcaded gallery. The courtyard is typically Tunisian in style and features an entrance to the prayer hall, marked by an arcade, which is horseshoe-shaped and in black and white marble. Wooden doors lead to the cells of the older students. The medersa was built in 1637 by Murad II, on the site of some Turkish army barracks that were destroyed during a rebellion.

Dar Hussein ⓲

Place du Château. *Tel* (71) 574 127. ◻ (courtyard only) summer: 8am–2pm, winter: 9am–1pm, 2:30–5:30pm.

This is one of the finest restored palaces of the medina. Built in the 18th century, it is a stately place,

and was erected on the site of an 11th-century palace. Today it houses the National Institute of Arts and Archaeology and visitors are welcome to look around. As this is an official building, formal dress is required. It is reached via the short and narrow Rue du Château. Having passed through the *skifa* (vestibule), enter the spacious palace courtyard, which has a modern, sloping glazed roof. The courtyard is surrounded by cloisters with columns topped with Corinthian capitals. The walls are covered in colourful ceramic tiles (the work of Italian artisans) that feature floral motifs and intricate geometrical patterns. The wooden vaults have also been beautifully decorated.

Dar el-Haddad ⓳

Impasse de l'Artillerie 9. *Tel* (71) 570 937. ◻ (courtyard only) summer: 8am–2pm, winter: 9am–1pm, 2:30–5:30pm. ◼ Fri. Admission free.

Hidden away in a labyrinth of narrow alleys, this is one of the oldest palaces in the medina and was built in the late 16th century. Restored in 1966, it now houses a branch of the National Heritage Institute. The easiest way to

Cloisters around Dar Hussein's arcaded courtyard

get here is from the west (from Boulevard Bab Menara), via Souk Sekkajine (turning into Rue ben Mahmoud), or via Rue du Château (also turning into Rue ben Mahmoud). From the 18th century, the palace belonged to the wealthy Haddad family, who arrived from Andalusia following the fall of Granada. The courtyard is surrounded by porticoes on three sides and its columns are topped with capitals from the period of the Hafsids.

Exquisitely decorated arcades around the patio of Dar el-Haddad

The minaret of the Kasbah Mosque

Kasbah Mosque ⓴

Place de la Kasbah.

The Kasbah Mosque gets its name from the fort that stood above the medina during the Hafsid reign. Badly damaged during a revolt by Turkish troops in 1811, only the mosque and parts of the wall running along Rue el-Zouaoui have survived. Protected by mighty walls, the kasbah was once the venue of the sultan's council gatherings and this was where the sultan held audiences.

Adjacent to the kasbah were the army barracks and city guard quarters. These were used as the sultan's residence until Husaynid times (18th century) and continued to retain a military function. During the time of the French Protectorate, they were occupied by French troops. The barracks were eventually demolished in 1957.

The mosque is well worth visiting, if only to see its minaret (the tallest in the medina), which served as the model for the Great Mosque's Malekite minaret. Five times a day, the call to prayer is signalled by briefly flying a white flag from the minaret.

Rue du Pasha ⓴

During the Ottoman period, this cobbled street bisected the town's smartest district. Today, it is a popular tourist route and divides the medina from north to south. It is worth taking a closer look at the small courtyards, window shutters, and the main doors along its route. The size and grandeur of each door is directly related to the size and grandeur of the residence behind it. Almost every door in this street is still furnished with its traditional doorknocker. Some of the houses have more than one knocker. These used to indicate the number of people who once lived inside and date from a time when different sounding "knocks" were used to signal the identity and gender of guests (men, women and children each had different doorknockers). One of the most elaborate of these doors can be found at No. 29.

Rue du Pasha is also full of intricately decorated façades and window shutters, and is an ideal place for taking some photographs.

Visitors can discover a variety of unusual places, such as the former palace at No. 71. Dilapidated but full of charm this once-grand building stands beyond a small garden planted with jasmine and banana trees. It now houses the headquarters of the Tunisian Red Crescent (volunteers are pleased to show visitors around).

Rue de la Hafsia ⓴

This district occupies the northern part of the medina. It was once inhabited by Jews, who towards the end of the 19th century moved to the Ville Nouvelle. Neglected and derelict, it gained a reputation as one of the seedier parts of town.

There were calls to demolish it but in the early 1980s the Hafsia area was redeveloped in a way that respected traditional styles and urban values.

Dar Lasram ⓴

Rue du Tribunal 24.
◯ summer: 8am–2pm; winter: 10am–7pm; Ramadan: 10am–2pm, 9–11:30pm.

Dar Lasram is one of the most stately and expertly renovated palaces in the entire medina. Visitors have access to the courtyard as well as some of the main rooms including the library, which has several displays of maps, plans and photographs.

Construction of the palace began in the latter part of the 18th century and was continued by Hammoud Lasram, a rich landowner and high-ranking officer. His descendants inhabited it until 1964. The palace is arranged over three storeys: the ground floor was occupied by the servants, the raised first floor was the main portion of the house, and the top floor was set aside for guests.

Rue du Pasha – an ancient street

Magnificently decorated rooms of Dar Lasram

Visiting the palace offers a unique insight into how the wealthy lived in 19th-century Tunis. The main door opens up to the *driba* (entrance hall), which was used by the owner of the house to receive visitors. The room to the right of the entrance is the *bayt-al-sahra* (evening room). During the day, it was used by teachers but in the evening it became a venue for all-male gatherings, which were livened up by female dancers.

Women also had their own soirees. For these, the servants would sprinkle the carpets and pond with rose and jasmine petals, fill the censers with ambergris, incense and aloe and arrange cushions on the floor. After the women had taken their seats, a large tray would be brought in, laden with sweets and glasses of tea.

Much of the decoration is in keeping with this lavish lifestyle. The wall containing the door to the *dar al-kebira* (state rooms) is lined with pink sandstone while the white stuccowork above the door resembles intricate lace. Look out for the arches supported by Doric columns that feature charming stucco decorations.

It is perhaps no surprise that such a stunning palace is now the home of the Association de Sauvegarde de la Medina (The Medina Conservation Society).

Sidi Mehrez Mosque ㉔

Rue Sidi Mehrez. ⬤ *to non-Muslims.*

This mosque stands in the northern part of the medina, in the El-Hafsia district. Begun in 1675, it was named after the town's patron saint – Sidi Mehrez – a prominent 10th-century marabout (Islamic holy man) and theologian, who arrived here from Kairouan. It was to him that Tunis owed its recovery in 944. The mosque architecture and decorations are reminiscent of the traditional Muslim buildings of Istanbul. One of the best views is to be had from the north side of Bab Souika.

Richly ornamented interior of Sidi Mehrez Mosque

THE CORSAIRS

The glamorous but violent world of the corsairs played a significant role in shaping the history of Tunisia from the mid-16th century until the early 19th century. The most notorious corsair was the Turkish-born Khair ed-Din Barbarossa (Red Beard), who based himself on the island of Jerba and in 1534 captured Tunis. Under the Ottomans there was great wealth to be taken at sea and corsairs flourished during the Husaynid period as a major Tunisian enterprise. During the late 17th and early 18th centuries some maritime nations even paid bribes to Tunisia so that their ships would not be attacked.

Barbarossa, once the most notorious corsair in Tunisia

The whole building is topped by a large white dome, surrounded by four smaller ones (also white). The courtyard is surrounded on three sides by arcades; and the walls of the prayer hall are richly ornamented.

Opposite the entrance to the mosque is the mausoleum of Sidi Mehrez (also known as Mehrez ibn Chalaf). The tomb is revered by Muslims and Jews alike. Sidi Mehrez was famous for his tolerance and won a number of concessions for the Jews. Thanks to him, those who traded in the local souks were granted the right to settle within the city walls and no longer had to leave the city at nightfall.

Hôtel Majestic ㉕

Avenue de Paris. **Hotel and restaurant** for renovation until 2012.

The Hôtel Majestic stands in Avenue de Paris, in the Ville Nouvelle. Built in 1914, it has a beautiful white façade with gently curved corners typical of Art Nouveau architecture. It also boasts several lovely balconies. The hotel is built over four-storeys: the first floor has a terrace where guests once took afternoon tea. The surroundings have changed somewhat: the once quiet street is now a busy avenue, full of shops, people and cars. Nevertheless, the hotel retains some of its old charm. A ten-minute walk along Avenue de Paris will bring visitors to Avenue Habib Bourguiba.

Hôtel Majestic, once among the best hotels in Tunis

Cathedral ㉖

Place de l'Indépendance.

The Cathedral of St Vincent de Paul and St Olive, to give it its full name, stands at the very centre of the Ville Nouvelle, close to Bab el-Bahr. Construction began in the 1890s, on the site of a Catholic cemetery dedicated to St Antoine. Mentioned in a number of early 17th-century texts, this cemetery was originally destined for deceased slaves who had previously been captured by corsairs operating out of Tunis. The cathedral, with its

Façade of the Cathedral of St Vincent de Paul

tall twin towers which form the entrance, is an odd mix of Byzantine, Gothic and North African architecture. This echoes the varied history of Christianity in the region and resembles the Christian basilica in Henchir Khira, near Béja, with a Byzantine-style dome rising above the nave and the transept intersection. A mosaic above the main entrance depicts Christ.

Inside, the church has a broad mix of styles and imagery. The arcade is crowned with the figure of Abraham blessing the Jews, the Christians and the Muslims. The painting in the apse depicts the Assumption of St Vincent de Paul who is surrounded by the figures of North African saints and

martyrs, led by the famous bishop of Carthage – St Cyprian. The green-blue stained-glass window on the left (south transept) depicts the Assumption of the Virgin Mary, while the red-gold window on the right (north transept) shows the descent of the Holy Spirit at Pentecost.

The main altarpiece mosaics are composed of alabaster and marble, and are fashioned in a typical Tunisian style. Built in 1921, the cathedral's organ is generally regarded as the finest in North Africa. The cathedral is occasionally used as a venue for concerts.

Théâtre Municipal ㉗

Avenue Habib Bourguiba.

This theatre was built by the French in the early 20th century and is a classic example of Art Nouveau, with distinctive white stucco, soft flowing floral forms and fantastic carved figures. It is still used as a theatre today and is a good venue for concerts of both classical and Arabic music as well as films and talks.

Ornate stuccowork on the façade of the Théâtre Municipal

Ville Nouvelle Architecture

During the period of the French Protectorate (1881–1956), the population of Tunis began to move beyond the walls of the medina. New structures appeared and wealthy Tunisians gave up the narrow labyrinthine alleys of the medina for the wide avenues and apartments of the Ville Nouvelle. The building of the new town coincided with the development of Art Nouveau in France and Italy, followed later by Art Deco. Perhaps no other European style has merged so successfully with Islamic architecture as Art Nouveau. The arabesque, an ornament typical of Islamic art, blended perfectly with the curves and undulating surfaces of Art Nouveau, as did the Islamic taste for ornate stuccowork and florid decorations.

Street lamps *with fanciful decorations protecting their glass shades illuminate and decorate Avenue Habib Bourguiba – one of the finest streets in the European district of Tunis.*

The Oriental style *featuring domes, arched windows and courtyards, combines with European elements and can be seen in the buildings around Place du Gouvernement.*

Art Nouveau *houses, adorned with stunning balconies are common on Avenue de Paris, Rue ibn Khaldun and Rue Ali Darghouth.*

Architecture *inspired by Baroque and Renaissance styles is the most prevalent in Tunis's modern town. Frequently, each storey of a building is constructed in the style of a different era. The extremely rich, heavily ornamented façades are also reminiscent of Islamic architecture.*

The colonial style *is represented mainly by apartment blocks and public buildings. These were built in clusters in styles fashionable in Europe during the late 19th century.*

Architectural details *including floral motifs and figures adorn the façades of most houses built during the colonial era.*

Imposing clock tower standing at the end of Avenue Habib Bourguiba

Avenue Habib Bourguiba ㉘

The main street of Tunis's Ville Nouvelle, Avenue Habib Bourguiba runs like an artery through the city linking the harbour and TGM train station with the medina. Along the way it cuts through Place du 7 Novembre 1987 (which commemorates the day when Bourguiba was replaced by Zine el-Abidine Ben Ali) and Place de l'Indépandance. From here it becomes Avenue de France. About half way along, Place du 7 Novembre has a fountain and a prominent clock tower decorated with fine tracery. In the evenings the illuminated clock and the multicoloured fountain become a popular meeting places for the youth of Tunis.

The section between here and the cathedral is the busiest part of this tree-lined promenade and there are plenty of smart cafés and fashionable restaurants to tempt visitors. Café de Paris, situated near Hôtel Africa, is the birthplace of the Ecole de Tunis, founded in 1949, which was an influential group of Tunisian painters. The café is still a popular meeting place, although little has remained of its artistic atmosphere. Moving on towards the medina, you pass

on the left hand side the lovely Art Nouveau façade of the Théâtre Municipal (see p82). Next to it is a large modern shopping centre, the Palmarium. At No.47 Avenue Bourguiba there is a craft workshop run by women, Mains des Femmes, selling good quality Tunisian crafts and souvenirs.

Tunis Cathedral (see p82) stands in Place de l'Indépendance, not far from Bab el-Bahr. Opposite is the French Embassy. To the left, beneath the arcades, are several smart shops selling clothes and shoes, and also Magasin Général – a large self-service store where food and drink can be purchased on the ground floor.

Fishmonger's stall in the main market

Main Market ㉙

Rue d'Allemagne. ⬚ from the early morning until about 2:30pm.

This huge market hall is situated not far from Bab el-Bahr and is where many of the residents of Tunis come to do their weekly shopping. Built during the colonial era and now restored, it has a high-vaulted roof to protect shoppers from the rain or heat. A wide variety of goods is on offer. Articles include a large selection of excellent cheeses, dozens of varieties of the Tunisian harissa (chilli and garlic sauce), cooking oil, vegetables, fruit, meat and fish. On sale right by the entrance are flowerpots containing Tunisian herbs and other plants that include varieties of jasmine, bougainvillea, basil and rosemary. A large part of the hall is occupied by fruit and vegetable vendors trying to out-perform each other in the hope of getting passers-by to purchase their products. Any transaction may involve haggling. The market is worth visiting if only to witness these scenes of everyday Tunisian life.

◁ **A stall with lanterns, plates and hookahs in the medina**

Belvedere Park ⓺

Entrance on Avenue des Etats-Unis or Place Pasteur. 🚊 🚍 **Tel** (71) 89 0 386. @ ami.belvedere@planet.tn

Belvedere Park is located to the north of the medina, on the slope of a hill standing some 2 km (1 mile) from the end of Avenue Habib Bourguiba. Outside rush hour it is possible to get there by TGM train (the Tunisians refer to it as the metro) from République (get off at Palestine then walk).

This is Tunis's only major park and provides an opportunity to escape from the busy and somewhat cramped streets and alleys of the medina. The park was established in 1892 by Josepha de Laforcade, a landscape artist and one of Paris's top gardeners. Initially it was closed to the public (due to construction works and the natural plant growth cycle) and the official opening did not take place until 1910.

To this day it remains a favourite place for family outings, receptions and Sunday picnics. At the last count, it had over 230,000 trees and 80 species of plants including olive trees, pines and numerous varieties of cacti. The park also plays an important educational role. A visit to the Friends of Park Belvedere Park, which has a small office on the high ground near the park's entrance, will provide information on the many plants growing in the garden, and also on Tunisia's flora and fauna in general. Close to this is the **Centre d'Animation Équestre**, which organizes pony-trekking activities in the Tabarka region in summer, and in Nefta and Tamerza in winter. A little higher up is a fairly gentle assault course.

There is also a zoo in the southern section of the park which has a number of birds and animals native to Africa. The zoo has a small admission charge and attracts over a million visitors a year. If visiting the zoo, look out

Belvedere Park – a popular recreational area for residents of Tunis

for the Midha, a 17th-century ablutions room that was transported here from the Souk et-Trouk in the medina and was also displayed at the World Exhibition in Paris in 1900. Not far from the zoo there is an artificial lake.

Standing at the heart of the park, on a hill, is a lovely *koubba* or pavilion. Once part of Hammouda Pasha's rose garden in the suburb of Manouba to the west of Tunis, it was placed here in 1922 to serve as a resting place and viewpoint. It is an excellent example of Tunisian architecture. Its decoration tastefully combines a variety of styles – Italian white marble columns, Doric capitals, Moorish-Spanish ceramics and stuccoes, and Tunisian earthenware.

The Rose Palace, which remains in Hammouda Pasha's rose garden in Manouba, now houses a fine Military Museum.

Centre d'Animation Équestre
Tel (98) 652 085.
Fax (71) 880 262.

Jellaz Cemetery ⓷

Next to Bab Alleoua.

Located next to the bus station, this burial ground is the largest in Tunis. Visiting the graves of one's relatives is considered a duty, especially during Aïd el-Fitr, at the end of Ramadan. At this time the cemetery is visited by family groups, who clean and whitewash the tombs, which are all arranged to face towards Mecca. The first mass demonstrations against French rule took place here in 1911, costing the lives of 30 Tunisians and nine Frenchmen in the riot that ensued.

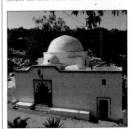

Entrance to Jellaz Cemetery – the largest burial ground in Tunis

For hotels and restaurants in this region see pp248–50 and pp272–5

Bardo Museum ⓷⓷

Ceramic decoration

Located on the outskirts of Tunis, the Bardo Museum occupies a former palace belonging to the Husseinite beys. The museum has an unrivalled collection of Roman mosaics dating from the 2nd to 4th centuries AD that once adorned the homes of some of Roman Africa's wealthiest citizens. Other exhibits include Punic funeral masks, Greek bronze statuary, Islamic tiles and finds from a ship that sunk off the coast of Mahdia in the 1st century BC.
Many exhibits may not be on view during renovations, which are ongoing until 2012.

2nd floor

★ Eros
(125 BC)
This bronze statuette is one of the most precious objects that was recovered from a ship that went down off Mahdia during the 1st century BC.

Mosaic with the image of Virgil

1st floor

★ Roman Sarcophagus (3rd century AD)
The relief depicts the three Graces and the four seasons of the year – a favourite Roman motif that often appears on tombs and in mosaics.

Ground floor

Minerva (2nd century AD)
The marble statue of Minerva, goddess of wisdom and war, patron of crafts, arts and literature, stands on the ground floor, in the corridor devoted to Roman sculpture.

STAR EXHIBITS

★ Eros

★ Julius Mosaic

★ Roman Sarcophagus

MUSEUM GUIDE

Roman mosaics are spread over all floors and Islamic art occupies rooms on the ground and first floors. Underwater finds from Mahdia are on the first floor. Punic and early Christian exhibits are on the ground floor. Some items may not be on view during renovation.

Entrance

Mosaics from the
Acholla baths,
near Sfax

VISITORS' CHECKLIST

Bardo 2000. 🚌 from Bab el-
Khadra, Nos. 3A, 3D, 16A, 16C,
30, 58 and 68. 🚋 4 from Park
Thameur. 🚇 **Tel** (71) 513 650.
Fax (71) 514 050. ⬜ Apr–mid-
Sep: 9am–5pm Tue–Sun; mid-
Sep–Mar: 9:30am–4:30pm
Tue–Sun. ⬤ Mon. 🖼️ 📷 📷

Mahdia Room
*In 1907 sponge
divers came across
the wreck of a ship
near Mahdia that
sank during the
1st century BC. It
contained marble
columns, reliefs,
sculptures and
bronze vases.*

Carthage Room
*This room has a
fine collection of
statuary from
Roman Carthage.
At its centre is a
monument to
Augustus from the
1st century AD. The
floor mosaics date
from the 3rd
century AD and
once decorated
wealthy homes
in Oudna.*

★ Julius Mosaic
*(3rd century AD)
This Carthaginian
mosaic belongs to
a series depicting
farming in North
Africa. Other
mosaics illustrate
scenes from
everyday life
and mythology.*

Dougga and Sousse Rooms
*The Dougga Room has an
intricately decorated ceiling
with floral and arabesque
motifs. In the adjacent Sousse
Room is a fine floor mosaic.
Recovered from a villa in
Sousse, it represents the
Triumph of Neptune.*

KEY

🟦	Roman art
⬜	Christian art
🟦	Punic art
⬜	Islamic art
🟦	Objects recovered from the shipwreck off Mahdia
⬜	Prehistoric art
⬜	Non-exhibition rooms

GREATER TUNIS AND CAP BON PENINSULA

*T*he coastal suburbs just east of Tunis, including La Goulette, Carthage and Sidi Bou Saïd, provide an alternative to the bustle of the city. Drawn by cooling sea breezes, many locals visit this area on hot summer evenings. Further east is the Cap Bon peninsula. A major agricultural region since Carthaginian times, Cap Bon has some fine beaches and has become one of Tunisia's main resort areas.

Poking out like a finger into the Mediterranean Sea, the Cap Bon peninsula is a mere 140 km (87 miles) from Sicily. Some geologists believe that it may once have provided a link between Africa and Europe until rising sea levels cut it off some 30,000 years ago. A range of mountains divides the peninsula lengthways into its eastern and western portions. The east coast, with its fine beaches and historic ruins, is mostly given up to resorts such as Hammamet and Nabeul while the west coast is more rugged and less frequently visited. Cap Bon is also one of the country's major industrial regions. La Goulette is a major port, and handles frequent passenger traffic from Europe.

The Carthaginians made the most of the fertile soil and by the time the Romans settled here the cape resembled a spectacular garden, and was named the Beautiful Cape or Cap Bon. When the French arrived in the 19th century they planted huge citrus groves and vineyards.

Even today, many farms thrive and, thanks to a high level of rainfall and efficient irrigation systems, Cap Bon provides the country with 80 per cent of its citrus fruit crop, 60 per cent of its grapes and almost half of its vegetables. Most Tunisian wines are also produced in this area, especially around the town of Grombalia, which has an annual wine festival in September.

Harvesting oranges in Cap Bon

◁ Striking white minaret of a mosque in Sidi Bou Saïd

Exploring Greater Tunis and Cap Bon Peninsula

Greater Tunis and the Cap Bon Peninsula have fine beaches, fertile land and unique historic sights. A visit to the ruins of Carthage, once the second city of the Roman Empire, is unmissable for anyone interested in this period. Just north of Carthage, the charming town of Sidi Bou Saïd looks out over the Gulf of Tunis, and has some fine restaurants. The gently rolling terrain and rugged coast of Cap Bon are perfect for exploring, as are the Roman ruins in Kerkouane. Nabeul, a little way from Hammamet, has a busy market and is famous for its ceramics. Spring is a good time to visit, when the scent of orange and lemon blossom is in the air.

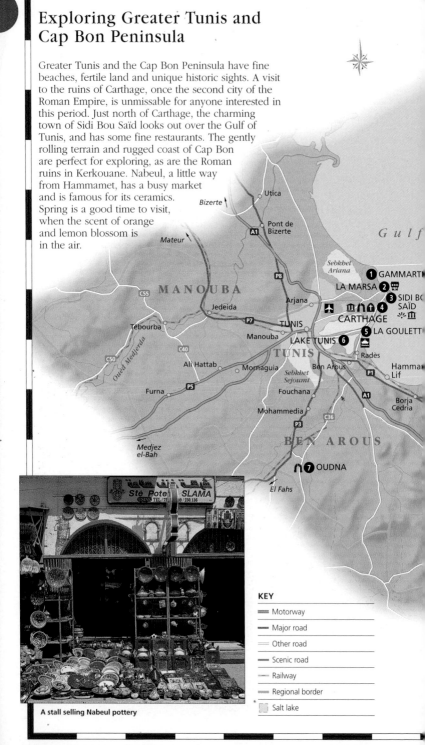

Bizerte

Utica

Pont de Bizerte

Mateur

Gulf

Sebkhet Ariana

1 GAMMART

LA MARSA 2

3 SIDI BOU SAÏD

MANOUBA

Arjana

4

CARTHAGE

Jedeida

TUNIS

Manouba

5 LA GOULETTE

Tébourba

LAKE TUNIS 6

TUNIS

Radès

Oued Medjerda

Ali Hattab

Mornaguia

Ben Arous

Hammam Lif

Sebkhet Sejoumi

Furna

Fouchana

Borj Cedria

Medjez el-Bah

Mohammedia

BEN AROUS

7 OUDNA

El Fahs

A stall selling Nabeul pottery

Ste Poteri SLAMA

KEY

- ▬ Motorway
- ▬ Major road
- ▬ Other road
- ▬ Scenic road
- ▬ Railway
- ▬ Regional border
- ▢ Salt lake

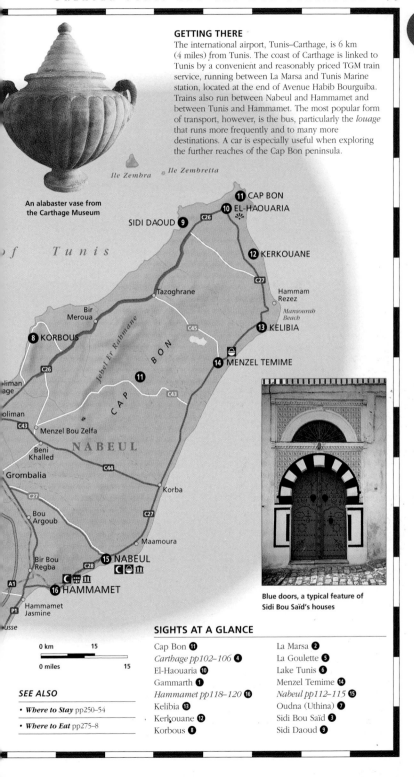

GETTING THERE

The international airport, Tunis–Carthage, is 6 km (4 miles) from Tunis. The coast of Carthage is linked to Tunis by a convenient and reasonably priced TGM train service, running between La Marsa and Tunis Marine station, located at the end of Avenue Habib Bourguiba. Trains also run between Nabeul and Hammamet and between Tunis and Hammamet. The most popular form of transport, however, is the bus, particularly the *louage* that runs more frequently and to many more destinations. A car is especially useful when exploring the further reaches of the Cap Bon peninsula.

An alabaster vase from the Carthage Museum

Blue doors, a typical feature of Sidi Bou Saïd's houses

0 km   15
0 miles   15

SEE ALSO

- *Where to Stay* pp250–54
- *Where to Eat* pp275–8

SIGHTS AT A GLANCE

A former beylical bathing pavilion on La Marsa beach

Gammarth ❶

Road map C1. 24 km (15 miles) northeast of Tunis.

The smart seaside resort of Gammarth is an upmarket place, with expensive hotels, magnificent beaches and lush greenery. In the past this was just a small fishing village nestled beneath cliffs. Holidaymakers have been visiting here since the 1950s and now tourism is the main source of the town's income. As well as the many four- and five-star hotels and some good restaurants, the town has some lovely private villas, hidden away in the hills.

Small sandy coves provide ideal conditions for swimming and most water sports. The town itself is small and its activities are firmly aimed at the holiday trade. During the high season, when it can become very busy, its narrow streets fill with boisterous visitors and those in the know often head a little way north in search of more remote and emptier beaches.

White houses perched on the high cliffs of Gammarth

La Marsa ❷

Road map C1. 22 km (14 miles) north of Tunis. *La Marsa Nights (Jul/Aug).*

La Marsa was once a district of Punic Carthage, and known as Megara. In the 7th century it became a port – Marsa er-Rum. Today, it is known for its beaches and is the favourite weekend playground for Tunis's residents. It is easy to get to by TGM train (from the end of Avenue Bourguiba in Tunis); the journey takes half an hour. It is worth stopping for a while at Café Saf-Saf at Place Saf-Saf, to enjoy a snack, a glass of mint tea or a Turkish coffee. Look out for the well on the terrace which dates back to the Hafsid period. Sometimes a camel working the well's wheel can be seen.

PAUL KLEE IN TUNISIA

"Colour has taken possession of me. Colour and I are one. I am a painter." So wrote Paul Klee (1879–1940), the Swiss-born painter associated with the Bauhaus, during his visit to Tunisia in 1912–14. Klee was taken aback by the festive colours he encountered in Tunis, Sidi Bou Saïd and Kairouan and his works from that period, such as those built up of coloured squares, were clearly influenced by the mosaics and arabesques that he so admired. His Tunisian-inspired paintings include *Sunrise over Tunis* and *Camels and Donkeys*.

Paul Klee

In the late 19th century, the Bey of Tunis built his residence here (Abdallia Palace). In order to make it possible for the ladies of the court to bathe discreetly, the palace was fitted with a specially constructed wooden terrace that rested on pillars over the sea. Openings were built into the floor that allowed the women to get in and out of the water well away from prying eyes.

The town has some good beaches and is a popular place. Looking from the beach towards the town, there are a number of small white houses standing on hillsides, hidden amid greenery. The smart, tastefully designed hotels all have direct access to the sea. With Sidi Bou Saïd and Tunis just a short train ride away, La Marsa makes a good base for a Tunisian holiday.

Beaches around Tunis

Tunis's suburbs include over 25 kilometres (16 miles) of beaches. They can easily be reached by car or by TGM train from the station at the end of Avenue Bourguiba. The coastline is varied – flat around Carthage and La Marsa, but rocky in the region of Gammarth and Sidi Bou Saïd. The small coastal towns have plenty of restaurants and cafés and are ideal for an afternoon or evening excursion.

Gammarth ⑤
Gammarth is famous for its exquisite fish restaurants and its magnificent sandy beaches. It can get busy during the summer and many of the hotels are often fully booked at peak times.

Sebkhet Ariana

La Marsa ④
This magnificent resort is at the end of the train line that links the coastal towns with Tunis. It has the region's best beaches and some expensive hotels.

Sidi Bou Saïd ③
Sidi Bou Saïd is worth visiting at any time of the year. The view from the main promenade over the gulf is truly breathtaking.

0 km   2
0 miles   2

La Goulette ①
The beaches of La Goulette, being the closest to Tunis, can get busy at peak times. Quieter spots can be found a short distance further afield, at Salambo for instance.

Salambo ②
This quiet little town is full of whitewashed villas and colourful flowers and makes a welcome alternative to the bustle of Tunis. Its wide, sandy beach runs along a cove that is protected by a breakwater.

Sidi Bou Saïd ❸

Road map C1. 20 km (12 miles) north of Tunis. 16,000. *Kharja Festival (Jun).*

Perched on top of high cliffs, Sidi Bou Saïd enjoys a commanding view over the Gulf of Tunis. It is named after Sidi Bou Saïd, a 13th-century Sufi holy man (1156–1231), who settled here on the return journey from his pilgrimage to Mecca. From then on, the village (known at the time as Jabal el-Menar) became a centre of Sufism, and attracted pilgrims from all over the country. The area around his tomb became the burial ground for other Sufis. Although there are no longer processions heading to the **tomb of Sidi Bou Saïd**, the grave and its adjacent small mosque are still visited by the Muslim faithful. It is

Sidi Bou Saïd's panorama, seen from the south

accessed via the narrow stairs, right behind Café des Nattes (see below).

In the early 18th century, Hassan ibn Ali Bey ordered a mosque to be built here, which was entered via a magnificent gate and stairway. Today, the stairway and entrance to Café des Nattes stand on exactly the same spot. In the 19th century Mahmoud Bey built his summer residence here. Soon afterwards, the charms of this pretty town, with its cobbled streets and narrow alleyways, were discovered by the wealthy residents of Tunis who came here hoping to escape the summer heat.

The **Café des Nattes** is the village's hot spot and was the favourite haunt of the 1920s avant-garde artists who came here. It remains highly popular to this day and a traditional glass of mint tea with pine kernels can still be enjoyed. During the day the café can get busy as tour buses stop off to explore the town. Early in the morning and later at night, it is a much quieter place and is taken over by locals who sit quietly reading their newspapers. The café's decor has not changed in years and the yellowed photographs lining the walls bear witness to its famous guests including Simone de Beauvoir, André Gide

and Jean-Paul Sartre. But, as the present owner of the café says, "The foreigners were only passing through here. They came and they went. But to our family, this place has always been a symbol of continuity and tradition."

Since the days when Paul Klee visited, the village has grown in size and beauty. Its smart streets are full of flowers; the freshly whitewashed walls reflect the strong midday light. Yet it remains an artists' village, full of galleries and studios, while the former palace of Baron d'Erlanger (now the Centre of Arab and Mediterranean Music) stages concerts of *malouf* music *(see opposite)*.

A summer day in Sidi Bou is broken by a long siesta, when a drowsy silence and calm descends upon its streets and

BLUE DOORS

A blue door with studded ornamentation

It was Baron d'Erlanger who gave Sidi Bou Saïd its blue and white colour scheme. The scores of blue doors in the village are only superficially identical. In reality, they differ from each other in terms of size and their ornamentation. The most popular motifs include moon crescents, stars and minarets. Blue and white dominate the streets and courtyards. The white walls provide a striking background for the deep blue shutters, ornate window grilles and colourful doorways.

The main street leading to Café des Nattes

For hotels and restaurants in this region see pp250–54 and pp275–8

alleyways. The hum ceases and the women, shrouded in white veils, disappear behind the houses' blue doors. It is only along the steep, main street of the village that shopkeepers remain open, waiting for holidaymakers to whom they offer Bedouin jewellery, intricate scent boxes and aromatic oils. Heat permitting, this can be a good time to explore the cobbled streets and alleys of Sidi Bou. The pretty, whitewashed houses rise and fall in line with the cobbled streets that climb the ridge of the hill. Their white walls are covered with purple bougainvillea and their gates are garlanded with scented jasmine.

A number of Sidi Bou's mansions are open to visitors. One of these is **Dar el-Annabi** at 18 Rue Docteur Habib Thameur, just off Place 7 Novembre. Several of the 55 rooms of this 300-year-old house are open to the public and a terrace offers magnificent views of the town and the gulf beyond.

Not far from Café des Nattes, the street turns into a promenade with an amazing view over the bay. From here head for the magnificently sited **Café Sidi Chabaane**. The zaouia (tomb) built here in 1870 is associated with Sidi Sheb'an – a mystic, poet and musician. Today, his tomb stands almost on the site of the café. Standing here, and looking in the direction of the sea, it is easy to see how much has remained from bygone days. It is also worth visiting the **fishing harbour** and the **yacht marina**. From here the whole village can be seen resting on the slope of a hill, amidst lush greenery.

Another place to look out for is Dar Ennejma Ezzahra, a former palace which now houses the **Centre of Arab and Mediterranean Music**. It was built between 1912–22 for Baron Rodolphe d'Erlanger, a member of a

Yachts in Sidi Bou Saïd's marina

A watercolour from a Sidi Bou Saïd gallery

rich French banking family of German descent. The Baron first visited Tunisia at the age of 16, fell in love with the country and swapped his banking career for a painter's easel. The site of the palace, which was built for his wife Elizabeth, was carefully chosen so as not to upset the character of the village. Built on the hillside, it overlooks the sea and village. As well as the architecture and wonderful gardens, the museum has a good selection of traditional musical instruments and some

rare recordings of Arab music.

An enthusiastic musicologist, the Baron was a major force behind the first Congress of Arab Music, which was held in Cairo in 1932 and it is possible to hear wonderful concerts of rare Arab music performed here. The Baron's tomb stands in the park that surrounds the palace.

Sidi Bou Saïd is easily reached by TGM train, which runs between Tunis and La Marsa. On leaving the small station, follow the road uphill and the street leads to Café des Nattes. Alternatively, climb up through the small, beautifully kept park on the right-hand side of the street that leads up to the village centre.

Most visitors stop here just for a few hours, but in order to soak up the atmosphere of the place it is well worth spending a night here. An overnight stay allows time to attend a concert of malouf music in the evening, and in the morning enjoy a drink of strong mint tea on the terrace of Café des Nattes.

🏛 **The Centre of Arab and Mediterranean Music**
Tel (71) 980 138. 🕐 Tue–Sun: 9am–noon & 2–7pm (summer); 2–5pm (winter). 📷

BIRDCAGES

Sidi Bou Saïd is famous for its beautiful birdcages. Made of wire and often painted white, they look like miniature mausoleums. The design of the birdcages resembles the curved window grilles found in the wooden shutters of traditional Arab houses. Tunisians are fond of pet birds, particularly canaries. Empty cages can often be seen in hotel reception areas, serving as decorations or as mailboxes for residents' letters and postcards.

An ornate wire birdcage

Artists in Sidi Bou Saïd

Among Tunisian artists, Sidi Bou Saïd enjoyed a reputation as an "artist's village" long before the arrival of the European painters, but it was the latter who made it world-famous. Enchanted with the place, artists such as Paul Klee, August Macke and Louis Moilliet visited in 1914 and stayed much longer than they originally planned. The Tunisian light transformed their painting. In the works of Paul Klee, for instance, brown and black graphics gave way to vivid colours. The arrival of European artists was to have a significant effect on Tunisian painting, and prompted the emergence of a salon that included European, Muslim and Jewish artists. Out of this grew the École de Tunis, which took Tunisian daily life as its subject matter and included paintings of cafés, markets and hammams.

Painting of flower-seller

A traditional lifestyle *was a frequent theme of painters from the École de Tunis. This picture by Ammar Farhat conveys the colour and mood of the Tunisian siesta splendidly. His paintings may be far removed from the popular image of Tunisia, but are essentially true.*

Brahim Dhahak *(1931-2004) was one of the most outstanding artists of the École de Tunis, although he is less well known than Yahia Turki.*

Portrait of an Old Woman *is the work of Yahia Turki (1902–69), one of the early members of the École de Tunis. The expressive sketch, drawn with ink and crayon, depicts in great detail not only a person but also her emotions. In the context of Tunisian art, this is an extraordinary work.*

Still Life with Fish *by Dhahak is proof that Tunisian artists are also skilled in the use of engraving techniques. This lithograph clearly shows the influence of modernist European artists.*

The Night Scene *is painted in pastels. The expressive power of many École de Tunis artists lies in their ability to depict mood through colour.*

Man on a Donkey *is the work of Brahim Dhahak. It captures the magnificent light and wonderful colours that once so entranced Paul Klee and August Macke.*

Remains of an 18th-century arsenal, constructed by Hammouda ibn Ali Bey, in La Goulette

Carthage ❹

See pp102–106.

La Goulette ❺

Road map C1. 15 km (9 miles) northeast of Tunis.

La Goulette – an old fort and the harbour for Tunis – lies a short distance from the capital. The town was first developed as a port and strategic outpost by the Arabs in the 7th century after they had captured Tunis. In the 16th century it was a stronghold for pirates who were allowed to stay here by the Hafsid sultan, Mohammed V, who feared an attack by the Spanish. The attack duly came and the pirates proved to be no match for the Spanish forces. In 1535 the Spanish King Charles V built a fort here. The fort was later destroyed and in its place the Ottomans built a massive kasbah, which remains to this day.

La Goulette began to grow rapidly in the 17th century, due to the construction of the harbour. Led by Dutch engineers, the development included the canal, the basin and the arsenal. The numbers of Europeans living in the town gradually increased from year to year. During the French Protectorate, the kasbah was used as a temporary prison. The name La Goulette – "the gullet" or "throat" that separates the sea from Lake Tunis – dates from those days.

Today La Goulette (along with Mahdia, Sfax, Kelibia, Tabarka and Bizerte) is a major fishing port and the coastal section of Tunis harbour. Here, fishermen can be seen returning in their rowing boats with their catch.

The country's long shoreline (over 1,300 km/800 miles) means that fishing still plays an important part in Tunisia's economy. Many of La Goulette's fishermen can be seen in the evenings, heading out to sea where they fish at night with lights, returning in the morning in time to deliver their valuable catch to the town's restaurants and markets.

Many Tunis residents come here to enjoy fish and seafood in one of the local restaurants as La Goulette is reputed to have the best fish restaurants in Tunisia. Depending on the season, fresh gilthead, bream or tuna are excellent.

La Goulette is also a major passenger port – almost all ferries going to Italy and France set off from here.

At one time La Goulette was also renowned for its religious tolerance. This is vividly illustrated by the 1995 Franco-Tunisian comedy *Un été à la Goulette*, which is set in 1967. The film tells the story of three teenage girls – one Christian, one Jewish and one Muslim – who decide to undergo their sexual initiation, each with a boy of a different faith. The girls' plan becomes public knowledge and causes a temporary upset in the staid life of the village.

La Goulette can be reached in less than ten minutes by TGM train from Tunis. The best time to visit the village is in the late afternoon or evening, on the way back from La Marsa's beach or a trip to Carthage. There is a beach near La Goulette, but in view of the harbour's proximity and the resulting pollution, it is better to swim elsewhere.

Lake Tunis ❻

Road map C1.

In the 9th century, the Arabs dug a canal about 10 km (6 miles) long to link Tunis with the sea. This created the artificial Lake Tunis. The widening of its mouth allowed two harbours to be built – one on each side of the canal. The lake – not particularly picturesque in itself – is now a brackish lagoon attracting various species of bird, including seagulls, white and grey heron, and, during the winter months – flocks of flamingoes and cormorants. The lake can be crossed by TGM train (Tunis-La Goulette-La Marsa) or by car.

Angler on the shores of Lake Tunis

For hotels and restaurants in this region see pp250–54 and pp275–8

Carthage ④

Scattered ruins are all that remain of one of the most powerful cities of the ancient world. Carthage was founded in 814 BC by Phoenician colonizers. By the 4th century BC it had become the major force in this part of the Mediterranean. The Punic wars led to the destruction of the city although it rose again under Roman rule. It was subsequently conquered by the Vandals, who were replaced by the Byzantines in the 6th century. Following its capture by the Arabs in AD 695, Carthage gradually fell into ruins.

St Louis Cathedral towering over the ancient city

Exploring Carthage

Carthage Museum stands on Byrsa Hill, right next to the Cathedral of St Louis. To the north of the museum, close by, is the 2nd-century Theatre of Hadrian, which stages performances in summer during the International Cultural Festival. Sights that should not be missed include the ruins of the Roman amphitheatre, the remains of the Roman villas, and the ruins of the Basilica of St Cyprian. From here, a road leads to the best-preserved fragment of Carthage – the Antonine Baths. In summer, there is a horse-drawn carriage that tours the main sites. It can be hired near Carthage Hannibal station. The trip lasts two hours and the price should be settled in advance.

🔒 📷 Cathedral of St Louis

Byrsa Hill. **Tel** *(71) 733 866.*
⬜ daily: 8:30am–7pm (summer); 9am–5pm (winter). 📷

The cathedral was built in 1890 by Cardinal Lavigerie. It was dedicated to the French King Louis IX who died of the plague while laying siege to Carthage in 1270. Cardinal Lavigerie was an enterprising person – he founded the Order of the White Fathers, which was active throughout Africa. Its nuns and monks proved to be outstanding archaeologists and were the first to begin investigations into Tunisia's past. Lavigerie was also responsible for resurrecting the Carthage bishopric.

The building has not served as a place of worship since 1964 and was rebranded in the 1990s as the **Acropolium de Byrsa**. It is now used as a venue for classical concerts and exhibitions.

🏛 Carthage Museum

See pp104–105.

Foundations of Punic houses unearthed on Byrsa Hill

⛰ Byrsa Hill

Climbing to the top of Byrsa Hill affords a magnificent view of the area and makes this a good place to begin a visit to Carthage. Under Punic rule it was the heart of the city and had a temple dedicated to the Carthaginian god Eschmoun. The Romans, after razing Carthage to the ground, levelled the top of the hill to accommodate their capitol and forum. In the process they buried some

---

HANNIBAL (247–182 BC)

Hannibal was one of the greatest military commanders of the ancient world. In the course of the Second Punic War he embarked upon a long and arduous march across the Pyrenees, southern Gaul and the Alps. Although his army was not large, it was exceptionally well trained.

Following his legendary crossing of the Alps, Hannibal took on the might of the Roman army. Despite early successes, the Carthaginians were eventually defeated and made to pay huge reparations. At home, an attempt to introduce democratic reforms brought Hannibal into opposition with the ruling classes and he was forced to flee Carthage. Unable to reconcile himself to the loss of his homeland, he committed suicide.

A marble bust of Hannibal

◁ Sun-drenched villa in Sidi Bou Saïd

Carthage's amphitheatre, capable of seating 3,000 spectators

VISITORS' CHECKLIST

Road map C1. 17 km (11 miles) north of Tunis. TGM Carthage–Hannibal. International Film Festival (Oct).

Several Christians were put to death on that occasion including St Perpetua who was gored by "a most savage cow" before being run through by a sword.

Punic villas that were later uncovered by French archaeologists. Byrsa Hill is now dominated by the Cathedral of St Louis and the Carthage Museum.

Antonine Baths

Avenue des Thermes d'Antonin. *Apr–mid-Sep: 8:30am–7pm Tue–Sun; mid-Sep–Mar: 8:30am–5:30pm.*
These 2nd-century baths were once the largest in Africa. Their soaring vaults rested on eight lofty columns made of grey sandstone, and the *frigidarium* was the size of a cathedral. Destroyed by the Vandals in AD 439, all that is left are ruins, including a handful of rooms and the remains of the vaults. Nevertheless, the complex still makes a deep impression.

Amphitheatre

Avenue du 7 Novembre. *Apr–mid-Sep: 8:30am–7pm Tue–Sun; mid-Sep–Mar: 8:30am–5:30pm.*
The amphitheatre was one of the largest in the Roman Empire. Games were the favourite recreation of the Carthaginians. In AD 203 a show was staged to celebrate the birth of the emperor's son.

The impressive ruins of the Antonine Baths

Roman Villas

Apr–mid-Sep: 8:30am–7pm Tue–Sun; mid-Sep–Mar: 8:30am–5:30pm.
The reign of Caesar Augustus brought with it stability and economic growth. The emperor created favourable conditions for land and sea trade, which resulted in the growing prosperity of the urban upper and middle classes, including natives of Tunisia. In the 2nd century AD, Carthage reached the peak of its development. The villas date from this period. Much of the site is overgrown, though the restored 3rd-century Villa de la Volières still has its original floor mosaics.

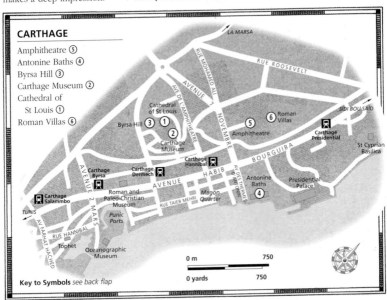

CARTHAGE

Amphitheatre ⑤
Antonine Baths ④
Byrsa Hill ③
Carthage Museum ②
Cathedral of
  St Louis ①
Roman Villas ⑥

Key to Symbols *see back flap*

Carthage Museum

The museum stands on top of a hill, surrounded by a beautiful expanse of grass. One of its terraces adjoins the foundations of the Punic villas, which were discovered by French archaeologists. The museum is arranged chronologically with Punic, Roman, Christian and Arab displays. Among these are inscriptions, marble sarcophagi, everyday objects from Punic and Roman Carthage, and colourful Phoenician masks.

Model of Carthage
Situated on the first floor of the museum, this model provides a good basis for appreciating the sheer scale of Carthage and its ports.

★ Mosaics
The museum displays only a handful of mosaics but all are very well preserved. Most are from the Roman-African period. The mosaic pictured here depicts a woman gathering fruit which symbolizes summer.

GALLERY LAYOUT

The museum houses exhibits dating from the Phoenician-Punic, Roman-African and Arab eras. The Phoenician-Punic exhibits occupy the ground floor. Here there are, among other things, Punic ceramics and Punic sarcophagi. The first floor is mostly devoted to exhibits from the Roman and Arab periods and includes some fine Roman sculptures and mosaics.

Jug (11th century BC)
Terracotta vessels were already being produced in the early days of Carthage. The most popular items included candlesticks, lamps and jugs made in fanciful shapes and decorated in blue and crimson.

Ground floor

PHOENICIAN ART

Characteristic of Phoenician art are sarcophagi with a human figure on the lid; other typical objects include terracotta figurines, jewellery products, ivory items and masks. Vast numbers of amulets made of a glass and silica compound bear witness to the important role played by magic in everyday life, as well as to the influence of Egyptian art and religion.

Punic tombstone of a man, from the Carthage Museum

KEY

☐ Mosaics
☐ Ceramics
☐ Archaeological finds

STAR EXHIBITS

★ Mosaics

★ Phoenician Coin

VISITORS' CHECKLIST

Byrsa Hill. *Tel* (71) 730 036. 🚃
Carthage–Hannibal. ⬜ Apr–mid-
Sep: 9am–5:30pm; mid-Sep–
Mar: 9am–4:30pm. 🎟

★ **Phoenician Coin**
*Phoenician coin dating
from the 5th century BC
from Tyre. Coins also
appeared in Ardos, Sydon
and Byblos at this time.*

Jug (7th century BC)
*Carthaginian ceramics include
jugs with an upturned top and
triple spouts. These items began to
appear in the late 8th century and
were produced until the end of
the 6th century BC.*

1st floor

Punic Vase
*Phoenician vessels were made
using a simple potter's wheel
and fired in tall round furnaces
which were built of brick.
The typical colour of Punic
ceramics was light red.*

Bronze Vase
*This exquisitely decorated vessel,
intended for water or wine, was
made in the 5th century BC.
Objects of this type were very highly
valued by the Phoenicians as well as
by their trading partners.*

Further Afield
On the other side of Avenue
Bourguiba is the Magon
Quarter where there are some
Punic floor mosaics. Further
on, along the main road to
Tunis, is the Roman and
Paleo-Christian Museum. A
little to the east of this are the
remains of the Punic Ports.
Another very interesting site
is the nearby Tophet
(Phoenician burial place),
which is also known as the
Tanit and Baal Hammon
sanctuary *(see p106)*.

⋔ St Cyprian Basilica
🚋 *TGM Carthage–Amilcar.*
St Cyprian, a prominent
writer and a theologian of
great standing, was a bishop
of Carthage. He preached
church unity based on the
unity of the College of
Bishops and was an advocate
of the bishop's power in his
own local community. He
died a martyr's death during
the persecution of Christians
under Emperor Valerian's
rule, in AD 258.

This Byzantine basilica that
bears his name was probably
the initial resting-place of the
saint, though that is open to
dispute. Situated at the north
end of the town, this eight-
aisle church is one of a
handful of the Christian
historic remains in Carthage,
along with the mighty
Damous el-Karita Basilica.

▦ Presidential Palace
Avenue Habib Bourguiba. 🚋 *TGM
Carthage–Presidence.* ◐ ⦸
The Presidential Palace stands
on a hill above the Gulf of
Tunis, near the Antonine
Baths. It is from here that the
best view of the palace,
engulfed by the greenery of
its vast garden, can be found.
When photographing the
Roman baths remember not
to point the camera at the
palace. In Tunisia it is
prohibited to photograph
government buildings,
soldiers and policemen. In
this case the law is strictly
enforced. The main entrance
to the palace is through the
gate at Avenue Bourguiba.
Following protests against the
government in 2011, the army
took over the duty of guarding the palace.

Former Punic Port at the south end of Carthage

🏛 Roman and Paleo-Christian Museum

🔵 *for renovation until 2012; access available from Carthage Dermish Park.*

This museum has objects dating from the Roman period of Carthage's history (5th–7th century AD). Also among the exhibits are some early Christian remains and some mosaic fragments. The origins of Christianity in the Roman Province of Proconsular Africa probably go back to the late 1st century. In the museum grounds are what little remains of the Basilica of Carthagenna (6th century AD).

⋔ Punic Ports

Avenue du Mars 1934.
🚉 *Carthage–Byrsa.*

Unfortunately, not much remains of these two ports which were once the powerhouse of Carthage's prosperity and the envy of Rome. Imagination is needed, therefore, to visualize the pride of the Punic fleet in these two small ponds. In

their heyday, these ports could accommodate 220 vessels. The southern square-shaped basin was for commercial shipping, while the northern circular basin was used as the naval harbour. The two harbours would have been linked. The entrance was via a channel in the sea which led to the commercial port. A scale model at the edge of the naval harbour gives some idea of just what a wonder these ports once were.

Between the two ports is an **Oceanographic Museum** which has aquariums and some interactive displays.

⋔ Tophet

Rue Hannibal. 🚉 *Carthage–Salambo.*
⬜ *Apr–mid-Sep: 8am–7pm Tue–Sun; mid-Sep–Mar: 8:30am–5:30pm.* 📷

These ruins are all that remains of the Tophet, or sanctuary, that was dedicated to the Carthaginian divinities Tanit and Baal Hammon (*see p110*). Sacrifice may well have

been the main act of this ancient Phoenician cult and this is the oldest surviving site of its kind in Carthage. Although no-one knows for certain, it is believed that offerings were made of animals, people (often foreigners and enemies), and most of all children. They were sacrificed to the goddess (originally the offerings were made to Baal Hammon, and only later to Tanit). According to some theories, the children were laid in the arms of a bronze statue, from where they fell into the flames. The parents were not allowed to cry, as their grief was believed to diminish the sacrifice.

When Agathocles defeated the Carthaginians in 310 BC, the town citizens reputedly sacrificed 300 children in order to appease the gods.

The oldest part of the Tophet includes the tiny Cintas shrine with a small niche carved into the rock where some 8th-century pots were found. In front of the building is a courtyard with an altar and three concentric walls forming a kind of labyrinth through which everyone wishing to enter the sanctuary had to pass.

DIDO AND AENEAS

According to Virgil's epic poem the *Aeneid*, Aeneas fled Troy after its destruction by the Greeks and set sail with a handful of refugees on a divine mission to found a new Troy in Italy. He was shipwrecked off Carthage and taken in by the Phoenician Princess Dido. Soon they fell passionately in love. Torn between his love for Dido and the will of the

gods, Aeneas left to fulfil his destiny and began a series of adventures that ended with the founding of Rome. Heartbroken, Dido stabbed herself, offering her life to Carthage. Her body was burned on a funeral pyre.

Dido Receiving Aeneas, Francesco Solimena

Tophet – a magnificent and tragic monument to Punic culture

Phoenician Culture

The Phoenicians were great explorers and during the early years of the first millennium BC they ventured as far as Spain and into the Atlantic, establishing a number of colonies including the one at Carthage. The Phoenicians brought with them a culture based on a blend of Egyptian, Anatolian, Greek and Mesopotamian influences. One of their greatest contributions was the alphabet, which

Coin dating from the Punic era

was adapted by the Greeks, and spread with the rise of the Roman Empire. The Phoenicians were also skilled in carving, metalwork, sculpture and jewellery. Many Phoenician remains were found at Carthage, and excavations carried out in Kairouan also reveal Punic houses containing well-preserved mosaics. Phoenician tombs have also been found in Cap Bon and in Utica.

Phoenician cemeteries *show that the Phoenicians and their Punic descendants believed in an afterlife. Embalmed bodies, elaborate sarcophagi and inscriptions warning against disturbing the dead indicate just how strong this belief was.*

The Punic alphabet, *with its elongated, gently curving letters, was widely used in Carthage and throughout the western Phoenician colonies.*

Altars *in the form of shrines (cippi) gave way in the 5th century BC to steles, with triangular tops. These often bear an engraved motif of a moon crescent or a stylized figure.*

Necklaces *made of glass compound were popular adornments. Jewellery played an important role in Carthage. Miniature masks, amulets, scarabs and golden plates were often added to necklaces.*

Terracotta female figures *were first produced around the 6th century BC. They may have been inspired by Egyptian art as figures unearthed at Carthage resemble those found on Egyptian sarcophagi. The use of masks in religious ceremonies was also widespread in Carthage.*

Oudna (Uthina), one of the oldest Roman colonies in Africa

Oudna (Uthina) **❼**

Road map C2. *30 km (19 miles) south of Tunis.* ☐ *Apr–mid-Sep: 9am–7pm Tue–Sun; mid-Sep–Mar: 8:30am–5:30pm Tue–Sun.* 🖼

This former Berber settlement is one of the oldest Roman colonies in Africa, and was founded during the reign of Octavian Augustus. The modern-day ruins of Roman Uthina (now called Oudna) divide into two main sections. Immediately by the entrance stands a complex of buildings, some of which have been reconstructed, including Roman villas, private and public baths, cisterns, a theatre and a 2nd-century amphitheatre. The second part, which includes the capitol, has been largely unexcavated and lies a few hundred yards away, adjoining a small village and the remains of the colonial buildings. This part of Oudna can be visited free of charge.

Founded at the beginning of the 1st century AD, Uthina was a typical Roman town and attracted wealthy veterans from the Roman army. The hub of its public life was the market square (forum), which was surrounded by the town's most important buildings including the capitol (the seat of the local authorities), a courthouse and the marketplace. One of the corners of the forum was usually adjoined by a smaller market square, known as the *macellum*.

The most valuable mosaics, including one depicting Venus bathing, are now on display in the Bardo Museum.

Environs
Before reaching Oudna, it is worth stopping in **Mohammedia** to see the ruins of the Palace of Ahmed Bey (1837–56) which was intended to rival Versailles in its grandeur. About 2 km (1 mile) from the village, running parallel to the Tunis–Zaghouan road, are the remains of a Roman aqueduct that once carried water to Carthage.

Korbous **❽**

Road map C2. *50 km (31 miles) northeast of Tunis.*

Korbous lies on the Cap Bon peninsula and is set in a deep ravine that opens to the sea near the village of Sidi Rais. Popular as a health resort since Roman times when it was known as Aquae Calidau Carpitanae, the waters here are believed by many Tunisians to to have health-giving properties. In the late 19th century, Korbous was developed by the French, while Ahmed Bey founded a spa resort here in 1901. Korbous is today Tunisia's main health resort and many of the local hotels and sanatoriums offer water and steam treatments to elderly Tunisians. The natural hot springs bubble up out of the ground at about 44–60° C (112–140° F) and contain high levels of sulphur.

Korbous is an unassuming place though there are now plans to convert this hitherto quiet resort into a large spa, with a marina and luxury hotels. The main attraction of the town is the **hammam** (bath), located in the former bey's palace.

Public bathing played a prominent role in the life of the Roman towns in North Africa. The custom of using alternate hot and cold baths, borrowed from the Greeks, assumed great importance in Rome and its dominions. Bath complexes were the centre of town life and often included playing fields, libraries and relaxation rooms with mosaic floors and frescoes. Wealthy people sometimes spent whole days in the baths – resting and enjoying discussions.

The local waters are thought to be good for curing arthritis and beneficial in cases of gastric ailments.

One famous landmark to look out for in Korbous is the **Zarziha Rock**, which can be found near the presidential palace. According to legend, it is supposed to cure infertility. The edges of the stone have been polished smooth by the hands of those who come here to seek its help.

Not much remains here of the old buildings. The fortress that towers over the town dates back to the Roman period. A hot spring, **Aïn el-Atrous**, can be found a short way north of town. Here water at 50° C (122° F) shoots out of the ground via an

Bathers in the hot springs in Korbous

underground pipe and falls over steps down to the sea. This is a very popular picnic spot, particularly at weekends.

Sidi Daoud ❾

Road map D1.

This fishing village located on the peninsula's headland, opposite the island of Zembra, is famous for tuna fishing. To this day the locals use an old-fashioned method known as *Matanza* that dates back to Roman times. This technique employs a huge net containing a series of chambers of decreasing sizes which is laid some 4 km (2 miles) out to sea. The fish are caught and swim from chamber to chamber until they all reach the smallest one. The net is closed and dragged to the surface. The fishermen then jump into the nets and set about the tuna with clubs, knives and harpoons. The *Matanza* takes place in May and June during the spawning season. For the rest of the year the village is quiet.

El-Haouaria ❿

Road map D1. ⬚ *daily: 8am–7pm (summer); 8:30am–5:30pm (winter).* 🎦 *Falconry Festival (Jun).*

El-Haouaria is perched high on the rugged headland of Cap Bon, surrounded by a

FALCONRY

Man training a falcon for hunting

Hunting with falcons has always been a favourite pastime of Arab kings and princes. Even today, falconry enjoys great popularity. Its main centre in Tunisia is El-Haouaria. In March, young peregrine falcons are caught in nets. Only the female birds are kept, because they are bigger and more predatory. These are then trained for a special falconry festival that takes place in June. After this, most of the birds are set free to resume their migrations.

turquoise sea. The view from here over the sea and its breaking waves is truly awe-inspiring. Two kilometres (1 mile) from the centre of the modern village is the site of the old Roman quarries from which marble was cut and transported by slaves to Carthage, El-Jem and other Roman towns. All that remains of them now are two dozen vermilion caves running along the coast. Some of these are 30 metres (98 ft) high. A little further out of town, the Chauves-Souris cave is inhabited by hundreds of bats. Visitors should make sure they have a guide – and a torch!

The village is famous for its June falconry show held on its outskirts, opposite the island of Zembra, during which trained

birds are used for hunting before being set free.

Environs

Almost directly opposite El-Haouaria, 15 km (9 miles) from Sidi Daoud, lies the picturesque island of **Zembra** and, separated from it by 5 km (3 miles) of water, the tiny island of **Zembretta**. Zembra was once popular with scuba divers but both islands and the waters that surround them have been declared a nature reserve and are now off-limits to visitors. In the spring and summer they provide resting points for migrating birds. They are also home to 260 species of plants, four of which are endemic. The surrounding waters support many types of fish.

El-Haouaria, site of a lifetime of slavery in the quarries

Peppers – one of Cap Bon's main crops

Cap Bon ⓫

Road map D1, D2.

A short way from Europe and within easy reach of Carthage, Cap Bon has long had an economic importance. Its main ports were once used as harbours for Phoenician ships, while the fertile coastal areas supported agriculture. Here, the Phoenicians cultivated cereals and grapes from which they produced wine. The Romans continued these traditions and it was only the Arab conquest that put an end to wine production. Under French rule, the Cap Bon peninsula was revived once again when it became an important area of European settlement. More vineyards were planted at this time, along with huge citrus groves.

Although tourism plays an increasingly important role, especially around the beaches of Hammamet and Nabeul, the production of vegetables and fruit still provides the main source of income. For this reason, the peninsula has preserved a quiet, rural character, particularly inland. In the small village of **Soliman** for instance, with its beds of spinach, beans and potatoes, time seems to have ground to a halt. In **Menzel Bou Zelfa**, orange and lemon groves fill the spring air with the heady scent of blossom.

On the east coast, Kelibia and Menzel Temime are famous for their colourful markets while the busy resort town of Nabeul is known for its ceramics and its magnificent beach. Just along the coast from Nabeul is Hammamet, once called the Tunisian Saint Tropez, although it is rather less exclusive than it once was. The main road along the rugged west coast runs inland where the scattered villages are isolated and little visited, apart from Korbous, which is renowned for its hot springs.

Kerkouane ⓬

Road map D1. ⬜ *9am–6pm daily.*

Kerkouane is situated on the high cliffs of Cap Bon. Between the 4th and the 2nd century BC this was a Punic town with a population of 2,000 and was controlled by Carthage. The Second Punic War put an end to the town's existence when it was abandoned. The town was rediscovered in 1952 by a French archaeologist.

Kerkouane has been remarkably well preserved and, from the remaining foundations, it is easy to see the checkerboard layout of the streets. Little was known about Punic architecture before the discovery of Kerkouane, but from the size of the houses and the wide streets, it is apparent that the town's inhabitants were not only sophisticated but also had a high standard of living.

GODDESS TANIT

From the 5th century onwards, the goddess Tanit occupied the highest position in the pantheon of the Punic gods. Associated with the cult of fertility, she was believed to be the personification of both the sun and the moon. Sometimes she is depicted by a crescent moon turned upside down and joined onto the disc of the sun. At other times, her image is formed from a triangle, a horizontal line and a circle.

Mosaic with the stylized symbol of the goddess Tanit

Most impressive of all are the houses' baths, with their well-preserved floors, walls and sanitary equipment. Many of the houses have their own bath, suggesting that the owners liked to bathe in private.

Very little is known about this town and it was named Kerkouane by the French

Kerkouane and its ruins of a Punic town

archaeologist who found it. From the artifacts that have been found here, it is probable that much of Kerkouane's wealth was based on the production of a dye, highly prized at the time, known as Tyrian purple (after Tyre, the Phoenician capital).

Kelibia ⓭

Road map D1. 50 km (31 miles) along the coast from Nabeul. ◯ 8am–6pm daily. 🎞 *Amateur Film Festival (Jul).*

Set at the very tip of Cap Bon, on its eastern side, this small town gives the impression of being fully surrounded by water. It dates back to Punic times (being for a while a trading outpost of Syracuse); as well as to the Roman Empire (as the Roman settlement of Clupea).

Its history resembles that of many other Punic hamlets in that it began life as a Berber settlement. Conquered by Agathocles in 310 BC, and by Regulus in 256 BC, it suffered devastating damage in the course of the Third Punic War, when the Romans nearly demolished it. Almost nothing remains from Punic and Roman times. The only relic that has survived is the late 6th-century Byzantine fortress. The lighthouse, dating from the early years of Arab rule, now houses a meteorological station and provides a magnificent panoramic view of the surrounding country. Kelibia is also known for its white wines, particularly the dry muscat.

The town's main sight is the old **fort** that overlooks the harbour. The present building was erected by the Byzantines in the 6th century AD and was further modified by the Spanish and the Turkish. The gun emplacements were laid here by German forces during World War II.

Next to Lake Ichkeul, Kelibia is the most important bird-breeding ground in Tunisia. The local lake changes its size and shape depending on the amount of

Kelibia – situated at the tip of Cap Bon

rain. At times of high annual rainfall its area grows to include the surrounding marshes. During the high season, the lake may attract over a quarter of a million birds. Unfortunately, low water levels have caused the number of birds to decrease significantly. Species still seen include heron and flamingo. The area around the lake is also visited by many species of birds that inhabit dry and desert areas. The best view of the lake is from its northeastern end, from the road near the GP2 and MC 48 junction. Kelibia's beach is small and often covered with seaweed, whereas **Mansourah beach**, 2 km (1 mile) to the north, is long, sandy and often almost deserted.

Market stalls in Menzel Temime

Menzel Temime ⓮

Road map D1. 🚌 *Tue.*

During the period of the Roman Empire, the wealth of this area was based almost entirely on the cultivation of cereals and olives, vineyards and fig orchards. Vast country estates brought great fortunes to their owners. It was here that the new colonial system was first introduced. It involved an annual tax, paid in kind – in the form of grain and oil – that was levied on large estates and used to feed the Roman populace.

Located a short way from Kelibia, Menzel Temime is known for its spices, the strings of sun-dried red peppers, and above all for its huge Tuesday market, where farmers from the entire peninsula congregate. Pyramids of fruit and vegetables create fantastic multicoloured mosaics.

Environs
A little further away lies the picturesque village of **Korba**. Korba is nicknamed the "red village" because of the quantity of tomatoes, peppers and strawberries that are grown here. There is much local produce worth buying in the village, including the homemade hot and spicy Tunisian sauce called harissa.

Nabeul

House in Avenue Habib Thameur

Just up the coast from Hammamet, Nabeul is the administrative centre of Cap Bon and is known for its beautiful beaches, busy market and wonderful ceramics. The original Punic town was destroyed by the Romans. Later on, Julius Caesar established a colony here, the ruins of which were accidentally discovered in 1964 during the construction of the first tourist hotel in town. With the arrival of the Arabs, the town became centred around the *ksar* (fortified granary). Today, this is the town's oldest district.

Shops along Rue el-Arbi Zarouk, the site of the market

Exploring Nabeul

Most people visit Nabeul on Friday and come for the weekly market. Virtually anything can be bought here from colourful spices, bowls and spoons to music cassettes and cotton shawls. Nabeul's large medina, with its complex network of narrow streets, gates and alleyways, is well worth exploring. Walking along Avenues Habib Thameur, Farhat Hached or Hedi Chaker takes the visitor past scores of shops and ceramic workshops selling colourful crockery, tiles, lamps, candlesticks, goblets and couscous dishes.

Market

Rue el-Arbi Zarouk. ☐ 6–10am Fri.
The market is held every Friday and attracts huge numbers of visitors. Originally it was a camel market, but camels are not usually on sale unless they are stuffed toys. During the peak season, however, there is the opportunity of paying for a camel ride. The thousands of day-trippers who visit here each week can be overwhelming and stall holders have no need to lower their prices. Little is to be gained from haggling.

Great Mosque

Rue de L'Orient and Rue Habib Karma. ● *to non-Muslims.*
Nabeul's mosque, hidden by the souk's arcades, is a typical example of sacral Islamic architecture. Its layout includes a courtyard and a large prayer hall decorated with some magnificent ceramic tiles and crystal chandeliers. Its green-white minaret is reminiscent of the mosque in Kairouan.

Decorative panel on the façade of the Great Mosque

Avenue Habib Thameur

Avenue Habib Thameur, whose continuation is Avenue Farhat Hached, runs in the direction of the souk and the market. Together with Avenue Hedi Chaker, it forms the town's commercial centre and is crammed with workshops and small shops selling ceramics. The heart of the town is Place du 7 Novembre, at the junction of Avenue Habib Thameur and Avenue Habib Bourguiba. The vast clay jug vessel here is meant to symbolize Nabeul's pottery traditions.

Ceramic bric-a-brac, such as ashtrays, small jars and plates can be bought fairly cheaply. Even larger plates or a beautifully decorated dish cost just a few dinars.

Although Nabeul is famous mainly for its pottery, it has also developed other forms of craft, including embroidery, wickerwork (straw mats) and stone carving. Nabeul embroidery is white or light blue and uses cotton or silk yarns. At one time it was used only on women's clothes but now it can also be found decorating tablecloths and linen napkins.

Courtyard of a pottery shop in Avenue Habib Thameur

Avenue Habib Bourguiba

Avenue Bourguiba, lined with palm trees and oleanders, is the town's swankiest street. It starts at the town centre and runs towards the sea, reaching the local beaches. It is over 2 km (1 mile) long. Along it are situated the station and the archaeology museum. Its northern section is full of shops. Heading south, it is worth taking a look at the beautiful villas belonging to the wealthy citizens of Nabeul.

🏛 Archaeology Museum

Av. Habib Bourguiba 44. **Tel** (72) 285 509. ⬜ Apr–mid-Sep: 9am–1pm & 4–7pm Tue–Sun; mid-Sep–Mar: 9:30am–4pm. 🎫

Several well-lit rooms in this small but interesting museum house items unearthed during archaeological excavations, including Carthaginian sculptures and Roman mosaics. The first room, immediately by the entrance, includes the plan of Roman Neapolis *(see below)* and a map of Cap Bon, showing the major archaeological sites. To the left of the entrance, in Room 1, are displays of Punic objects (7th–4th centuries BC) including oil lamps, jewellery and coins, mainly from the excavations in Kerkouane. Here vessels from Kelibia can also be found.

Along the corridor there are further displays of Punic and Roman objects, including clay statuettes of Baal Hammon and the Carthaginian goddess Tanit. The remaining rooms house a large collection of Roman mosaics excavated

Statue from the Archaeology Museum

from Kelibia (1st–3rd century AD) and Roman Neapolis (4th century).

♁ Neapolis

⬜ 1–5pm Tue–Sun.

This ancient site stands in the town suburbs, within the tourist zone, close to the Hotel Neapolis and opposite Pension Monia Club. Not much is left of the Roman town whose ruins were discovered accidentally when building the Hotel Neapolis and its large, fenced-off grounds are overgrown with grass and olive trees.

Nabeul was once a part of the senate province of Proconsular Africa. It was governed by the proconsul residing in Carthage. The reign of Caesar Augustus marked a period of stability, when colonies began to grow and new towns intended for Roman war veterans were established. Caesar ensured favourable conditions for trade, which resulted in the growing wealth of the

VISITORS' CHECKLIST

Road map D2. 🏘 60,000. 🚉 ONTT: Avenue Habib Bourguiba, (72) 223 006. **www**.nabeul.net. 🎭 Orange Blossom Festival (Mar/Apr); Summer Festival (Jul/Aug).

urban upper and middle classes, as well as of the native population. One of these towns was Nabeul.

Increasing wealth was accompanied by the growing influence of Roman culture. Not much has survived from ancient Nabeul, which the Romans called Neapolis, and all that can be seen is a handful of scattered stones and the remains of a wall that probably once surrounded a palace.

Excavation site in Neapolis

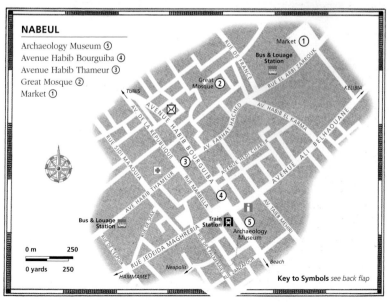

NABEUL

Archaeology Museum ⑤
Avenue Habib Bourguiba ④
Avenue Habib Thameur ③
Great Mosque ②
Market ①

Market ①
Bus & Louage Station
Great Mosque ②
TUNIS
KELIBIA
RUE DE FRANCE
RUE EL ARBI ZARROUK
AVENUE HABIB BOURGUIBA
AV. HABIB EL KARMA
AV. DE LA REPUBLIQUE
AV. FARHAT HACHED
AVENUE HEDI CHAKER
AVENUE ALI BELHAOUANE
RUE SIDI MAAOUIA
RUE MARBELLA
③
④
RUE HABIB THAMEUR
AV. TAIEB MEHIRI
Bus & Louage Station
Train Station
ⓘ
⑤
Archaeology Museum
RUE DE MAX
RUE JEDEIDA MAGHREBIA
RUE EL PALMERS
RUE ZANZAFOUR
Beach
0 m 250
0 yards 250
HAMMAMET
Neapolis

Key to Symbols *see back flap*

Nabeul Pottery

Tunisian pottery goes back to the Neolithic period when large jugs and vases were used for storage. In the early years of the Muslim era, during the Aghlabid dynasty (649–909), a new technique was introduced known as "mirror" dyeing that involved the use of metallic dyes. The periods of the Fatimids and Zirids (10th and 11th centuries) mark a revolution in the decorative arts of this region when figurative images began to appear on vases and mosaics. During those days, Tunisian ceramics were in high demand and were exported to Andalusia and Sicily.

Abstract designs – *arabesque and geometric patterns – first appeared during the Hafsid dynasty (1233–1574). At that time, the popular colours were cobalt blue and brown. These designs have survived though the range of colours has increased.*

Turkish influences *are in evidence from the 16th century onwards. The Ottoman Turks introduced polychromatic (many coloured) designs, with flowers being a frequently used motif. These techniques produced brightly-coloured designs on bowls, jugs, tiles, vases and all kinds of other vessels.*

POTTERY WORKSHOP

Workshops that produce ceramics are generally small. They employ a handful of people, often members of one family. Separate rooms are used for moulding, firing and decorating the items. Visiting tourists are generally invited to see the final stages of the process when artists decorate the bowls and jugs.

CERAMIC DECORATION

Craftsman decorating a bowl

The centre of Tunisian ceramics was once Guellala, on the island of Jerba. Its local craftsmen arrived at Nabeul in the 15th century, possibly attracted by the quality of the local clay. The Guellala potters often use Berber motifs and favour brown and beige colours. Nabeul craftsmen prefer floral designs. Each item is hand-decorated by an artist.

Nabeul pottery *uses a lively mix of colours but is predominantly in strong blues and greens.*

Andalusian, *Turkish and Italian influences are evident in 17th-century ceramics. Today, traditional green and yellow decorated objects, with brown motifs, are becoming increasingly rare.*

Artistic pottery products *are decorated with arabesques or geometric patterns combined with images of fish, birds, cypress trees and stylized flowers.*

Children learn the craft from an early age.

The quality of all finished vessels is carefully checked.

Ceramic tiles *are decorated with motifs that together form large multi-coloured compositions.*

All pots are moulded on a potter's wheel.

Ceramics shops *can be found in every street of town. Their courtyards display all possible forms of ceramics, and their small workshops are tucked away at the back.*

Jugs *– long and pointed – were produced during the Phoenician era. Roman times saw the introduction of red ceramics decorated with mythological and floral motifs.*

Hammamet

Hammamet lies on the coast, half-way between Tunis and Sousse, and has some of the best beaches in Tunisia. In the 2nd century, the Romans established a settlement called Pupput, close to the present town, which was later inhabited by the Normans. It was only in the 1920s, however, that the place was really put on the map when the Romanian millionaire George Sebastian built a villa here. Where he led others soon followed and today Hammamet attracts over half a million visitors a year.

Mermaids from the kasbah

Exploring Hammamet

The most pleasant time of the day in Hammamet is the late afternoon, when the streets and cafés fill with people emerging after their afternoon siesta, and the sun casts a warm glow on the walls of houses. The compact medina, built by the Hafsids, is well worth exploring and includes ancient bathhouses and shops hidden away in the narrow alleys. The Great Mosque and the kasbah are strategically located by the medina's main entrance.

At sunset, head for the café situated by the kasbah at the entrance to the medina. This delightful spot is a pleasant place to savour a cup of mint tea or coffee and watch the world go by.

The main streets of the modern section of town are Avenue Bourguiba and Avenue de la République, where most shops, banks, and some good restaurants are situated. At their junction stands the **Centre Commercial**, which was opened in 1979.

Narrow streets of the medina, providing shelter from the sun

♨ Kasbah

☐ Apr–Oct: 8am–1pm & 3–7pm. Outside high season: 8:30am–5:30pm.
Built in the 15th century, the kasbah (Arab fort) stands next to the main gate leading to the medina. It is approached by high stairs; its upper terrace provides a magnificent view of the glistening sea and the roofs of the old town houses on

which drying peppers, peas, sesame seeds and couscous often form colourful mosaics. Visitors can also stop for a cup of aromatic tea in the charming café next to it.

⊞ Medina

Through the main gate – Bab el-Souk – is the entrance to the medina. It is surrounded by high walls, erected in AD 904, and was rebuilt in the 13th century during the period of the Hafsid dynasty.

Immediately past the gate there are souvenir vendors with colourful stalls and small shops full of rugs, lovely oriental mirrors and old (or imitation) jewellery. In the first street to the left (counting from the gate) are the Turkish baths (open to men in the morning, and to women in the afternoon).

There is little need for a detailed map when wandering around Hammamet's medina, and it is easy to get into the rhythm of its narrow streets with its unique patchwork of alleyways. Walking around, there is a pleasant variety of details to take in – a doorknocker in the shape of the hand of Fatima, for example, or a flower-pot set against the white wall of a house. Visitors can step into **Dar Hammamet** in order to see a traditional Tunisian house with a collection of costumes which have been gathered together from all over Tunisia.

🏛 Dar Hammamet

Rue Sidi Abdallah. **Tel** (72) 281 206.
☐ 9am–1pm, 2–5pm daily. 🗀

☪ Great Mosque

🚫 to non-Muslims.
Standing in the medina, the Great Mosque was built in 1236 by Abu Am Othmar. Since then the mosque has been remodelled and has undergone two major renovations: one in 1727 was undertaken by Hussein Bey, the second in 1978–79 was overseen by the town authorities. The nearby Sidi Abdel Kader mosque was built in 1798; it now houses the School of Koranic Studies.

View from the kasbah walls over the medina and the sea

◁ *Chryses visiting Agamemnon* – a mosaic from Neapolis, now in the Nabeul Museum

A palm-shaded promenade on Avenue Bourguiba

Avenue Habib Bourguiba
The main thoroughfare of
Hammamet, Avenue Habib
Bourguiba is full of shops,
narrow passageways and
tourist restaurants. The
adjacent central square is the
site of the fish and vegetable
market, held every morning.
This is also the centre of
Hammamet's nightlife, with
clubs and restaurants open
until the small hours. In order
to see how the Tunisians
spend their free time, take a
seat for a while during the
late afternoon in one of the
local teahouses, in the area
where Avenue Bourguiba
reaches the walls of the
medina. The end of siesta
marks a time for coffee and
chichas (hookahs) or for

contemplating life over a cup
of strong mint tea. The busiest
people around this time of the
day are the jasmine sellers.

Fishing boats on one of
Hammamet's beaches

Men place the small fragrant
posies behind their ears;
women hold them in their
hands, turning them around.

Beaches
Hammamet has two main
tourist zones. The older, in
the north, is located between
Hammamet and Nabeul; the
newer, in the south, has been
named Hammamet Jasmine
and lies 8–10 km (5–6 miles)
from the town centre.
Thoroughly geared up for
visitors, these zones have
excellent beaches, clean
water and mounted police
patrols. The northern zone
offers a wider range of hotels
and restaurants. It is also
more lively, with small bars
and street vendors; and it is
closer to town. Hammamet
Jasmine maintains a higher
standard, with most hotels
having four or five stars. It
also has the largest Tunisian
marina. Tourist zones allow
visitors to behave in a more
relaxed way than would be
appropriate in the town.

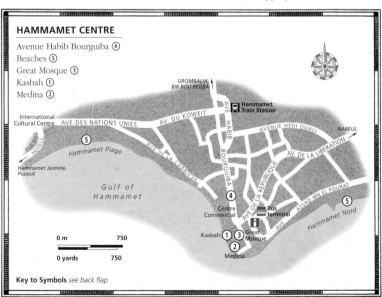

HAMMAMET CENTRE

Avenue Habib Bourguiba ④
Beaches ⑤
Great Mosque ③
Kasbah ①
Medina ②

0 m   750
0 yards   750

Key to Symbols *see back flap*

The former villa of George Sebastian

Further Afield

Beaches that are further from the town centre, as well as those located in parts of Hammamet Jasmine, are all within easy reach by taxi. A walk to the International Cultural Centre, which hosts performances in the summer, takes about 20 minutes. Also worth exploring, particularly on market days, are the villages around Nabeul.

🏛 International Cultural Centre

Avenue des Nations Unies. **Tel** (72) 280 410. ◯ 8am–6:30pm daily. 🎵 Jul, Aug.

The International Cultural Centre is housed in the villa that once belonged to George Sebastian, which was praised by the architect Frank Lloyd

Wright as the most beautiful house he had ever seen. The ground floor is occupied by a gallery, and the house is surrounded by a beautiful park. Visitors can stop and rest in one of its delightful nooks or sit in the waterside café, although it is open only in the summer. The centre hosts an Arab Music Festival during July and August in the park's amphitheatre. The concerts, including both classical and modern popular Arab music, are great fun.

Environs

Nearby, **Pupput** is situated 6 km (4 miles) south of Hammamet, on the road to Sousse. In the 2nd century AD this was a small Roman settlement. During the Byzantine era, the site was occupied by a fortress. Although little remains of the town's former glory, it is still worth coming here to see the 4th-century mosaics from Christian tombs.

Grombalia, 30 km (19 miles) north of Hammamet, comes alive on market days, although

to experience a truly festive atmosphere it is best to visit the town in September, during the wine festival that coincides with the all-important harvest.

Grombalia is one of Tunisia's wine-producing regions. Vines have been cultivated here since Punic times. In order to protect the plants from the heat, the vineyards were laid out facing north, the vines were planted in trenches and their roots were covered with stones to provide protection from rain and the summer heat. The Phoenicians were believed to have produced excellent wines. The Romans upheld these traditions, but with the arrival of Muslim civilization, wine production declined. Grapes continued to be cultivated, but on a much smaller scale. This is largely because the drinking of alcohol was not encouraged by the Prophet. This rule was strictly adhered to in the early days of Islam, but Imam ibn Hanifa and the Hanefite school of law allowed their followers to drink certain types of wine. Wine-drinking was widespread towards the end of the Ummayad dynasty. In some branches of Sufism, wine has come to symbolize the Absolute, with wine-induced intoxication regarded as a state of mystic ecstasy in which the Sufi draws closer to God.

Monument to wine making, in Grombalia

Bir Bou Regba, a small town close to Nabeul, is fairly quiet but gets busier on market days. Visitors usually head for the dried-out riverbed of Faoura. The target of their trips is the small waterfall (also sometimes dry) a short distance up the course of the river. Water flowing from the spring runs over the stones that are believed to be the remains of a Roman aqueduct. One of the ravines in the valley used to contain a sanctuary devoted to the Punic god Baal Hammon and the goddess Tanit (see p110).

🎭 Pupput

◯ Apr–Sep: 8am–1pm & 3–7pm daily. Oct–Mar: 8:30am–5:30pm.

GEORGE SEBASTIAN

In the early 20th century, Hammamet became the favourite haunt of artists, aristocrats and politicians including Winston Churchill, who worked on his memoirs here. This is largely due to George Sebastian, a Romanian millionaire who liked it so much that he decided to make it his home. He built a magnificent villa (now the International Cultural Centre) set in a beautiful park. George Sebastian used it to entertain many writers and artists, including Paul Klee and André Gide. Word spread and he was soon not the only foreign resident. The town also lured the American couple John and Violet Henson and their house became a meeting place for the artistic elite from all over the world.

Bust of Sebastian

Tunisian Doors

In Tunisia, doors are regarded as symbols reflecting the fortune and happiness of the households within. They are therefore solidly built of palm wood, reinforced with sheet metal and often set within richly decorated portals. They are usually painted blue, though they can be brown or yellow. Only the doors leading to public baths or marabout mausoleums are painted in green or red.

Carved portal of a house in Kairouan

Under the Hafsids (13th–16th century) Tunisian doors were almost entirely devoid of decoration. In the 16th and 17th centuries, the Moorish style introduced geometric patterns, which under Turkish rule were supplemented with stylized plants and flowers. In the 19th century, European fashion influenced the colouring and the decorative motifs of Tunisian doors.

Ornament and opulence *are the hallmarks of this sturdy 18th-century door. It is studded with nails that form complicated designs. Frequently used motifs include stars, plants, flowers and crescents. The side posts are decorated with spiral columns supporting a typically Islamic horseshoe arch.*

Doorknockers *are present on every door. They are often in the shape of a large circle or a hand. The ones on the left are usually used by women, the ones on the right by men.*

An Italian influence *is clear in the semicircular wrought-iron grille in the top section of this door. The light blue colouring is inspired by the European fashion and appeared in the 20th century.*

Motifs *most frequently seen on Tunisian doors include the crescent, star, minaret and stylized palm leaves.*

European influence *led to hearts and stylized flowers on rectangular tiles replacing doorway decorations produced with studs and nails.*

NORTHERN TUNISIA

For many years Northern Tunisia was little appreciated by visitors who preferred other parts of the country such as the east coast of Cap Bon and the resorts around Tunis. This situation is gradually changing and the mild Mediterranean climate, rugged coast, magnificent beaches and Roman sites such as Bulla Regia are attracting visitors in increasing numbers.

The indigenous population of the northern regions of Tunisia were the Berbers, but it was the Phoenicians who established the earliest settlements here – including present-day Utica, Bizerte and Tabarka. They were attracted by the fertile soil of the region and its calm bays, in which they could safely anchor their ships.

Following the downfall of Carthage, Rome took over the former Punic settlements, turning them into fast-growing military colonies. Towns such as Béja, Bulla Regia, Utica and Bizerte owe their prosperity to grain and trade. The fertile soil of the Medjerda Valley was the granary of Phoenicia and Rome, and it remains agriculturally important today. The region owes much to the Arab immigrants who arrived from Andalusia in the 17th and 18th centuries. Besides cereals and vegetables they began to grow almonds, figs, citrus fruit and grapes. The vineyards of Raf Raf and Béja produce fine Coteaux D'Utique wines.

Bizerte and Tabarka – northern Tunisia's largest towns – have long-established maritime traditions dating back to Phoenician times. Both were once major ports, pirate strongholds and naval bases. Today their economies are based on industry and on a steadily growing tourist trade, with numerous resorts and hotels springing up. Bizerte, nicknamed the "Venice of the North", has a lovely old harbour and a charming medina, while at Tabarka there is a coral reef and a first-class golf course.

Rolling hills around Testour

◁ **Working on the fishing boats in Ghar el Melh harbour**

Exploring Northern Tunisia

The northern section of Tunisia is not as popular as the coast of Sahel and Jerba, yet the region has a great deal to offer. Those who enjoy hiking or hunting should head for the Khroumirie Mountains where there are many trails leading through wooded hills. The beaches around Tabarka, Bizerte and Raf Raf are perfect for swimming and relaxing while Lake Ichkeul, used as winter quarters by many thousands of migrating birds, is an ornithologist's paradise. Bulla Regia, to the south, has unique underground villas and is one of the most archaeologically important Roman towns in the world.

A ceramic statuett from Sejnane

Les Aiguilles by the Tabarka beach

SIGHTS AT A GLANCE

Béja ⑥
Bizerte ⑫
Bulla Regia pp132–3 ⑤
Cap Blanc ⑬
Cap Serrat ⑨
Chemtou ④
Ichkeul National Park pp136–7 ⑩
Khroumirie Mountains ③
Menzel Bourguiba ⑪
Sejnane ⑧
Tabarka ①
Testour ⑦
Utica ⑭

Tours
Around Tabarka pp128–9 ②

SEE ALSO

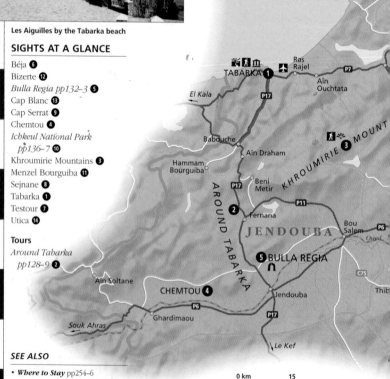

0 km   15

0 miles   15

GETTING THERE
The main airport for the northern coast is Tunis. Two roads link the capital with Tabarka: the northern P7 and the southern P6 from which drivers must turn north onto the P17. Bizerte can be reached by the A1 motorway or P8 highway. The scenery around Béja, Téboursouk and Testour is remarkable, although the roads are narrow. Access to the coast in places other than Tabarka and Bizerte is difficult.

An underground villa in Bulla Regia

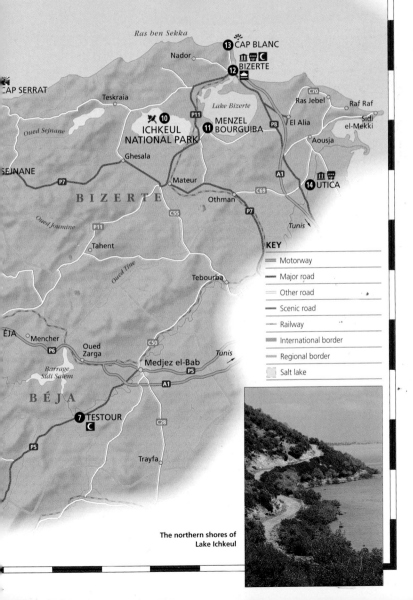

The northern shores of Lake Ichkeul

KEY
▬▬	Motorway
▬	Major road
═══	Other road
▬	Scenic road
┄┄	Railway
▬▬	International border
───	Regional border
░░	Salt lake

Fishing boats, with Tabarka's Genoese fort in the background

Tabarka ❶

Road map B1. ⚐ *13,700.*
🛈 ONTT: Commissariat regional au tourisme, Blvd. 7 Novembre 32, *(78) 673 028.* 🎵 *International Jazz Festival (late Jun–Jul).*

Tabarka is just 22 km (14 miles) from the Algerian border and is one of the greenest towns in Tunisia. Its picturesque setting includes beaches to the north and gentle hills overgrown with cork oak, pine and mimosa to the south.

The town stands on the site of a former Phoenician colony, Thabraca. During Roman times Tabarka was an important port used for shipping grain from Béja and marble from Chemtou to Rome. As well as its forests full of game, Tabarka's greatest asset was its coral reef. In the 16th century the exclusive rights to coral fishing were granted to the Genoese who built an offshore fort close by. With the advent of the French Protectorate, in 1881, coral rights were taken up by the French and Tabarka and Le Kef were two of the first towns to be occupied.

Tabarka is quite small. It centres round two streets running parallel to the coast, where most of its restaurants and cafés can be found. The red-tiled roofs of the **Genoese fort** can be seen from almost any point in town but the best view is from the jetty. The beautifully located hotel **Les Mimosas** also affords a magnificent panoramic view of the town, the gulf and the surrounding area. A little further west from the harbour stands an ochre-coloured rock formation – **Les Aiguilles** (The Needles), sharpened by the constant erosion of wind and rain.

Tabarka has quiet beaches and a number of golf courses. It also has some of Tunisia's best diving. Local diving clubs regularly organize diving excursions to various sites along the coral reef just off the coast. There are trips which are suitable for beginners as well as more experi-

CORAL

Coral, brought up by divers and fishermen from the seabed, has been in high demand throughout North Africa for many years. Since the 15th century, when the Europeans discovered its beauty, coral jewellery has fetched a high price. Tabarka is a centre for jewellery made from coral and shops sell necklaces, pins and brooches with coral inserts. It has long been used as a talisman: red coral is believed to bestow vitality, pink coral is conducive to pleasant thoughts, while white coral clears the mind. Coral is becoming scarce, however; some visitors choose not to buy it for this reason.

Coral and shell necklaces for sale at Tabarka's market

enced divers. About 60 km (37 miles) north of Tabarka is the Galite archipelago, which can also be reached by boat from Tabarka. Details of diving excursions can be obtained from any of Tabarka's diving clubs *(see p307).*

Les Aiguilles (The Needles) as seen from Tabarka's beach

Coral Reef

Tabarka's coral reef is close to the shore. Just 10 minutes away by boat is a rock surrounded by black and red corals. A little further on is a magnificent complex of tunnels, grottoes, underwater caves and caverns. Warm waters mean that the reef teems with life. Flitting between coral branches are colourful marine fish and luminescent jellyfish.

Other marine occupants include sponges, sea urchins, sea cucumbers and sea squirts. Deeper waters are inhabited by halibut, moray eel and wrasse. Diving for coral is popular along the entire northern shore of Tunisia, but the most beautiful specimens come from the waters around Tabarka. Its popularity means that coral is an endangered species.

Rainbow wrasse *is a colourful fish belonging to the perch family. Only active during the day, it buries itself in the sand at night.*

Swallowtail sea perch *is a small predatory fish that lives in large shoals. Its bright colouring makes it highly conspicuous. It can be seen grazing near entrances to underwater caves in which it seeks shelter when threatened.*

Fish *graze near the bottom of the sea, searching for food in rock crevices and amongst the coral where they can hide. They often assume the colour of the reef, which makes them invisible to predators.*

The dusky grouper *is a very large, slow-swimming fish. It can sometimes be curious about divers and therefore presents an easy target for spearfishing. Reefs provide it with plenty of hiding places, although it does not have many natural enemies other than mankind.*

Wrasse *favour rocky coastal waters and reefs. Here they find the small fish, as well as snails, mussels, crabs and other invertebrates that make up their staple diet.*

Red coral knolls *grow on the rocky bottom of the Mediterranean Sea. As well as being collected with nets, coral is also cut using a special device consisting of heavy, metal-reinforced beams. These are set in the shape of a cross, weighted with a stone in the centre and have loosely weighted nets at the corners. The cross is pressed into crevasses and the nets wind themselves around the coral, breaking it off the bedrock.*

Around Tabarka ❷

Rising immediately behind the town are the steep slopes of the Khroumirie Mountains. These are densely forested and are a marvellous region for exploring. The deep ravines and numerous springs and streams provide welcome cool in the summer heat. Villages such as Hammam Bourguiba and Aïn Draham are long-established resorts and make good starting points for hikes. The cool climate and wonderful scenery make this area popular with Tunisians.

EL-KALA

Hammam Bourguiba ①

The village lies in a valley surrounded by hills dense with cork oak and pine. The excellent climate combined with hot springs has made it popular with elderly Tunisians including (at one time) President Bourguiba.

Bulla Regia ⑥

These Roman ruins include baths, a temple complex and theatre, as well as villas that were built underground to escape the heat.

Beni Metir ④

Beni Metir was built in 1956 to house French builders. It is close to a lake and surrounded by a forest of oak and myrtle.

Chemtou ⑦

These local quarries used to provide Rome with marble. On top of the hill the Numidians erected an altar to Baal. The Romans used this to worship Saturn. For the Muslims it became a centre for marabouts (Islamic holy men).

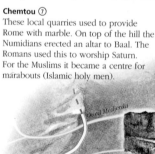

Oued Medjerda

Ghardimaou ⑨

This quiet village lies almost on the border with Algeria. It is worth visiting mainly for its beautiful mountain scenery as part of a tour that also takes in Chemtou.

SOUK-AHRAS

Babouche ②
The road to Babouche runs steeply upwards. The village is 5 km (3 miles) from Aïn Draham at the entrance to a gorge. From here the road leads to a deer park. This is a good starting point for hikes through the forest.

TIPS FOR DRIVERS

Length: *About 90 km (56 miles).*
Stopping-off points: *Jendouba, Aïn Draham and Hammam Bourguiba have accommodation. There are plenty of restaurants.*
Other attractions: *The road that runs between Bou Salem and Téboursouk is particularly scenic.*

Aïn Draham ③
Perched on the western side of Jebel Bir (1,014 m/3327 ft), Aïn Draham was popular with the French. Aïn Draham's steep red-tiled roofs help cope with the winter snow and lend the town an Alpine atmosphere.

Fernana ⑤
Around Fernana the mountainous landscape gives way to a plain. Every Sunday the village holds a market selling fruit, vegetables and livestock. According to legend it was here that the Khroumirie chiefs came to ask a thousand-year-old oak tree how much tax they should pay to the Bey of Tunis. The tree would rustle its leaves in response.

KEY

- Suggested route
- Other road
- Unmetalled road
- Viewpoint

Jendouba ⑧
The provincial capital, surrounded by fields, is half way between Tabarka and Le Kef. In the evenings the men sit down to a cup of tea and a *chicha* (hookah) in one of the small restaurants along the main road from Tabarka to Le Kef. It is a good base to visit the ruins at Bulla Regia.

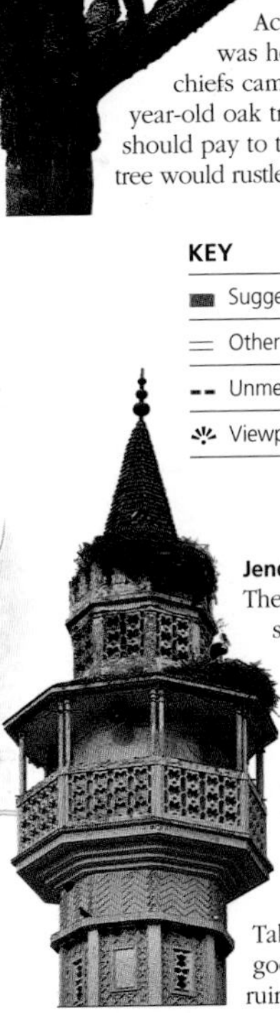

Hilltop field and olive trees, flanked by the Khroumirie Mountains

Khroumirie Mountains ❸

Road map B2.

The Khroumirie Mountains begin to rise just a few miles outside Tabarka and stretch some 50 km (31 miles) south to Fernana, reaching a height of about 1,000 m (3,281 ft). They owe their name to the Khroumirie tribes who were renowned for their bravery. When French troops invaded in 1881, it was the Khroumirie who put up the fiercest resistance. The forests were once the favourite hunting grounds of local tribes, as well as visiting Europeans. The last lion was killed in 1891; all hunters have been left with is wild boar. In summer, the forests are popular with mountain hikers.

Although holly, eucalyptus, mimosa, elm, birch and willow all grow here, the most abundant tree is the cork oak, which has been grown for its bark by the villagers of the Khroumirie for thousands of years. Used to make anything from tiles to wine corks, the red-stained trunks of freshly-stripped trees can be seen everywhere.

Chemtou ❹

Road map B2. 27 km (17 miles) north of Jendouba. ⏛ *Apr–Oct: 9am–6:30pm Tue–Sun; Nov–Mar: 9am–5pm Tue–Sun.* 🖼

Not much has survived in Chemtou from the former Roman colony of Simithas, which was established in the 1st century BC. Chemtou owed its existence to the quarries which provided a dark-yellow marble that was highly prized by the Romans. Blocks of marble were marked with the name of the emperor and were transported on carts to Tabarka across the mountains.

The site included workers' homes, baths, a theatre and a workshop. Aerial photographs taken in the late 1960s revealed a large labour camp. It was built in AD 154 and housed the slaves who worked in the quarries. The quarries remained active until Byzantine times, but were abandoned after the arrival of the Arabs (7th century).

The site was first excavated in 1968 and many of the finds from this dig can be found in the excellent **site museum**, which was opened in 1990. Among the displays are a detailed explanation of the excavation, a working model of an ancient flour mill and over 1,600 gold coins that were discovered when the museum was being built.

One surprise of the excavation work was the discovery of a Numidian temple to Baal Hammon at the top of the hill. Dating from the 2nd century BC, the find suggests that the Numidians had a more sophisticated culture than historians had once believed.

The quarries are located opposite the museum. The huge holes dug into the rock attest to the amount of sheer effort and human endurance that went into working them.

Further on up the hill are the ruins of a temple. Originally a Numidian site, it was converted into a temple dedicated to Saturn by the Romans. Particularly interesting among Chemtou's other relics are the rock carvings found on the western and northern sides of the hill.

Red trunk of a freshly stripped cork oak, an important resource of the Khroumirie Mountains

Bulla Regia ❺

See pp132–133.

The ancient quarries at Chemtou

Béja ❻

Road map B2. 🏠 *70,000.*

The road from Tabarka to Béja (which in ancient times was called Vaga) runs amid gently rolling hills covered with eucalyptus, stone-pine and oleander. The town – the capital of the province – is 250 m (820 ft) above sea level, and lies in the valley of the Medjerda River. Béja is an important grain town and a weekly market has been held here since Roman times. The town was attacked and destroyed by the Vandals in the 5th century, only to be rebuilt by Emperor Justinian who named it Theodoriana, in honour of his wife. The ruins of the Byzantine kasbah that dominate the old town date from that period.

The most charming part of modern-day Béja is its small medina. It is a busy and atmospheric place and the many mosques, *zaouias* (tombs), Islamic schools and public baths are punctuated by colourful market stalls. Head for Rue Farhat Hached for a fine view from the medina over the town and the surrounding countryside.

Environs
Some 13 km (8 miles) south of Béja stands **Trajan's Bridge**. Built in AD 29, it linked Carthage with Bulla Regia *(see pp132–3)*. Heading north, towards Beni Metir, 8 km (5 miles) beyond Béja, is **Henchir el-Fouar**. Excavations begun in 1960 unearthed the ruins of Roman villas, a small forum and two basilicas, which formed the Roman town of Belalia Major. It is worth stopping for a while in **Tebourba** – a little town on the banks of the Medjerda River, set in gardens and olive groves. Tebourba has a pleasant medina, laid out on a regular grid pattern. As well as a number of market stalls, the town has a 17th-century Great Mosque and a handful of smaller mosques and *zaouias*. The oldest of the *zaouias* is dedicated to Sidi Thabet and dates from the 7th century.

A medersa's green-tiled dome, Testour

Testour ❼

Road map C2. 🏠 *8,000.*
🎵 *Malouf Music Festival (Jun).*

Testour is one of Tunisia's Andalusian Muslim towns. In the 17th century, 80,000 Arabs who were expelled from Andalusia after the Christian reconquest arrived in Tunisia. The wealthier refugees were allowed to settle in Tunis but the poorer farmers had to make do with the uninhabited regions of the country's interior. After petitioning the authorities they were granted the right to settle on the Roman site of Tichilla, which became present-day Testour.

The farming techniques brought from Andalusia helped the newcomers turn the barren land into fertile oases and their attachment to Andalusian traditions injected a European flavour into the Arab settlements. Testour's central square became the focal point of the town layout. Windows now faced the streets and mosques acquired their distinctive arches. Testour's main square is one of the earliest products of the 17th-century Spanish influence. It contains several cafés, the Great Mosque and the hammam and is planted with numerous orange trees and jasmine shrubs. Leading to the square is the town's main street – Avenue Habib Bourguiba.

Testour used to have 14 mosques. Five of them remain open to this day. The main one – the **Great Mosque** (17th century) is open only to Muslims and is a good example of Tunisian Moorish architecture. The square base of the tiled minaret is crowned with two octagonal towers, one built into the other, and is reminiscent of a Castilian bell tower. The most striking evidence of Andalusian influence is the clock on the minaret's south face. Besides the fact that a clock is not seen on a minaret anywhere else in the world, the other surprising feature is the hours, which go backwards, revealing, perhaps, the refugees' desire to turn back time and return to their homeland.

Nearby, in El-Andalouse Square, are the ruins of the first Great Mosque (1610). Rue du Mars, running parallel to Avenue Bourguiba, contains the Abdellatif Mosque, also known as the Hanefite mosque.

For most of the year, Testour is a quiet town but it can get busy in June during the Festival of Malouf music.

Green fields dotted with olive trees near Béja

Bulla Regia ❺

The important archaelogical site of Bulla Regia is famous for its underground villas, which were built by the Romans in the 2nd and 3rd centuries AD to escape the fierce heat of the Tunisian sun. The site also includes a temple, baths, fort and a market square, but it is the houses which are the main attraction. Each of the villas has been named after the mosaics that were found within them. Some of these beautiful mosaics are still *in situ*, while others have been moved to museums such as the Bardo in Tunis (*see pp88–9*).

★ House of Amphitrite
The house, found at the north end of the cluster of underground villas, is famous for its exquisite mosaics, which are in the basement.

★ House of the Hunt
Of all the surviving underground houses this one is the most striking. Its colonnaded basement courtyard is especially impressive.

The Byzantine fort is a very modest structure, devoid of any defensive features. It was erected in the 6th century.

Byzantine Church
The church was built in the 6th century. Visible among the fallen columns are fragments of the floor mosaics featuring Christian motifs.

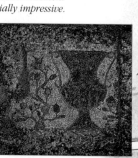

0 m   50

0 yards   50

STAR SIGHTS

★ House of Amphitrite

★ House of the Hunt

Roman cisterns were later used to store food.

Southern baths

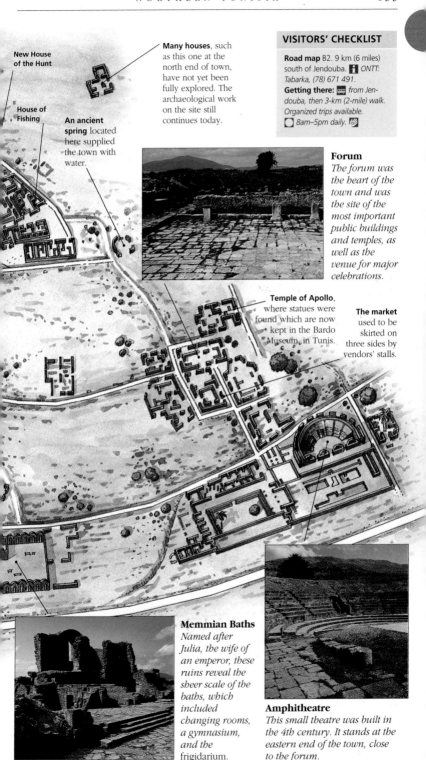

New House of the Hunt

House of Fishing

An ancient spring located here supplied the town with water.

Many houses, such as this one at the north end of town, have not yet been fully explored. The archaeological work on the site still continues today.

Forum
The forum was the heart of the town and was the site of the most important public buildings and temples, as well as the venue for major celebrations.

Temple of Apollo, where statues were found which are now kept in the Bardo Museum, in Tunis.

The market used to be skirted on three sides by vendors' stalls.

Memmian Baths
Named after Julia, the wife of an emperor, these ruins reveal the sheer scale of the baths, which included changing rooms, a gymnasium, and the frigidarium.

Amphitheatre
This small theatre was built in the 4th century. It stands at the eastern end of the town, close to the forum.

Sejnane ❽

Road map B1. 🚶 2,000.

Sejnane – a small village hidden among the hills overgrown with laurel, oleander and eucalyptus – lies along the road that links Bizerte with Tabarka. Quite close to Béja and Cap Serrat, the village is inhabited by Berber tribes who lead a semi-nomadic life. The air here is suffused with the smell of pine resin and the bread baking in outdoor ovens.

Sejnane is famous for two things: its lovely beige pottery and its numerous storks' nests. The storks, of which there were 24 pairs at the last count, build their nests each spring. The birds seem fairly indiscriminate as to where they site their nests and can be seen on the roofs of local houses, the train station, electricity transformers and on some abandoned mining apparatus.

Berber ceramics from Sejnane region

The techniques used to create the pottery made here date back thousands of years. The clay is shaped by hand, then decorated. Some of the decorations are drawn directly onto the wet clay and the grooves are filled with a black resin from the mastic tree. The items are baked on open fires in the yards of the houses. Pots of various shapes and sizes and animal figurines, which are painted by hand by the Berber women using traditional motifs, are most common. The typical colours of the Sejnane products are beige, rust-red and black.

Originally, such pottery was intended for domestic use or as talismans created to bring success and happiness. Sejnane pottery includes heavy plates, water jugs, deep platters, animal statuettes and censers. These are filled with herbs and aromatic resins, and the sweet-smelling smoke is believed to purify the house of all evil influences. The women also purify their skirts and dresses with the smoke.

The decorative patterns on the vessels all have symbolic meanings. The stylized triangles symbolize fertility; the crosses, large and small, are intended for protection and healing. A wavy line placed on a dish will ensure the abundance of water.

Much of the pottery produced here is from the outlying villages and is sold on roadside stalls. Many of these can be found on the road to Bizerte.

North from Sejnane, across the wooded hills, are the beautiful Sidi Mechrig beach and Cap Serrat.

Cap Serrat ❾

Road map B1.

Cap Serrat is situated away from the busy tourist centres. Its steep cliffs drop down to the sea and the views from the top are truly breathtaking. The remote beach on the eastern side of this little peninsula is long, sandy and, for much of the time, virtually deserted. It is visited mainly by local Tunisians who come here in family groups. A small café next to the beach caters for campers during the summer.

The road between Cap Serrat and Cap Negro is an exceptionally scenic one. It is fringed with laurel, mimosa and pine trees. Cap Negro (its name is associated with the Genoese settlers) is an old trading post, built in the 16th century by the French who traded in grain. It is now occupied by the National Guard. The area is beautiful, but has virtually no roads and is best explored on foot.

The region between Cap Serrat and Tabarka is full of pine, eucalyptus, mimosa, oleander, cork oak and fruit orchards. Sometimes described in brochures as "Green Tunisia", it is a long way from the typical Tunisian image of desert and beaches.

Environs

About 40 km (25 miles) off the coast from Cap Serrat is the volcanic archipelago of **La Galite**. Consisting of seven volcanic islands, this was already known to the Phoenicians. During Roman times it was called Galathea. The waters around the islands are rich in marine life and are a superb place to go diving. There is no regular transport between the islands and the mainland, but it is possible to get here by boat from Tabarka. Details can be obtained from one of Tabarka's diving clubs (*see p307*). Although remote, the islands are inhabited by a handful of families who make their living from fishing and cultivating grapes.

Leading a horse to water in Cap Serrat

Tunisian Birds

Tunisia is visited by many migrating birds that fly here from the north for the winter. The Gulf of Gabès is the winter home of some 350,000 birds – almost half of the bird population that winter in the Mediterranean region. Here flamingoes and many varieties of shorebirds, such as curlew, plover and dunlin, can be seen. Lake Ichkeul is a perfect habitat for waterfowl and a paradise for ornithologists. About 200,000 ducks, geese and coots also settle here during the winter. Birdwatchers tend to visit Tunisia in March.

Thekla lark in full song

Flamingoes *live in colonies, feeding on small water animals and plants. In Tunisia they can be seen in and around the Gulf of Gabès and also in Ichkeul National Park.*

Lesser black-backed gulls *are the most commonly seen bird on the Tunisian coast. The biggest flocks of these birds can be seen around the Gulf of Gabès.*

Lanner falcons *live in the border areas, between the mountains and the desert. This bird of prey builds its nest in rock crevices and hunts in open spaces. It catches birds and small rodents. Unlike many other species of falcon it can also catch its prey on the ground.*

Boobys *are among the largest birds that can be seen on the Tunisian coast. They inhabit the steep craggy shores in the north of the country.*

Common cranes *can be seen in many parts of northern Tunisia, including the salt lake at Sebkha Kelbia. They feed on plants and small animals.*

Houbara bustards *inhabit the edges of the desert, in areas of low-growing vegetation where they can hide. Although a protected species, hunting for bustards with falcons is a popular local sport.*

Ichkeul National Park ⑩

This government-protected nature reserve was established in 1980. Covering 60 sq km (23 sq miles), it is one of the main wintering grounds for migrating waterfowl in the entire Mediterranean basin. The shallow, freshwater lake and its surrounding marshes are a sanctuary to thousands of waterfowl which nest here during the mild winter *(see p135)*. Other animals inhabiting the reserve include toads, terrapins, porcupines, jackals, wild boar and foxes. There is even a herd of water buffalo, which is descended from Asian buffaloes brought here in the 19th century.

Otter
This predator inhabits low-lying areas surrounding the lake; it feeds mainly on fish.

Lake Ichkeul

Greylag Goose
Some 10,000 of these birds arrive here each year. Wintering on the waters of the lake, the geese can easily find food.

Genet —
Genets hate water. Their hunting grounds are the shrubs that cover the hillsides. They hunt for small birds and rodents and also feed on birds' eggs.

JEBEL ICH

TABARKA   P7

TUNIS

0 km   2

0 miles   2

KEY

━ Minor road

═ Other road

— Park boundary

∿ River

☀ Viewpoint

Jebel Ichkeul
Several sandy footpaths lead through the hills, which are overgrown with wild olive trees, pistachio and euphorbia shrubs. The best view of the lake is from here.

For hotels and restaurants in this region see pp254–6 and pp278–80

VISITORS' CHECKLIST

Road map C1. 35 km (22 miles) southwest of Bizerte. **Getting there:** *The best way is by car.* 🏛 **Eco-museum** ⬭ *9am–noon & 12:30–4:30pm daily;* **Park** *7am–6pm daily.* **Other info:** *Best to visit from Oct–early Mar.*

Water Buffalo
A pair of buffalo was introduced here in the 19th century. Hunters brought the animal to the verge of extinction in the 1960s. Now it can be seen on the northern shore of the lake.

Grey Heron
This species can be seen from the lake-shore throughout the year, although they are more plentiful during the winter.

Tinja

Kestrel
This small falcon is one of the few birds of prey that can be seen in the park.

Idjane

Eco–museum
Displays illustrate the natural assets of the region, which in 1996 was placed on the UNESCO List of World Cultural and Natural Heritage Sites.

Coastal Marshes
The marshes dry out in the summer as waters fall below the level of the sea that feeds the lake.

Fishing boats in Bizerte's Old Port

Menzel Bourguiba ⓫

Road map C1. 👤 *30,000.*

Menzel Bourguiba is a small industrial town situated 24 km (15 miles) south of Bizerte. To get here take a car or *louage* (shared taxi) which can be hired in front of Bizerte's railway station. The town was established by the French in 1897. Originally called Ferryville, it was built on the ruins of a Spanish fortress, and was intended for European immigrants. The French built an arsenal and five dry docks here that were once the biggest in Africa. In the early 20th century the small town that sprung up around the arsenal was nicknamed "Little Paris".

Not much remains of the original provincial town. Since 1963 Menzel Bourguiba has been developing as an important centre of the textile and metal industries. It has a large harbour that links directly with the Mediterranean through the Bizerte Canal. Menzel Bourguiba's main street has an impressive modern mosque.

Bizerte ⓬

Road map C1. 65 km (40 miles) northwest of Tunis. 👤 *90,000.*
ℹ️ *Next to Bizerte Resort Corniche (Sidi Salem), (72) 436 966.* 🎭 *Bizerte International Festival (17 Jul–17 Aug).*

Bizerte, the oldest city in Tunisia, is the principal town on the northeast coast of Tunisia and is situated on the canal that links Lake Bizerte with the sea. A modern-day commercial port, Bizerte has long had a strategic importance. It was the Phoenicians who first settled here and dug a channel linking the lake to the sea, thus producing one of the safest harbours in the Mediterranean. They named their town Hippo Zarytus. The Romans destroyed it in 146 BC only to rebuild it again as Hippo Diarrhytus. It was subsequently renamed Benzert by the Arabs. Under the French Protectorate the town became a major naval base. During World War II it was occupied by German troops and suffered considerable damage in the course of Allied bombardments. The magnificent, almost empty beaches and scenic dunes stretching along the Corniche (the road that runs parallel to the coast) have prompted the

Top of the Great Mosque's minaret

building of many hotels. A modern marina has also been developed. Stretching from the entrance of the old port along the Corniche, it encompasses residential apartments, shopping malls, cafés, restaurants and nightclubs, as well as impressive recreational facilities and a yacht harbour.

The picturesque old town and the fishing harbour run along the lake with the canal. The newer European part of the town begins at the point where the canal joins up with Lake Bizerte. The most attractive part of Bizerte is its **Old Port**, built on the canal that links the lake with the sea. Here, the quay is lined with quaint cafés where it is pleasant to sit out and watch the boats heading out to sea. The Old Port is entered through a huge gate, 35 m (115 ft) wide. The promenade that starts by the kasbah runs in a gentle arc along the canal. The kasbah and the small

Seaside promenade beside the beach in Bizerte

◁ **Green hills between Testour and Téboursouk**

11th-century citadel, standing on the opposite side, once formed parts of the fortifications that guarded the medina and the harbour. Built by the Arabs on the site of a Byzantine fortress, the traditional Byzantine brick arrangement can be seen to this day.

The **kasbah** dates from the 17th century. Behind its huge walls, which are up to 10 m (33 ft) high in places, is a self-contained town within a town which includes atmospheric streets and alleys, a mosque, baths and a number of homes. The Fort Sidi el-Hanni tower now houses the **Oceanography Museum**, which has a small collection of sea creatures.

Originally, there was only one gate leading to the medina, which is now hidden behind the façades of the houses that line the banks of the canal. Until the 19th century it was surrounded by a 6-m (20-ft) high wall that was 3.5 m (11 ft) thick. All that remains of it now is the segment between the Andalusian district and the so-called Spanish Fort.

The **Spanish Fort** is actually Turkish in origin and was built in the 16th century. Little of its original structure remains, though a Muslim cemetery lies within its defensive walls. The fort's terrace offers a magnificent view over the surrounding area, including the Old Port and the modern harbour. In summer it serves as a venue for concerts.

The **Great Mosque** at the centre of the medina was built in the 17th century. Its octagonal minaret is crowned with a balcony that can be seen from every point along the promenade. The mosque is surrounded by a number of small *zaouias* (tombs), but the most important of them, the Zaouia of Sidi Mostari, is situated some distance away.

This tomb was built on the orders of Murad Bey, in 1673. It features an ablutions room, a dome-covered sanctuary containing El-Mostari's tomb, and a beautiful galleried courtyard.

The kasbah defending the harbour entrance, Bizerte

It is worth visiting the Andalusian quarter where the Arab refugees from Spain settled in the 17th century. Once situated beyond the town walls, it had its own mosque, with a square minaret topped by a roof of green tiles. The houses here also have a distinctly Spanish character with light blue doors decorated with studs and nails. However, with the passage of time, the town wall vanished and the Andalusian quarter lost much of its identity.

Returning to the medina, to the quayside promenade, it is worth stopping in **Café Le Pasha**. In the evening its

Picturesque houses of the medina, Bizerte

terrace provides a lovely view of the canal and the colourful lights of the nearby cafés. Immediately behind the café, situated between the souks, the Old Port and the harbour, is **Place Lahedine Bouchoucha**. Here, a 17th-century mosque featuring an octagonal minaret is decorated with an external gallery. One section of the square is occupied by a market selling fish, fruit and vegetables.

The main street that runs along the quay leads to the beach, and further on to the tourist zone.

Head west from the town centre along Avenue Habib Bourguiba to reach the Military Academy and, further on, the European cemetery with the nearby Martyrs' Monument commemorating victims of the 1961 pitched battle between the French garrison and Tunisian forces that included many barely-trained volunteers.

The road leading to the former French part of town and the Ras Jebel peninsula goes over a vast draw-bridge. Cap Blanc, situated 10 km (6 miles) away, is often taken as the northernmost point of the African continent.

Craggy coastline around Cap Blanc

Cap Blanc ⓭

Road map C1. 10 km (6 miles) north of Bizerte.

Cap Blanc is often given the title of the northernmost point of Africa, though a map reveals that this claim to fame should actually go to Ras ben Sekka situated just a short distance to the west.

The road from Bizerte runs along Habib Bougatfa, following the coast. Passing the tourist zone and the pebbly beaches, the road climbs gently upwards. The greater the height, the lovelier the views become. Seen from the beach or the road, Cap Blanc appears to be a big green mountain whose summit has been replaced by a sugar-loaf. The mountain drops sharply towards the sea. The surrounding waters are much favoured by divers. The area is quiet and can be windy. It is possible to stop for a while in Nador (the last village before Cap Blanc) to rest and have a bite to eat in the Rif Rif restaurant.

Utica ⓮

Road map C1.

Utica is an older sister of Carthage. It lies 10 km (6 miles) from the sea, southeast of Bizerte. The Phoenicians established Utica as their trading post perhaps as early as the 10th century BC. The site's main feature is the House of Cascades, named after the fountains that once

decorated this palace. Other objects found here include amulets, rings, scarabs, painted vessels, lamps and numerous amphorae.

Not much is known about the early days of Utica's history. Scarce information began to appear in ancient Greek texts but only after the founding of Carthage. Utica is regarded as the second most important ancient town after Carthage in this region. At its height, it had its own harbour and merchant fleet and fought alongside Carthage against Greece and Rome. However, in the course of the Third Punic War (149–146 BC) it switched allegiance, declaring itself on the side of Rome. Following the destruction of Carthage it was granted autonomy in AD 146 and became the capital of the Province of Africa. It remained as such until the rebuilding of Carthage. The town's economic growth reached its zenith in the 2nd and 3rd centuries when it derived most of its revenue from trade. Today Utica no longer borders the sea as the deposits carried by the Medjerda River have clogged up the bay.

Statue of Hercules in the Utica museum

Reminders of the town's Punic heritage include a **pottery workshop** and the **necropolis**. The **baths** and two **theatres** date from Roman times as do the **Treasury Building**, the **House of the Hunt** and the **House of the Cascades**. The latter has a colonnaded inner courtyard and was once a villa belonging to a wealthy Roman citizen. Its other features of note include a fountain and marble slabs with mosaics portraying maritime themes. One of the loveliest mosaics, depicting a dolphin playing with a cherub, was taken from here to the Louvre.

The **House of the Historic Capitals** is a spacious villa built on the site of a Punic structure. The inner court is surrounded by colonnades.

Utica's **museum** is also worth visiting. It displays some interesting mosaics, jewellery, funeral accessories and Punic sarcophagi of children that were probably sacrificed.

🏛 **Museum**
By the entrance to the town.
◻ Apr–mid-Sep: 8am–7pm daily; mid-Sep–Mar: 8:30am–5:30pm daily. ◙

Ancient ruins in Utica

Northern Tunisia's Beaches

East of Bizerte is a range of hills covered with olive groves, vineyards and orchards of almond and fig trees. In spring the entire area blossoms and resembles one big, colourful garden. The local beaches are, for the most part, undeveloped, empty and incredibly picturesque. The shore falls steeply into the crystal clear water. The most beautiful beaches of the region are to be found in Raf Raf and Sidi Ali el-Mekki.

Ras Jebel ①
The small farming town of Ras Jebel has its own beach. The water here is clear, but the currents are very strong. The beach has not been developed. It is popular as an unofficial campsite.

Raf Raf ②
The coast here is craggy, and the beach is relatively narrow, but it is a beautiful setting. The place is ideal for diving. The village is known for its grapes which make an excellent Muscat wine.

Sidi Ali el-Mekki ③
Sidi Ali el-Mekki is famous for its lovely quiet beach and the tomb of Sidi Ali el-Mekki. A network of caves leads to the tomb hidden deep in the mountain.

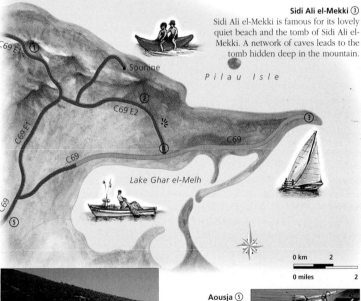

C69 E1 ①

Soumne

Pilau Isle

C69 E2 ②

C69 ③

C69 ①

Lake Ghar el-Melh

C69

C69

⑤

0 km 2

0 miles 2

Ghar el-Melh ④
This small town, sometimes referred to as Porto Farina, has been here since Punic times. Sites worth visiting include the fortress of Osta Murad Dey and the old port. The town lies on the shores of a lake and is linked to the sea by a canal.

Aousja ⑤
The best time to visit this picturesque village, situated some 2 km (1 mile) southwest of Ghar el-Melh, is in August, during its festival. There is a local restaurant that serves tasty fish caught by the village fishermen.

THE SAHEL

*L*ong sandy beaches, sparkling emerald waters, jasmine-scented nights: these are the images usually associated with the Sahel. The eastern coast of Tunisia (Sahel is Arabic for coast) stretches from Nabeul, through Sfax and the Gulf of Gabès, to Libya. It is here that Tunisia's most famous resorts and yacht harbours are found, as well as the historic towns of Mahdia, Sfax and Sousse.

To the Phoenicians and Romans the Sahel was one of the most important regions with thriving Roman towns and colonies including Hadrumetum (Sousse) and El-Jem, which was one of the richest towns in Roman Africa. Such municipia were able to fund ambitious construction projects including the amphitheatre at El-Jem, which is one of the most impressive monuments of Roman civilization in Africa. The citizens of El-Jem had their own administration and possessed civic rights on a par with the citizens of Rome.

The wealth of the region was based on the trade in olives. The oil was valued by the Romans for its flavour but was also used in lamps. With some 15 million olive trees, the Sahel accounts for over two-thirds of Tunisia's olive oil production.

Great towns such as Mahdia, the former capital of Tunisia, and the Sahel's ribats (fortified Islamic monasteries) are a reminder of the region's past when it was under constant threat from piracy and Christian invaders. Monastir's historic ribat is particularly interesting as it is not only the oldest and the best-preserved in present-day Tunisia, but is also one of the few along the entire African coast that admitted women as teachers and students. Islamic holy men are still held in great esteem in this part of the country and the *zaouias* (tombs) are more than mere relics of the past.

French influence can be seen in the "new towns" (*villes nouvelles*) of Sousse and Sfax although the ancient medinas of these two ports still have much of their maritime atmosphere.

Fishing boats in Mahdia's harbour

◁ Hotel bungalows in one of the Sahel's tourist zones

Exploring the Sahel

Situated along Tunisia's east coast, the Sahel has the country's best beaches, an abundance of wildlife, and numerous historic sites. Located between Hammamet and Mahdia are Tunisia's most popular resorts, while Port el-Kantaoui and Hammamet Jasmine have the country's biggest marinas. The once-isolated Kerkennah Islands, near Sfax, have been steadily developing their tourist infrastructure. Sousse and Sfax are the region's major towns and have ancient walled medinas and interesting museums. Magnificent examples of Islamic architecture can be seen in Monastir, Sousse and Mahdia.

Woman from Hergla selling wicker baskets

The distinctive dome of Khalaout el-Koubba in Sousse

GETTING THERE

The Sahel region has three airports – Monastir, Sfax and Enfida International Airport; the latter handles the majority of flights for the area. The Métro du Sahel (which has a stop-off at Monastir's airport) provides a comfortable transport link between Monastir, Mahdia and Sousse. The entire coast up to Sfax has railway links with Tunis; many trains run from Hammamet to Sousse (change at Bir Bou Regba). The *louage* (shared taxi) also provides a convenient means of transport; private taxis are popular on the route between Sousse and Monastir. A hired car is best for a trip inland.

SIGHTS AT A GLANCE

SEE ALSO

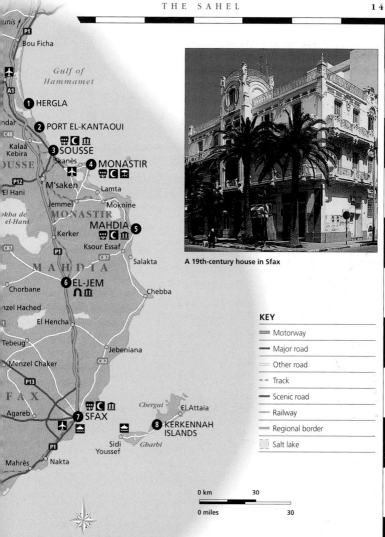

A 19th-century house in Sfax

KEY

▬▬	Motorway
▬▬	Major road
▬▬	Other road
- -	Track
▬▬	Scenic road
▬▬	Railway
▬▬	Regional border
▨	Salt lake

0 km   30

0 miles   30

Beach in Chafaar, on the Gulf of Gabès

Hergla ❶

Road map D2. 32 km (20 miles) north of Sousse. 🚶 6,000. 🚌 Thu.

Perched on a cliff, Hergla spreads out on both sides of a fishing harbour. The original village, known as Horraea Coelia, was founded in the 2nd century AD by the Romans. Its remains are a short way from the village centre. The village was totally destroyed in the course of the Arab invasion, but with time it rose from the ashes. In the 18th century it acquired an attractive mosque.

Today this pleasant seaside village is quiet and largely undiscovered, with pretty, whitewashed houses and a sandy beach. In the town's 18th-century mosque is the tomb of Sidi Bou Mendil, a 10th-century holy man who is said to have flown back from Mecca on his handkerchief.

A cemetery on the outskirts of Hergla

Fountain at the centre of Port el-Kantaoui

Port el-Kantaoui ❷

Road map D2. 10 km (6 miles) north of Sousse. 🚶 6,000. 🚃 tourist train. 🛈 ONTT: Marina Kantaoui, (73) 246 903, Port el-Kantaoui (73) 225 755.

This garden harbour (el-Kantaoui means "garden") of the Mediterranean fully deserves its name. It is immersed in flowers, while its marina is the second largest in Tunisia. Port el-Kantaoui was built in the late 1970s as a tourist zone and represents the up-market end of Tunisia's thriving holiday machine, with a complex of smart hotels that is situated directly on the beach.

Not surprisingly, there is plenty for holidaymakers to enjoy. The beach, of course, is first class, although much of it is taken up exclusively by the five-star hotels. The hotels, built in an Arab style, are surrounded by lush greenery such as jasmine and bougainvillea. In the evenings most of them put on their own entertainment including concerts, folk shows and belly dancing. The town's championship quality golf club has a course that winds through the olive groves next to the marina. Cruises are popular, with many agencies organizing sea trips. Club Sdanek can provide information about diving and also offers lessons.

For children, there is **Hannibal Park**, which has a merry-go-round and other rides. Next to this, **Acqua Palace** has water chutes, slides and pools.

At the heart of Port el-Kantaoui lies its colourful marina. The yacht basin is full of boats swaying gently on their moorings. A replica of a pirate ship takes visitors on sailing trips. The marina is fringed by restaurants, cafés and shops selling souvenirs. Street vendors sell fruit juice and posies of fresh jasmine.

JASMINE

The white jasmine plant was probably brought to Tunisia from Arabia, Persia or India. The strong fragrance of its delicate flowers is believed to lift the spirits and act as an aphrodisiac. Tunisians can often be seen carrying small posies of jasmine when out strolling or when sitting down to dinner. Posies are sometimes given as welcoming or parting gifts. Men place them behind their ears or carry them in their hands. Women frequently wear garlands of threaded flowers made into fragrant white necklaces. Small bottles of jasmine oil are readily available.

Street vendor selling posies of white jasmine

Yachts moored in Port el-Kantaoui's busy marina

Beaches of the Sahel

The Sahel's beaches are among the most visited in Tunisia; many of the region's hotels can be found close by. Yasmine Hammamet, a tourist area that opened in Hammamet in 2001, includes Tunisia's largest marina. The resort town of Port el-Kantaoui has a long stretch of pristine sand. The once-deserted beaches on the Kerkennah Islands are gradually becoming popular with visitors.

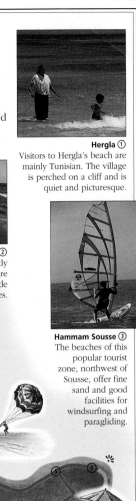

Hergla ①
Visitors to Hergla's beach are mainly Tunisian. The village is perched on a cliff and is quiet and picturesque.

Port el-Kantaoui ②
Here, the stretches of beach are mostly owned by the hotels, though parts are open to the public. The facilities include hire of diving equipment and water bikes.

Sebkhet Halk el-Menzel

A1

Hammam Sousse ③
The beaches of this popular tourist zone, northwest of Sousse, offer fine sand and good facilities for windsurfing and paragliding.

Sousse ④
Sousse's main beach is wide and long and runs next to the town's main promenade. The white sandy beach close to the main high-rise hotels can get very busy, though there are some quieter parts further out of town.

0 km   3

0 miles   3

Skanès ⑤
The beaches of this tourist zone have fine sand and are within easy reach of the hotels.

Monastir ⑥
Curving round a bay, Monastir's main beach provides a good view of the ribat and the Great Mosque. The hotel beaches are west of town.

Sousse ❸

The capital of the Sahel and the third largest town in Tunisia, Sousse was founded by the Phoenicians in the 9th century BC and was, for a time, Hannibal's naval base. Throughout the Punic wars it was one of the Phoenicians' most important towns, along with Carthage and Utica. Modern-day Sousse is a popular resort town with a sandy beach, an historic walled medina and, occupying part of the kasbah, an excellent museum with mosaics from the 2nd and 3rd centuries AD.

Exploring Sousse

The medina is entered from Place Farhat Hached or from Place des Martyrs. The medina includes the 9th-century Great Mosque and the ribat (fortified monastery). Nearby is the Turkish-built Zaouia Zakkak. One of the more picturesque fragments of the medina starts uphill, near Bab el-Gharbi. Down towards El-Caid souk are antique stores, workshops and cafés. Not far from here is the Sofra cistern complex. Narrow streets lead down towards the main market. Near Bab el-Gharbi is the kasbah and museum.

Interior of the Great Mosque, viewed from the courtyard arcades

🏛 Place Farhat Hached

This colourful square is the centre of Sousse and the entrance to the medina. This is where the town's main streets originate (even the railway cuts through it). It is a popular meeting place for the young people of Sousse and is also busy with street vendors. To the north of the square, beyond the railway line, is Avenue Bourguiba, a modern thoroughfare with shops, banks and department stores. This runs down to the coast and to the seashore boulevard – Avenue Hedi Cheker. Entering the square from Avenue

Bourguiba there is a several-storey-high **Artisanat** on the right. It is a good idea to step in here for a while before entering the medina, to get some idea of the prices. To the southeast of the square is Sousse's harbour.

🏛 Place des Martyrs

Adjoining Place Farhat Hached is Place des Martyrs. The 16th-century Sea Gate – Bab el-Bahr – provided entry to the inner harbour. The 18th-century fort that once stood on this site was destroyed during a World War II bombing raid.

🏛 Great Mosque

Rue el-Aghlaba. ⬭ 8am–2pm Sat–Thu, 8am–1pm Fri (to courtyard).
🖼

The Great Mosque stands at the edge of the medina and not – as is more common – at its centre. Together with the ribat and the medina walls it formed part of the town's defensive system. This is reflected in its architectural design that resembles a fortress rather than a mosque. Built in 851, at the peak of the Aghlabids' golden age, it was modelled on Kairouan's mosque. Its vast courtyard (the only part open to visitors) is surrounded by columns; carved above them are words from the Koran, the date of completion and the names of the mosque's builders. From one corner of the building high stairs lead to an octagonal sundial. The minaret that rises above the mosque was built two centuries later. Before that time, the faithful were called to prayer from the tower of the neighbouring ribat. The prayer hall's arched vault rests on massive supports. Its walls are dust of stones laid out in an intricate pattern providing an austere decoration for the interior.

⚓ Ribat

Rue de Smyrne. ⬭ 9am–6pm daily.
🖼

Sousse's ribat, dating from the Aghlabid period, is one of the most famous and best-preserved monastic fortresses in Tunisia. Work on its construction began probably in AD 787 and was completed in AD 821. It was then that the Nador – the 27-m (89-ft) high watchtower – was added at the southwest corner. The ribat was built at a time when Christians invading from Italy were a constant threat and the tower would have been used as a lookout point as well as a beacon for passing on messages. Today it offers a view over the entire town.

The garrison consisted of mercenaries paid by the state. A ribat offered shelter to travellers and merchants and,

Monument commemorating Tunisian nationalism, Place des Martyrs

For hotels and restaurants in this region see pp256–9 and pp280–83

The unassuming main entrance to the ribat

building of the kasbah in the southwest part of the medina, the ribat lost some of its military importance and began to fall into ruin. It was restored in 1722 and turned into a Koranic school. Some additional restoration work was carried out in the 1950s.

at times of extreme danger, to the local population as well. The square-shaped structure is surrounded by walls over 13 m (43 ft) high. Vast bastions were placed at the corners and halfway along each wall. The inner yard is skirted by rows of portico-shaded cells. On the ground floor these surround the yard on all four sides; on the first floor – on three sides only; the fourth side is taken up by a large oratory that confirms the religious character of the building. During times of peace, the ribat was used as a place of study. Following the

C Zaouia Zakkak
Rue Tazerka.

A little way west of the ribat stands an octagonal minaret whose style is reminiscent of Renaissance architecture. It belongs to the Zaouia Zakkak complex, which was built during the Ottoman era. The complex includes a mosque, a medersa (school) and a mausoleum and owes its name to the holy man who lived and worked here in the 10th century. On his death he was buried in his own house, which was later turned into a medersa. The porticoed entrance leads to the courtyard that is flanked on three sides by students' cells. The south end of the *zaouia*

Octagonal minaret of Zaouia Zakkak

(tomb) was destroyed in 1943 during a bombing raid. The dome-covered mausoleum, built in the 18th century, stands in the northeast corner of the complex.

Rue el-Aghlaba
Rue el-Aghlaba – one of the medina's most picturesque streets – starts immediately beyond the ribat and runs westwards, past the Great Mosque, going deep into the medina. One of its offshoots is Rue d'Angleterre that runs southwards to the covered markets. The many stalls and shops found here form the commercial heart of Sousse and are a riot of colour and activity.

VISITORS' CHECKLIST

Road map D3. 492,000.
Skanès/Monastir.
ONTT: Avenue Habib Bourguiba 1, (73) 225 157.
Sidi el-Kantaoui Festival (Jul); International Sousse Festival (Jul–Aug); Folklore Festival (Aug).

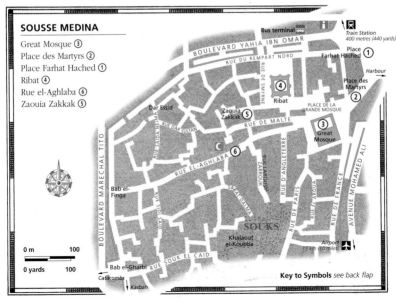

SOUSSE MEDINA

Great Mosque ③
Place des Martyrs ②
Place Farhat Hached ①
Ribat ④
Rue el-Aghlaba ⑥
Zaouia Zakkak ⑤

Bus terminal
Train Station 400 metres (440 yards)
BOULEVARD YAHIA IBN OMAR
RUE DU REMPART NORD
Place Farhat Hached ①
Harbour
RUE DE SMYRNE
④
Ribat
Place des Martyrs ②
Dar Essid
Zaouia Zakkak ⑤
PLACE DE LA GRANDE MOSQUE
RUE DE MALTE
③ Great Mosque
RUE SAIDA NEUMA
RUE DAR SULTAN
BOULEVARD MARECHAL TITO
⑥ RUE EL-AGHLABA
RUE D'ANGLETERRE
RUE DE PARIS
AVENUE MOHAMED ALI
Bab el-Finga
RUE SIDI ALOUA
SAFAI DAMIA
ZARROUK
RUE LARGUES
RUE D'ALOUA
RUE DE FRANCE
SOUKS
Khalaout el-Koubba
Airport 15 km (10 miles)
0 m 100
0 yards 100
Bab el-Gharbi RUE SOUK EL CAID
Catacombs Kasbah
Key to Symbols see back flap

Walls of the medina, dating from the 9th century

♣ Medina Walls

The medina's western and southern extremes are well preserved and exceptionally picturesque. It is worth taking a stroll around here to get a taste of the everyday life of the medina's inhabitants.

In the 7th century Oqba ibn Nafi's army destroyed the Roman town of Hadrumetum. In its place, the Arabs built Soussa and, some 200 years later, during the Aghlabid period Soussa (which was renamed Sousse) became a major port for the Aghlabid capital – Kairouan.

The 9th-century walls that surround the medina date from this time. They were built to replace the earlier Byzantine walls. To this day they encircle the town with a ring of stone that is broken only near Place des Martyrs, which was bombed during World War II. At one time there were eight gates. Only four now remain standing – Bab el-Gharbi, Bab el-Finga, Bab el-Jerid and Bab el-Khabli. The only section of wall open to the public is within the kasbah's museum (*see below*).

♣ Kasbah

Boulevard Maréchal Tito. *Tel* (73) 219 011. ☐ *Apr–mid-Sep: 8am–noon & 3–7pm Tue–Sun; mid-Sep–Mar: 9am–noon & 2–6pm Tue–Sun.* ⬤ *for renovation until 2012.* 🖼

A visit to the kasbah, which is located just outside the medina's walls to the south, should also include a tour of the **Archaeology Museum**.

Built originally in 1100 it was rebuilt and reinforced around 1600. It houses an excellent museum that displays mosaics dating from the Roman and Byzantine periods, and has a variety of objects found in the vicinity of the Great Mosque and the harbour. Set under the arcades of its small courtyard are some fine mosaics displaying geometric patterns, animal and mythological motifs and Christian symbols that were found in the city's Christian catacombs.

Roman mosaic from the kasbah's museum

Room No. 3 houses the most precious mosaics including a 3rd-century AD depiction of Bacchus in Triumph being drawn along in a chariot by lions and tigers. At the north end of the courtyard there are some Christian epitaphs taken from the catacombs and also the sarcophagus of a woman named Theodora.

The large, garden-like courtyard of the kasbah, where there is some pleasant shade during summer, contains an exhibition of sculptures, sarcophagi, columns and capitals. The roof terrace provides a good view of the medina.

🏛 Khalaout el-Koubba

Rue Zarrouk. ☐ *summer: 10am–6:30pm daily; winter: 8:30am–1pm, 3–6pm daily.* 🖼

Not far from the covered souks and stalls on Rue d'Angleterre is the Khalaout el-Koubba. This building, crowned with a distinctive *koubba* (dome), dates from the 11th or 12th century. Its original purpose remains a mystery. It was probably some kind of tomb for a major spiritual leader or a meeting place. The most distinctive feature of the Koubba is its dome, which is decorated with a zigzag frieze. This type of decoration can also be found on some of the domes in Fès and Marrakech (Morocco), dating from the Almoravid period. The central court was added at some later date, probably in the 17th or the 18th century.

The building was used as a *fondouk* (inn) in the 14th century and later became a café. It was restored in 1980 and today houses the **Museum of Popular Arts and Traditions**, which is devoted to the history of the medina with life-size tableaux illustrating marriage customs and everyday activities.

Zig-zag patterned dome of Khalaout el-Koubba

🏛 Dar Essid

Rue du Rempart-Nord 65.
Tel (73) 220 529. ☐ 10am–7pm
daily (summer); 10am–6pm daily
(winter). 🖼

This fascinating museum is
situated in a beautiful home
that adjoins the walls of
Sousse's medina. A small,
private museum, its
collections include costumes,
jewellery and everyday items.
The decor has been recreated
in the style of a well-to-do
Arab household from the 19th
century and includes family
rooms surrounding a tiled
courtyard. It is a charming
place and succeeds admirably
in conjuring up the
atmosphere of an affluent
Arab home. The house itself
dates from AD 928 and is one
of the medina's oldest homes.

The walled-off area between
Bab el-Finga and Dar Essid is
Sousse's red-light district.

**Catacombs – the final resting place
for 15,000 Christians**

Catacombs

About 2 km/1 mile from the town
centre, close to Rue Hamed el-
Ghazali. The easiest way to get to the
catacombs is from the bus station or
the louage stand in Avenue des
Catacombes. ☐ Apr–mid-Sep:
9am–7pm Tue–Sun; mid-Sep–Mar:
9am–5pm Tue–Sun.

In 1888 a vast complex of
Christian catacombs was
discovered on the outskirts of
Sousse in the west part of the
town. This labyrinth of
chambers and corridors was
carved out of the soft rock
between the 3rd and 4th
century AD. Its wall niches
contain the remains of 15,000
Christians. The galleries

stretch over 5 km
(3 miles), though
only a small fraction
is open to the
public. The
**Catacombs of the
Good Shepherd**
date from the late
3rd century. They
are 1.6 km (1 mile)
long and include
6,000 graves; the
Hermes Catacombs
date from the 3rd
century and contain
2,200 graves.

The section of
catacombs open to
the public consists
of a 100-m (328-ft)
long segment of the
Catacombs of the
Good Shepherd. Most of
the graves are bricked up,
but a few have glass
windows displaying the
human remains.

Environs

The areas around Sousse are
planted with olive groves that
have been cultivated here
since Punic times. Although
the Romans used oil mainly
for industrial purposes, it was
– along with wheat – Tunisia's
main agricultural product.
Now over 50 varieties of olive
trees are grown here.

Some 43 km (27 miles)
northwest of Sousse is **Enfida**,
which has a World War II
cemetery and a Sunday
market. The town also has a
Christian church that has
been turned into a museum,
where you can see early
Christian mosaics from the

Ken village – a handicraft centre

nearby site of Upenna. In
July, Hammam Sousse hosts
the Sidi el-Kantaoui Festival.

The village of **Ken**, 20 km
(12 miles) north of Sousse, is
a purpose-built craft village
that produces and sells a
variety of handicraft items
including blown glass, textiles
and furniture. The village's
eclectic architecture embraces
a variety of traditional
Tunisian building styles
and methods.

Park Friguia, situated in
Bou Ficha, 58 km (36 miles)
from Sousse, is a large
recreation area that combines
a zoo with an amusement
park. Run in collaboration
with the Tunisian forestry
commission, the zoo is home
to some 25 species of African
animals including giraffes and
elephants. The zoo also has a
restaurant and puts on folk
shows at peak times.

TUNISIAN DOLLS

This warrior-doll is a typical Tunisian souvenir.
The dolls are made by hand and come in a
variety of colours and sizes but always include
the same basic elements. The head is carved
from wood and sports bushy whiskers, while
its trunk is fashioned from wood and wire.
The warrior is dressed in wide trousers
with a colourful tunic over the top. In his
hand he holds a metal sword. The origin
of the doll is not clear, though its clothes
would suggest that it comes from Turkey.
Wooden puppets such as these are hung
on metal wires and can be seen in almost
all Tunisian markets.

Tunisian doll dressed in a colourful costume

Monastir ❹

Monastir was founded by the Phoenicians as a port and is a little way south of Sousse. Julius Caesar camped here before the Battle of Thapsus in AD 46 but the town's main claim to fame, aside from being a popular resort, is as the birthplace of ex-president Habib Bourguiba. Bourguiba lived here until his death in 2000. He is now buried in the cemetery on the town's northern edge.

Mausoleum's minaret

Exploring Monastir

Monastir is a university town and provincial capital and stands on a small rugged headland in the Gulf of Hammamet. It is also a major player in the Tunisian tourist industry and large hotel complexes and souvenir shops are everywhere. The signs of Habib Bourguiba's presence here are also commonplace and include a statue of Bourguiba as a schoolboy, streets named after members of his family and a Bourguiba Mosque.

Relics of the town's Phoenician and Roman

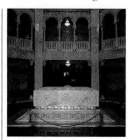

Habib Bourguiba's sarcophagus in the mausoleum

heritage are still evident. The main attraction is the town's famous ribat (fortified Islamic monastery), which was built in AD 796 as a coastal defensive fortress, and the first on the African continent. The Great Mosque, just south of the ribat, dates from the 9th century. After 1534 Monastir, along with Sousse and Sfax, enjoyed a high degree of autonomy. At this time it resembled a small republic and often gave shelter to pirates.

In the 20th century, Habib Bourguiba tried to make Monastir into a smart modern metropolis. He ordered the National Palace to be built near the Phoenician settlement of El-Kadima and encircled the ribat with a magnificent esplanade. At the same time,

HABIB BOURGUIBA

Habib Bourguiba was born in 1903. Having studied law in Paris he returned to Tunisia and embarked upon intensive political work, campaigning against the French occupation of his country. Initially a member of the Destour Party, he founded the Neo-Destour Party in 1934. When Tunisia regained independence in 1956, Bourguiba became its first prime minister and then president.

the town also acquired a large marina.

A walk around Monastir should begin at the medina. Its most striking feature is the yellow-stone Ali el-Mezeri mosque (closed) and the Bourguiba Mosque. Towards the sea are a wide esplanade and the ribat (see pp156–7). The ribat's south gate adjoins the Great Mosque. Stretching before it is a wide avenue flanked by administration buildings. The Bourguiba Mausoleum is a little further to the west. The Métro Sahel station, in the medina's western section, has frequent services to the airport, Sousse, Tunis and Gabès.

⚰ Habib Bourguiba Mausoleum

◘ 8am–6pm daily.

This marble mausoleum with its gilt cupola stands to the north of the ribat, and dominates the Sidi el-Mezeri cemetery. With its gilt cupola and twin minarets, it is hard to miss the building in which are the remains of Habib Bourguiba's family and, within a marble sarcophagus, the great man himself. Elsewhere in the cemetery are the tombs of marabouts and various spiritual masters. Particularly striking is the 12th-century tomb of Sidi el-Mezeri after whom the cemetery is named.

⚰ Tomb of the Unknown Soldier

Rue de Tunis.

This modest octagonal structure is on the right at the beginning of the avenue that leads to the Bourguiba mausoleum. It is a symbolic grave for all Tunisians who fought for the freedom of their homeland.

Tomb of the Unknown Soldier

Great Mosque, standing next to the ribat

⚜ Ribat
See pp156–157.

🇨 Great Mosque
Route de la Corniche.
The Great Mosque stands next to the ribat, and was built in the 9th century and further extended during the Zirid dynasty (972–1152). Its courtyard is flanked by arcades resting on columns with pointed arches. The Roman columns that support the arches were taken from the ruins at Ruspina.

🇨 Bourguiba Mosque
Rue de l'Indépendance. ☐ 8am–11:30am (courtyard only). ● Fri.
Habib Bourguiba Mosque was built in 1963 to a design by Taieb Bouzguend and was inspired by the Hammouda

Pasha Mosque in Tunis. This large structure has undoubtedly spoiled the general layout of the medina. The building and its spacious interior (the prayer hall can accommodate a congregation of up to 1,000) combine many features of modern architecture with the requirements laid upon traditional Islamic buildings.

🏛 Museum of Traditional Costume
Rue de l'Indépendance. ☐ 8am–1pm & 3–6pm daily. 📷
This little museum, situated not far from the tourist office, has a handful of rooms containing folk costumes from virtually every region of Tunisia. Particularly interesting is the collection of wedding costumes that includes items of jewellery.

Fountain in the courtyard of the Bourguiba Mosque

VISITORS' CHECKLIST

Road map D3. 🏘 40,000.
🚌 🚆 ℹ️ ONTT in Monastir: (73) 521 016, ONTT at the airport: (73) 520 894.
📅 Sat.

🚏 Place du Gouvernorat
This large square lies between the medina and a seaside boulevard (Route de la Corniche). Towards the sea and the ribat there is a well-stocked Handicraft Centre (Artisanat) that sells a good range of Tunisian souvenirs. The items sold here carry the government certificate of authenticity and are generally of a reasonable quality.

The square is flanked by government buildings; the congress hall and the theatre are located nearby. Look out for the eye-catching golden statue of Habib Bourguiba, who is depicted as a schoolboy. Bourguiba's school originally stood on the same spot as the statue.

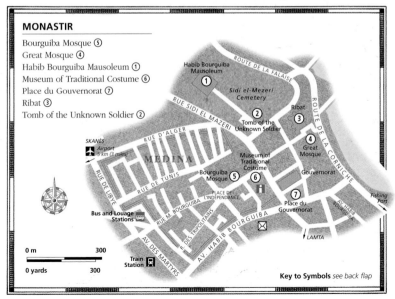

MONASTIR

Bourguiba Mosque ⑤
Great Mosque ④
Habib Bourguiba Mausoleum ①
Museum of Traditional Costume ⑥
Place du Gouvernorat ⑦
Ribat ③
Tomb of the Unknown Soldier ②

0 m 300
0 yards 300

Key to Symbols see back flap

Ribat

The Holy War against Christians, the constant skirmishes with the Berbers and the plans to carry out military forays to Europe prompted the building of ribats from the 8th century onwards. Monastir's defensive fortress was originally known as the Ribat de Harthama and combined religious and military functions by assembling soldiers and mystics under the same roof. It is one of the oldest and best preserved in Tunisia and was used for scenes in Zeffirelli's *Life of Christ* and *Monty Python's Life of Brian*.

Side Entrance
The ribat could originally be entered through any one of its four gates. Each gate was on a different side of the fortress, guarded by mighty bastions that were constantly being enlarged, even in the 19th century.

★ **Defensive Walls**
The walls were completed in the 11th century and included accommodation for soldiers.

Defensive corner turret

Large courtyard

Islamic Art Centre
A museum devoted to Islamic art is in the ribat's prayer room and includes Arab coins, fabrics and pottery.

Battlements
Some sections of the walls are crenellated. The battlements were usually simple, but provided protection for archers shooting from the walls.

VISITORS' CHECKLIST

Av. Harthoume ibn el-Aychine.
☐ May–Sep: 9am–2pm & 2:30–
6pm Tue–Sun; Oct–Apr:
2–5:30pm daily. 🏛 **Islamic Art
Centre** ☐ 8am–7pm daily. 📷

Decorative Details
*As in many ribats,
there is little in the way
of decoration. Most
heavily decorated are
the window surrounds
and column capitals;
much of this has worn
away over the years.*

Minaret –
towering
over the
ribat and the
town

**The main
entrance**
to the ribat
is from the
south.

STAR FEATURE

★ Defensive Walls

Parasols on a Monastir beach

Further Afield
The area around Monastir
abounds in olive trees, which
have been cultivated here
since Roman times. Of more
interest to the visitor,
Monastir has several long,
sandy beaches and small
coves. The most popular of
them are around Skanès.

🚢 Port
Route de la Falaise.
A little way to the southeast
of Monastir, the old fishing
harbour is no longer very
important to the economy of
the town, which derives its
main revenue from tourism,
olive oil production and sea
salt excavation. There is,
however, an attractive marina
not far from the ribat. Fringed
by restaurants and cafés, it
provides a pleasant place to
escape from the summer heat.

🏖 Beaches
The town's main tourist
complex is around Skanès.
This tourist zone provides

9,000 hotel beds. The beach
is wide and well kept. As
well as bathing, equipment
can be hired on the beach
for water sports such as
paragliding. A frequent train
service and taxis provide easy
access to town. There are
numerous beach bars. Beach
vendors offer light snacks and
ensure that no-one goes
hungry. The beaches around
Khniss are quieter.

Environs
It is worth stopping for a
while in **Lamta**, some 15 km
(9 miles) southeast of
Monastir – which was once
the Roman colony of Leptis
Minor, the smaller sibling of
Leptis Magna, which can be
found in Libya. Following the
downfall of Carthage, this was
one of the six free towns.
Even then, the region was
famous for its olive groves.
Another local speciality was
the fish sauce called *garum*,
which was much valued
throughout the Roman world.

MARABOUTS
Marabouts were mostly members of Sufi brotherhoods.
Revered as mystics and Islamic holy men or saints, many
were believed to have divine powers. To this day many
Tunisians believe that a marabout has
received a special gift from God
(Allah), allowing him to plead
successfully for Allah's mercy
(*baraka*) on their behalf. Many
Muslims make
pilgrimages to a marabout's
tomb (also known as a
marabout). One of the most
revered of Tunisia's
marabouts is Sidi Mehrez
– the patron of Tunis.

A plain marabout in Blidet

Mahdia

The first Fatimid Caliph, Obeid Allah, known as El-Mahdi (the Saviour of the World), waited until the astrologers identified the most propitious moment before founding this coastal town. Work started in AD 916 and the town was given the name of Mahdia, in honour of the charismatic caliph. Today Mahdia is a major port. It is one of Tunisia's most attractive towns and is famous for its house decorations. The busy quayside is lined with palms and has an engaging maritime atmosphere.

Rue Obeid Allah el-Mahdi – the main shopping street in Mahdia

Exploring Mahdia

Mahdia has retained much of its medieval charm. Its medina is entered by a vast gate, Skifa el-Kahla. Standing close to Place du Caire is the Mustapha Hamza Mosque and the Great Mosque. Further along the narrow boulevard are the Municipal Museum, the ruins of the former docks, the armoury, the emir's palace and the Great Tower – Borj el-Kebir, which provides a splendid view of the town and the bay beyond (*see p162*).

🚇 Rue Obeid Allah el-Mahdi

This is one of Mahdia's main streets and leads through the heart of the medina. The bright house walls stand in contrast with the colourful shops selling ceramics, carpets and leather goods. Along its side streets are workshops where weavers work on upright looms making silk fabrics destined for wedding dresses. Silk weaving is a big business in Mahdia and was brought here by Jewish immigrants from Libya in the 19th century. The loom workers are highly skilled and are usually happy to talk to visitors about their work.

🏛 Municipal Museum

Rue Obeid Allah el-Mahdi.
◐ *Apr–mid-Sep: 7:30am–6:30pm Tue–Sun; mid-Sep–Mar: 8am–5pm Tue–Sun.*
This modern archaeological museum houses some fine Punic, Roman and Christian statues and ceramics, mosaics from El-Jem (*see p163*) as well as a number of oil lamps and a delightful collection of perfumes in intricate bottles made of coloured glass, which are arranged on brightly painted, wooden shelves. A section is devoted to Islamic art and includes mosaics, calligraphy (*see p167*) and some examples of local costumes including exhibits relating to their manufacture. Mahdia is famous for its house decorations and the museum also has some good examples of the local passion for interior decoration.

☪ Mustapha Hamza Mosque

Rue Obeid Allah el-Mahdi. ◐
This mosque, with its lovely façade, was built in the 18th century during the town's Ottoman period. Its octagonal minaret towers over the entire district and is typical of Turkish design.

Minaret of the Mustapha Hamza Mosque

🚇 Skifa el-Kahla

Rue Obeid Allah el-Mahdi.
The huge gate that leads to the town was built in the 10th century by Obeid Allah. Its "dark passage" (which gave the gate its name) was once the only entrance to the city and led through a wall that was 10 m (33 ft) thick in places. At the time, Mahdia was the private property of its ruler. All who did not belong to the court were forced to live outside the walls and huge iron grilles were lowered to deny anyone else access to the city. The original gate was destroyed by the Spanish in 1554 but rebuilt the same year. The former city entrance today contains a covered market selling perfume and items of jewellery.

🚇 Place du Caire

This small square at the centre of the medina functions almost as a salon. The locals, especially the old

Relaxing in the shade of the trees in Place du Caire

◁ **Habib Bourguiba Mausoleum in Monastir**

men, gather here to discuss the latest events, to meet with friends, read a newspaper or simply ponder over a glass of tea. It is pleasant to stop here for a while and survey the proceedings from one of the cafés overlooking the Mustapha Hamza mosque.

Detail, façade of the Slimen Hamza Mosque

C Slimen Hamza Mosque

Place Kadhi en-Noamine. ◐
This building, which stands facing the Great Mosque, is in an Ottoman-style design. Mosques of this kind generally have a rectangular structure that is crowned with a dome and include a slim minaret, which is usually octagonal in shape. Tunisian minarets dating from the Ottoman period have a much greater diameter than their Turkish counterparts, however, the prayer hall is large and much brighter than those found in Kairouan-type mosques. There is very little ornamentation and the only furnishings and decorations consist of carpets and calligraphic inscriptions.

More attention is paid to the light and the mosque contains stained-glass windows and exquisite lamps. A lamp in the mosque is the symbol of God's presence and appears on the prayer mats.

C Great Mosque

Rue de Borj. ◯ 8am–noon daily.
◐ to non-Muslims.
The Great Mosque was founded by Obeid Allah in AD 921. Destroyed when Charles V and his troops entered the town, little of the original building remains and what is seen today is a reconstruction from the 1960s and 1970s that was designed as a replica of the original Fatimid mosque. The most obvious Fatimid element is the monumental entrance gate, which was used exclusively by the caliph's family. In the prayer hall this segregation is also apparent, with a central aisle that was

VISITORS' CHECKLIST

Road map D3. 🏘 27,000.
🚊 🚌 🛈 ONTT: Rue el-Moez,
(73) 680 604 or 680 000. 🎭
Fête de la Mer (Jul), International
Festival of Symphonic Music, also
at El-Jem (Jul–Aug). 🛒 Fri.

reserved for the ruler and his privileged entourage. Original parts of the structure that can still be seen are the remains of the mihrab (niche indicating the direction of Mecca) and the monumental portal leading to the courtyard.

Arcaded walkway of the Great Mosque

MAHDIA

RUE SIDI TABEUR
RUE HAJ MOHAMED ABESSALEM
Slimen Hamza Mosque ⑥
AVENUE 7 NOVEMBRE
RUE IBN EL FOURAT
RUE DU CAIRE
PLACE KADHI EN NOAMINE
Borj el-Kebir, Fatimid Port
Place du Caire ⑤
RUE OBEID ALLAH EL-MAHDI
Skifa el-Kahla ① ③ 🛈 ④ Mustapha Hamza Mosque ⑦ Great Mosque
Municipal Museum ②
RUE DES FATIMIDES
RUE DE BORJ
Mediterranean Sea
PLACE L'INDÉPENDANCE
KSDUR ESSAF, Salakta
Market

0 m   50
0 yards   50

🚃 Train Station
300m (330 yards)
🚌 Bus and Louage Stations
3 km (2 miles)

Key to Symbols see back flap

Further Afield

Standing beyond the walls of the medina is an old Fatimid port, a Muslim cemetery established in the 16th century, scenically located on top of a hill, and the Punic necropolis – the second largest after Carthage. Among the objects discovered here is a clay statuette of a naked goddess, wearing a crown. A short way southwest, in Ksour Essaf, is the *zaouia* (tomb) of Sidi Ali Mahjub.

♠ Borj el-Kebir

Rue de Borj. ◻ *Apr–mid-Sep: 7:30am–6:30pm Tue–Sun; mid-Sep– Mar: 8am–5pm Tue–Sun.* 🖼

This 16th-century Turkish fort stands on the site of Obeid Allah's palace. A narrow corridor leads to the courtyard flanked by rows of small cells and a mosque. The fortress was rebuilt several times. Until the 16th century it had a rectangular ground plan; the mighty bastions were added in the 18th century. The southwestern bastion includes the entrance, from which a gently curving corridor leads to a gate adorned with a stone rosette. The gate opens to a barrel-vault passage resembling Skifa el-Kahla, which leads to the reception hall that was restored during the colonial days. Stairs from the small courtyard lead to the first floor, where the fort's commander had his quarters. The castle's terrace provides

Muslim necropolis near a lighthouse

a wonderful view of the surrounding area. In the 16th century Mahdia was a pirate stronghold and became closely linked with the intrigues of the superpowers of the day such as Spain and Turkey. The most famous corsair residing in Mahdia was Dragut.

⋒ Fatimid Port

The port's construction is generally attributed to caliph Obeid Allah. It was most probably built on the site of the old Punic port. The Fatimids had a very strong fleet, which they inherited from the Aghlabids. Obeid Allah wanted Mahdia to be both a fortress and a strong naval base. The 15-m (49-ft) long canal that leads to the port was guarded by two towers. Fragments of their foundations can be seen today. The basin was a

rectangle and could accommodate 30 ships. During the times of Obeid Allah the port had its own defensive walls. Now only a small section of these walls remains, on the south side of the port.

Remains of 10th-century Fatimid fortifications

Environs

The small town of **Ksour Essaf**, 11 km (7 miles) south of Mahdia, is famous for its textiles and contains the 18th-century *zaouia* (tomb) of Sidi Ali Mahjub. The dome of the sanctuary is decorated with grooved terracotta ornaments. Inside the mosque is an unusual mihrab, placed on wheels.

In **Salakta**, 14 km (9 miles) from Mahdia and a short taxi ride from Ksour Essaf, are the ruins of the Roman port and fishing village of Sullectum. The port was probably used for shipping lions that were destined for the gladiatorial arena at El-Jem. The nearby beach is a pleasant place to stroll and has some further Roman remains including a bath and some villa walls.

Bastion of Mahdia's main fort – Borj el-Kebir

For hotels and restaurants in this region see pp256–9 and pp280–83

El-Jem ❻

This former Punic town – Thysdrus – declared itself
on the side of Rome during the Third Punic War in
AD 146. It proved to be a wise move and after the fall
of Carthage El-Jem was awarded the status of a free
town. In the mid-3rd century it became a Roman
colony. It was among the richest towns in Roman
Africa. The most magnificent historic relic of El-Jem is
its 3rd-century amphitheatre.

VISITORS' CHECKLIST

Road map D3. 🏠 12,000. 🚌 🚇
🏛 Amphitheatre. ⬜ Apr–mid-
Sep: 7:30am–6:30pm Tue–Sun;
mid-Sep–Mar: 8am–5pm Tue–
Sun. 🏛 **Museum** ⬜ As above.
🎭 Symphonic (Jul–Aug). 📷

★ Amphitheatre
*Built in 230–238 this is the world's third largest Roman
amphitheatre and the best-preserved Roman relic to be
found in Africa.*

Corridors
*The corridors lead to all
levels of the auditorium,
which measures 427 m
(1,401 ft) in
diameter.*

Elliptical arena, measuring
65 x 39 m (213 x 128 ft)

The highest seats
provide a breathtaking
view. The games could
be watched by over
30,000 spectators.

Mosaics
*As well as some
gladiatorial scenes,
the mosaics
displayed in the
museum have some
more abstract and
stylized designs.*

★ Museum
*The museum is housed in one of
Tunisia's best-preserved Roman villas,
on the outskirts of El-Jem.*

STAR SIGHTS

★ Amphitheatre

★ Museum

Sfax ❼

A mosque decoration

The port of Sfax is Tunisia's second largest city and its major commercial centre. Once a Roman settlement, its prosperity was founded on its shipping fleet and the trade in olive oil. Sfax is known for its unhurried atmosphere and has a compact medina with wonderful covered souks and two excellent museums. A regular ferry route runs from the port to the Kerkennah Islands *(see p172)* a little way offshore.

Bab Diwan standing at the end of Avenue Hedi Chaker

Exploring Sfax

The city stretches between the medina walls and the harbour. Rebuilt in the late 1940s, modern Sfax resembles any large European city, with wide avenues, squares and public parks. Hedi Chaker Avenue runs from Hedi Chaker Square to Bab Diwan – one of two gates leading to the old town. Beyond it lies the medina. It is well worth taking a stroll along Rue Mongi Slim, stopping for a while at the colourful spice market in Rue des Aghlabites.

Rue de la Grande Mosquée – full of shops and always busy

⚓ Bab Diwan

Bab Diwan is the medina's main entrance and is located on the south side. It was built in the early 14th century, but was extensively remodelled in the 17th and 18th centuries. It was finally restored in the 20th century.

Along with Bab Jebli in the north, Bab Diwan was once one of only two entrances to the city. Its ironclad doors would have been closed tightly at night to protect Sfax from intruders.

Bab Diwan was designed to complement the 9th-century walls built by the Aghlabids. These walls originally marked the boundaries of the city, although modern Sfax has long since outgrown these limits. Beyond the walls were olive groves, which flourished thanks to earlier Roman irrigation systems. One of the gate's towers now houses a charming Moorish-style café.

⛩ Rue de la Grande Mosquée

One of the main streets of the medina, it starts at the Grand Mosque and runs south in a straight line towards the medina walls, which are parallel to Rue Mongi Slim.

🄲 Great Mosque

🌀 *to non-Muslims.*

Begun in AD 849 by the Aghlabids, the Great Mosque was modelled on its famous contemporary in Kairouan. It stands at the heart of the medina, at the junction of its two main roads. The mosque has been modified several times and was rebuilt extensively in 988 and 1035. In the 12th century the courtyard was reduced by half, allowing for the enlargement of the prayer hall, which still maintains an L-shaped layout. By the 18th century the mosque was in its present form.

The minaret, rising at the north end of the courtyard, is a replica of the minaret adorning Kairouan's Great Mosque. It is three storeys high and is richly decorated with Kufic script and floral motifs. The mosque is closed to non-Muslims, its eastern wall being the only section that is visible. The best view of the minaret can be had from Rue des Aghlabites, which runs along the north side of the mosque.

Men relaxing inside the Great Mosque

🏛 Dar Jellouli Museum

See pp168–9.

⛩ Rue Borj Ennar

This narrow street follows the southern section of the walls, from Rue de la Grande Mosquée to the fortress of Borj Ennar. This is a typical medina street, lined with workshops, small shops and rows of unassuming doors

Borj Ennar, built into a section of the city wall

district of Sfax. Borj Ennar now houses the Association de Sauvegarde de la Médina, a group responsible for preserving the medina, where a detailed street map of the old town and also more about the medina's history can be obtained.

leading to private homes. It also contains a number of small mosques such as Amar Kamoun mosque, between Nos. 50 and 52, which was built in the 14th century and substantially modified four centuries later.

♦ Borj Ennar
Rue Borj Ennar. ☐ 8:30am–6pm Tue–Sun.

Borj Ennar – the "Tower of Fire" – owes its name to the beacons that used to be lit on its tower as signals. Located at the southeast corner of the medina walls, this was one of the main defensive towers of old Sfax, and was built at the same time as the medina walls. From the top, there is a splendid view over the entire medina and the French

Further Afield
Other places worth visiting include Sidi Abu el-Hasan's mausoleum, located a short distance to the west of the

A small mosque in a row of houses in Rue Borj Ennar

mosque; and the blacksmiths' souk, situated to the north. In the 10th century this was a *fondouk* (inn) and featured in Anthony Minghella's 1996 film *The English Patient*. Beyond the walls, stretching out to the north, is the new town, which suffered heavy damage during World War II. Hedi Chaker and Avenue Habib Bourguiba are streets with beautiful 19th-century houses. A little further on, to the southwest, is Sfax's port and a thriving daily fish market.

⊞ Place de la République
Place de la République is at the junction of Avenue Habib Bourguiba and Avenue Hedi Chaker and dates back to the French Protectorate, when the administration centre was built outside the medina walls. Much of this area was destroyed during wartime bombing raids, although several colonial buildings have survived. The square contains a monument to Habib Bourguiba.

VISITORS' CHECKLIST

Road map D4. 🏘 340,000.
🚍 🚆 🛈 ONTT: Avenue Mohammed Hedi Khefacha, (74) 497 021. 🎭 (Jul–Aug). 🛒 Fri.

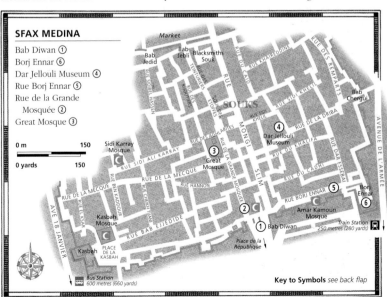

SFAX MEDINA

Bab Diwan ①
Borj Ennar ⑥
Dar Jellouli Museum ④
Rue Borj Ennar ⑤
Rue de la Grande Mosquée ②
Great Mosque ③

0 m   150
0 yards   150

Key to Symbols *see back flap*

🕎 Kasbah

⬜ 9:30am–4:30pm Tue–Sun. 📷

Sfax's kasbah can be found in the medina's southern quarter. Part of the building is 12th century but it was gradually extended until, by the 17th century, it had reached the size of a large fortress. Initially it served as a watchtower and later as the residence of the Hafsid governor. After that, it became the headquarters of Sfax's military commander.

Today, the kasbah houses the **Museum of Traditional Architecture** and contains exhibits on religious, private and public Tunisian building. A number of the exhibits are outdoors. These include a model illustrating the design of the medina walls and the construction methods used by their builders. Best of all, a trip to the kasbah provides an opportunity to walk along the battlements.

Shady entrance to Sfax's historic kasbah

🕎 The Souks

Strolling through the shady streets and alleyways it is not hard to see that Sfax's medina is one of the loveliest and best preserved in the whole of Tunisia. Indeed, much of Sfax's market district was used as a stand-in for Cairo in the film *The English Patient*.

The narrow alleys can be crowded but become quieter during siesta hours. The old town is divided into markets (souks) – specializing in perfumes, spices, textiles, bags, gold, carpets and food.

Souk ar-Rabi, situated in the northern part of the medina, specializes in the production of *chechia* hats, while the former Rue el-Bey is now the blacksmiths' souk and rings to the sound of hammering.

Two-colour façade of the modern town hall

When shopping for a carpet, head for Souk des Etoffes, which was also used as a setting in *The English Patient*. The narrow streets surrounding Rue des Aghlabites are full of stalls and shops selling a variety of spices, herbs, gum arabic and blue talismans that protect the wearer against the "evil eye". Squeezing through a narrow medina entrance at the end of Rue Mongi Slim, visitors emerge into a modern, but very pleasant, covered market where fruit, vegetables and spices are on sale. At the back is a butcher's hall.

In Rue de la Driba, not far from Dar Jellouli Museum, there is Hammam Sultan, which is Sfax's oldest bathhouse. It was restored in the 18th century and is still open to the public.

Avenue Hedi Chaker

Hedi Chaker is one of Sfax's smartest streets. It runs from the square in front of the town hall to Bab Diwan – the main gate leading to the medina. Along it there are travel agents, pharmacies, restaurants, music shops, banks and a theatre.

Vegetable souk at the edge of the medina

🕎 Town Hall

Place de la République. **Tel** (74) 229 744. **Archaeological Museum**
⬜ Sep–Jun: 8:30am–1pm & 3–6pm; Jul–Aug: 8am–3pm. ⬛ Sun.

The town hall was erected during the French Protectorate in the early 20th century. Built in a Moorish style it features a tall, minaret-like clock tower at the corner. A dome covers the main hall.

The ground floor of the building now houses a small **Archaeological Museum**, with exhibits ranging from prehistoric to Roman and Arab times. These include flint items, pottery, glass, tomb steles (grave stones) and a variety of objects dating from the Punic, Byzantine and Roman periods.

The most interesting sections include the collections of coins, frescoes, terracotta, Roman drinking vessels, Muslim books, jewellery and mosaics.

Avenue Habib Bourguiba

Situated in the new part of town, this runs from the railway station in the east to the harbour in the west and crosses Avenue Hedi Chaker. It is one of the town's main thoroughfares and is lined with restaurants and hotels as well as nightclubs, banks, travel agents' offices and a post office. Here, modern offices stand next to stylish apartment blocks reminiscent of 19th-century Parisian architecture.

Arabic Calligraphy

For Islamic countries calligraphy, or the art of handwriting, has a special importance and copying the Koran is a highly esteemed skill. The Islamic edict prohibiting representation of the human form further promoted calligraphy as a kind of decoration. Arabic calligraphy is based on the Kufic script. This almost geometric style was ideal for carving in stone. Some fine examples of Kufic script can be seen on the eastern wall of Sfax's Great Mosque. By the end of the 12th century, Kufic had been largely replaced in North Africa by a style of calligraphy known as Maghribi, which arrived in Tunisia via Granada (Spain) and Fès (Morocco).

Kufic script *was used as a highly decorative element in Islamic architecture. Its earliest forms were characterized by rigid, angular lines.*

Tomb steles *were often decorated with Kufic script. Its appearance evolved with time, tending towards richer forms. This resulted in a variety of types, including floral kufi, interwoven kufi, and kufi enclosed within floral or geometric borders. From the 12th century onwards the Kufic script was used only for decoration.*

Decorative calligraphic compositions *painted on glass became popular in the 19th century. Their roots can be found in Ottoman art. Highly colourful, they were often used to display Koranic verses.*

Paper *was first used by the Arabs in the 8th century. Blue paper is very rare and surviving examples of early Arab script on blue paper are highly valued by collectors.*

El-bijazi, *though not ornamental, is a popular form of the Arabic script. This private letter was written on parchment using sepia ink.*

The most valuable copies of the Koran *are embellished with gold letters. From the 13th century onwards, literary and scientific works were also decorated.*

Dar Jellouli Museum

Occupying a 17th-century courtyard house in Sfax that once belonged to the wealthy Jellouli family is the Dar Jellouli Regional Museum of Popular Arts and Traditions. The building has a classic layout with an arched entrance and a porticoed courtyard surrounded by rooms. The first floor features a lovely wooden balustrade. From the magnificently decorated ceilings to the walls lined with faience tiles and the doors painted in bright colours, the interiors conjure up a period of opulence and affluent ease.

Colonnades surround the courtyard at the first floor level.

★ Costumes
Tunisians attached great importance to their clothes, which also marked the social rank of the wearer. A typical woman's outfit consisted of a tunic, a scarf and a veil, complemented with items of jewellery.

The kitchen has been reconstructed with the same degree of precision as the other rooms.

Ceilings
Houses belonging to the wealthy were heavily decorated. Window and door frames were intricately carved; ceilings were decorated in geometric or other patterns.

1st floor

Rooms
Rooms within grand houses had a T-shaped floor layout. Wall shelves were used as cabinets and displayed bric-a-brac and lamps. Low sofas were usually arranged facing each other, or placed around the walls of a niche.

GALLERY LAYOUT
Many of the museum's exhibits have been designed to create the impression that the Jellouli family still live here. The ground floor contains furniture, kitchen appliances and vessels. Here visitors can learn how to make harissa, the traditional spicy Tunisian sauce, or study the art of creating aromatic oils used for producing perfumes. The first floor is given over to a collection of traditional costumes (including wedding garments) and jewellery.

STAR EXHIBITS

★ Alcove

★ Costumes

★ Jewellery

★ Jewellery
Women always wore plenty of jewellery. Jewelled headgear was a standard piece of attire for a wedding or other formal occasion.

VISITORS' CHECKLIST

Rue de la Driba. *Tel* (74) 221 186.
⬜ 8am–noon, 3–6pm Tue–Sun
(9:30am–6pm Sep–Mar). 🎟 📷
The museum is situated in the eastern part of the medina; the way to it from Rue de la Grande Mosquée is marked with arrows.

Glass Paintings
Dar Jellouli houses an interesting collection of glass decoration. This includes quotes from the Koran and decorative calligraphic characters of symbolic significance.

★ Alcove
Dar Jellouli would have had a strictly divided space. The upper floors were used mainly by women. The ground floor rooms (apart from the kitchen) were the male section. Women were not admitted to most gatherings held in the house.

Chest
Richly ornamented chests were used by the family to store valuable fabrics, clothes and thick quilts, which were used as beds.

Windows
Windows were fitted with intricate wooden grilles, which were designed to protect women from the gaze of strangers.

KEY

🟦	Jewellery
⬜	Costumes
🟪	Calligraphy
🟫	Historic interiors
⬜	Non-exhibition rooms

Ground floor

Entrance

A Traditional Arab Town

In the 9th and 10th centuries a new type of Arab town emerged, laid out on a grid pattern. The towns built in this style include Kairouan and Mahdia. In order to protect their population from invasion, towns began to develop districts known as medinas in the 11th and 12th centuries that were guarded by gates and surrounded by a high wall. At the medina's centre stood the Great Mosque, with markets and public baths nearby. The urban landscape was enriched by further religious buildings, including Islamic schools and *zaouias* (tombs).

Walls *surrounding the town were broken in four places by gates. It was customary to use the grounds immediately next to the gates, inside or outside, for cemeteries.*

The medina's streets are narrow and shady.

The turrets of the defensive walls

Kasbahs *were normally sited on hilltops or close to harbours. They had high walls and small windows. Some of the most beautiful examples can be seen in Sousse, Le Kef and Tunis.*

The roof *was and still is an integral part of a Tunisian house and a scene of everyday life for its inhabitants with tables and a carpet on the floor. This is where family and friends might meet over coffee.*

SFAX'S MEDINA

This is one of Tunisia's best-preserved old quarters and conforms to Islamic principles of architecture. At its centre is the Great Mosque, which is surrounded by the town's souks. The souks, according to custom, are located in a hierarchy. Incense and candle dealers are closest to the mosque while noisy blacksmiths and vendors serving the caravan trade were located at the medina's edge.

The towers at the four corners of the medina walls were supported by buttresses and crenellated; they were built into the walls that formed part of the fortifications.

Souks, *besides being markets, were also scenes of political discussions and plotting. They also included a wide variety of places where people could go for a glass of mint tea and listen to professional storytellers.*

Dars *were homes of the medina's elite. Externally they did not differ much from the surrounding buildings but the beauty and the riches of their interiors were stunning.*

The gates *guarding the entrance to towns usually numbered between two and six. During the day markets would be held close by. At night the gates were closed.*

Smaller mosques *(some the size of a living room) were often situated on the ground floors of other buildings. They were used for Friday prayers from the 12th century onwards.*

The Great Mosque *was and still is the most important and usually the most beautiful of an Arab town's mosques. Communal Friday prayers are the busiest time. In the early days of Islam this was the only mosque that had a* minbar *(pulpit).*

Interior of the 12th-century Sidi Driss Mosque

Kerkennah Islands ❽

Road map E4. 🏚 *15,000.*
🚢 *Av. Mohammed Hedi Khefacha.*
🎪 *Festival of Octopus (Mar); Festival of Mermaid (Jun).*

Located just 20 km (12 miles) off the coast of Sfax, the Kerkennah Islands were once a place of exile. Hannibal was sent here, as were Roman outlaws and, much later, Habib Bourguiba. Even today the 180 sq km (70 sq miles) of archipelago, comprising seven islands, has a desolate feel and only two of the islands (Gharbi and Chergui) are inhabited.

Depending on the time of year, up to five car ferries provide daily transport links with the mainland. The journey takes about 75 minutes. The ferries sail to Sidi Youssef on Gharbi. On the northeastern coast lies the islands' capital – El-Attaia. The main attractions include fine white sand, quiet surroundings and excellent conditions for snorkelling. The islands are flat (the highest point is only 13 m/43 ft above sea level) and are therefore ideally suited for cycling. The main resort is Sidi Frej on Chergui, which lies west of Ouled Kacem. From here it is possible to walk along the beach to the Roman ruins at Borj el-Hissar.

Gulf of Gabès ❾

Road map D4, D5.

Stretching south from Sfax all the way to the Libyan border, the Gulf of Gabès's sandy marshes provide a winter home for half of the entire bird population that migrates to the Mediterranean basin from the north. The winter migrants number around 400,000 and include several varieties of gull and heron as well as tern, plover, oystercatcher and flamingo.

The main town on the shores of the gulf is Gabès. Its foremost historic relic is the 12th-century **Sidi Driss Mosque**. Other attractions include a **Museum of Popular Arts and Traditions**, which is housed in a former medersa, and a trip to the local oasis. For visitors and Tunisians alike, however, Gabès is famous mainly as the centre of henna production, which can be purchased here cheaply.

Underground houses in Matmata, providing shelter from the heat

Matmata ❿

Road map D5. 🏚 *8,500.* 🚌

The Berber village of Matmata lies 650 m (2,133 ft) above sea level and is 40 km (25 miles) south of Gabès. This is the biggest and best known of the troglodyte villages, where the houses have been dug out of the rock to escape the intense daytime heat. This building tradition, which allows the rooms to maintain an even temperature of about 17° C (63° F) throughout the year, goes back hundreds of years. In the 1960s the three biggest cave compounds were turned into hotels. Many houses are still occupied and they inspired George Lucas, the creator of the *Star Wars* films, to spend many days shooting scenes here.

The current centre of the region is New Matmata, which is situated about 15 km (9 miles) from old Matmata.

SPONGES

Tunisia is a good place to purchase real sponges, which have been collected for hundreds of years from the Gulf of Gabès. Sponges are marine creatures and spend their lives

Cutting sponges in a workshop

motionless, attached to rocks or the sea bed; they do not have any nerve cells or muscles, and do not display any reaction to external stimuli. They filter organisms and organic matter by letting a constant stream of water flow through their bodies. Sponges have amazing powers of regeneration. Even a tiny fragment, consisting of just a few cells of the same kind, is able to reproduce a new sponge.

The Hammam

It would be hard to imagine a Tunisian town without a bathhouse. The custom of building them was passed down from antiquity and the need for them was kept up by the Islamic requirement for ritual cleanliness, particularly the ablutions carried out prior to prayers. At one time there

Women at the Baths by **Dominique Ingres**

was at least one bathhouse in every street, and in large towns they could number several hundreds. Visitors would undress in a special room, put on a thin towel and enter the water. Washing was originally carried out using oil of jojoba or soapwort in place of soap.

Hammams *were a vital part of life in Roman times and served a social function as well as an hygienic one. Everything needed for a bath could be bought from a vendor who stood by the front door. The attendants cleaned the rooms and scrubbed the slabs, which were heated with hot air.*

Hammam rooms *serve a variety of purposes. Some are used for bathing; others – filled with steam – for opening the pores and cleansing the skin.*

Temperatures *in a Tunisian hammam are not as high as in a sauna. Nevertheless, the steam and the hot-water pool will warm the body in no time at all.*

Massages and haircuts *are among the treatments offered in hammams. Hammams once employed barbers who were also skilled in bloodletting. Payment for a visit is made on leaving.*

Women *used to visit hammams around midday. This provided them with an opportunity to go out (shopping was done by men). Older women would scrutinize the younger ones, searching for wives for their sons.*

JERBA AND THE MEDENINE AREA

*T*he island of Jerba lies at the southern end of the Gulf of Gabès, 5 km (3 miles) from the mainland. It is known for its wonderful sandy beaches, its warm climate and its picturesque capital of Houmt Souk. Other attractions include fortified smallholdings (menzels) and Ibadite mosques. Back on the mainland, the area around Medenine has scenic hills and ancient villages.

Were it not for the dogged determination of its people, Jerba would remain no more than a scrap of desert. The inhabitants of the island have managed to turn the barren island into one big garden, however, with olive and orange groves and orchards. There are about 4,000 wells on the island, and the tourist zone is supplied with water by an aqueduct. Beautiful whitewashed mosques and traditional *menzels* hidden behind high hedges add to Jerba's charm.

According to myth, Odysseus landed here and nearly lost his crew to the amnesia-inducing food of the resident lotus-eaters. From the 4th century BC, Jerba was ruled from Carthage; later on it passed into the hands of the Romans. The island's prosperity is derived from trading in fish, olive oil and ceramics. The advent of Islam in the 7th century was accompanied by the arrival of the Ibadites, an austere Islamic school of religious thought and practice that was hostile to authority. Their descendants still inhabit western parts of the island. In the 16th century the Malekite school began to gain popularity and now the majority of Jerba's population is Sunni Muslim. There is also a small but significant Jewish contingent, whose ancestors arrived here some 2,000 years ago. Hara Sghira's synagogue is still a place of reverence for Jews.

Medenine was once an important stopping point for caravans and is a good base for forays into the villages scattered among the nearby hills.

Wickerwork products for sale in Houmt Souk

◁ The mosque and flat-roofed houses of Toujane, northwest of Medenine

Exploring Jerba and the Medenine Area

Jerba occupies an area of 538 sq km (208 sq miles) and is virtually flat. It is one of Tunisia's most popular tourist destinations. As the temperature on the island never falls below 15° C (59° F) even in winter, it is a popular resort all year round. Zarzis, on the mainland, is slowly beginning to rival Jerba as a tourist area, but it is more difficult to reach. The Zarzis peninsula is the region's main area for growing citrus fruits and olives. Medenine, 40 km (25 miles) southwest of Jerba, provides a good starting point for a tour of the *ksour* (fortified villages).

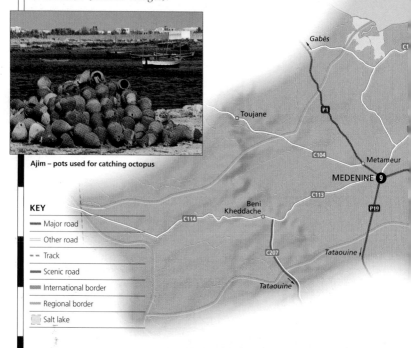

Ajim – pots used for catching octopus

KEY

━━ Major road

══ Other road

▬ ▬ Track

━━ Scenic road

▬▬ International border

━━ Regional border

▨ Salt lake

SIGHTS AT A GLANCE

Aghir ❻
El-Ghriba ❷
El-May ❸
Guellala ❼
Houmt Souk pp178–9 ❶
Medenine ❾
Midoun ❺
Ras Remel ❹
Zarzis ❽

Tours

*Around the Gulf of Bou Grara
    pp188–9* ❿

Crocodiles in an amusement park in Jerba

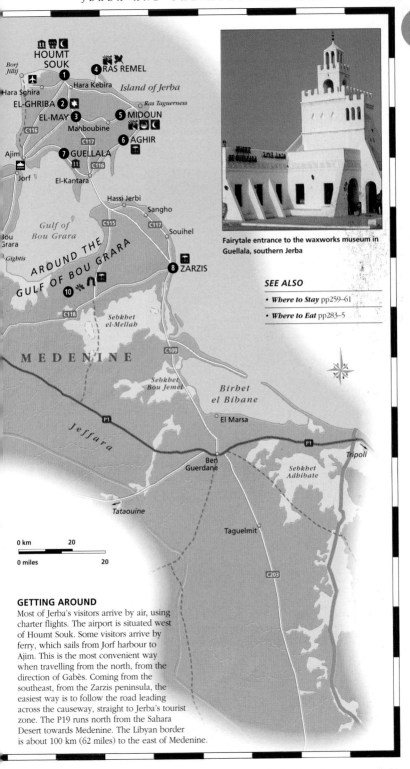

Fairytale entrance to the waxworks museum in Guellala, southern Jerba

GETTING AROUND

Most of Jerba's visitors arrive by air, using charter flights. The airport is situated west of Houmt Souk. Some visitors arrive by ferry, which sails from Jorf harbour to Ajim. This is the most convenient way when travelling from the north, from the direction of Gabès. Coming from the southeast, from the Zarzis peninsula, the easiest way is to follow the road leading across the causeway, straight to Jerba's tourist zone. The P19 runs north from the Sahara Desert towards Medenine. The Libyan border is about 100 km (62 miles) to the east of Medenine.

0 km 20
0 miles 20

Houmt Souk ❶

Jerba's charming capital lies on the island's northern shore. Houmt Souk literally means "market quarter", revealing the long-standing importance of trade to the town, and its narrow streets and ancient souks are full of shops selling jewellery, clothes and souvenirs. Also of interest are the *fondouks* that were built as inns for travelling merchants during the Ottoman period, and the 13th-century fortress, Borj el-Kebir, which provides stunning views along the coast.

Avenue Bourguiba, a thoroughfare and a place of relaxation

Exploring Houmt Souk

To the north of the town lies the harbour, and close to it the Borj el-Kebir. The old town centre is fairly compact. Rue Mohammed Ferjani leads to the shady Place Hedi Chaker. Nearby is the Mosque of the Turks, which serves as a market venue. Rue Moncef Bey, running parallel to Rue Mohammed Ferjani, has an interesting *fondouk* with a large courtyard. On the left hand side of Place Sidi Brahim is the tomb of Sidi Brahim. On the opposite side of the road is the Mosque of the Strangers. A walk along Avenue Abdel Hamid el-Kadhi leads to the Museum of Arts and Popular Traditions, housed in the mausoleum of an Islamic holy man.

🕌 Avenue Habib Bourguiba

This is the main street, cutting across the town from north to south. Its northern section is fringed with houses built in various European styles at the end of the 19th century. The street's southern section is shady.

🕌 Souks

Place Bechir Saoud, Avenue Abdel Hamid el-Kadhi.

The town's old quarter is a maze of narrow alleys and small shops selling leather goods, jewellery and handmade fabrics. The only covered souk is Souk ar-Rab. The old *fondouks* are among the most interesting and picturesque features of Houmt Souk. These former lodging houses combined the functions of stores and inns and were used by travelling merchants. Some of the *fondouks* have now been converted into hotels or youth hostels.

Fish auction at the souk

🅲 Mosque of the Strangers

Avenue Abdel Hamid el-Kadhi.
Tel (75) 606 4715. 🌑 *to non-Muslims.*

In Houmt Souk there are three mosques standing next to one another. Each belongs to a different Islamic school. The multi-domed Mosque of the Strangers is used by the Malekites and is topped with an ornate minaret. The El-Sheikh Mosque is the main mosque of the Ibadites, while the Mosque of the Turks is used by the Hanefites.

🕌 Zaouia of Sidi Brahim

Place Sidi Brahim. 🌑 *to non-Muslims.*
The entire complex consists of a school, the tomb of Sidi Brahim, a hammam (bath) and a bakery. The school was founded in the 17th century by the Muradids, with the aim of promoting the Malekite school of Islam. The medersa's large courtyard is flanked on three sides by arcades and on the fourth by the prayer hall. Small steps lead from the courtyard to the first-floor gallery.

🕌 Place Hedi Chaker

Rue Mohammed Ferjani leads to this square, which is in the town centre. A lively place, it makes an excellent spot to sit down for a while, order a cup of coffee or tea and take in what is going on.

🅲 Mosque of the Turks

Avenue Mohammed Ferjani.
🌑 *to non-Muslims.*
The Mosque of the Turks, covered with seven white domes, is the town's largest mosque and dates from the 17th century. It is used by the followers of the Hanefite school of Islam, which proclaims rationalism and tolerance towards other religions. This branch of Islam reached its peak of popularity during the Ottoman period but is still popular in Tunisia.

Further Afield

The town's life centres around Avenue Bourguiba and the souks. The Museum of Arts and Popular Traditions can be found a short way to the east of the centre. To the north, a little way along the beach, is

Stone bridge leading to Borj el-Kebir

the Borj el-Kebir. Lying beyond this is the harbour.

🏛 Museum of Arts and Popular Traditions

Tel (75) 650 540. ◯ 9am–7pm Sat–Thu.

Occupying the Zaouia of Sidi Zitouni, this modest museum has a collection of traditional costumes and other items illustrating various aspects of the traditions and customs of Jerba's population.

🏯 Borj el-Kebir

◯ Apr–mid-Sep: 8am–noon & 3–7pm; mid-Sep–Mar: 9am–6pm ● Mon. ◗ Mon & Thu.

This fort stands on the seafront. Its foundations date back to Roman times, but the

first fortress on the island was built by the king of Sicily, Roger de Lluria, in 1289. It was reinforced in the 14th century. In its design, the fortress combined defensive elements with religious features and was the most important part of the island's defence system. In the 16th century the famous pirate Dragut reinforced its walls and extended the entire structure.

🏯 The Monument of Skulls

Situated between the harbour and Borj el-Kebir is a small obelisk. The site was formerly occupied by a gruesome 11-m (36-ft) high pyramid of human skulls placed here by Dragut following a massacre of Spanish Christians in 1560.

VISITORS' CHECKLIST

Road map D5. 🏯 63,000. ✈
ℹ (75) 622 666. 🚌 Mon, Thu.

The pyramid stood here until 1848, when the human remains were buried at the local cemetery.

Harbour

Houmt Souk's small harbour looks its best at sunset, when the fishermen return with their day's catch. The local fish include tuna, gilthead and shrimp. In winter, fishermen use clay pots to catch squid and octopus. The harbour is located at the end of Rue du Port, which is an extension of Avenue Bourguiba.

Fishing boats moored at Houmt Souk

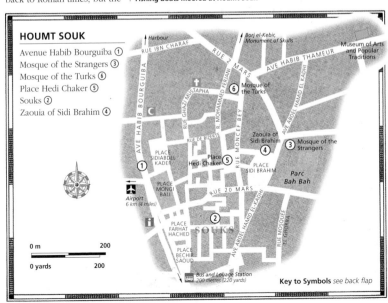

HOUMT SOUK

Avenue Habib Bourguiba ①
Mosque of the Strangers ③
Mosque of the Turks ⑥
Place Hedi Chaker ⑤
Souks ②
Zaouia of Sidi Brahim ④

0 m   200
0 yards   200

Key to Symbols *see back flap*

El-Ghriba ❷

Road map D5. ◯ *Sun–Fri*
9:30am–5pm.

The country's most famous synagogue is El-Ghriba, which is a short way south of Hara Sghira. This is the oldest site of a synagogue in the world and dates back to 586 BC; the present structure was built in the 20th century. It is an important place of pilgrimage for Jews from all over North Africa, especially during the Passover Festival. Although relations between Muslims and Jews are generally good on the island, El-Ghriba was subject to a terrorist attack in 2002 which killed 21 people and damaged part of the interior.

FORTIFIED MOSQUES

The nave of an underground mosque

Besides being important spiritual centres, Jerba's mosques were also military defence establishments. Their thick walls provided shelter from attacks, while their minarets were used as watchtowers. As well as fortress-style minarets, the local population also built underground mosques. It is likely that these were used by the Ibadites for secret prayer meetings. One such mosque – Jama'a el-Baldawi – can be found near the village of Ajim. Its façade was built in modern times. Underground mosques are distinguished by their austerity and functionality. Ibadite doctrine does not permit any ornamentation within the mosque, as this could distract the faithful from prayer.

The interior of the El-Ghriba synagogue

Increased security since then means that you will need your passport if you wish to visit.

The prayer hall's 12 windows allude to the Zohar – the principal book of the Kabbala – and symbolize the 12 tribes of Israel. The interior is decorated with rich fabrics, wood-carvings and ceramic tiles. It houses many items donated by pilgrims from all over the world. In order to maintain the high status of the synagogue, the Rabbi of Jerba decreed it to be the only place on the island where religious scrolls are to be kept. Particularly striking elements of the interior furnishings include a beautiful Torah cabinet and Hanukkah lamps made of wood and silver.

El-Ghriba ("the miracle") is said to have been founded on the spot where a holy stone fell from heaven. A mysterious woman arrived at the same time to oversee construction.

Jerba's Jewish community is concentrated mainly in two villages – Hara Sghira (Er Riadh) and Hara Kebira (Es Souani). At first glance these two villages (which are about 5 km/3 miles apart) are identical to any other Tunisian village with palm trees and white houses with distinctive blue doors and windows. It is

only when the streets fill with boys returning from school wearing skull-caps, or when Sabbath candles are lit inside the houses, that visitors may get the impression of being in a district of Jerusalem rather than in a Tunisian village. The two villages have a number of synagogues. Some bear stern notices: "If you talk in the synagogue, where do you pray?"

The island's Jewish community is ultra-orthodox and celebrates the Sabbath and other holy days as well as observing religious rituals. At a son's circumcision, a red blanket is hung on the door, inviting everyone to come and witness the ceremony.

El-May ❸

Road map D5.

This village lies at the centre of Jerba and is 9 km (6 miles) south of Houmt Souk. Once it used to separate the eastern part of the island, inhabited by the Ibadites, from its western part, populated by the Wahbis. The Ibadites (a moderate faction of Kharijism) recognized man's free will. The Wahbis, who renounced all other factions of Islam, proclaimed the necessity for *jihad* – holy war. The 16th-century Mosque of Umm et-Turkia (closed to non-Muslims) was formerly also a fort.

The mosque in El-May, at the centre of the island

Ras Remel – a site of wintering birds and a weekend recreation spot

Ras Remel ❹

Road map D5.

The Ras Remel peninsula in the north of Jerba is just under 10 km (6 miles) from Houmt Souk, and is an ideal spot for daytrips and picnics. Its main attractions are the wintering flocks of pink flamingoes that migrate here from southern France and Spain, joining the fledglings who spend the entire year here. The waters surrounding Ras Remel are shallow and the muddy bottom provides the birds with plenty of food. A short distance from the headland lies Flamingo Island. Most hotels situated in Houmt Souk's tourist zone organize trips to the island, which are often combined with lunch and swimming.

Environs
At the furthest northwestern tip of the island is **Borj Jillij**, a mere 3 km (2 miles) from Mellita Airport. A lighthouse was first built here in the 16th century. This was replaced in the 18th century by a fort, which is once again being used as a lighthouse. From here it is possible to walk to Ajim along a narrow and quiet country road.
Ajim – ancient Tipasa – is situated 22 km (14 miles) southwest of Houmt Souk. Occupying the point closest to the mainland it has regular ferry links with Jorf (the ferry can be busy, especially at weekends). The village is also

a centre for sponge diving (*see p172*). The MC116 road runs among palm and olive groves. Fans of the first *Star Wars* film may want to search out the mosque that is 3 km (2 miles) up the coast towards Borj Jillij – this was used as the exterior of Obiwan Kenobi's house.
The small village of **Mahboubine** lies in the eastern part of the island, 3 km (2 miles) southwest of Midoun, and is surrounded by green fields and gardens. Its El-Katib Mosque is a copy of the Hagia Sophia in Istanbul. It was built in the 19th century by Ali el-Katib.

The village of **Arku** lies at the centre of the island, not far from the coastal town of Aghir, which marks the end of the tourist zone. The village's population consist mainly of the descendants of former slaves, who were brought to Jerba from Central Africa. Following the abolition of slavery in 1846, the majority of the island's black inhabitants chose to stay. Some adopted the surnames of families for whom they worked. Today their main occupation is agriculture, as well as basket- and mat-weaving. They are also renowned as outstanding musicians and dancers.
Unlike the centre of Jerba, which resembles one big garden, with palm, fig and olive groves, as well as orange and apple orchards, Jerba's **west coast** is largely uninhabited. A dirt road runs from Ajim to Borj Jillij with traditional Jerban houses and small fields scattered here and there. The coastline is rocky and not good for swimming, which means that there are few tourists. The dirt roads and lack of facilities, however, make it popular with campers and cyclists who don't mind putting up with a little hardship in order to get away from the bustle of the resort areas.

Ras Remel flamingo

MENZELS

Menzels are self-sufficient agricultural smallholdings. Although many have been abandoned, some remain in use. The internal area consists of a yard surrounded by white walls and buildings. The buildings provide accommodation for people and domestic animals; the yard also contains a granary and a water cistern. The entire area is surrounded by a garden and a palm grove. *Menzels* used to be interconnected with a maze of roads to other *menzels* and the mosque. In this way, news of approaching danger could be passed around instantly.

A fortress-like *menzel* on Jerba

Midoun ❺

Road map D5. 👥 *48,000.* 🚌 *Fri.*

Surrounded by gardens, and orange and palm groves, this is Jerba's second town, after Houmt Souk. Midoun's population includes many descendants of African slaves, who were brought here from sub-Saharan Africa. The weekly Friday market attracts crowds of people from all over the island, as well as from the nearby mainland villages. The market is held at the centre of the town's small medina. It sells a variety of souvenirs, including local ceramics, wood carvings, leather goods and olive oil.

The other local event – "Fantasia" – is staged every Tuesday during the summer and includes a mock wedding ceremony accompanied by music and folk dancing, as well as displays of horse and camel riding. At the centre of Midoun, close to the junction that leads to Houmt Souk and the tourist zone, is an underground *massera* (oil press), covered with a white dome at ground level.

Mosque and fountain in front of the town hall, Midoun

Aghir ❻

Road map E5.

The hotel zone that starts about 8 km (5 miles) east of Houmt Souk stretches up to the village of Aghir, on the eastern side of the island, which has been transformed into a hotel resort. Even so, as well as the souvenirs sold

Reconstructed dye-works in Guellala's waxworks museum

by local shops everyday groceries can also be bought. There is a regular bus service to Houmt Souk and Midoun.

From Aghir it is not far to Ras Taguerness, which is distinguished by a 54-m (177-ft) tall lighthouse. Aghir is also convenient for a visit to the small village of Arku *(see p181)* or for a walk along the beach to other complexes in Séguia or Ras Lalla Hadria. Aghir's sandy beach has been divided into a public area and a number of private sections belonging to local hotels.

Guellala ❼

Road map D5.

Guellala, the ancient town of Haribus (meaning a "pot"), owes its name to the skill of the local potters, who mastered the potter's wheel several thousand years ago. The village lies on the south coast of Jerba and is the only place on the island where the Berber language is spoken.

Since ancient times this was the island's main pottery centre. Jerba was for centuries the sole manufacturer of ceramics in Tunisia, and its products were famous throughout the Saharan region. Even as late as the 19th century the island paid the beys tax, which was paid in kind, in the form of jars and pots that were used for storing food.

The range of Jerba's traditional ceramics includes amphora-like jars, which are still used today. Most of the production now centres on enamelled goods that are intended for visitors, however. There are about 450 small pottery shops working in this area.

Traditional Jerba ceramics are made of clay that is excavated from mines up to 80 m (262 ft) deep. It is dried for two to three days and then mixed with water. The products are left out to dry for a further 60 days, and only after that are they fired for four days in kilns, which are half-buried in soil.

Guellala's **museum** is a little way north of the village on the road to Cedouikech. The colourful displays, using waxwork tableaux, conjure up scenes of traditional Tunisian life such as a shepherd with his flock or a weaver at work.

🏛 **Guellala Museum of Popular Traditions**
Tel (75) 761 114. 🕐 *8am–6pm (until 8pm in summer).* 📷

Ceramic workshop and retailer, Guellala

Jerba's Jewish Community

A Jewish resident

There are fewer than 1,000 Jews living in Jerba. According to legend, a group of Jewish clerics arrived on the island following the fall of Jerusalem in 586 BC. They brought with them a door from the destroyed Jewish temple and included it in the new El-Ghriba synagogue. From Jerba, Jewish colonies sprang up across Tunisia and by the 2nd century AD Tunisia was the home of the majority of North African Jews. Many Jews worked as jewellers and established Jerba's reputation as a commercial centre. During the 19th century Jews here were forced to wear distinctive black clothes to mark them out and anti-Jewish discrimination only lessened with the arrival of the French in 1881. Many Jews left Jerba for a new life in Israel and France in the 1950s and 60s.

El-Ghriba *is the most important synagogue on the island and is open to foreign visitors. It is closed only on the Sabbath, when it is used by the Jewish islanders for services.*

Lag Ba'omer *is a major festival and an occasion when several thousand Jews from all over the world congregate in Jerba. The holiday celebrates the 33rd day of Omer, a period of abstention and mourning, that is counted from Passover.*

Pilgrimage – *El-Ghriba (the miracle) is an important site of pilgrimage for Jews from all over North Africa.*

Library – *this is the place for studying the Torah (Jewish holy book). El-Ghriba has one of the oldest Torahs in the world and is a centre of Jewish study.*

Sabbath services *take place once a week, beginning at sunset on Friday evening and continuing until sunset on Saturday, when Jerban synagogues fill with the faithful.*

Zarzis ❽

Road map E5. 🏛 *11,000.* 🚌.

Zarzis is a large town and is located 20 km (12 miles) southeast of Jerba. In geographical terms this area belongs to the Jaffara Plains that stretch between Gabès and the Libyan border. Since the 7th century this region has been inhabited by Arab nomads and a population that led a semi-nomadic lifestyle.

Zarzis is surrounded by vast olive and palm groves, with about 700,000 olive trees and 110,000 date palms. The town itself was built in the 19th century by the French, who established their garrison here. The tourist zone has fine sandy beaches and starts 4 km (2 miles) outside town. The zone stretches for about 8 km (5 miles) along the coast. It is becoming increasingly important as one of Tunisia's tourist regions.

Medenine ❾

Road map E6. 🏛 *18,000.* 🚌.

This is an excellent base from which to explore the outlying villages. The town, which is split into two by a river bed (the Arab word "medenijin" means "two towns"), was once an important stopping point for caravans. During the French Protectorate it housed a military garrison. As the main market town, to which goods were brought from the entire southern region, it

Beach in Zarzis's tourist zone

became the administrative centre of southern Tunisia.

Initially Medenine consisted of a large *ksar*, which in total had over 6,000 *ghorfas* (rooms). The nomads used them for storing valuables, mainly corn, seed and vegetables, but they also left in them articles that were not needed on the journey.

Each family had its own *ghorfa*. During the 1960s most of the *ghorfas* were demolished. Today the handful of remaining *ghorfas* have been turned into tourist souvenir shops.

Such *ksour* (plural of *ksar*) are symbols of an old way of life, although they are increasingly being abandoned and falling into ruin, as the villagers store their grain in

modern silos on the outskirts of the towns. Nevertheless, there are still many well-preserved *ksour* in the neighbouring area. The best way to get to them is by car *(see pp196–7)*.

Environs

A large *ghorfa* complex can be seen in **Metameur**, 6 km (4 miles) west of Medenine. The village inhabitants are semi-nomadic. Some of them are descended from Sidi Ahmed ben Adjel, a holy man who founded the village in the 13th century. The best time to visit Metameur is on Friday, when the nomads leave their pastures and gather here for their Friday prayers. The most important building in town is the 600-year-old *ksar*, which has three storeys of *ghorfas* built around three courtyards.

From Metameur a road (MC104) leads to **Toujane**, a small half-deserted village below the ruins of a kasbah. Its flat roofs, made of olive wood, resemble terraces.

Some 80 km (50 miles) southeast of Medenine is the small town of **Ben Guerdane**, which has 3,000 inhabitants. Every Friday there is a market here. As with Zarzis and Medenine, it was founded by the French in the late 19th century. From here it is only 32 km (20 miles) to the Libyan border.

Souvenir shop in a *ghorfa* in the centre of Medenine

◁ **Traditional Jerba pottery**

Jerba's Beaches

Jerba's beautiful beaches stretch along the northeast coast of the island, all the way from Ras Remel to Ras Taguerness. However, access to them is often restricted by a virtually unbroken line of hotels. There are some attractive beaches on the east coast, in the region of Aghir. The less-frequented beaches on the island can be found around Ras Remel.

Bravo Club ②
Most hotels have their own stretch of beach, with umbrellas, loungers and other facilities including paragliding and water bicycles for the sole use of guests.

Ras Remel ①
This beach lying at the tip of the headland is often deserted and can only be reached by car over unmetalled roads. It is best to travel with a guide to avoid getting lost.

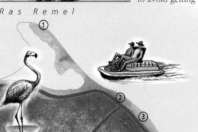

Beach Traders ③
Vendors can often be seen roaming the tourist zone beaches. They offer drinks, ice cream and fruit and also sell beach toys and souvenirs.

Sport ④
Banana rides, sailing and a variety of other attractions are available on the tourist zone beaches.

Beach Rides ⑤
The most popular local activities include camel rides along the beach. On some parts of the beach horse riding is also available.

0 km   1

0 miles   1

Dar Jerba ⑥
The gardens and terraces of this large hotel complex, which has bars, restaurants and nightly entertainment, lead directly to the sandy beach.

Around the Gulf of Bou Grara ❿

A journey around the Gulf of Bou Grara reveals just how diverse and attractive this section of the coastline is. As well as ancient ruins, picturesque floodplains and golden beaches, there are high rugged cliffs, a modern tourist zone and hundreds of acres planted with olive and orange trees. It is also worth venturing a little further to visit the exotic bazaar in Ben Guerdane, which sells a variety of Libyan-made goods.

El-Kantara ①
This is the starting point for the causeway leading to Jerba. It provides a lovely panoramic view of the island.

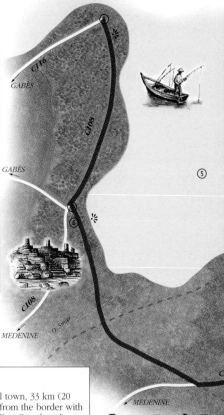

Jorf ⑧
Visitors have to pass Jorf when travelling to Jerba from the direction of Gabès. Every quarter of an hour or so the only ferry to the island leaves from here.

Bou Grara ⑦
This tiny fishing village would not have much to recommend it were it not for the magnificent scenery, which includes a high shore line and sandy beaches.

BEN GUERDANE

A small town, 33 km (20 miles) from the border with Libya, Ben Guerdane has a good market where almost anything can be bought, though not always at a low price. The market is used mainly by Tunisians. Along the road to Ben Guerdane are small petrol stations, which also sell inexpensive Libyan jewellery.

Rug stall at Ben Guerdane

Gightis ⑥
This ancient village, on the shore of the bay, was founded by the Phoenicians. The existing ruins represent a later period dating from the 2nd century AD.

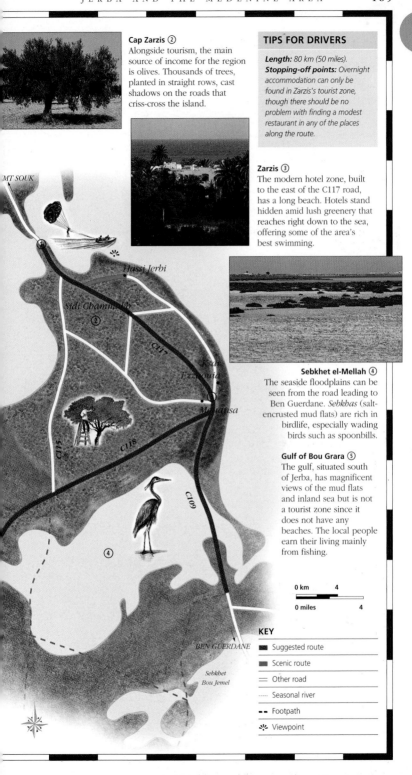

Cap Zarzis ②
Alongside tourism, the main source of income for the region is olives. Thousands of trees, planted in straight rows, cast shadows on the roads that criss-cross the island.

TIPS FOR DRIVERS

Length: 80 km (50 miles).
Stopping-off points: Overnight accommodation can only be found in Zarzis's tourist zone, though there should be no problem with finding a modest restaurant in any of the places along the route.

Zarzis ③
The modern hotel zone, built to the east of the C117 road, has a long beach. Hotels stand hidden amid lush greenery that reaches right down to the sea, offering some of the area's best swimming.

Sebkhet el-Mellah ④
The seaside floodplains can be seen from the road leading to Ben Guerdane. *Sebkhas* (salt-encrusted mud flats) are rich in birdlife, especially wading birds such as spoonbills.

Gulf of Bou Grara ⑤
The gulf, situated south of Jerba, has magnificent views of the mud flats and inland sea but is not a tourist zone since it does not have any beaches. The local people earn their living mainly from fishing.

0 km   4

0 miles   4

KEY

▪▪	Suggested route
▪▪	Scenic route
=	Other road
·····	Seasonal river
--	Footpath
❀	Viewpoint

SOUTHERN TUNISIA

*S*ome of the country's most interesting sights are to be found in
this part of Tunisia. Oases and ancient ksour; a sea of golden
sand and green palm groves; troglodyte houses; Bedouin bread
baked on the scorching sand; modern musicals performed in the
desert and the largest salt lake in Africa – all these make a visit to
southern Tunisia a truly unique experience.

Southern Tunisia lures visitors
with the sheer diversity of its
landscape. It holds special
appeal to holidaymakers who
simply wish to relax on the
beaches of the Sahel but is
also increasingly popular
with adventure-seekers. Only
a small section of the Sahara –
the world's largest desert,
shared by 11 African countries –
belongs to Tunisia. Nevertheless, in
view of its relative safety, transport
facilities and tourist infrastructure, it
is this section of the Sahara that is
most easily accessible.

Here, visitors can journey along the
routes of former trade-caravans or
choose to follow in the footsteps of
Star Wars director George Lucas.
Nights can be spent in Bedouin
tents, remote mountain oases or
luxury hotels that resemble oriental

palaces. Pomegranates and
dates can be picked ripe from
the tree. Some visitors choose
to spend several days touring
the desert on camelback.
Others prefer to relax in
ancient Berber villages
or lose themselves in
meditation amid the ancient
mosques of Sufi Nefta.

The Tunisian section of the
Sahara comprises three main
types of desert: the rocky
hamada; the pebbly *serir* and the
sandy *erg*. The latter is the most
picturesque and occupies the eastern
end of the Great Eastern Erg. Its
most impressive dunes can be seen
around Ksar Ghilane.

During the summer, this region can
become unbearably hot. For this
reason, spring and autumn are the
best times to visit.

The main courtyard of Ksar Ouled Soltane

◁ **Palm trees of a Saharan oasis**

Exploring Southern Tunisia

With so much choice, it could be difficult to decide what to see in southern Tunisia. Visitors keen on ancient ruins will find little of interest here, but those who seek spectacular, breathtaking scenery cannot fail to be enchanted with the region, which includes ancient mountain oases, the shifting colours of Chott el-Jerid, and the green oases of Nefta – the cradle of Tunisian Sufism. Ksar Ouled Soltane, perched on top of a mountain, has some extremely well-preserved *ghorfas*. Most impressive of all, perhaps, is the Sahara Desert, which can be admired while perched on a camel's back during an organized trek into the dunes, or explored on foot with a guide.

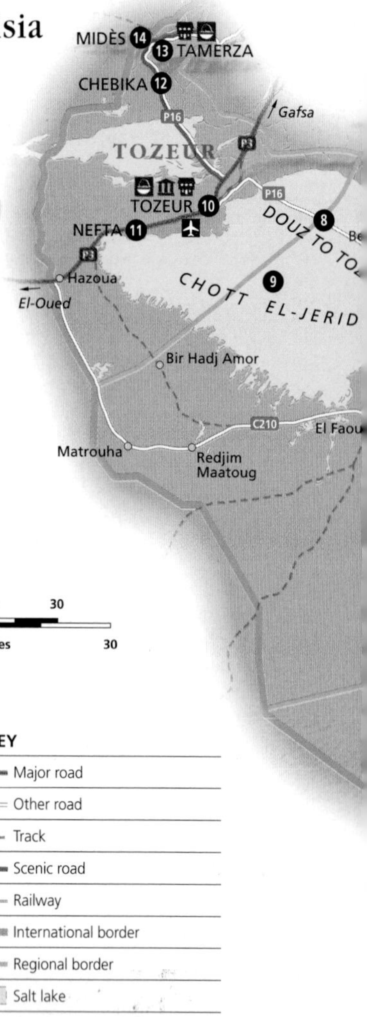
MIDÈS 14
13 TAMERZA
CHEBIKA 12
P16
Gafsa
TOZEUR
P3
TOZEUR 10
P16
NEFTA 11
DOUZ TO TO
8
P3
Hazoua
El-Oued
CHOTT EL-JERID
9
Bir Hadj Amor
C210
El Faou
Matrouha
Redjim Maatoug
0 km 30
0 miles 30
KEY
Major road
Other road
Track
Scenic road
Railway
International border
Regional border
Salt lake

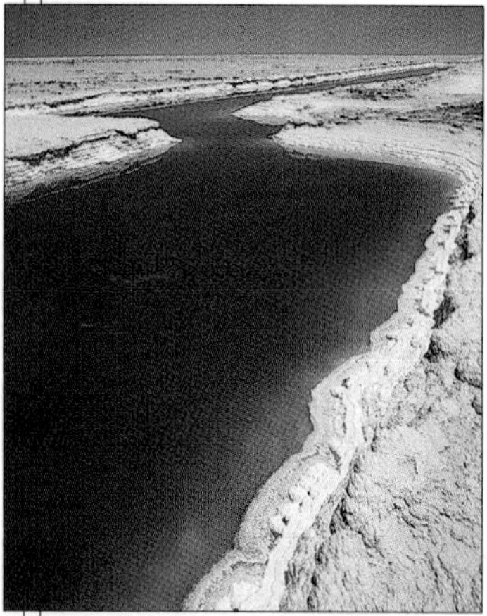

Chott el-Jerid – a seasonal salt lake

SIGHTS AT A GLANCE

Chebika 12
Chott el-Jerid 9
Douz 6
Ksar Ghilane 5
Ksar Haddada 1
Ksar Ouled Soltane 3
Midès 14
Nefta 11
Remada 4
The Sahara pp200–1 7
Tamerza 13
Tataouine 2
Tozeur 10

Trips

Douz to Tozeur pp206–7 8

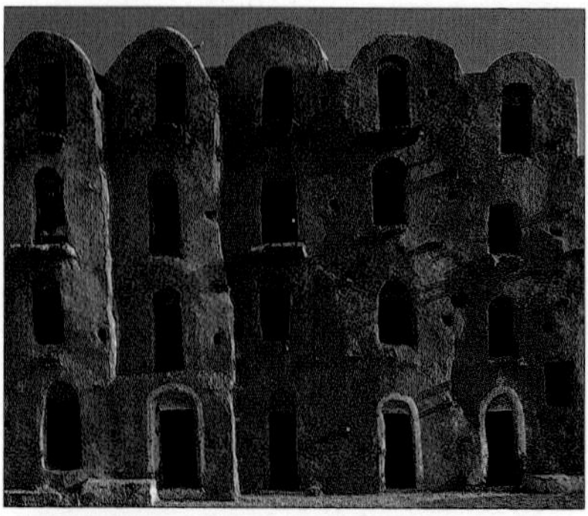

Ksar Ouled Soltane – the best-known *ksar*

For additional map symbols *see back flap*

Camel-train waiting for tourists in front of a Douz hotel, on the edge of the Sahara Desert

GETTING THERE

The Tunisian Sahara is skirted by roads on its northern and eastern sides. Douz – the northern gate of the Sahara – can be reached from Gabès via the P16, or from the direction of the mountain oases via the causeway that runs across Chott el-Jerid. From here on, visitors can explore the Sahara only with a guide. To reach Ksar Ghilane turn west from the P19. Finding this, the most popular oasis, is no easy task, since during high winds the roads become covered in sand. The P19 road running from Medenine ends in the south at Remada.

A maze of alleys in Ksar Haddada

Ksar Haddada ❶

Road map D6. 29 km (18 miles) northwest of Tataouine.

The main point of interest of this small village is its superbly restored *ksar*, which is one of the most striking complexes of former fortress-granaries to be found in southern Tunisia. It stands at the very centre of the village, in close proximity to the mosque, which is across the road.

A large notice in front of the main gate informs visitors that in 1997 George Lucas used this place as a location for the *Star Wars* prequel, *The Phantom Menace*.

It is worth diving deeper into the maze of stairways, terraces and small courtyards and peeping into some of the granary niches known as *ghorfas*. These were once used to store food by the local Haddada and Hamdoun tribes, and by two other tribes which probably arrived here from Libyan and Moroccan territories.

Today, a section of the *ksar* has been converted into a small hotel, which combines the unique atmosphere of an ancient *ksar* with a tinge of Hollywood. The hotel's kitchen offers a simple menu; the rooms, although equipped with bathrooms, are fairly austere. Right by the entrance to the *ksar* is a pleasant little café where a glass of mint tea can be enjoyed with a puff on a hookah if desired.

Tataouine ❷

Road map D6. 125 km (78 miles) south of Gabès. 🏠 7,000. ℹ ONTT: Avenue Habib Bourguiba, (75) 850 686. 📷 *International Saharan Ksour Festival (Mar–Apr); Festival of the Olives (Jan).* 🗓 Mon, Thu.

Variously known as the "gateway to the Sahara" and the "mouth of the springs" (from the Berber "foum tataouine"), this is Tunisia's southernmost tourist base. It is situated 50 km (31 miles) from the Mediterranean coast, along the popular tourist trail that links Jerba with Matmata and Douz with the Saharan oasis of Ksar Ghilane. Some fans of *Star Wars* may also realize that Tataouine provided the name for Luke Skywalker's mythical and wind-blown home planet of Tatooine.

Traditional flutes on sale at Tataouine's market

Some 150 million years ago this area was inhabited by dinosaurs before being flooded by the sea. Mankind has been forced to adapt to the barren land and arid climate. To this day the Berbers show great respect for the natural environment. Berber women occupy themselves with handicrafts, weaving rugs and carpets and sewing warm camel-wool cloaks. The men produce shoes called *balgha* which have flattened toe-ends.

Tataouine was founded in 1892 by the French and is today a major administration centre of this region. It is known for its hotels which are distinguished by their interesting architectural style and locations, and for its colourful markets selling fruit, olives and Berber fabrics. There is also a weekly livestock market during the early part of summer which is popular with tribespeople from the outlying villages.

Apart from the hotels and markets Tataouine has little tourist appeal though it does provide a very convenient base for exploring the local *ksour*, such as Ksar Haddada (29 km/18 miles), Ksar Ouled Soltane (20 km/12 miles), and Remada (78 km/48 miles). The nearest one is Ksar Megabla – only 2 km (1 mile) from the centre of Tataouine (in the direction of Remada). Though this former fortified village has been largely destroyed, it does offer a lovely view of the surrounding area.

The local delicacy is the sweet honey-and-almond bread *(kab el-ghazal)* baked in the shape of a gazelle horn. The annual Saharan Ksour Festival (a five-day event at the end of March/beginning of April) provides an opportunity to witness camel races and Berber wedding ceremonies and to sample some of the delicious local cuisine.

Tataouine is also only 18 km (11 miles) from **Chenini**, a Berber village occupying a scenic position on a high hill, which is famous for its ancient cave dwellings.

Ksar Ouled Soltane ❸

Road map D6.

Ksar Ouled Soltane is the most interesting and best-preserved fortified village in Tunisia, and is situated 20 km (12 miles) south of Tataouine. It is still used to store grain and olives and is inhabited by the Ouled Chehida tribesmen (in between their regular migration to pasturelands to tend their sheep, goats and camels). Surrounded by an additional set of defensive walls, the complex consists of over 300 granaries – *ghorfas*. Rising up to four storeys they are set round two courtyards that are linked by a narrow corridor made of palm wood. The older courtyard dates from the 15th century; the newer one was built in 1881. The place is worth visiting particularly on Friday, after the main Muslim prayer session, to witness the lively discussions between the Ouled Chehida tribesmen.

The larger of the two *ksar* courtyards is also sometimes used as a venue for folk shows, especially during the Ksour Festival. The traditional Berber music and dancing of the ancient community are in perfect harmony with the architecture of this beautifully restored fortified village.

Steep stairs leading to upper floors in Ksar Ouled Soltane

Remada ❹

Road map D6.

This small oasis lies 50 km (31 miles) from the Libyan border. A smallish Roman fort once stood here. Under the French Protectorate, the town once again became a military base. Due to its close proximity to Libya, Remada has remained a garrison town. The only eye-catching feature in the central Place de l'Indépendance is a former abattoir building, covered with 15 small domes. This is a border zone, and any trip to the desert requires special permission from the military authorities.

Borj Bourguiba, 41 km (25 miles) southwest of Remada, is where the first president of Tunisia, Habib Bourguiba, was kept prisoner during the early 1950s.

STAR WARS

George Lucas – the creator of *Star Wars* films – was fascinated by the landscape of southern Tunisia and used many of its most exotic sights and interiors as locations for his epic space adventures. Luke Skywalker's home at the beginning of the first *Star Wars* movie was actually the interior of the Sidi Driss Hotel in Matmata for instance, while the natural features of Ksar Haddada were used to conjure up slave quarters in *The Phantom Menace*. The worldwide success of *Star Wars* helped to promote many of Tunisia's tourist attractions and a percentage of the revenue obtained from the sale of tickets when the first film was released in 1977 went to the National Solidarity Fund that helps the poorest regions of the country in their fight against the desert. Newly-established tourist agencies have since begun to offer trips that follow in the footsteps of George Lucas – there are even some local road signs that point to *Star Wars* sites.

Remaining fragments of *Star Wars* film set

Star Wars robot

The Ksar

This centuries-old feature of the Tunisian landscape is a strongly fortified Berber village that is difficult to access. Originally the word *ksar* (or *ksour* in the plural) meant a fortified granary with *ghorfas* (rooms), which were placed cylindrically around an inner courtyard with a well-concealed entrance. Later on, *ghorfas* came to be used as dwelling places for local tribes. Ksar Ouled Soltane is considered to be Tunisia's best-preserved fortified village, and is still used by the Ouled Chehida tribe as a home and granary.

Berber fortified villages and granaries *have for centuries been part of the everyday life of people in southern Tunisia.*

Courtyards *were a feature of every* ksar. *Some larger* ksour *had more than one courtyard, linked with a special passage. Surrounded by* ghorfas, *courtyards were the main scene of Berber social life.*

Stairs *provided internal connections within a* ksar. *This was particularly important since* ghorfas *were usually two to four storeys high.*

The well in a *ksar's courtyard was surrounded by green plants.*

KSAR OULED SOLTANE

This is one of the most southerly *ksour* and has been restored to its original state. The *ksar* is still inhabited by a Berber tribe. The entrance to it is from the plateau, through a small courtyard. The *ksar* is at its best at sunset.

External walls *ensured the safety of the inhabitants and protected their granaries. The* ghorfas *facing the courtyard also provided a natural defence with no access via their back walls. For added security, an additional wall was sometimes added.*

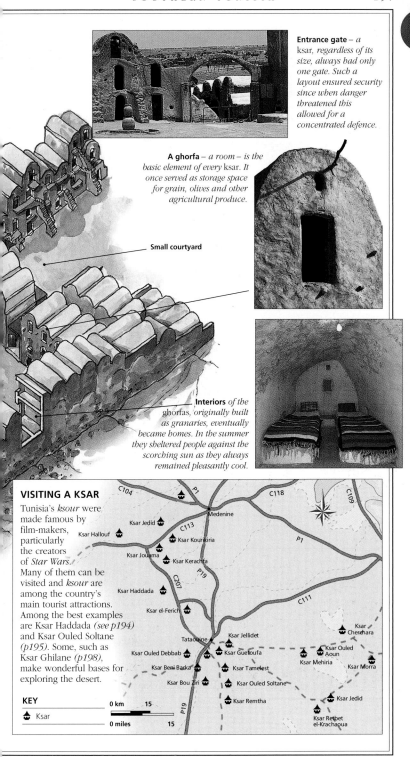

Entrance gate – *a ksar, regardless of its size, always had only one gate. Such a layout ensured security since when danger threatened this allowed for a concentrated defence.*

A ghorfa – *a room – is the basic element of every ksar. It once served as storage space for grain, olives and other agricultural produce.*

Small courtyard

Interiors *of the ghorfas, originally built as granaries, eventually became homes. In the summer they sheltered people against the scorching sun as they always remained pleasantly cool.*

VISITING A KSAR

Tunisia's *ksour* were made famous by film-makers, particularly the creators of *Star Wars*. Many of them can be visited and *ksour* are among the country's main tourist attractions. Among the best examples are Ksar Haddada *(see p194)* and Ksar Ouled Soltane *(p195)*. Some, such as Ksar Ghilane *(p198)*, make wonderful bases for exploring the desert.

C104
P1
C118
C109
Medenine
Ksar Jedid
C113
Ksar Hallouf
Ksar Kourikiria
P1
Ksar Jouama
Ksar Kerachfa
P19
Ksar Haddada
C207
C111
Ksar el-Ferich
Ksar
Cherchara
Ksar Jellidet
Tataouine
Ksar Ouled
Aoun
Ksar Ouled Debbab
Ksar Guetoufa
Ksar Mehiria
Ksar Beni Barka
Ksar Tamelest
Ksar Morra
Ksar Bou Ziri
Ksar Ouled Soltane

KEY

♣ Ksar

Ksar Remtha
Ksar Jedid

Ksar Retbet
el-Krachaoua

0 km 15

0 miles 15

P19

Camels resting at a desert watering place

Ksar Ghilane 🟡

Road map C6.

Surrounded by the dunes of the Great Eastern Erg, this small Saharan oasis is 147 km (91 miles) southeast of Douz and 100 km (62 miles) west of Chenini. The Romans built a frontier fort on this desolate spot and the ruins of a citadel can still be seen close by. The only way to get to Ksar Ghilane is by four-wheel-drive car or by camel. It is well worth stopping here for a few days to see the shifting reds, golds and yellows of the desert sand.

Accommodation is not a problem. Tourist camps with Bedouin tents are furnished with camp-beds and blankets. Some campsites have canteens offering a limited menu; some even have showers (though these are not always working). For more fastidious visitors there is a luxury campsite with air-conditioned Bedouin-style tents, complete with refrigerators and satellite TV. Some meals are served with genuine Bedouin bread – a large flat cake that is tossed into fire embers. After ten minutes it is turned over and left for a while longer. Bread baked this way is delicious.

One special attraction of Ksar Ghilane is bathing in the palm-fringed pool that is fed by the waters of a natural hot sulphur spring. In the winter, when the night temperature drops to just a few degrees above freezing (from over 20° C/68° F during the day),

bathing in the desert, amid swaying palm trees under starry skies, is a unique experience. The pool is surrounded by small cafés and restaurants where souvenirs can be purchased such as a desert rose or a warm woollen cloak with a hood – the traditional clothing of the desert people.

Market stall selling locally-made footwear in Douz

Douz 🟡

Road map C6. *123 km (76 miles) southwest of Tozeur.* 🏠 *7,000.* 🛈 *ONTT: Avenue des Martyrs, (75) 470 351.* 🎭 *International Festival of the Sahara (Nov–Dec).* **www**.festivaldouz.org.tn 🛒 *Thu.*

Nicknamed "the gateway to the Sahara", this small town lies on the edge of the Great Eastern Erg that stretches westwards, all the way to Morocco. The oasis, which is literally on the verge of the vast desert dunes, is a major springboard for exploring the Sahara. This is where the asphalt road ends and any further journey southwards can be made only by a four-wheel-drive vehicle (approximately seven hours to Ksar Ghilane) or on camelback (five days to Ksar Ghilane).

A good time to visit is during the International Festival of the Sahara, normally in November or December. The festival, which has been taking place for over 30 years, is an opportunity to witness the ceremonies that have marked the pace of life of the local nomadic tribes. These include wedding ceremonies, sheep-shearing, duels, hunting and camel races.

From Douz, groups can ride scooters over the dunes. Sweet dates can be bought here, as well as Berber jewellery and leather goods. The tourist zone starts a short way from the centre, on the edge of the dunes.

TUNISIAN CONDIMENTS

Harissa – a traditional Berber paste made with hot dried red pepper, garlic, spices and olive oil – appears on every Tunisian table and is eaten with almost everything. It is thought to strengthen the appetite and invigorate and disinfect the body – including the respiratory tract. Harissa is

sometimes served with small pieces of tuna and olives. Other herbs and spices used in Tunisian cuisine include fresh and dried mint leaves, coriander, aniseed, saffron, cumin, cinnamon and caraway.

Multicoloured herbs and spices

Caravans

In ancient times groups of merchants travelled along the Silk Road that linked China with the West. During the Middle Ages such caravans provided the only safe way of travelling across North Africa and were the sole means of transporting goods and merchants, troops and pilgrims. Tunisia lay at the crossroads of major caravan routes to the far corners of the African continent.

Warning sign: Attention! Camels!

Caravans also used mules and donkeys, but in the harsh desert environment the camel proved to be the most effective. As well as goods, caravans helped the spread of Islam, the scriptures and the written language. Many of the roads that were once travelled by caravans have now become highways. It is possible, however, to join an adventure caravan and travel over the desert dunes.

Camels *have been domesticated for thousands of years. They can drink 130 litres (28.6 gallons) of water at a time and go for up to two weeks without drinking again. Much of the camel's fat is in its hump, enabling it to lose heat more easily. The Arabic language has over one hundred terms to describe camels.*

Special contraptions *facilitated travel on camelback, while at the same time protecting the rider against sun and sand. The most difficult operations are mounting and dismounting. Riders must hold on tight to the horn of the saddle that is placed in front of the hump.*

Oases *and deep wells hidden among the desert sands ensured a caravan's survival. Any camel-driver is able to lead the caravan to an oasis or a well, without needing to refer to a map.*

Present-day caravans *still travel over the sands of the desert. Their nomadic owners are able to recognize their camels just from the camel's footprints.*

Visitors *may go for short trips or embark on camel treks lasting several days between oases and ksours, stopping at night in ghorfas or pitched Bedouin tents.*

Typical desert terrain near Gabès

The Sahara ❼

Road map B6, C6, D6.

The Sahara is the world's largest desert and occupies one third of the African continent (9,000,000 sq km/ 3,474,000 sq miles). It stretches from the west coast of Africa to the Red Sea. Its area lies within 11 African states, one of them being Tunisia, which controls only a small section of the desert. However, in terms of safety, transport facilities and tourist infrastructure this section of the Sahara is the most accessible. It is also the patch of desert that most often features in the movies.

The image of a desert as an ocean of sand, stretching off to the horizon, was created by fiction writers and film-makers such as Bernardo Bertolucci in *The Sheltering Sky*. In reality the desert is more often than not a stony plain – grey and dull, or an arid land criss-crossed with mountain ranges that are punctuated by mountain oases such as Chebika, Tamerza and Midès.

The Tunisian section of the Sahara features all three main types of desert: the rocky *hamada*; the pebbly *serir* and the sandy *erg*. The latter, most frequently associated with the image of the Sahara portrayed in films and literature, lies at the eastern end of the Great Eastern Erg,

A palm-shaded oasis in the middle of the desert

which runs all the way from Morocco. It starts south of Douz and its most striking sand dunes can be seen in the vicinity of Ksar Ghilane. In the north they are preceded by vast steppes occasionally interspersed with sand dunes which are bordered by vast, dry salt lakes. The causeway that crosses the largest of these – Chott el-Jerid – is the spot where mirages are most likely to occur.

Wildlife is scarce in the desert. Wild camels are rarely encountered in Tunisia's arid areas. The ones that are seen are usually part of someone's herd. The North African fox, its ears pointing up like radar aerials, can now be seen only in zoos. At times a gazelle can be spotted. There is no shortage of desert lizards, poisonous adders and scorpions. Here and there, desert areas feature clumps of esparto grass, which is used to make paper and mats.

The driest areas of the Sahara have no more than 25 mm (0.985 inches) of annual rainfall. The oases are surrounded by a sea of sand. Every scrap of greenery, every well or pasture, once belonged to a clan or a tribe and was cherished, cared for and fought over. Strangers were perceived as a threat and as competition. Even the *sa'alik* – the knight errant of the desert, the intractable outcast of various tribes – would join in groups in order to survive. An expulsion from a community meant death amid the sands. Tribal awareness, although not as

---

SAFETY IN THE SAHARA

The rule is never travel alone in the desert, even when using a four-wheel-drive jeep. There must be at least two cars, preferably driven by Tunisian drivers. Any excursion made by car or on camelback must always be reported to the National Guard and may only be made with their permission (travel agents can usually arrange these formalities). Excursions made on foot also have to be reported and are best made with a guide. It is essential to take sunscreen products. Also useful are wraparound sunglasses, a down-filled sleeping bag, a groundsheet, a pair of loose trousers, a large cotton headscarf that can cover the entire head and neck from sun and wind, and as much water as you can carry. High-sided shoes will provide protection against scorpions.

---

vital as in the old days, is still strong. The ties of blood protected people and gave them a feeling of security. Several families descending from a common ancestor formed a clan. A group of related clans formed a *kabila* – a tribe. A tribe used to surround the home of their chieftain with a circle of tents – the *dawwar* – creating something like a small, sovereign autonomous state.

Family, tribes and the association of tribes formed the bedrock of Bedouin society. Warrior-sons and guards led the caravans, procured domestic animals and, in the course of plundering raids, defended the honour of their clans and took women captives. Their bravery and courage ensured the clan's safety and prosperity. Women were regarded as the property of their families. They were expected to be obedient and bear the maximum possible number of sons. Their situation changed for the better with the arrival of Islam, for although Mohammed preserved the form of marriage that left a woman in the power of her husband, he nevertheless set

Camel train travelling across the desert

Sand dunes in the Sahara

Horses – a frequent sight on the edges of the Sahara

out a number of rules aimed at protecting women. He made the woman the owner of her own dowry and regulated the legal position of orphans, of women abandoned by their husbands and of widows, granting to all of them rights to at least some portion of the estate.

Time seems to flow very slowly in the desert. Sand shifts from one dune to another. Colours also shift: white, occasionally yellow and golden-red mounds move along, changing their shape and position.

Though beautiful, the desert can be extremely treacherous. Sand immobilizes wheels on vehicle and hinders travellers' legs, while its minute grains find their way into camera lenses, even without a sandstorm. At the same time the sand is so velvety that it can be rubbed against the cheek without causing a scratch.

Tozeur, Nefta and Jerba all represent fairly convenient starting points for forays into the Sahara, but to truly make the most of your desert adventure, the best places to start are Douz, Zaafrane and Ksar Ghilane. Here, the sense of wonder will not be limited to just sleeping in Bedouin tents, the proximity of the desert or the taste of Bedouin bread baked in the hot sand – your trip will also include the sight of quirky cafés built of old metal cans or palms, appearing unexpectedly over dune tops.

DIRECTORY

TRIPS TO THE SAHARA FROM DOUZ

Douz Voyages
Place de l'Indépendance, Douz.
Tel (75) 470 178/179.
Fax (75) 470 315.
www.douzvoyages.chez.com

Ghilane Travel Services
Avenue Taieb Mehiri 38, Douz.
Tel (75) 470 692.
Fax (75) 470 682.
@ gts@planet.tn

Horizons Deserts Voyages
Rue el-Hanni 9, Douz.
Tel (75) 471 688/788.
Fax (75) 471 688.
@ h.deserts@planet.tn
www.horizons-deserts.com

Libre Espace Voyages
Avenue Mohamed, Marzougi, Douz.
Tel (75) 470 620.
Fax (75) 470 622.
@ contact@libre-espace-voyages.com
www.libre-espace-voyages.com

Mrazig Voyages
Avenue 7 Novembre, BP 126, Douz.
Tel (75) 470 255.
Fax (75) 470 515.

Desert Oases

The oasis was once a haven for caravans and lost travellers and was used by tribes who lived in the desert. Even today, oases are a vital lifeline for people who must survive in extreme conditions. Desert oases have grown up around natural springs, ground water and wells. The typical desert oasis consists of cultivated plots of land shaded by palms and screened with palm-frond fences. Some oases, such as Gabès and Douz, have grown into large towns.

Berber tents, *put up specially for visitors, are a popular way to experience life in the desert oases. Some luxury tents are even air-conditioned.*

A sophisticated irrigation system *is indispensable to the life of an oasis. It must ensure an even distribution of water. In large oases, such as Nefta and Tozeur, water must be collected from hundreds of sources.*

The date harvest *in Tunisia is one of the biggest in the world. Dates are both sweet and nutritious and are an essential part of the staple diet of the oasis's inhabitants. Dates and either milk or water mark the end of the Ramadan fast.*

Arable fields under palm trees *are possible as a result of irrigation. Crops that can be cultivated include carrots and semolina, which is used to make couscous.*

THE OASIS

The modern oasis exists purely thanks to human intervention. Irrigation systems make the most of natural water sources, making it possible not only to water the camels, but also to grow plants.

Shaft craters collect valuable rainwater.

Camels *that live in Tunisia have only one hump. The oases provide them with places of rest and shade, where they can also top up their stores of water.*

Underground springs also supply the oasis with water.

The pathways *that criss-cross the oasis are not only used for transport, but also mark out the watered plots. The locals travel around on foot, on camelback or on donkeys.*

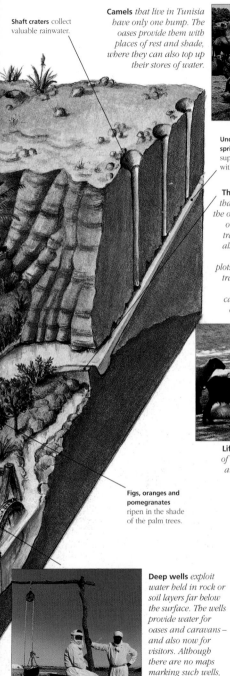

Figs, oranges and pomegranates ripen in the shade of the palm trees.

Life in an oasis *revolves around the tending of crops and animals (camels, horses, sheep and goats). The irrigation systems are vital and require constant attention.*

Deep wells *exploit water held in rock or soil layers far below the surface. The wells provide water for oases and caravans – and also now for visitors. Although there are no maps marking such wells, every good camel driver knows their locations by heart.*

Natural pools, *fed by deep underground springs and artificial reservoirs, provide oases with a constant supply of water for bathing.*

Douz to Tozeur ❽

This is one of the most interesting routes in Tunisia and crosses the Chott el-Jerid – a vast, glittering salt lake that stretches as far as the eye can see. The route forms an important section of a longer tourist trail that leads from Tozeur (via Matmata) to Jerba. Until the mid-19th century it was used to transport slaves to the vast slave market in Kebili. The road is remarkably scenic, and it is worth allocating extra time for the journey.

Chott el-Jerid ⑦
The contours of salt lakes as drawn on most maps correspond with the winter rains season. The actual sight seen by visitors is usually only the dry bottom of the lake.

TAMERZA

GAFSA

P16

P3

Chott el-Gharsa

El-Mahassen

El-Hamma du Jerid

P16

Causeway ⑨
This is where desert mirages are most often seen in Tunisia. Some people imagine they see passing caravans of camels, or even a railway train.

Chott el-Fejej ⑧
This is a natural offshoot of the Chott el-Jerid, and forms a narrow corridor running to the desert oasis of El-Hamma, near the shore of the Gulf of Gabès.

P3

NEFTA

Degache ⑩
Oases such as Degache are inhabited by descendants of ancient nomadic tribes who still travel with their herds of camels, sheep and goats in search of fresh pastures. Life in this arid land is only possible thanks to the existence of oases.

DESERT ROSE

This is the most famous and least expensive souvenir of a visit to southern Tunisia. Sometimes artificially coloured (in shades of light green, blue and red) its beauty nevertheless resides in its natural colour – grey bordering on brown. It is usually found under several metres of sand. In chemical terms this is made of gypsum (crystals of calcium sulphate) that crystallizes from underground water and takes on the form of an open rose flower.

Desert rose – a symbol of the Sahara

Tozeur ⑪
Tunisia's "Hollywood" is the town of poets and of unusual yellow brick architecture. It is also a good base for trips to the mountain oases, to Nefta and to the dunes of the Great Eastern Erg.

◁ Camel train making its way across the desert

Bechri ⑥
This 64-km (40-mile) long causeway crosses the Chott el-Jerid. It links Bechri (near Kebili) with Kriz (near Tozeur).

Kebili ⑤
Kebili is the main market town of the Nefzaoua oases (market day is Tuesday). It is an important oasis along a former caravan route.

TIPS FOR DRIVERS

Length: 161 km (100 miles).
Stopping-off points: Hotels can be found in Douz, Tozeur, Nefta and Bechri. A cup of coffee and a light meal are available anywhere, even on the causeway.

Blidet ④
This hill surrounded by palm groves, on which the village stands, is one of the better places from which visitors can admire the panoramic view of the Chott el-Jerid.

El-Faouar ③
El-Faouar – an oasis on the southern shore of the Chott el-Jerid – gives a foretaste of the great adventure.

Zaafrane ②
Along with nearby Douz and Ksar Ghilane, Zaafrane is a major tourist centre from where classic camelback expeditions to the desert can be embarked upon.

Douz ①
Douz is the main springboard for desert trips. Any further journey south requires the use of a four-wheel-drive vehicle. Douz is also the venue for the International Festival of the Sahara.

KEY

- ▬ Suggested route
- ▬ Scenic route
- = Other road
- ☀ Viewpoint

Chott el-Jerid ⑨

Road map B5.

One of Tunisia's several salt lakes, Chott el-Jerid was created by tectonic movements of the earth's crust some 1.5 million years ago. It is the largest of the North African salt lakes (51,280 sq km/19,794 sq miles) and lies between the Gulf of Gabès and the Algerian border. For most of the year it is dry, with only a thin layer of water remaining here and there, becoming an intriguing desert "carpet" that consists of minute salt crystals shimmering with blue, white and pale-green hues. The view of the lake at sunset is unforgettable. Mirages are a common occurrence.

The lake can be crossed on a 64-km (40-mile) long causeway that is open all year round. The route links Kriz (near Tozeur), with Bechri (near Kebili). It is best not to stray away from the road, as the lake bed in this area may be dangerous.

Halfway along the causeway there is a handful of small cafés, built of reed, where souvenirs such as amethyst and desert rose stones (*see p206*) can be bought. These can also provide toilet facilities. A trip on the causeway is one of the main tourist attractions along the Douz-Tozeur route.

Museum courtyard in Tozeur

Tozeur ⑩

Road map B5. 🏠 21,000. ℹ️ Abu-al Qasim Shabbi, (76) 454 503. 🚪 Tue, Sun. 🎫 Festival of the Oases (Nov–Dec). **www**.planet-oasis.com

Tozeur is a major town and tourist centre, and it has one of the country's most beautiful oases containing a vast palm grove. There are thousands and thousands of palm trees here, as well as fig trees, pomegranate trees, and banana groves spread over 10 km (6 miles). The area is fed by natural springs that produce millions of litres of water a day. The town is also known for growing the best dates in Tunisia. They are translucent, sweet and juicy; nearby Nefta is also famous for them.

Tozeur house decoration

The oldest part of town is Ouled el-Hadef, which dates from the 14th century and has a distinctive high wall made of handmade bricks. The yellow stones of Ouled el-Hadef's houses are arranged so that they form Koranic verses and floral motifs.

On the outskirts of Tozeur is a private museum, **Dar Cheraït**, which is devoted to southern Tunisia's

history and everyday life. A separate section of the museum transports visitors to the realm of the *Thousand and One Nights*. This collection of anonymous tales written over several centuries includes traces of Indian, Persian, Egyptian, Greek, Mesopotamian and Arab influences. In the Arabian Nights grotto visitors can meet, among others, Ali Baba, Sinbad the Sailor and Scheherazade. The folk tales are accompanied by descriptions of everyday life.

A separate **museum** on Rue de Kairouan is devoted to local traditions and includes costumes used in circumcision ceremonies and a collection of door knockers that produce a variety of sounds (making it possible to identify the caller).

Tozeur also has a **botanical garden** and a **zoo**. The latter provides a rare chance to see some desert wildlife.

Planet Oasis is a vast cultural centre near Tozeur. Its huge stage, set on the Saharan sand, has state-of-the-art laser effects to accompany musical shows and other entertainment. The centre also claims "the largest Berber tent in the world".

🏛 **Dar Cheraït**
Rue Touristique. ⏱ 8am–midnight.
Tel (76) 454 888.

🏛 **Museum of Popular Arts and Traditions**
Rue de Kairouan. ⏱ 8am–noon & 3–5pm

Salt on the edge of Chott el-Jerid

For hotels and restaurants in this region see pp261–3 and pp285–7

Nefta

Road map A5. 23 km (14 miles) southwest of Tozeur. 🚶 18,000.
ℹ️ *ONTT: Avenue Bourguiba, (76) 454 088.* 🎪 *Festival of the Dates (Nov–Dec).* 🛒 *Thu.*

The oasis town of Nefta is Tunisia's second holiest site after Kairouan. It is situated on the shores of the Chott el-Jerid, near Tozeur. During the Roman occupation it was known as Aggasel Nepte; in the 16th century it became a centre of Sufism *(see below)*. At that time Nefta had 100 mosques, dozens of Islamic schools and a *zaouia*. Today, it is frequently visited by film-makers who come for the unique scenery. It is worth stopping here, even if only for one night, to make a trip in a horse and cart around the entire oasis or to stroll along the narrow alleys of Ouled ech-Cherif.

Ouled ech-Cherif is the oldest part of Nefta and lies in the western portion of the town. There are some interesting streets and alleys to be explored here and many of the houses repay a second glance. The doors and window shutters have been built in a wide range of shapes and colours and have intricate fixtures and door handles. The door handles are often in the shape of the Hand of Fatima.

The town wakes up after siesta, two hours before sunset. At the foot of the ancient mosques young boys play football, vendors open their shops and old men sit on street benches. With a bit of luck it may be possible to strike up an acquaintance with a local, get invited to a typical Arab house and in its courtyard be treated to fresh dates and camel milk. The row of restored mosques towering over La Corbeille – a deep, palm-filled gulley – is well worth a photograph. The best views are to be had from the **Café de la Corbeille**.

In the heart of Nefta's oasis is the **mausoleum of Sidi Bou Ali**, a Moroccan-born 13th-century mystic who founded one of the earliest Sufi brotherhoods. It was his fame that turned Nefta into a major spiritual centre of the Islamic world. The reverence which many Muslims pay to Sidi Bou Ali is still strong today and his mystical powers of healing, passed on to his successors, continue to attract people to Nefta. The mausoleum is not open to non-Muslims.

The date plantations in the oasis belong to many private owners. Some will invite visitors (for a small fee) to taste the drinks made of palm juice, or try a cigar wrapped in palm leaves. Here, visitors can also find one of the many oasis springs or go for a stroll along the shady country lane that crosses the entire valley.

Palm trees in La Corbeille gulley in Nefta

SUFISM

Sufism is a branch of Islam that originated in the Middle East in the late 8th to early 9th century and spread to Central Asia and India. Followers of Sufism attempt to arrive at the Ultimate Truth through the "shedding of the veil" – discarding the shackles of everyday reason and senses that constrain us. Some of these devotional practices, such as walking on hot coals, have led to Sufis being distrusted by other Muslims.

Whirling dervishes: the best-known followers of Sufism

Mosques towering over the oasis in Nefta

Chebika – a mountain oasis shaded by palm trees

Chebika ⑫

Road map A5. 60 km (37 miles)
northwest of Tozeur; 5 km (3 miles)
south of Tamerza. 🏠 35,900.

This is one of the three
best-known Tunisian
mountain oases (along with
Tamerza and Midès). All
three villages are situated
near Tozeur, close to the
border with Algeria. As
recently as the 19th century
they were major stopping-off
points along one of the two
main caravan routes that
linked the east and west
coasts of the African
continent. During the years of
the Roman Empire they were
used as military forts where
the legionnaires, making use
of high-rise sentry posts,
communicated with each
other using mirrors.

For centuries the villages
produced only what they
needed to feed their
population. This balance was
upset when phosphate
deposits were discovered
nearby and many people left
their homes to work in the
mines. This also brought
about changes in the local
customs and traditions as
agricultural production
gradually diminished. Even
greater changes were caused
by the onset of mass tourism.
Today, visitors travel in large
numbers to this area, arriving
by jeep for a day trip from
Tozeur. This is also the
destination for those wishing
to take the Lézard Rouge
train route *(see p216).*

Chebika is a small village,
built of stone and clay and

clinging to the side of a
mountain. It was probably
built on the site of an earlier
Roman outpost, Ad
Speculum. Following severe
flooding in 1969, the old
village was abandoned. Now
the village layout is almost
the same as that of nearby
Tamerza. Small side streets
branch off the main road that
leads to the market. The main
point of interest in Chebika is
its picturesque spring
featuring a small palm grove
and a waterfall, which can be
found a little way beyond the
village. The spring is fed by a
series of small underground
mountain streams (and the
network of underground
canals that feed the wells).
This supply of water means
that the otherwise barren land

can produce apricots,
peaches, pomegranates, citrus
fruit, bananas and olives.
Tobacco is grown in the
shade of the palm trees.

According to a Tunisian
proverb, the ultimate ruler
here is the rain, and in day-
to-day life water is more
precious than petrol. The
reason the oasis flourishes is
its sophisticated irrigation
system. To ensure local
harmony, the system must
maintain an even distribution
of water to all plots. To meet
this need, Chebika once had
a curious "hourglass room" (it
can still be seen behind the
village's only public toilet). It
contains a simple timer,
consisting of two large jugs
with handles, painted yellow
with a green stripe (typical of
Berber style). The jugs were
hung from a rope and the
water poured from one jug
into the other. Based on the
time it took for the lower jug
to fill, an attendant would
open and close appropriate
gates within the irrigation
system, sending water to
each arable plot in turn.

Tamerza ⑬

Road map A5. 65 km (40 miles)
northwest of Tozeur. 🏠 1,500.
🎭 *Festival of the Mountain
Oases (Mar).*

Known as the
"hanging balcony
overlooking the
Sahara Desert",
Tamerza (sometimes
spelt "Tameghza") is
the largest of the
mountain oases and
is the only one that
has a public transport
link with the outside
world (buses leave
daily for Redeyef,
Touzeur and Tunis).
It is renowned not
only for its scenic
views but also for the
most beautifully
situated hotels in
Tunisia. The four-star
Tamerza Palace
towers majestically
over a large gorge (a
dry river bed), facing
the white houses and
domes of the old

Tamerza's waterfall

town standing on the opposite side. Guest hotels and terraces look out onto magnificent scenery made famous by the film *The English Patient*. Tamerza, like Chebika, was abandoned following floods in 1969. The old village is now falling into ruin but maintains the general layout of an oasis, including the main road running from east to west and a labyrinth of narrow alleys that branch off it, climbing upwards.

Several marabouts (Islamic mausoleums) are still maintained in the abandoned village. The most interesting of these is the **mausoleum of Sidi Tuati**, which stands out clearly amid the devastated houses. It contains the holy man's tomb and rooms for pilgrims.

The present sanctuary is supposed to have been formerly occupied by a church. This claim was made by, among others, the medieval Arab traveller and author Tidjani. His belief may be supported by the presence of Christian churches which were active in the Jerid region in the 14th century. Some of these inspired the style of several mosques built in this area, which clearly display the influence of an 18th-century Italian style. Nevertheless the building materials are mainly local, including palm tree wood, typical of the Jerid region.

Another interesting sight in Tamerza is the pointed dome of the prayer hall belonging to the **mausoleum of Sidi Dar ben Dhahara**. The

Steep walls of the gorge surrounding Midès

mihrab (niche indicating the direction of prayer) of this sanctuary has been incorrectly placed and does not point accurately towards Mecca, a rare thing in Islamic art.

The abandoned houses and ruins of old Tamerza are increasingly visited by hikers and photographers. They are most impressive when the town becomes illuminated by the light of the setting sun.

New Tamerza has been built just above a waterfall. Close to its top stands the Hotel des Cascades, which is popular with globetrotters. Another waterfall can be seen a short way out of town on the road to Chebika.

Midès

Road map A4.

Midès is the smallest mountain oasis in this area and is situated just a short walk from the Algerian border. The village is perched on the edge of a deep gorge (it flanks it on three sides). The gorge's red-soil floor is overgrown with lush green palm trees. The wavy vertical walls of the gorge present a particularly impressive sight. As with Tamerza and Chebika, the production of pomegranates, citrus fruit and dates plays an important role in the village economy.

Close to the modern settlement is an abandoned **Berber village**. The deserted houses can be seen on the other side of the gorge. Next to the village is a café and stalls selling souvenirs, such as desert roses and semi-precious stones, as well as cold drinks and mint tea, indicating that tourism is becoming increasingly important to the economy here.

The area around Midès was used as a location for the aircraft crash scenes involving the main character in the film *The English Patient* (1996).

The ruins of old Tamerza

CENTRAL TUNISIA

*T*he central region of the country is dominated by vast mountainous areas of the Tell and Saharan Atlas ranges. Its extraordinary scenery includes the flat-topped Jugurtha's Table and the green hills of Jebel Zaghouan. Kairouan, one of Islam's four holiest cities, is well worth exploring, as are the Roman remains at Dougga, Sbeïtla and Thuburbo Majus.

The hills of Jebel Zaghouan and Jebel Chambi are covered in dense forest dominated by Aleppo pine. The oases of Gafsa grow date palms, and the fertile areas around Kasserine are the country's second major bread-basket, after the Medjerda Valley. Little grows in the harsher parts of the interior apart from thick clumps of esparto grass, which is used for making paper and household items such as baskets.

Central Tunisia has four major national parks including Chambi, where hyena, gazelle and a variety of birds can be seen as well as many species of plant.

Central Tunisia's watercourses often dry out, but during the rainy season they rapidly fill with water. Numerous dams are built to prevent flooding and to stop the waters from rising too rapidly. These also preserve much-needed fresh water. Temperatures in this part of the country are higher than in the Sahel.

Kairouan is the largest town of the central region. It has the country's most famous mosque and is also a centre for carpet making. Kairouan is followed by Le Kef, 45 km (28 miles) east of the Algerian border, which has always been an important political centre. During World War II it was the seat of government in areas liberated from German occupation.

Central Tunisia has some of the country's most important historic sites where ancient temples, theatres and baths from the period of the Roman Empire can be explored.

Berber women walking near Sbeïtla

◁ **Interior of the Great Mosque in Kairouan**

Exploring Central Tunisia

Kairouan is Central Tunisia's largest town and, along with Mecca, Medina and Jerusalem, one of Islam's four holy cities. Kairouan's original Great Mosque was the first of its kind to be built in North Africa. The fortress town of Le Kef, to the south, includes a mighty kasbah and the sanctuary of Sidi Bou Makhlouf. Situated towards the Algerian border are some magnificent rock formations, including an extraordinary mountain known as Jugurtha's Table. The Roman sites in this region are some of the most impressive in Tunisia. Dougga, for instance, is North Africa's best-preserved Roman town, while the ruins at Sbeïtla include ancient temples, baths and a theatre built in the 3rd century AD.

Interior of the mosque of Sidi Sahab in Kairouan

SEE ALSO

SIGHTS AT A GLANCE

0 km   25

0 miles   25

GETTING THERE

The central region of Tunisia is best explored in a hired car. A kind of long-distance transport that's popular with many Tunisians are *louages* (large shared taxis). These run more frequently than buses but are often driven at high speeds and can be uncomfortable. *Louages* marked by a yellow stripe are licensed to travel only within the local district; those marked by red stripe are allowed to cross the district boundaries. The closest airport for Central Tunisia is Sfax, which is about 135 km (85 miles) southeast of Kairouan. A train service runs between Tunis, Gafsa and Metlaoui and frequent bus services run between Tunis, Sousse and Gafsa, with some services to Sbeïtla, Tozeur, Medenine and Gabès.

KEY

- Major road
- Other road
- -- Track
- Scenic road
- Railway
- International border
- Regional border
- Salt lake

Ruins of the Temple of Caelestis, on the edge of Dougga

Gafsa ❶

Road map B4. 93 km (58 miles)
from Tozeur. 🏠 *61,000*. 🚍 🚃
🚉 *ONTT: Place des Piscines
Romaines, (76) 221 664.* 🛍 *Tue.*

Built round a large oasis
on the border between the
mountain and the desert,
Gafsa is the main transport
hub for the region. It isn't the
most inspiring of Tunisia's
towns but the surrounding
area has vineyards, olive
plantations and some striking
scenery. Gafsa itself has a
handful of attractions
including restored palaces
and some baths left behind by
the Romans.

Gafsa has a long history. In
the 2nd century BC this was a
settlement belonging to the
Kingdom of Numidia.
Destroyed in 106 BC by the
Roman commander Marius, it
was subsequently rebuilt and
turned into a garrison. Under
the Emperor Trajan it acquired
the status of a colony and
became an important Roman
town. It was destroyed in 680
in the course of an Arab raid
but rebuilt by the Hafsids in
the 15th century.

Situated at the southwest
end of Avenue Habib
Bourguiba are the **Roman
Pools** (Piscines Romaines).
These are two 4-m (13-ft)

deep reservoirs,
linked by a tunnel
and filled with water
from a warm spring.
Though it is not
encouraged, the
youth of Gafsa can
often be seen diving
and swimming in the
water. Nearby is a
small museum, which
has some mosaics
from Sousse.

The minaret
attached to the Great
Mosque dominates
Gafsa's skyline. The
mosque probably
dates from the
Aghlabid dynasty
(9th–10th centuries),
although a large
section of the
complex was not
added until the 14th
century. The prayer
hall is decorated with
blue ceramic tiles.

At the heart of Gafsa is Habib
Bourguiba square, situated in
the eastern part of the town. It
contains a variety of shops,
government offices and a
pleasant small park.

When exploring the medina,
it is worth stepping into **Dar
Loungo**, a traditional 17th-
century house, and **Dar el-
Shariff**, which was built by a
wealthy 18th-century landlord,
Haj Osman el-Shariff.

The Roman Pools in Gafsa

> 🏛 **Dar Loungo**
> Adjacent to the National Museum of
> Gafsa. ⬜ *8:30am–noon & 3–6pm
> Tue–Sun.* ⬛ *Mon.*
>
> 🏛 **Dar el-Shariff**
> Rue Mohammad Khodouma.
> ⬜ *Oct–May: 8am–noon & 3–5pm;
> Jun–Sep: 8am–1pm.*

Metlaoui ❷

Road map B5. 42 km (26 miles)
southwest of Gafsa. 🏠 *43,500* 🚍 🚃

Metlaoui is Tunisia's main
centre of phosphate mining.
It was built by the French at
the end of the 19th century
and lies at the foot of the
Tell Atlas. The phosphate
deposits were discovered in
1886 by Philippe Thomas, a
veterinary surgeon in the
French army and amateur
palaeontologist. In 1896 a
mining licence was granted.

The main reason to come to
Metlaoui is to climb aboard
the **Lézard Rouge**, a narrow-
gauge railway line, which was
opened in 1899 by the Bey of
Tunis. The train runs through
the 15-km (9-mile) long Seldja
Gorge and takes one and a
half hours for the round trip.
The carriages are early 20th
century and are fitted with
red leather seats. Tickets can
be obtained from Metlaoui's
main train station.

Lézard Rouge in the Seldja Gorge, near Metlaoui

For hotels and restaurants in this region see pp263–5 and pp287–9

Sened village, scenically located in a valley

Sened ❸

Road map C4.

The easiest way of getting to Sened is from the modern Sened Gare hamlet, which once had a railway station. The village of Sened is tucked away among the hills of Jebel Biada (1,163 m/3,816 ft above sea level). Sened's houses are unusual in that they are built from stone with gypsum mortar – Berber houses are usually built with clay. After they have been harvested, red peppers are sometimes laid out to dry on flat roofs. This area has been inhabited for thousands of years and nearby caves were once the dwellings of prehistoric humans.

Environs

Some 30 km (19 miles) to the southwest of Sened and 18 km (11 miles) southeast of Gafsa is **El-Guettar**, a busy oasis town on the road from Gafsa

to Gabès. A further 7 km (4 miles) to the southeast from Sened is the beautiful oasis of **Lalla**. During the 1880s the nomads of this region put up fierce resistance to the French army before escaping to the Turkish territory of Libya. It was several years before the nomads returned. As well as refreshments, the café just beyond the river provides a good view of the oasis.

Sidi Bouzid ❹

Road map C4. 🏘 112,000

In Sidi Bouzid – a small district capital town – life passes slowly. Having a glass of mint tea, a *chicha* (hookah), or a game of cards are all long-drawn out activities. Much time is spent just talking. This is not surprising, since in the summer the scorching sun can raise the temperature to 45° C (113° F).

The centre of town has several modern buildings, which include offices, shops, a post office and a hotel. Most of the town buildings are single-storey, modest houses with solid doors.

Sidi Bouzid and the surrounding area played an important role during World War II. In February 1943 the Afrika Korps, commanded by Field Marshal Rommel, clashed with the American 1st Armoured Division and elements of the British First Army, which led to heavy Allied losses.

South of Sidi Bouzid, on the way to Gafsa, there are some old Berber settlements spread along the mountain range that runs from Gafsa to Sfax. Situated away from well-trodden paths, this region has some excellent hiking areas. Many of the villages are semi-deserted and can be reached only on foot or in a four-wheel-drive car.

THE DAKAR RALLY

In 1977 a French motorcyclist, Thierry Sabine, was taking part in the Abidjan-Nice motorcycle rally and lost his way. After wandering about for several days amid the sands of the Libyan Desert, he was miraculously found at the last moment. Thierry Sabine returned to France and decided to organize a rally that would provide its participants with a chance to challenge the forces of nature and their own limitations. He achieved his aim on 26 December the same year when drivers competing in the first staging of the event set off from Paris heading for Dakar. The rally was open to anyone who had a vehicle able to travel over the sands. The race still takes place and anybody who has suitable equipment may take part.

Racing in the Dakar Rally

Sbeïtla ❺

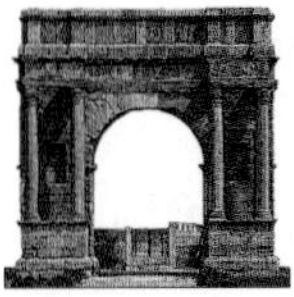

Arch of Diocletian, to the south of town

Sbeïtla is a modern town 30 km (19 miles) east of Kasserine and is fringed with olive groves and arable fields. Close by is the site of the Roman town of Sufetula. Initially Sufetula had the status of a municipium (independent city) and later became a Roman colony. In the 3rd century Christians settled here; most of the local churches date from that period. The ruins are particularly well preserved and include baths, a stunning forum and a capitol containing temples to Juno, Jupiter and Minerva.

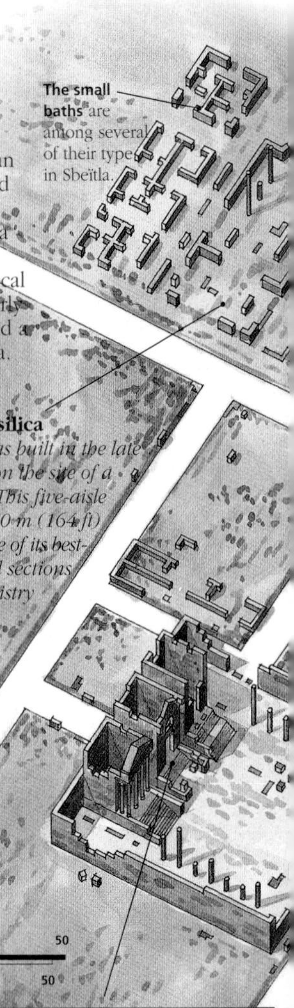
0 m
50
0 yards
50

The small baths are among several of their type in Sbeïtla.

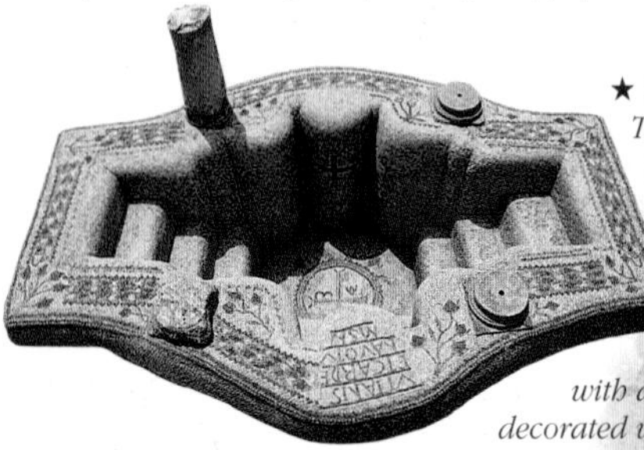

★ St Vitalis Basilica

The church was built in the late 5th century on the site of a large villa. This five-aisle edifice is 50 m (164 ft) wide. One of its best-preserved sections is the baptistry with an oval basin decorated with mosaics.

STAR SIGHTS
★ Capitol
★ Entrance to Forum
★ St Vitalis Basilica

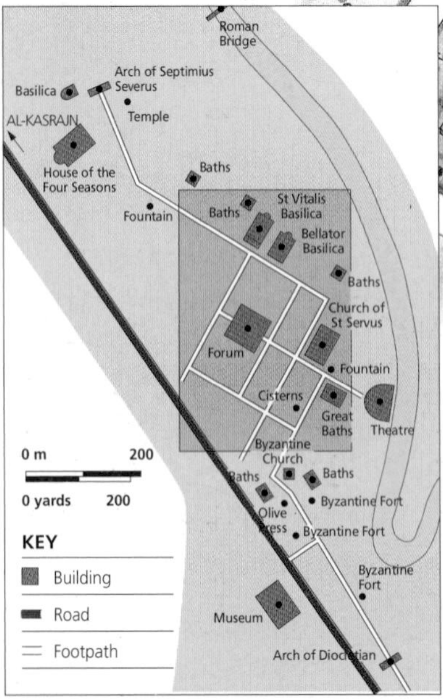
Roman Bridge
Arch of Septimius Severus
Basilica
Temple
AL-KASRAJN
House of the Four Seasons
Baths
Fountain
Baths
St Vitalis Basilica
Bellator Basilica
Baths
Church of St Servus
Forum
Fountain
Cisterns
Great Baths
Theatre
Byzantine Church
Baths
Baths
Byzantine Fort
Olive Press
Byzantine Fort
Byzantine Fort
Museum
Arch of Diocletian
0 m
200
0 yards
200
KEY
Building
Road
Footpath

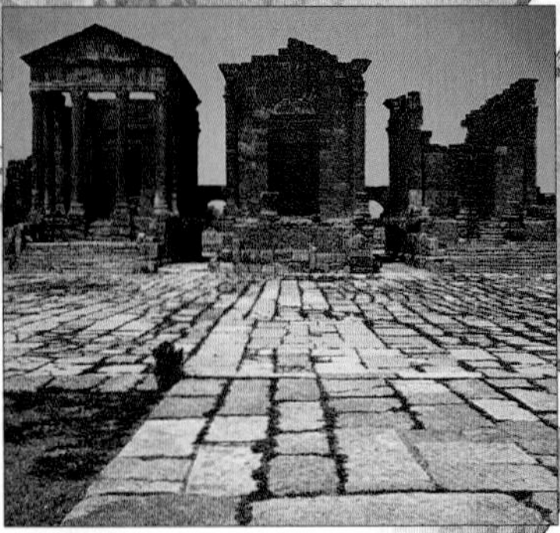

★ Capitol

The northwestern corner of the forum is occupied by the capitol consisting of three temples dedicated to Juno, Jupiter and Minerva. The forecourt of Jupiter's temple once had a speaker's podium (rostrum).

For hotels and restaurants in this region see pp263–5 and pp287–9

Bellator Basilica
The church was built in the early 4th century AD on the foundations of a Roman temple. Its name comes from an inscription found on the site.

VISITORS' CHECKLIST

Road map B3, B4. Sbeïtla–Kasserine road. Rue du 2 Mars. **Ruins and museum:** *Tel* (77) 465 813. ☐ 7am–7pm daily (summer); 8:30am–5:30pm (winter).

★ Entrance to Forum
The forum is among the best-preserved in North Africa. The entrance to it was through the Arch of Antoninus Pius (AD 139) and led onto a paved area. During the Byzantine era it was surrounded by a 4-m (13-ft) high wall.

Church of St Servus
Recognizable by its four surviving pillars, this church was erected on the site of a pagan temple. It is likely that this was the cathedral of the Donatists who were active in the early 4th century (see p50). To the south are the Great Baths and an amphitheatre.

The cistern
was a tank intended for storing water, which would have fed the baths.

Vendors' Stalls
The remains of market stalls can be seen around the forum. Here, a variety of goods was sold, but mainly oil (the remains of an olive oil press are near to the fort). Equally well-preserved are pavement slabs that lead to the stalls.

The main square at the centre of Kasserine

Kasserine ❻

Road map B3. 120 km (75 miles) south of Le Kef. 🚌 🚍 *40,000.* 🚉 *Tue.*

Kasserine lies on the central Tunisian upland, on the banks of the Oued el-Habeb. This is a major industrial town and transport hub. Since 1963 the town has produced cellulose and paper made from the local esparto grass. Kasserine was established by the Romans in the 2nd century

BATTLE OF KASSERINE

During World War II, on 14 February 1943, the German 21st and 10th Panzer divisions, supported by an air task force, broke through American positions at Kasserine, and advanced towards the Algerian border. US troops bore the brunt of the onslaught and it took a week of hard fighting and the arrival of British reinforcements to halt what proved to be one of the last German offensives in North Africa.

British tank in Kasserine

AD, and named Cillium. Following the fall of the Roman Empire it lost its status and remained an insignificant centre for local villages until it regained some of its lustre during the period of the French Protectorate. The French built a railway line and expanded the town. In its eastern section they erected a new colonial town, cut across by the long main street (Avenue Habib Bourguiba). Even today this area has most of the town's administrative buildings. It also contains the railway station (goods trains only), bus station and numerous shops. Ancient monuments, including a large mausoleum, are found on the other side of town (towards Gafsa).

A short way out of Kasserine, next to the Oued Derb, is the well-preserved **Mausoleum of the Flavii**. The walls of this triple-tiered monument are covered with a poetic inscription consisting of 110 lines; the middle section has Corinthian pilasters; above this is a niche that once housed a statue of Flavius. The whole structure was once covered with a triangular roof. In the western part of Kasserine, on the edge of the dry river bed, there is another mausoleum, which is now in ruins.

South of the town, to the left of the road leading to Gafsa, are the ruins of **Roman Cillium**, standing on top of a hill. Only a small section of the site has been unearthed. Its best-preserved

relic is a 3rd-century Triumphal Arch. Nearby are the foundations of a Christian basilica, tombs (which are carved in rock) and a small Byzantine fortress. The 1st-century theatre situated on the slope of the hill affords a magnificent view over the surrounding area.

Environs

About 15 km (9 miles) east of town is Tunisia's highest mountain, **Jebel Chambi** (1,554 m/5,098 ft). In 1981 this area was declared a national park. Halfway up the slope is a tourist information bureau and a small museum. From Kasserine the GP17 road leads to the village of Chambi.

A capital from the theatre ruins in Haïdra

Haïdra ❼

Road map B3. **Archaeological station** ☐ *daily.*

Situated close to the Algerian border, Haïdra – formerly the Berber settlement of Ammaedara – was on the trade route that linked Hadrumetum (Sousse) with Carthage and Theveste (Tebessa) in Algeria. The Romans took control of it around AD 75 and established a camp here, which was used to station the famous Third Augustan Legion. Soldiers' graves can be seen beside the road.

An ancient road runs parallel to the modern one that leads to the site of the ruins. It is worth visiting the three-aisle **Basilica of the Martyrs** (5th–7th century).

Jugurtha's Table – a conspicuous flat rock jutting above the plain

The mosaics that once decorated the floor are now kept in Tunis's Bardo Museum. Standing to the northeast of the basilica is the **Arch of Septimius Severus** (AD 195) that was later included in the Byzantine citadel. This is the best-preserved Roman relic in Haïdra. On the other side of the road are the ruins of a late 3rd-century theatre, and further north are the remains of a basilica dating from Vandal times.

The best-known historic relic of Haïdra is the **Byzantine Fort** built during the reign of Justinian (527–565). This is the largest fortress to be found in any of the Maghreb countries. The north side of the fort was rebuilt in 1840 but the south side has since been destroyed by floods. At the centre of the fort are the remains of the Byzantine Chapel of the Citadel. To the north of the chapel are the ruins of the 4th-century Mellus Basilica, in which four tombs were discovered including that of Bishop Mellus; it is possible that the tomb of St Cyprian is also situated here.

Jugurtha's Table ❽

Road map B3

Close to the small town of Kalaat es-Senam, this flat-topped mountain rises abruptly out of the slightly undulating landscape that surrounds it. It owes its name to the Numidian king Jugurtha who held out against the Romans here between 112

and 105 BC. Numidia's kingdom was situated in what is now present-day Algeria and western Tunisia and competed with Carthage. In about 300 BC Numidia fell under the control of Carthage. The Numidian leader, Massinissa, supported Rome during the Second Punic War, which ensured a high degree of political freedom after the fall of Carthage. Massinissa's successor, Micipsa, continued with this policy. Following the death of Micipsa, however, Rome imposed Jugurtha (illegitimate grandson of Massinissa) as ruler.

The Arab name of the mountain (and also the nearby town) is Kalaat es-Senam or "Senam's Citadel", which originates from the chief of the bandits who used this mountain as his stronghold.

From Kasserine the GP17 road runs towards Tajerouine. Immediately past the mosque

in Kalaat es-Senam, the road climbs up towards Aïn Senan. From there a narrow footpath leads to the top of Jugurtha's Table. The climb takes about an hour and a half. The trail leading up the side of the mountain is spectacular. Its last section (a 15-minute climb) is steep and requires the use of hands. Standing immediately before the summit is a gate built by the bandit chief. At the top, at 1,271 m (4,169 ft), are the ruins of a Byzantine fortress, some troglodyte caves and a tiny shrine containing the tomb of an Islamic holy man – Sidi Abd el-Juada. This is a popular local pilgrimage destination. The shrine is open to non-Muslims.

When setting out, be sure to take along plenty of drinking water (it is not possible to buy anything along the route). On reaching the summit, stop for a picnic and enjoy the view.

BERBER TATTOOS

Berber tattoos are often associated with magic. The first tattoo – *ayasha* (the one that protects life) – is introduced immediately after birth. It is cross-shaped and usually placed on the cheeks or forehead. Tattoos are used for protection, to ensure good luck and prosperity, and also as an adornment. They are also placed on wrists and the chest. Women like to sport *fula* (triangles) on their chins.

Tattooed Berber woman

Roman Baths with well-preserved floor mosaics

Makthar ❾

Road map B3. 114 km (71 miles) west of Kairouan. 🚹 19,600. 🚌 *Mon.*

Makthar is situated between the steppes and the upland in Tunisia's second largest agricultural region (after the Medjerda Valley). It has splendid Roman remains, which are the most important in Tunisia along with Dougga and Bulla Regia.

In the 2nd century BC the small town of Makthar belonged to the Numidians, who built a fort here giving them control over local trade routes. Following the fall of Carthage in 146 BC many Punic refugees arrived here, as the town lay beyond the borders of Roman Africa. However, in 46 BC it was included in the province of a new Roman territory – Africa Nova. The Punic and Roman population coexisted peacefully. Romanization was a slow process that took some 200 years to accomplish. The numerous tomb steles (grave stones) and the tophets (sacrificial sites), preserved to this day, provide evidence of a considerable Punic influence.

In the 2nd century AD, during the reign of Emperor Trajan, the town was granted independent status, and under Marcus Aurelius it became a colony. The inhabitants were granted Roman citizenship and rights on a par with those enjoyed by the Romans. Makthar rapidly became the district's richest town, and maintained considerable

influence over the surrounding villages. During the Byzantine era the town was fortified, but following the Hilalian invasions in the 11th century it was destroyed.

A small **museum** houses a collection of tomb steles (1st–3rd century BC). Some of these bear Punic inscriptions and symbols (crescents, doves, grapes, peacocks and fish). The Roman era is represented by sculptures and architectural fragments; the Byzantine by bronzes, olive lamps and some 4th-century floor mosaics.

Past the museum are the remains of a temple that has been converted into a basilica. A paved Roman road leads to the amphitheatre and to the triumphal arch. Erected in AD

Christian stele tomb stone

116 to celebrate the town being granted the status of a municipium, Trajan's Arch overlooks the forum. Beyond it are the ruins of a basilica with a baptistry flanked by four columns. Here, too, is the tomb of Hildeguns – a 5th-century king of the Vandals. South of the Basilica of Hildeguns are the ruins of the Great Baths (2nd century).

A paved road running westwards from the Great Baths leads to the old forum. Slightly to the north is the temple of Bacchus (though only its crypt remains). To the right are the North Baths, which have some attractive floor mosaics. The road running past the Punic forum leads to the Schola Juvenus (AD 88). This was a kind of youth club where well-to-do children were taught how to be good Roman citizens.

Further on is the temple of Hathor Miskar (an Egyptian goddess of love) and the temple of Venus; immediately past this is the Roman forum, paved with white marble. Other interesting sights include the 1st-century AD Punic mausoleum, which was turned into a church in the 4th century and, next to the Great Baths, some Numidian tombs. At the very end of Makthar, beyond the **excavation site**, stands Bab el-Aïn – one of the town's oldest gates. Here, close to the stream, there once stood a tophet dedicated to Baal Hammon.

This ancient site was rediscovered in 1887 by Captain Bordier, a French officer, who founded a new town that now faces old Makthar across a ravine. Set at nearly 1,000 m (3,281 ft) above sea level, it is a spectacular spot.

🗼 **Excavation Site**
🕐 *Mid-Sep–Mar: 8:30am –5:30pm daily; Apr–mid-Sep: 8am–7pm daily.*

Ruins of Trajan's Arch dating from AD 116

◁ **Sun setting on the Roman ruins at Sufetula**

Roman Mosaics

Mosaics were a popular decorative element during Roman times. The mosaics would have been laid by travelling teams of artisans and were used to line the floors and walls of public baths and to adorn the façades of public buildings. Mosaics were composed of *tesserae* – tiny pieces of stone, marble or brick. From the 3rd century onwards, wealthy people began to use them to decorate their houses. Subjects were taken from everyday life, religion, agriculture and so on. Later on they began to feature images from mythology as well as floral and aquatic motifs. Favourite subjects included hunting and feasting and the seasons of the year. Games, held in amphitheatres, were also a popular subject.

Colourful mosaic featuring a bird

***Virgil and the Muses** – besides realistic scenes of everyday life, mosaics often featured images of well-known artists or rulers. Virgil was the favourite author of educated North Africans.*

***Animals and plants** were frequent motifs of Roman mosaics. Craftsmen often used their own colour schemes.*

Geometric patterns *represented another style of mosaic art, which was developing along with a realistic trend. This ornamentation is typical of the later mosaics, found in Christian churches.*

***Neptune's Triumph** – figurative mosaics from the Roman period used mainly mythological subjects and usually portrayed gods.*

***Ulysses and the Sirens** – this mosaic (AD 260) comes from Dougga. It depicts the temptation of Ulysses, a scene from Greek mythology.*

Le Kef

Road map B2. 170 km (106 miles) southwest of Tunis; 42 km (26 miles) from the Algerian border. 🏛️ 30,000. 🚍 🚉 🚌 Thu.

Le Kef ("the rock" in Arabic) enjoys an exceptionally scenic location on the slopes of Jebel Dyr, close to the border with Algeria. The site was occupied early and both Neolithic tools and Numidian tombs have been found here. Following the First Punic War it fell to Carthage and was known as Sicca. Later, the Romans took over the town, naming it Sicca Veneria as a mark of respect to the goddess Venus. Most of the population fled as a result of a Vandal raid but the town was slowly rebuilt and captured by the Arabs in AD 688.

With the arrival of the Ottomans in the 16th century, the town became known as Le Kef. As a border area it was a subject of contention between Algeria and Tunisia and Le Kef was the first town occupied by the French in 1881. During World War II it was the seat of the Protectorate authorities, and in 1942 it was used as the provisional headquarters of liberated Tunisia.

A tour may be started from Place de l'Indépendance, where there is an old Roman spring, Ras el-Aïn, which once supplied some huge Roman cisterns to the north of town. An open-air café here is a favourite meeting point of the locals. Close by stands a small altar

Nomadic tent in the Museum of Popular Arts and Traditions, Le Kef

dedicated to Lalla Ma – goddess of water. Rue de la Source leads to an early Roman bath complex. A walk uphill, along Rue Farhat Hached, leads to the Church of St Peter, also known as Dar el-Kousse. The church dates from the 4th century and contains a well-preserved apse. Early Christian symbols can be seen on the wall by the entrance.

The town's most interesting spot is Place Bou Makhlouf, where there is a kasbah and, at the top end, the Great Mosque, known now as the Basilica. This building no longer functions as a mosque and is used as a venue for cultural events.

Nearby is the Mosque of Sidi Bou Makhlouf, which is named after the patron saint of Le Kef. Next to this is a *zaouia* (tomb) where the saint is buried along with members of his family. Inside this mausoleum is a garden, the remains of mosaics and some steles. This 17th-century *zaouia* is an interesting sight, and features two domes and an octagonal minaret. Sidi Bou Makhlouf, founder of the sanctuary, was a Sufi master, and a disciple of El-Hadi Beness el-Mekhnessi

Cannon in the kasbah's courtyard

– a Moroccan Sufi and the originator of Aissaouia, a form of religious music. Members of the Aissaouia brotherhood used music as a means of entering into a trance. Religious meetings accompanied by Aissaouia music are held near the tomb of the master every Friday. Close to the tomb is the complex of Sidi Ali ben Aissa (1784) and the headquarters of the Rahmania Brotherhood. Today, it houses the **Regional Museum of Popular Arts and Traditions**, which has a collection of traditional costumes including wedding gowns, as well as jewellery, Bedouin tents, everyday objects, textiles and ceramics.

Below the square stands the mausoleum of Ali Turki, which also contains the tomb of his second son, Husayn bin Ali, founder of the Husaynid dynasty (1705–1957).

Le Kef's kasbah contains two forts. The smaller of the two is 12th-century and was built on the site of a Byzantine fortress. The larger one was built in 1679 by Mohammed Bey. The tower provides a spectacular view over the surrounding area. The building now houses a museum and is used as a venue for cultural events.

🏛️ **Regional Museum of Popular Arts and Traditions**
⏰ summer: 9am–1pm, 4–7pm; winter: 9:30am–4:30pm. 📷

Zaouia of Sidi Bou Makhlouf

National Parks

The process of founding national parks in Tunisia began in the 1980s. These parks represent a wide range of landscapes. For bird-lovers a visit to Lake Ichkeul is a must. Those interested in botany should head for Boukornine, near Tunis, especially when the cyclamens are in bloom. The islands of Zembra and Zembretta are not only oases of peace and quiet, but also veritable laboratories of natural science. A long walk through Chambi National Park and a climb up Jebel Chambi, Tunisia's highest peak, provides an opportunity to see wild gazelle and hyena, as well as a variety of birdlife.

Antelope in Bou Hedma

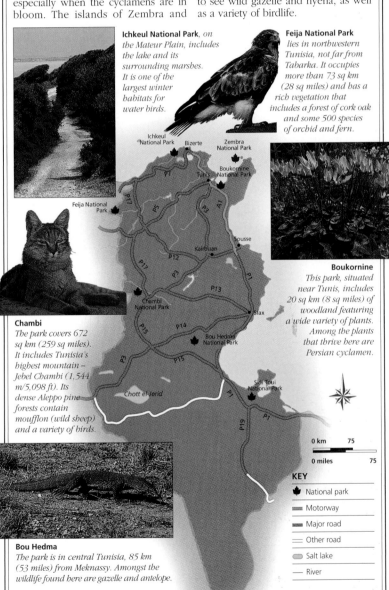

Ichkeul National Park, *on the Mateur Plain, includes the lake and its surrounding marshes. It is one of the largest winter habitats for water birds.*

Feija National Park *lies in northwestern Tunisia, not far from Tabarka. It occupies more than 73 sq km (28 sq miles) and has a rich vegetation that includes a forest of cork oak and some 500 species of orchid and fern.*

Boukornine *This park, situated near Tunis, includes 20 sq km (8 sq miles) of woodland featuring a wide variety of plants. Among the plants that thrive here are Persian cyclamen.*

Chambi *The park covers 672 sq km (259 sq miles). It includes Tunisia's highest mountain – Jebel Chambi (1,544 m/5,098 ft). Its dense Aleppo pine forests contain mouflon (wild sheep) and a variety of birds.*

Bou Hedma *The park is in central Tunisia, 85 km (53 miles) from Meknassy. Amongst the wildlife found here are gazelle and antelope.*

Map labels: Ichkeul National Park, Bizerte, Zembra National Park, Boukornine National Park, Tunis, Feija National Park, Kairouan, Sousse, Chambi National Park, Sfax, Bou Hedma National Park, Chott el-Jerid, Sidi Toui National Park

Roads: P7, P17, P5, P3, A1, P12, P17, P3, P13, P1, P15, P14, P3, P15, P19, P7

0 km 75
0 miles 75

KEY

⚜ National park
▬ Motorway
▬ Major road
= Other road
⬭ Salt lake
— River

Dougga ⑪

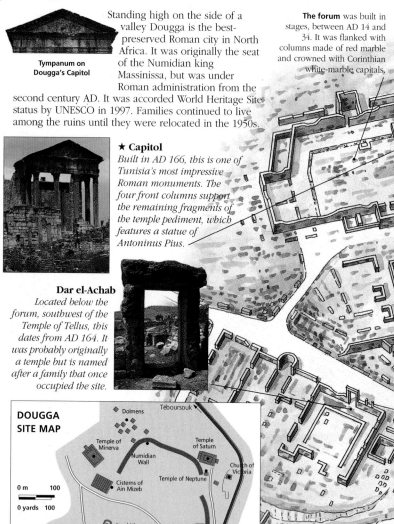

Standing high on the side of a valley Dougga is the best-preserved Roman city in North Africa. It was originally the seat of the Numidian king Massinissa, but was under Roman administration from the second century AD. It was accorded World Heritage Site status by UNESCO in 1997. Families continued to live among the ruins until they were relocated in the 1950s.

Tympanum on Dougga's Capitol

The forum was built in stages, between AD 14 and 34. It was flanked with columns made of red marble and crowned with Corinthian white-marble capitals.

★ Capitol
Built in AD 166, this is one of Tunisia's most impressive Roman monuments. The four front columns support the remaining fragments of the temple pediment, which features a statue of Antoninus Pius.

Dar el-Achab
Located below the forum, southwest of the Temple of Tellus, this dates from AD 164. It was probably originally a temple but is named after a family that once occupied the site.

DOUGGA SITE MAP

Dolmens
Téboursouk
Temple of Minerva
Numidian Wall
Temple of Saturn
Temple of Neptune
Church of Victoria
Cisterns of Aïn Mizeb
0 m   100
0 yards   100
Cisterns of Aïn el-Hammam
Amphitheatre
Theatre
Temple of Caelestis
Alexander Severus Arch
Temple of Augustan Piety
Forum
Temple of Concordia
Temple of Frugifer and Liber Pater
Temple of Pluto
Temple of Tellus
Lycinian Baths
Dar el-Achab
House of Dionysus and Ulysses
Fountain
House of the Trefoil
Arch of Septimius Severus
House of the Gorgon
Cisterns of Aïn Doura
Libyo-Punic Mausoleum

0 m   25
0 yards   25

KEY
- Building
- Road
- Footpath

STAR SIGHTS

★ Capitol

★ Lycinian Baths

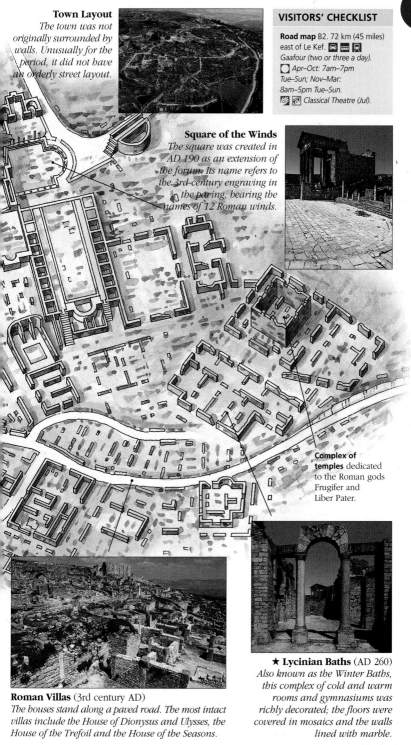

Town Layout
The town was not originally surrounded by walls. Unusually for the period, it did not have an orderly street layout.

VISITORS' CHECKLIST

Road map B2. 72 km (45 miles) east of Le Kef. 🚗 🚌 🚉
Gaafour (two or three a day).
⏰ Apr–Oct: 7am–7pm Tue–Sun; Nov–Mar: 8am–5pm Tue–Sun.
🎫 📷 Classical Theatre (Jul).

Square of the Winds
The square was created in AD 190 as an extension of the forum. Its name refers to the 3rd-century engraving in the paving, bearing the names of 12 Roman winds.

Complex of temples dedicated to the Roman gods Frugifer and Liber Pater.

★ Lycinian Baths (AD 260)
Also known as the Winter Baths, this complex of cold and warm rooms and gymnasiums was richly decorated; the floors were covered in mosaics and the walls lined with marble.

Roman Villas (3rd century AD)
The houses stand along a paved road. The most intact villas include the House of Dionysus and Ulysses, the House of the Trefoil and the House of the Seasons.

Thuburbo Majus – one of the most scenic ancient ruins in Tunisia

Thuburbo Majus ⑫

Road map C2. 67 km (42 miles) west of Hammamet. ☐ *Apr–mid-Sep: 7am–7pm Tue–Sun; mid-Sep–Mar: 8:30am–5:30pm Tue–Sun.*

Thuburbo Majus lies in a beautiful valley surrounded by hills, and is – along with Dougga, Bulla Regia, Makthar and Sbeïtla – one of the most important Roman remains in Tunisia, with many impressive monuments. A convenient café and toilet are at the entrance.

The Roman settlement was established in 27 BC, close to the Punic town. In AD 128, after a visit by the Emperor Hadrian, Thuburbo Majus was granted the independent status of a municipium, and later, in AD 188, it became a colony.

Located on the trading route between Sousse and Carthage, surrounded by fertile land, Thuburbo Majus grew rapidly. Most of the public buildings and homes decorated with mosaics date from the 2nd and 3rd centuries. In the 4th century some of the buildings were extended and the town's name was changed to Res Publica Felix Thuburbo Majus. However, the continuing conflicts

The colonnaded exercise yard

between Donatists and Catholics, Vandal raids and finally the Arab invasion led to the town's downfall.

On this site, immediately past the gate is the forum (each of its sides is 49 m/161 ft long), which is flanked on three sides by vast Corinthian columns. Its most important feature is the Capitol temple (one of the largest in Africa), which is dedicated to Jupiter, Juno and Minerva. Fragments of the 70-m (230-ft) statue of Jupiter are kept in the Bardo Museum, in Tunis *(see pp88–9)*. On the forum's southwestern side stands the Temple of Mercury (3rd century), which has eight column bases arranged in a circle. The southeastern side of the forum features a small temple and was once the site of the town's administrative buildings.

Beyond the forum, just to the right, are the Summer Baths. These occupy an area of 2.8 sq km (1.1 sq miles). They were once decorated with statues of Aesculapius, Hercules, Mercury and Venus and with exquisite mosaics that can now be seen in the Bardo Museum. The entrance led to the changing room; further on was the *frigidarium* with three pools, the *tepidarium* (the warm room), the *caldarium* (the steam baths) and the *sudatorium* (the sweat room). Adjacent to it was the Palaestra of the Petronii (AD 225), an exercise yard enclosed within Corinthian columns that is named after the rich family who funded it. The letters engraved on the pavement at the south end form the board of the "36 letters" game that was widely used to learn the alphabet. Higher up the hill are the Winter Baths, a well-preserved complex with a black-and-white mosaic floor.

The southern section of Thuburbo Majus contains a temple dedicated to Baal – the layout indicates Roman and Punic influence in equal measures. To the east of it stood the sanctuary of Caelestis, which was later converted into a three-aisle church. The Roman cellar became the baptistry and the forecourt of the temple was turned into a cemetery. Occasionally, a procession is held here in honour of St Perpetua, a saint who died a martyr's death at Carthage.

Zaghouan ⑬

Road map C2. 👥 10,000.

Zaghouan is a charming little town that lies at the foot of Jebel Zaghouan (1,295 m/4,249 ft). During the time of Tunisia's Roman occupation the place was called Ziqua. Little remains from this period apart from the large triumphal arch standing in the main street. This street has a number of local restaurants and climbs upwards to a small square that is dominated by two minarets – one octagonal, one square. The square minaret was added to the church building that has been converted into mosque. A further climb along a narrow street to the left of the square leads to the tomb of the town's patron saint Sidi Ali Azouz (who is also venerated in Tunis). Zaghouan clearly displays Andalusian influences, following an influx of refugees in the 17th century – house windows are hung with light blue curtains and drinking fountains are decorated with mosaics.

Ruins of the fountain in Zaghouan

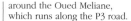

Aqueduct for ancient Carthage

Zaghouan is famous for the superb quality of its water and its mountain springs. It is worth taking a walk further out of town (about 1.5 km/1 mile), along the road leading through orchards and shaded by old trees towards the **Temple des Eaux**, a Roman fountain with 12 niches – one for each month of the year. The fountain was built in the 2nd century AD on the orders of Emperor Hadrian.

The small square hall of the fountain, framed by a portico, was built next to a spring (now, alas, dry). On the opposite side are water tanks in a figure of eight shape. This was the starting point of the 124-km (77-mile) long aqueduct that used to supply Carthage with fresh water. Its most famous sections are around the Oued Meliane, which runs along the P3 road.

Environs

Some 35 km (22 miles) from Zaghouan is the spa resort of **Jebel Oust**, where the natural brine springs come out at 55° C (131° F). The town has a small balneotherapy centre, which continues the traditions of the Roman hot baths. At the summit above Jebel Oust there is a temple devoted to Aesculapius and Hygeia, which in Christian times was turned into a church.

Jebel Zaghouan ⑭

Road map C2.

This craggy mountain is clearly visible behind the Temple des Eaux and its surrounding woodland. It appears to have been cut into halves. A little way up, above the fountain, is a resting point. Close to the summit, at 975 m (3,198 ft), is an excellent viewpoint and a TV transmitter. In ancient times this area was covered with cypress trees. The northern slopes of the hill are overgrown with Aleppo pine, breadfruit trees and wild olives. The scent of the pine trees blends with the fragrance of the sun-warmed meadows and rosemary. From 600 m (1,969 ft) up, green oak and turpentine trees can be seen. Maple and cherry trees become more numerous nearer the top. A hike around this area is steep, with rugged terrain and few signposts, but it provides a good opportunity to get away from the bustle of the tourist centres.

The mountain is rich in birdlife, especially birds of prey. Birdwatchers may be able to spot the king eagle and the Bonelli eagle, as well as vultures and falcons.

The green slopes of Jebel Zaghouan

Kairouan ⑮

Kairouan was founded in AD 670 by Oqba ibn Nafi, who, according to legend, chanced upon a golden goblet in the sand that turned out to have been lost in Mecca. When the goblet was picked up water sprang from the ground. The city's main sight is the Great Mosque (*see pp238–9*), which is an important pilgrimage destination. Kairouan has many other interesting things to see and the city was declared a UNESCO World Cultural Heritage Site in 1988.

Ceramics stall on Avenue 7 Novembre

Exploring Kairouan

Visitors to Kairouan are welcomed by the sight of two vast Aghlabid cisterns. The entrance to the medina, surrounded by impregnable walls (7 km/4 miles long) is through monumental gates. The usual entrances are Bab Tunis or Bab ech-Chouhada. These are linked by Avenue 7 Novembre (formerly Avenue Ali Belhouane). To the right of Bab ech-Chouhada is the tomb of Sidi el-Ghariani. A little further down towards the medina's centre is the Mosque of the Three Doors. At the centre of the medina, in Rue des Cuirs, is Bir Barouta, a well named after a 13th-century holy man. Further on, in Avenue de la République, is the 16th-century tomb of Sidi Sahib (also known as the Mosque of the Barber). The Great Mosque, or Mosque of Sidi Oqba, is on the northern edge of the medina, adjacent to the walls.

A **global ticket** covering a day's entry to the city's major attractions can be purchased at the Great Mosque and the Aghlabid Basins.

🏛 Avenue 7 Novembre

The main route of the medina leads through the souks. Most of the street dates from the 17th and 18th centuries. Workshops producing traditional Tunisian handicrafts can still be seen.

Bab ech-Chouhada is the best gate for the heart of the medina, which contains the al-Halfaouine café, the Bir Barouta and the Mosque el-Bey. Further along, on the left, is the Mosque el-Maalek. At the end of the avenue is Bab Tunis, which was built in 1772.

🏛 Medina Walls

The first walls surrounding Kairouan were built in AD 762. At that time they had six gates and enclosed a smaller space than they do today, with the Great Mosque at the centre. The walls have been repeatedly destroyed and rebuilt. The town was sacked during the 11th-century Hilalian invasion and the medina's walls were not rebuilt until the 18th century, when they were reinforced with twenty round towers. Today the walls contain four gates: Bab Tunis, Bab el-Khoukha, Bab Djedid and Bab ech-Chouhada.

Decorated niche in the Zaouia of Sidi el-Ghariani

🅲 Zaouia of Sidi el-Ghariani

Rue Sidi Abid el-Ghariani. ☐ summer: 8am–2pm; winter: 8am–noon, 3–6pm. 🔲 Sat afternoon & Sun.
The tomb of Sidi el-Ghariani stands to the right of Bab ech-Chouhada. It was built in the 14th century by the philosopher El-Djadid, though the building is now named after his disciple. The courtyard is surrounded by two storeys of colonnades. From here, it is possible to enter the mausoleum, which is lined with ceramic tiles. The intricately carved doors are worthy of note, as is the stuccowork and the wooden ceiling in the tomb.

🏛 Bir Barouta

☐ 8am–5:30pm Sat–Thu, 8am–noon Fri. Entrance: Rue des Cuirs.
The well was probably dug in the 8th century, though the building that surrounds it is 17th-century. The water is

Medina walls, over 7 km (4 miles) long

◁ Roof of a carpet shop near the Great Mosque, Kairouan

Bir Barouta's famous camel drawing water

VISITORS' CHECKLIST

Road map D3. 80,000. Rue ibn al-Aghlab, (77) 270 452; ONTT: Place des Martyrs, (77) 231 897. www.kairouan.org

drawn by a camel that turns the wheels of the mechanism. Some believe that the well was found by Oqba ibn Nafi and that it is connected to Mecca. The well is said to have special properties – anyone who drinks from it is certain to return to Kairouan one day.

Souks

Kairouan's medina is one of the best-preserved in Tunisia. The centre of town, which once adjoined the Great Mosque, was moved during the Hafsid dynasty to the site that is now occupied by the souks (markets). The maze of streets is full of shops and workshops producing copper

pots, leather goods and, above all, Kairouan's famous carpets *(see pp237 and 241).* Perfumes, clothes, jewellery, hats and condiments can also be obtained here. The busiest part of the medina lies between Bab Tunis and Bab ech-Chouhada.

Mosque of the Three Doors

Rue de la Mosquée des Trois Portes.
to non-Muslims

The Mosquée des Trois Portes dates from the 9th century and is one of the medina's oldest religious buildings. It was founded by Mohammed bin Kairouan el-Maafri but owes its name to its three arched doorways. One is intended to

be used by men, one by women and the other by children. The mosque's 9th-century façade is covered with Kufic script and floral ornaments. The minaret in the northeastern corner of the mosque was added during the Hafsid period. This square tower features two blind horseshoe arches framed with blue mosaics.

Carved stone façade of the Mosque of the Three Doors

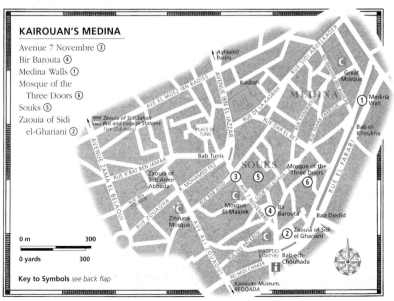

KAIROUAN'S MEDINA

Avenue 7 Novembre ③
Bir Barouta ④
Medina Walls ①
Mosque of the Three Doors ⑥
Souks ⑤
Zaouia of Sidi el-Ghariani ②

0 m 300
0 yards 300

Key to Symbols *see back flap*

One of Kairouan's Aghlabid Basins

Further Afield
The sights situated beyond the medina's centre can be easily explored on foot. Particularly worthy of note are the Aghlabid Basins – a masterpiece of Arab hydraulic engineering. These ensured that even during times of drought the fields around Kairouan were green and supplied the town with grain. The Zaouia of Sidi Sahab (Sidi Abou Zammaa el-Balaoui) is a splendid architectural example of an Arabic sanctuary, while the Zaouia of Sidi Amor Abbada has some interesting examples of Tunisian wrought iron.

🏛 Aghlabid Basins
Avenue 7 Novembre.
⭘ *7:30am–6pm during high season;*
8:30am–6pm at other times.
The Aghlabid Basins are about a kilometre (half a mile) north of the medina and were built in 860 on the orders of the Aghlabid prince Abu Ibrahim Ahmed, under the supervision of a freed slave named Chalaf.

When they were completed, the cisterns formed part of an extended hydro-technical system that is considered to be one of the most important hydraulic masterpieces of the Arab world. The vast cisterns belong to a system of 15 water reservoirs that once supplied the town with water.

The basins are huge. The largest of them measures 128 m (420 ft) across and is 4.5 m (15 ft) deep. It can hold over 57 million litres (12 million gallons) of water. The water was collected partly during the winter rains

and was also fed in along a 35-km (22-mile) long aqueduct from Jebel Cherichera. Most of Kairouan's inhabitants also had their own wells and small cisterns in their homes, but the water stored in the reservoirs made the town independent of the vagaries of the weather. In the middle of the main pool the remains of a number of pillars can be seen. These pillars once supported a pavilion where the Aghlabid rulers would come to cool off on hot summer evenings.

🏛 Zaouia of Sidi Sahbi
Avenue de la République.
⭘ *8:30am–5:30pm daily.*
This sanctuary dates from the 15th century and was originally just an octagonal structure, surrounded by a wall. It was built to honour Abou Zammaa el-Balaoui, who was killed in a battle 50 km (31 miles) from Kairouan, before the town was founded. In the 17th century Hammouda Pasha restored the mausoleum and began the construction of additional buildings, but

Zaouia of Sidi Sahbi

most of the work was carried out under Mohammed Bey between 1681 and 1685. The mausoleum can be found in the northwestern corner of the complex and is covered with a dome (1629) under which stands the tomb of Sidi Sahbi, clad with green and white marble. According to legend, Sidi Sahbi was a companion of the Prophet and always carried with him three hairs from Mohammed's beard – the *zaouia* is sometimes referred to as the Mosque of the Barber for this reason. The vast courtyard is dominated by a minaret, which dates from 1690. The *zaouia* has long been a holy place for Muslims and a *fondouk* (inn) was added in the 17th century for pilgrims along with an Islamic school and a mosque.

🏛 Zaouia of Sidi Amor Abbada
Rue el-Gadraou. ⭘ *summer: 8am–2pm; winter: 9am–4pm.*
The seven-domed tomb was built in 1860 to house the tomb of Sidi Abbada and

Zaouia of Sidi Amor Abbada

is one of Kairouan's principal pilgrimage destinations. Sidi Abbada was an illiterate blacksmith who was regarded as a holy man. He was a colourful character by all accounts and many legends and stories about him have survived to this day. Sidi Abbada specialized in prophecies. One of them predicted that "three vast scaly snakes, breathing fire and iron, will surround Kairouan and finding the town undefended will enter it. This will be the punishment for the transgressions committed over centuries by the inhabitants". The prophecy was believed by some to have been fulfilled when tanks of the Allied Forces entered the medina in 1943.

As well as making prophecies, Sidi Abbada was also known for producing large works in iron. Placed around his tomb are various articles made by him including a giant anchor, large chains and smoking pipes. Two giant swords, believed to protect Kairouan from attack, were stolen in 1996. A pair of giant anchors (which Sidi Abbada claimed to have come from Noah's Ark) stand beyond Bab Djedid, just north of Place des Martyrs. They are supposed to attach Kairouan to the earth.

🕌 Medersa of Husayn
🔲 8:30am–1pm & 3–6pm daily
⬤ Fri & Sun.
Built in 1710 by a Husaynid prince, Husayn bin Ali, this is the oldest of Kairouan's Islamic schools to have survived to our times. Its entrance, adorned with an arch, leads to a courtyard that is flanked on three sides by a gallery. The latter consists of arched arcades resting on columns crowned with capitals dating from the Ottoman period. There are 11 cells around the courtyard. The southeastern end is occupied by a mosque. The mihrab (niche indicating the direction of prayer) is crowned with a semicircular arch. The school underwent renovation works in 1980 and now serves as a town hall.

Minaret of Zitouna Mosque, within the thick walls

🄲 Zitouna Mosque
Avenue Ali Zouaoui.
The Zitouna Mosque (Olive Mosque), although not as famous as its counterpart in Tunis (see pp70–71), represents a typical example of Kairouan architecture. Its courtyard, surrounded by a colonnade, is the forum for religious discussion and repose. The minaret that towers over the mosque has a rectangular base. Its top section is adorned by a widow framed with blue ceramic tiles. It is worth remembering that minarets were added to mosques much later. In the early days the muezzin called the faithful to prayer from the roof of the mosque; only later on were separate towers built for this purpose. Formerly, the voice of the muezzin reverberated around the district five times a day; these days a recording is increasingly used instead.

🏛 Kairouan Museum
Avenue Ali Zouaoui.
Tel (77) 232 013.
🔲 summer & Ramadan: 8am–2pm; winter: 8:30am–1pm, 3–5:30pm.
The tradition of carpet-weaving in the city goes back to the 8th century, but it was only in Ottoman times that Kairouan became famous for carpet production.

The Kairouan Museum has many examples of carpets produced by nomadic weavers, who offered their services to richer nomads. The technique and the patterns used in these carpets show strong Turkish and Anatolian influences. One of the most distinctive features of these products is their red background, with colourful geometric patterns surrounded with white cotton thread. The carpets are usually made of camel or goat wool (see p241).

Carpets are on sale in many outlets in Kairouan but not all are of the highest quality. In an attempt to keep standards high, the Tunisian government issues stamped certificates, which include information about the article's type, size and the date of production. Such certificates are a guarantee of a carpet's quality. The Kairouan Museum is the ideal place to buy a certified product, and also to see examples of antique carpets. It is also a good source to obtain reliable information about the prices of carpets, and to become familiar with the details of their production.

Modern and antique rugs on display in the Kairouan Museum

The Great Mosque

A column-crowning capital

Kairouan's Great Mosque, in the centre of the medina, is also known as the Mosque of Sidi Oqba after the city's founder. The original mosque was built in AD 670 but was completely destroyed. Most of what exists today dates from the 9th century, though it has been remodelled many times since then. This is one of the oldest (and largest) places of prayer in the Islamic world and the fourth most important pilgrimage destination after Mecca, Medina and Jerusalem. According to Muslims, seven visits here are equivalent to one visit to Mecca.

Capitals
Most of the column stems and their capitals were taken from other buildings, both pagan and Christian. Some, however, were produced by local craftsmen.

★ Minaret
The base of this minaret was built between 724 and 728 and is one of the oldest surviving structures of its kind. It set the pattern for all minarets in this part of the Islamic world. The remainder of the 35-m (115-ft) high minaret is 9th-century and towers over the mosque's vast courtyard. Stairs with 129 steps lead to the top floor.

Well-heads are used to draw water from the cisterns, which is used for ritual ablutions.

The sundial in the courtyard marks the hours of prayer.

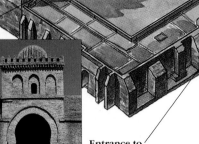

Cistern
The courtyard slopes towards the centre to deliver rainwater into a cistern below. The intricate decorations covering the hole are designed to filter out impurities before the water reaches the well.

Entrance to the Courtyard
The wall surrounding the courtyard has six gates. The main entrance is through a gate crowned with a dome.

For hotels and restaurants in this region see pp263–5 and pp287–9

Arcades
The cloisters skirt the courtyard on three sides, forming long aisles that cast a shadow and provide shelter from the sun.

Mihrab Dome
This dome marks the position of the mihrab, which points in the direction of Mecca. It has richer decorations than the mosque's other domes.

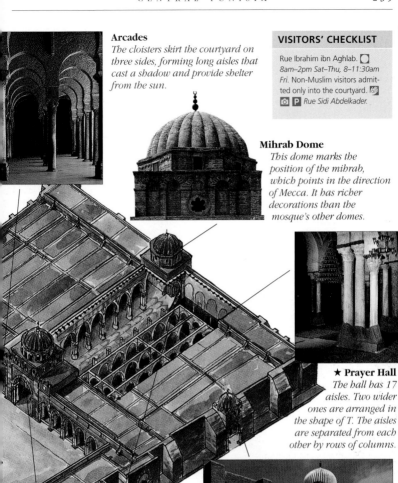

★ Prayer Hall
The hall has 17 aisles. Two wider ones are arranged in the shape of T. The aisles are separated from each other by rows of columns.

Pulpit – made of teak, this was produced around AD 863, on the orders of the Aghlabid Emir, Abu Ibrahim.

Entrance to the Mosque
There are two entrances to the mosque from the street, both leading through dome-crowned gates. One is on the southeastern side, the other on the southwestern.

Decorations
The mosque's floral motifs are inspired by ancient Hellenic traditions. The geometric patterns come mainly from early Christian and Berber designs.

STAR SIGHTS

★ Minaret

★ Prayer Hall

Pool in the courtyard of Kairouan's former kasbah

♣ Kasbah
Avenue ibn el-Jazzar.
Built into the northwestern walls of the medina, the kasbah formed part of Kairouan's defensive system. Its high walls and small windows are characteristic of this type of structure. Today, the kasbah houses a hotel. A heated pool is in the central courtyard, while a café is in the former prison.

♛ Zaouia of Sidi Abdel Qadir el-Djilani
Rue de la Kasbah.
This architectural complex is devoted to Abdel Qadir el-Djilani – the founder of the Sufi Qadiriyya group, one of Islam's most popular spiritual groups or *tariqas* (literally spiritual "ways"). The main site of the cult is the Sidi Abdel Qadir mausoleum in Baghdad. *Zaouias* devoted to el-Qadiriyya are also found elsewhere in the Muslim world. Sufis emphasise meditation and recital of the holy text.

Environs
Some 9 km (6 miles) south of Kairouan is **Reqqada**, which contains the ruins of a former Aghlabid palace. Along with Mahdia and Abbasiya, this was one of the four Tunisian capitals. In AD 876 the Aghlabid prince, Ibrahim II, built a magnificent residence – Qasr el-Fath (the Victory Palace) – on the outskirts of Kairouan which was soon turned into a luxury

summer residence. Soon afterwards, other similar palaces were built elsewhere in the country. The building materials used, including brick and timber, were typical of the region. The ornamental motifs were mainly floral and geometric. As well as palaces, Reqqada also contains the remains of Aghlabid baths and *fondouks* (inns).

The **National Museum of Islamic Art** occupies a former presidential palace at Reqqada. It displays objects found in the palace, as well as items from other parts of the country. A special exhibition is devoted to exhibits from Sabra – a palace just outside Kairouan that was built by Caliph el-Mansour in the mid-10th century. The entrance hall to the museum has a model of Kairouan's Great Mosque and a reproduction of its mihrab (niche indicating the direction of prayer). Other rooms house a collection of Fatimid and Zirid coins, some 10th-

Ancient coin from Reqqada's museum

century inscriptions from the Koran and examples of 9th-century ceramics.

The nearby village of **Sidi Ali ben Nasrallach** is inhabited by semi-nomadic tribes and stages "Fantasia", a spectacular horse-riding show, in September.

About 60 km (37 miles) northwest of Kairouan is **Ksar Lemsa**, a 6th-century Byzantine fortress, which once guarded routes into the fertile Tell region. A few kilometres further on is the Berber village of **La Kesra** and a huge forest of Aleppo pine. Some 36 km (22 miles) west of Kairouan is the village of **Haffouz**, which has a war cemetery for Muslim soldiers who served in the French army. A short way further on, close to Oued Cherichera, are the remains of the **aqueduct** that once supplied Kairouan with water.

⛪ National Museum of Islamic Art
Tel (77) 323 337. ◯ 8am–2pm Tue–Sun (until 4pm winter except Fri).

Entrance to the Zaouia of Sidi Abdel Qadir, close to the Great Mosque

Kairouan's Carpets

Carpet weaving in Kairouan goes back hundreds of years. It is said that the carpets produced here were so precious that the Aghlabid princes paid

A carpet of Berber design

their taxes in them to the Abbasid Caliphs. Two main types of carpet are made in Kairouan – knotted and woven. Woven carpets tend to be cheaper. In the 19th century a loop stitch was introduced. Camilla, daughter of the town's Turkish governor, is said to have taught this to the locals. This type of carpet features mainly red, blue and green colours and geometric patterns.

More than 4,000 women *in Kairouan are employed to weave carpets (men stick to selling) and work mainly from home. At one time, brightly coloured carpets were the main part of a bridal dowry.*

Buying a carpet *is a ritual, and many people visit Kairouan Museum (see p237) for advice. Visitors can also buy carpets with certificates of authenticity here.*

Mergoum, or woven carpets *are of Berber origin. This type of carpet has brighter colours and a purely geometric pattern; it is also much lighter in weight and is further decorated with embroidery.*

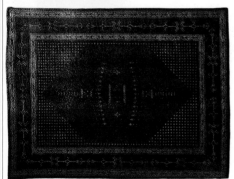

Carpets *sold by street vendors are predominantly of beige, white and black colouring. They are decorated with geometric patterns and floral motifs.*

The basic knot *used in Kairouan carpets is of Turkish origin. The value of a carpet depends on the density of knots, the quality of material and the weaving technique. Silk carpets can have as many as 500,000 knots per square metre.*

TRAVELLERS' NEEDS

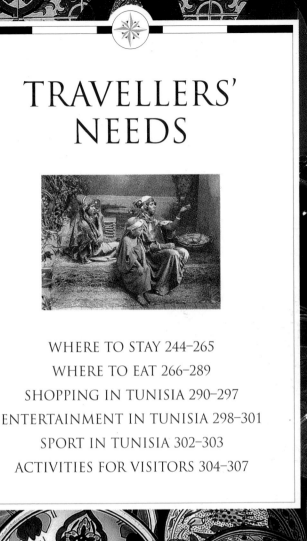

WHERE TO STAY

Tunisian hotels are mostly of a good standard and even the more basic ones are generally perfectly clean and comfortable. Independent travellers may like to consider staying in well-kept, small family hotels that are located in old mansions or in one of the former *fondouks* (inns for travelling merchants). When visiting Berber villages it is possible to stay in a troglodyte home, as many have

A hotel porter in Monastir

been converted into small hotels. Most hotels in tourist resorts are set in scenic surroundings. Many offer extensive recreational facilities and have modern decor. Some can dazzle visitors with their exotic splendour. Hotels situated away from the main resorts are more modest. Many are aimed at Tunisian holidaymakers and do not provide the same facilities, such as nightly entertainment.

Hotel lobby in Kairouan

TYPES OF HOTEL

The choice of hotel in Tunisia is dictated not only by its price but depends also on whether the hotel caters mainly for independent travellers or the package holiday market. As with almost everywhere in the world, a package holiday is usually a less expensive option but will not always provide the most interesting accommodation.

All hotels in tourist resorts, from three-star upwards, will have a swimming pool but in towns even a five-star hotel may not have a pool.

The choice of where to stay includes ancient *fondouks* (inns) and former palaces, troglodyte homes and Bedouin tents pitched at an oasis.

Another category is the so-called "hôtels de charme". These independently-run upmarket establishments generally have a small number of rooms and offer chic accommodation. Many distinguish themselves with stylistic flourishes such as minimalistic "designer" decor or original artwork by Tunisian artists on display in the rooms.

When checking into a less expensive hotel, particularly in the summer, check if the room is air-conditioned. At

the very least, it should have a fan and the use of a bathroom. If there is a hotel restaurant, ask for a room well away from the kitchen or dining area to avoid the potential bouquet of smells.

HOTEL CATEGORIES

Hotels in Tunisia can be divided into three categories: the non-classified (NC), the classified (from one to five stars) and those classified within holiday resorts. The latter are far superior to their urban equivalents in terms of standards, comfort and recreational facilities, and they usually offer a beautiful location. Bear in mind that a five-star hotel in Tunisia may be equivalent to a four-star hotel in Europe; however, some of the newest resort hotels measure up quite well.

One- and two-star hotels are sometimes situated in older buildings which reflect earlier colonial times. Sometimes, they are tucked away in the alleyways of ancient medinas. Most rooms

Hotels surrounding the harbour in Port el-Kantaoui

◁ Colourful ceramics from Nabeul

Swimming pool in one of Tunisia's tourist zones

have en suite bathrooms or hot showers. Three-star hotels are mostly aimed at package holidaymakers. Four- and five-star establishments cater also for business travellers. In tourist resorts these upmarket hotels will usually have much larger rooms than the ones offered by their town equivalents, while their decor is more likely to be inspired by local designs and tradtional architecture.

HOTEL CHAINS

The main hotel chain in Tunisia is Abou Nawas. It runs some good four- and five-star hotels located in many of the towns and tourist resorts. El-Mouradi is another major chain which has very good four- and five-star hotels. Several other international hotel chains operate in Tunisia, specializing in seaside holidays. These include Riu, Club Mediterranée and the Golden Tulip chain.

PRICES

Prices charged by four- and five-star hotels are determined by the Ministry of Tourism. They depend on the time of year, the location and the overall standard. An extra surcharge may be made for a room with a sea view. In the higher category hotels the price often includes breakfast. This however is not a hard and fast rule, so check in advance. Five-star hotels in towns charge about

160–230 TD per night for a double room. Ask about any special offers as there is often a substantial discount for a longer stay or an out-of-season visit.

Three-star hotels and those catering mainly for tourists offer a wide range of prices. The price of a single or double room varies between 50–75 and 100–120 TD per night, respectively. One- or two-star hotels are cheaper and cost between 40–70 TD per night. Small and non-classified hotels cost around 10–15 TD per night for a double room with an en suite bathroom. Slightly higher-class hotels – outside the peak July and August period – cost about 22–30 TD for a double room with an en suite bathroom. For a room in one of the cheapest hotels, with a shared bathroom, it is about 5 TD per night. These can be found in many parts

Plaque of a "tourist-class" hotel

of Tunisia, including Tunis's medina. During the peak holiday time, however, it can be difficult to find accommodation in Tunis for under 30 TD. For example, a double room in a two-star seaside hotel, with half-board, will cost about 45–50 TD during the peak season. Accommodation in a four-star hotel during peak times will be about 145 TD.

BOOKING

Tunisia has a large number of hotels, particularly in the resorts, so generally speaking there is no problem securing accommodation. The best way to book a hotel room on arrival is by going to the ONTT airport desk.

However, booking ahead is advised, particularly in the summer and during peak holiday periods. The situation is somewhat different with the many medium-category hotels and "hôtels de charme", where there is often a shortage of rooms.

Other than through a travel agent, the best way to book a hotel room before arriving in the country is on the Internet. However, this will involve making a credit card payment for at least one night. Booking by fax is not advised as it may not guarantee a room.

Booking a room in a less expensive hotel is best done by telephone. You should be aware that things can go awry, however, and this method also does not absolutely guarantee a room.

Rooftops among the palm trees in the tourist zone, Aghir

TOURIST ZONES

A tourist zone *(zone touristique)* is a purpose-built holiday town. The main advantages of such zones include their close proximity to entertainment, lush green surroundings and direct access to the sea and beach. Tourist zone hotels are generally of a higher standard than city hotels. Standards of behaviour are also more relaxed and visitors may act much more freely than in towns or the countryside.

Tourist zones tend to be quieter than towns. Their location may, however, disappoint those who put sightseeing above time spent under a beach umbrella because they are rarely close to the major sights. A definite disadvantage of tourist zones is their lack of local cafés and restaurants serving traditional Tunisian cuisine. In addition, prices in tourist zones are generally much higher than in town.

YOUTH HOSTELS

Tunisia offers a choice of two types of youth hostels: the **auberges de jeunesse** and the **maisons des jeunes**. Try to find the former because they are usually located in historic buildings such as *fondouks* (inns) or palaces. The rooms, often arranged around flower-filled courtyards, differ in terms of size and furnishings. They are usually quite simple

Fairytale shapes of a tourist-zone hotel near Hammamet

with just a bed, a wardrobe and a small table, but they are very clean. The staff contribute to a very pleasant atmosphere though the regulations and rules can be fairly strict (many hostels close at 10pm and allow a maximum stay of three nights). This type of hostel includes the charming *auberge de jeunesse* on Jerba, where small cushions embroidered with roses are placed on each bed. The hostels are also very popular with Tunisians.

The *maisons des jeunes*, on the other hand, are part of a charmless, government-run organization which in high season usually occupy schools or colleges. A major disadvantage of these hostels is their poor location, well away from town centres. A big plus is the fact that they can be found in almost every town. Many of them have small kitchens, which can be used for a small additional fee. Both types of hostel give preference to members of the International Youth Hostel Association. A night in a two- or three-bed room costs about 3–4 TD. Breakfast will cost 1 TD; the remaining meals about 3 TD. The country's southern regions feature *marhalas*, which are slightly more expensive than the typical

Swimming pool of a hotel in Hammamet

youth hostels found elsewhere. These are excellent places for a low-budget overnight stay and are hospitable, well-equipped and serve traditional food.

CAMP SITES

There are few camp sites in Tunisia and their standard is very low. With the permission of the landowner or the local authorities a tent may be pitched on private or public land, or on a site belonging to a youth hostel. There are camp sites in Remel Plage, near Bizerte, in Hammamet (Ideal Camping), Nabeul (Les Jasmines), Sousse (Green Pub), Tozeur (Le Belvedere), Douz (Paradis), Zarzis (Sonia Camping 'n' Caravanning) and on Jerba, by the Sidi Slim Hotel. When travelling in the south of the country, it's possible to sleep in a Bedouin tent for a small fee.

DISABLED PERSONS

Most Tunisian hotels are not accessible to wheelchair users. Modern hotels are more likely to be wheelchair-accessible but you should check this before booking.

Information on facilities for the disabled can be obtained from the **Association Générale des Insuffisants Moteurs**, the main organization for people with impaired mobility in Tunisia.

CHILDREN

Tunisians love children and are eager to cater for their

needs and wants. When planning a holiday with children, ask the travel agent about hotels that offer specific entertainment for families with young ones.

All tourist zone hotels will have highchairs for infants and serve special menus for young children. They should also be able to provide a cot, though few hotels provide dedicated baby-changing rooms. Baby food, disposable nappies and food supplements can all be purchased in local shops.

Most hotels offer discounts of between 30 to 40 per cent for children aged under 10.

The major resort hotels usually have well-maintained playgrounds and shallow paddling pools. While many of the tourist beaches are patrolled, it is always wise to keep a watchful eye on the children.

Sunset over the swimming pool of a hotel in Tamerza

HOTEL ENTERTAINMENT

Most tourist zone hotels put on entertainment (known as animation) for their guests including social evenings, competitions and themed parties, which enable visitors to get to know the other hotel guests – this can be especially useful for those travelling with children. However, for visitors who simply wish to relax quietly an evening's entertainment may be unwelcome. Loud music from the hotel dance floor or the amplified voice of an enthusiastic compere can penetrate even into a tightly shut room. Most entertainment programmes are run in hotels aimed at families with children; in five-star hotels the entertainment is lower key.

Some hotels host evenings of cultural entertainment. This may consist of a folk show, for instance, or belly dancing or traditional *malouf* music, with the chance to try a *chicha* (hookah) in one of the hotel cafés. The larger hotels also organize excursions to some of Tunisia's most interesting sights. An additional fee is usually required for these trips.

The main pavilion of the Hammam Bourguiba resort

DIRECTORY

HOTEL INFORMATION

Tunisian Tourist Office
77a Wigmore Street, London, W1U 1QF
Tel (020) 7224 5561.
www.cometotunisia.co.uk

HOTELS ON THE INTERNET

www.planet.tn
www.tunisia.com
www.tunisiehotel.com
www.tourismtunisia.com/hotels
www.hoteltravel.com
www.hotels-tunisiens.com
www.tripadvisor.com

HOTEL CHAINS

Abou Nawas
www.abounawas.com

Orangers
www.orangers.com.tn

Dar Hotels
www.darhotels.com

Sol Meliá Hotels and Resorts
www.solmelia.com

Golden Yasmine
www.goldenyasmine.com

Groupe Sassi
www.groupe-sassi.com

Iberostar
www.iberostar.com

Tunisian Travel Service
www.tts.com.tn

YOUTH HOSTELS

Association Tunisienne des Auberges et Tourisme de Jeunes
Rue d'Alger 8, 1000 Tunis.
Tel (71) 353 277.
Fax (71) 352 172.
www.atatj.planet.tn

Tunis Medina
Rue de Saida Ajoula 25.
Tel (71) 567 850.
Fax (71) 567 850.

Bizerte
Route de la Corniche.
Tel (72) 431 608.

Nabeul
Rue Mongi Slim.
Tel (72) 285 547.
Fax (72) 285 547.

Houmt Souk
Rue Moncef Bey 11.
Tel (05) 650 619.
Fax (05) 650 619.

Hammamet
Tel (72) 280 440.
Fax (72) 278 960.

Hammam-Sousse
Tel (73) 362 644.
Fax (73) 362 888.

INFORMATION

Association Générale des Insuffisants Moteurs
Tel (70) 605 264.

Choosing a Hotel

Hotels of various price categories have been chosen on the grounds of their location, standard and good value. The chart below first lists hotels in Tunis, and this is followed by a list of places to stay in each of the other regions of Tunisia. Map references refer to the road map of Tunisia on the back inside cover.

PRICE CATEGORIES
For a standard double room, with bath or shower, including service and tax. Prices are in Tunisian dinars.

TD Under 30 TD
TD TD 30–65 TD
TD TD TD 65–100 TD
TD TD TD TD 100–150 TD
TD TD TD TD TD Over 150 TD

TUNIS

Auberge de Jeunesse

25 Rue Saïda-Ajoula, 1000 **Tel** *71 56 78 50* **Fax** *71 56 78 50* **Rooms** *6*   Map *C1*

At the heart of the medina, this is a great and atmospheric youth hostel with four double rooms, one dormitory for women and one for men. The rooms have old tiles, and the dining room has an amazing 18th-century decorated ceiling. Clean showers and toilets, but take your own bed linen. Book ahead in summer. **auberge.medina@topnet.tn**

Continental

5 Rue de Marseille, 1001 **Tel** *71 25 98 34* **Rooms** *20*   Map *C1*

The Continental is an old-fashioned budget hotel in a lovely building just off Avenue Habib Bourguiba on a lively pedestrian street. The rooms are clean and spacious, with high ceilings, basic beds and basins. The communal toilets and showers are reasonably clean, and the staff are friendly if a little sleepy.

El-Medina

1 Rue des Glacières & Place de la Victoire, 1001 **Tel** *71 32 74 97* **Fax** *71 32 54 52* **Rooms** *24*   Map *C1*

In a 1930s sparkling white building with typical blue shutters and at the entrance to the souks, El-Medina is a hotel with character, offering large, spartan but clean rooms, some of which have fans. The communal bathrooms are clean enough, and there is a café terrace with a restaurant overlooking the lovely square.

Hotel de Suisse

5 Rue de Suisse, 1000 **Tel** *71 32 38 21* **Rooms** *26*   Map *C1*

The Hotel de Suisse's rooms are very spartan, with a shower and basin in the corner, and all are fairly clean. Some rooms have balconies, but street noise can be a problem. The hotel staff are friendly enough, but it's still a good idea to lock up your belongings here. All in all, this is a reasonable budget option.

Hotel du Soleil

32 bis Rue de la Kasbah, 1000 **Tel** *71 32 30 65* **Fax** *71 32 30 65* **Rooms** *12*   Map *C1*

The traditional blue and white colours of its surroundings predominate at this typical, no-frills medina hotel. The rooms are on the small side and reasonably clean, with decent communal toilets and showers, for which you need to pay extra. The hotel is on one of the medina's main streets, right in the action but noisy. No breakfast.

Marhaba

5 Rue de la Commission, 1000 **Tel** *71 32 76 05* **Fax** *71 32 54 52* **Rooms** *14*   Map *C1*

An option for hardened backpackers, this small hotel is laid back, with very welcoming and helpful staff. It is conveniently located at the main entrance of the medina, opposite the Bab el-Bahr. Breakfast is not served at the hotel, but there are plenty of cafés on the square. Showers (additional cost) and toilets are clean and shared.

Agriculture

25 Rue Charles de Gaulle, 1000 **Tel** *71 32 63 94* **Fax** *71 32 16 85* **Rooms** *28*   Map *C1*

This downtown hotel is in a very lively street so the rooms are not the quietest in town. All the small rooms are painted in the typical white and blue, and are equipped with a shower, toilet, central heating, and some also have air-conditioning, while the others just have fans. The staff are friendly, and there is a cafeteria attached.

Grand Hotel de France

8 Rue Mustapha M'Barek, 1000 **Tel** *71 32 62 44* **Fax** *71 32 33 14* **Rooms** *56*   Map *C1*

Very close to the Porte de France, this hotel is both convenient for the centre of town and the old medina. It is a charming hotel in colonial style, with spacious rooms, high ceilings and old furniture as well as clean bathrooms. Check out several rooms before taking one, as the condition of beds varies. **hotelfrancetunis@yahoo.com**

Hotel de Russie

18 Rue de Russie, 1000 **Tel** *71 32 88 83* **Fax** *71 32 72 67* **Rooms** *27*   Map *C1*

A typical budget Ville Nouvelle hotel in a colonial Moorish-style building with a colourful and elegant, if slightly faded, decor. All the cosy rooms have air-conditioning/heating, a clean en suite bathroom and a TV. The rooms on the street side can be very noisy, particularly at weekends. **hotel-russie@yahoo.fr**

Key to Symbols *see back cover flap*

La Maison Dorée

3 Rue el-Kufa, 1000 **Tel** *71 24 06 31* **Fax** *71 33 24 01* **Rooms** *49*

Map C1

Travel back in time at this wonderful old colonial hotel in a grand period building. The current French owner, whose grandfather started the hotel, keeps up the high standards. The immaculate rooms are large with dark furniture, adding to the old-world atmosphere. Some rooms have en suite bathrooms. There may be noise from the nearby metro.

Naplouse

20 Rue de Naplouse, 1001 **Tel** *71 33 88 44* **Fax** *71 33 17 98* **Rooms** *36*

Map C1

The Naplouse is a good-value budget option in the centre of town which attracts both tourists and businessmen. The hotel is in a well-kept modern building with a few traditional style elements. Rooms are clean, and all have en suite bathrooms, mini bar and satellite TV. Friendly staff. **www.hotel-naplouse.com**

Salammbo

6 Rue de Grèce, 1000 **Tel** *71 35 07 32* **Fax** *71 33 74 98* **Rooms** *60*

Map C1

A typical old Ville Nouvelle hotel with spotless, slightly faded rooms, which can be noisy on the street side as it is right in the middle of things. For a little extra you get a room with an immaculate tiled bathroom; others have shared bathrooms. Friendly welcome and the possibility of sleeping on the roof in summer. **hotel.salammbo@gnet.tn**

Transatlantique

106 Rue de Yougoslavie, 1000 **Tel** *71 24 06 80* **Fax** *71 34 40 14* **Rooms** *45*

Map C1

The Transatlantique is a comfortable old-style hotel in a wonderful Maghrebi Art Deco building near the medina and the central market. The large rooms have a basin and shower in the room, clean communal toilets are found in the corridor. The hotel has seen better days, but it is clean and full of atmosphere. Some noise from the adjacent metro line.

Belvédère Fourati Tunis

10 Avenue des États Unis d'Amérique, 1002 **Tel** *71 78 31 33* **Fax** *71 78 22 14* **Rooms** *69*

Map C1

A modern business hotel near the Belvedere Park and commercial district of town, with large rooms equipped with private bathrooms, internet connection, satellite TV and mini bar. The ground level has a popular bar and an international restaurant. A good choice for businessmen. **www.belvederefourati.com**

Carlton

31 Avenue Habib Bourguiba, 1001 **Tel** *71 33 06 44* **Fax** *71 33 81 68* **Rooms** *82*

Map C1

The best hotel in this price category, the Carlton is in a beautifully restored Art Deco building and offers clean and comfortable rooms, right in the hub of town, within easy walking distance of the medina. The staff are very friendly and helpful, and the hotel has a good business centre. **www.hotelcarltontunis.com**

El Oumara

42 bis Rue Ali Dargouth, 1000 **Tel** *71 33 31 22* **Fax** *71 33 80 30* **Rooms** *59*

Map C1

El Oumara is a comfortable hotel convenient for the train station, and seemingly popular with local businessmen. The good-size rooms are spotless and all have satellite TV, a clean bathroom, a comfortable bed and air-conditioning, or heating in winter. Avoid the rooms above the nightclub on the second floor. **hotel.eloumara@planet.tn**

Excel

35 Avenue Habib Bourguiba, 1001 **Tel** *71 35 51 61* **Fax** *71 34 19 29* **Rooms** *45*

Map C1

In a modern building on the city's main artery is the Excel, which has small but comfortable and bright rooms similar to the Carlton's next door, with private bathrooms, satellite TV and air-conditioning. The rooms overlooking the avenue are slightly noisier but have more character, although all are soundproofed. **www.hotelexcel.com**

Golf Royal

51/53 Rue de Yougoslavie, 1000 **Tel** *71 94 14 34* **Fax** *71 34 81 55* **Rooms** *60*

Map C1

This three-star hotel is in a modern building in the centre of town, and has standard, simple but spotless rooms equipped with en suite bathrooms and satellite TV. The hotel has a cafeteria where breakfast and drinks are served, called "The Bunker", and a bar which is popular with locals. **www.golfroyalhotel.com.tn**

Les Ambassadeurs

75 Avenue Taieb Mehiri, 1002 **Tel** *71 84 60 00 / 71 78 80 11* **Fax** *71 78 00 42* **Rooms** *145*

Map C1

The city's largest green zone, the Belvedere Park, faces this comfortable three-star hotel near the business district and embassies. All rooms have satellite TV, internet connection, safe, mini bar and a good-sized bathroom. The hotel has the Consul restaurant, which offers international and Tunisian cuisine. **www.hotel-ambassadeurs.com**

Diplomat

44 Avenue Hedi Chaker, 1002 **Tel** *71 78 52 33* **Fax** *71 78 16 94* **Rooms** *167*

Map C1

The Diplomat is a large modern business hotel, 20-minutes walk from the medina. The rooms are spacious and comfortable, with great views, and are well equipped with all modern conveniences. The hotel has several conference rooms, a bar, an international restaurant and a café-terrace. **www.diplomat-hotel-tunis.com**

Hotel Le Consul

84 Rue de Palestine, 1002 **Tel** *71 28 47 84* **Fax** *71 78 58 24* **Rooms** *44*

Map C1

You will be welcomed as friends by the staff at this charming hotel just five minutes from the Medina. Nothing is too much trouble, from organizing cars, excursions and more. The building is rather non-descript but is nicely appointed with modern furnishings and decor. All rooms have internet connection. **www.hotelleconsul.com**

Hotel du Parc

Avenue de l'Arabie Saoudite, 1002 **Tel** *71 84 30 22* **Fax** *71 84 94 03* **Rooms** *51*   **Map** *C1*

This modern small resort-style hotel near the Belvedere Park has large grounds with lots of sporting facilities, including a great gym and football pitches, popular with international sports teams visiting the country. The spacious rooms are well-appointed and bright, with en suite bathrooms. **www.hotelduparc.com.tn**

Yadis ibn Khaldoun

30 Rue du Kuwayt, 1002 **Tel** *71 83 22 11* **Fax** *71 83 16 89* **Rooms** *130*   **Map** *C1*

Yadis ibn Khaldoun is a large, modern business hotel, slightly off the beaten track, with small rooms. It is not necessarily a first choice option, but acceptable if everything else is full. The rooms have air-conditioning and en suite bathrooms, though the whole place lacks character and the service can be slow. **www.yadis.com**

Abu Nawas

Avenue Mohamed V, 1080 **Tel** *71 35 03 55* **Fax** *71 35 28 82* **Rooms** *313*   **Map** *C1*

Huge, modern and elegant hotel overlooking the city centre and the Gulf of Tunis, with comfortable large rooms, well equipped with mini bars, satellite TV and good-sized bathrooms. The hotel is particularly popular with business-men, and has several restaurants, including a Lebanese, a Tunisian and an Italian.

Dar El-Medina

64 Rue Sidi ben Arous, 1006 **Tel** *71 56 30 22* **Fax** *71 56 35 20* **Rooms** *12*   **Map** *C1*

The first mansion in the medina to be converted into a cosy boutique hotel, with 12 rooms/suites set around two peaceful courtyards. The traditional layout, atmosphere and style have been kept, but there are contemporary additions, inspired by the old ways, that bring it up to date. **www.darelmedina.com**

El-Hana International

49 Avenue Habib Bourguiba, 1000 **Tel** *71 33 11 44* **Fax** *71 34 11 99* **Rooms** *198*   **Map** *C1*

Huge, 1970's Soviet-style mastodon that is a landmark on the town's main avenue, with tired-looking but good-sized and comfortable rooms. The hotel is conveniently located for both the medina and the Ville Nouvelle. The bar and café-terrace on the ground floor are very popular with locals. **inter.elhana@planet.tn**

La Maison Blanche

45 Avenue Mohamed V, 1002 **Tel** *71 84 47 18* **Fax** *71 79 38 42* **Rooms** *48*   **Map** *C1*

This hotel is close to the diplomatic and business area so is not really convenient for the tourist sights, but it has a character all of its own. The lobby and piano bar are in a black and white Art Deco style, while the rooms are spacious and bright, equipped with all modern conveniences and comfortable beds. **maison.blanche@planet.tn**

El-Mechtel

Avenue Ouled Hafouz, 1002 **Tel** *71 94 14 34* **Fax** *71 81 96 13* **Rooms** *270*   **Map** *C1*

This is one of the biggest hotels in town, and is particularly popular with business travellers. The rooms are rather standard but comfortable, and there are several restaurants and a popular nightclub playing loud house music. **heberge.elmechtel@planet.tn**

El-Mouradi Africa

50 Avenue Habib Bourguiba, 1001 **Tel** *71 34 74 77* **Fax** *71 34 74 32* **Rooms** *212*   **Map** *C1*

Africa offers five-star luxury in a Tunis landmark. The tower on the city's main avenue is as central as it gets, both for the medina and the new town. The spacious and comfortable rooms are equipped with all modern conveniences, and have great views over the city. There are several bars and good restaurants here too. **www.elmouradi.com**

Sheraton

Avenue de la Ligue Arabe, Tunis Carthage, 1080 **Tel** *71 78 21 00* **Fax** *71 78 22 08* **Rooms** *285*   **Map** *C1*

The Sheraton Tunis offers renovated rooms and suites, decorated in a contemporary Moorish style. All rooms have a balcony with views over the city, an en suite bathroom, satellite TV and mini bar, and the hotel has several trendy dining options and bars, as well as a good swimming pool and large grounds. **www.starwoodhotels.com**

Tunisia Palace

13 Avenue de France, 1001 **Tel** *71 24 27 00* **Fax** *71 24 25 55* **Rooms** *49*   **Map** *C1*

At the gate of the medina, this hotel is found in a grand Belle Epoque building. The large and elegant rooms are well equipped and have sumptuous bathrooms. The hotel boasts a small spa, an Italian restaurant with views over the city *(see p273)*, a gourmet restaurant and a bar. Staff are rather brusque. **www.goldenyasmin.com/tunisia-palace**

GREATER TUNIS AND CAP BON PENINSULA

CARTHAGE Amilcar

Zone Touristique, Carthage Amilcar, 2016 **Tel** *71 74 07 88* **Fax** *71 74 31 39* **Rooms** *235*   **Map** *C1*

Gigantic hotel below Sidi Bou Saïd's cliff. The hotel's architecture, in a very unattractive 1970's style, has little going for it but the large rooms are clean, comfortable and have great sea views. The hotel has a fresh water swimming pool set in a lush garden, a large sun terrace and a pleasant poolside bar. **www.hotel-amilcar.com**

CARTHAGE Résidence Carthage

16 Rue Hannibal, 2016 **Tel** *71 73 07 86* **Fax** *71 73 07 86* **Rooms** *10* **Map** *C1*

Résidence Carthage is an elegant and quiet little hotel in a residential quarter of Carthage, with spacious classic rooms overlooking a garden full of flowers. This is the kind of hotel people come back to again and again. The restaurant, Le Punique, is renowned for its excellent Moroccan cuisine.

CARTHAGE Villa Didon

Byrsa Hill, 2016 **Tel** *71 73 34 33* **Fax** *71 73 34 88* **Rooms** *10* **Map** *C1*

Splash out at this spectacular boutique hotel with just 10 suites, all with floor-to-ceiling windows overlooking the whole bay of Tunis, the sea and Carthage ruins, with furnishings by Ron Arad and Philippe Starck – including a Jacuzzi in the room. The restaurant *(see p275)* and the bar are excellent, and there is a small spa. **www.villadidon.com**

EL-HAOUARIA Dar Toubib

El-Haouaria, 8045 **Tel** *72 29 71 63* **Fax** *72 29 71 63* **Rooms** *11* **Map** *D1*

This small budget hotel is popular with backpackers who like the laid-back atmosphere. The basic rooms, set around a garden patio, are bright, roomy and clean with en suite bathrooms. There's no air-conditioning, but the breeze from the sea is usually cooling enough. The hotel is a 10-minute walk from the main square.

EL-HAOUARIA L' Épervier

3 Avenue Habib Bourguiba, 8045 **Tel** *72 29 70 17* **Fax** *72 29 72 58* **Rooms** *14* **Map** *D1*

This modest, modern two-star hotel is situated on the main street of this small town. The rooms have balconies, are well kept and comfortable, with spotless bathrooms and air-conditioning, or heating in winter. This is a pleasant little hotel with a wonderful restaurant *(see p275)* attached, that has an excellent reputation.

EL-HAOUARIA Les Grottes

Route Les Grottes **Tel** *72 26 90 72* **Fax** *72 26 90 70* **Rooms** *30* **Map** *D1*

Les Grottes consists of a set of modern bungalows arranged around a garden with two swimming pools and several reputed restaurants serving international and Tunisian cuisine. Since it is set on top of a hill, there are good views and there is also a tranquil atmosphere. **www.centregrotte.com.tn**

GAMMARTH La Tour Blanche

Avenue Taieb Mehiri, 2078 **Tel** *71 74 68 35* **Fax** *71 74 72 47* **Rooms** *35* **Map** *C1*

Smaller than most resort hotels, the pleasant, two-star Tour Blanche is situated on a beautiful strip of beach on the northern coast of Tunisia. The rooms are simple but well kept, with en suite bathrooms, and the garden has a lovely pool surrounded by greenery. **www.tourblanche.com**

GAMMARTH Golden Tulip

Avenue de la Promenade, 2078 **Tel** *71 91 30 00* **Fax** *71 91 39 13* **Rooms** *264* **Map** *C1*

Large, modern hotel built on top of a hill in Gammarth with extensive grounds, and commanding good views of the sea and Tunis. The five-star rooms are spacious and sumptuous, and the hotel has several restaurants, swimming pools, a hammam or Turkish bath, and offers several sports facilities. **www.goldentulipcarthagetunis.com**

GAMMARTH La Résidence

Les Côtes de Carthage, Raoued, 2079 **Tel** *71 91 01 01* **Fax** *71 91 01 44* **Rooms** *164* **Map** *C1*

This, the most luxurious resort in the region, is decorated in a Moorish style with work by contemporary Tunisian artists, and has sumptuous rooms overlooking the beach or large garden. The hotel has several excellent restaurants, a renowned marine spa and two swimming pools as well as a private beach. **www.theresidence-tunis.com**

GAMMARTH Karthago Le Palace

Complexe Cap Gammarth, 1057 **Tel** *71 91 20 00* **Fax** *71 91 14 42* **Rooms** *291* **Map** *C1*

Le Palace offers spacious rooms equipped with satellite TV and an en suite bathroom, and most also have a terrace overlooking the sea. The hotel boasts several restaurants and bars, a health spa, swimming pools and a beach club. Businessmen can make use of the business centre and conference rooms. **www.karthagopalace.com**

HAMMAMET Résidence Amine

Avenue de la Libération, 8050 **Tel** *72 76 55 00* **Rooms** *12* **Map** *D2*

Pleasant little hotel in the centre of Hammamet with very friendly and welcoming management. Some rooms are larger than others, though all are spotless and have good en suite bathrooms, and are decorated with lovely colourful tiles. The decor is simple but the welcome is warm enough to make you feel at home.

HAMMAMET Samaris

Avenue des Nations Unies, 8050 **Tel** *72 22 63 53* **Fax** *72 28 50 73* **Rooms** *16* **Map** *D2*

The rooms here are old fashioned and have definitely seen better days, but they are clean and acceptable. The main reason people like it at Samaris is that the rooms are set around a courtyard and a lovely peaceful garden away from the road, in which it is also possible to pitch your own tent in the shade.

HAMMAMET La Résidence

60 Avenue Habib Bourguiba, 8050 **Tel** *72 28 07 33* **Fax** *72 28 03 96* **Rooms** *184* **Map** *D2*

Good-value hotel in the centre of Hammamet, with a choice of clean and comfortable studios, which all come with a small kitchenette and en suite bathroom. The hotel has several restaurants, a bar, a pool on the roof terrace, a small garden, private beach and little supermarket where alcohol is available. **www.hammamet-residence.com**

HAMMAMET Les Citronniers

Rue de Nevers, 8050 **Tel** *72 28 16 50* **Fax** *72 28 26 01* **Rooms** *57*   *Map D2*

Les Citronniers is a pleasant budget package hotel with two floors of spacious rooms, all equipped with satellite TV, air-conditioning and en suite bathrooms. The hotel has a swimming pool, a pleasant café-terrace and its own private stretch of beach. The rooms have balconies, some overlooking the sea. **www.hotellescitronniers.com**

HAMMAMET Résidence Romane

Avenue Assad ıbn el-Fourat, 8050 **Tel** *72 26 31 03* **Rooms** *25*   *Map D2*

This small holiday resort has both standard double rooms and self-contained flats for two or four people. The rooms are spacious and airy, very well kept and tastefully decorated in traditional local colours. The pool is set in a lovely garden with a good-sized sun terrace and sunbeds. **rommene.sami@gnet.tn**

HAMMAMET African Queen Hotel

Rue Kerkouane, Zone Touristique, 8050 **Tel** *72 31 11 11* **Fax** *72 31 12 22* **Rooms** *4*   *Map D2*

Built in Afro-Asian style, this hotel is set in tropical gardens not far from the medina and close to two golf courses. The spacious rooms all have en suite facilities and the majority have sea views. There's a children's pool and also an indoor pool for use during the colder months. Sports activities, car hire and excursions can be arranged.

HAMMAMET Dar Zakariya

Next to the medina, Hammamet Yasmine, 8050 **Tel** *72 24 85 00* **Fax** *72 24 85 51* **Rooms** *96*   *Map D2*

A relatively small beach resort hotel that was awarded four stars but which should really be three-star, frequented mainly by French package tourists. The rooms are spacious enough, equipped with all modern conveniences, including a good-sized bathroom, and the hotel has several swimming pools and a garden. **dar.zakariya@gnet.tn**

HAMMAMET Grand Oasis

Yasmine Hammamet, 8050 **Tel** *72 22 77 33* **Fax** *72 22 73 15* **Rooms** *135*   *Map D2*

Grand Oasis is a five-star, all inclusive hotel with several restaurants, including French and Japanese, bars, swimming pools, sauna, spa and a wide choice of sports activities and children's entertainment. The rooms are pleasant and cosy, mostly overlooking the sea, and have all the expected facilities.

HAMMAMET Dar Hayet

Route de la Corniche, 8050 **Tel** *72 28 33 99* **Fax** *72 28 33 99* **Rooms** *48*   *Map D2*

The service is friendly at this very pleasant, bright blue and white hotel right on the beach. It is within easy walking distance of the medina and centre of Hammamet, and perfect for a tranquil, old-fashioned beach holiday. The rooms have delightful balconies overlooking the sea. The food in the restaurant is good. **www.darhayethotel.com**

HAMMAMET Hasdrubal Thalassa

Avenue de la Medina, Hammamet Yasmine, 8050 **Tel** *72 24 40 00* **Fax** *72 24 48 95* **Rooms** *211*   *Map D2*

Large, luxurious hotel facing the Mediterranean, renowned for its state-of-the-art thalasso spa and excellent facilities – some of the best in Hammamet. The rooms overlook the sea and are particularly sumptuous, and the hotel boasts some excellent gourmet restaurants and lots of sports facilities. **www.hasdrubal-hotels.com**

HAMMAMET Iberostar Saphir Palace

Boulevard du 7 Novembre, Yasmine Hammamet, 8051 **Tel** *72 24 16 00* **Fax** *72 24 12 22* **Rooms** *236*   *Map D2*

Large holiday beach resort with many restaurants, bars, shops, swimming pools, sports facilities and a luxurious spa. The modern white hotel, in a contemporary Moorish style, has large rooms with a balcony overlooking the sea, marble floors, attractive bathrooms and satellite TV. The staff are friendly and most speak English. **www.iberostar.com**

HAMMAMET Les Orangers Beach Resort

Rue de Nevers, 8050 **Tel** *72 28 05 44* **Rooms** *380*   *Map D2*

This enormous, all-inclusive beach resort is popular with European families in summer and during the holidays, and with older people in winter because of the attractive rates. The hotel has well-appointed rooms with spotless bathrooms, and a wide range of sports activities, restaurants and bars. Child-friendly too. **www.tunisia-orangers.com**

HAMMAMET Melia Flora Park Boutique Hotel

Hammamet Yasmine, 8050 **Tel** *72 22 77 27* **Fax** *72 22 66 01* **Rooms** *100*   *Map D2*

Tunisian style and colours predominate at this modern beach resort, with comfortable rooms overlooking the sea or the large garden, all equipped with en suite bathrooms, satellite TV, safes and mini bars. The hotel has a choice of restaurants and bars, a private beach, several swimming pools and a lovely Moorish café. **www.solmelia.com**

KELIBIA Pension Anis

Avenue Erriadh, 8090 **Tel** *72 29 57 77/ 72 27 31 28* **Fax** *72 27 31 28* **Rooms** *12*   *Map D1*

Both Tunisians and visitors like to holiday in this very friendly family pension, with warm and welcoming staff and very cosy and pleasant rooms. The place is spotless, with communal bathrooms on the landing, although the two larger suites have en suite bathrooms. Good restaurant and in the centre of town.

KELIBIA Palmarina

Near the harbour, 8090 **Tel** *72 27 40 63* **Fax** *72 27 40 55* **Rooms** *36*   *Map D1*

Palmarina is one of the better hotels in Kelibia, with two swimming pools and two restaurants. The quiet rooms, on just two floors, are pleasant and clean, with balconies overlooking the sea. The rooms could, however, do with a splash of paint to smarten them up a little. **www.hotelpalmarina.com**

Key to Price Guide *see p248* **Key to Symbols** *see back cover flap*

KERKOUANE Dar Zenaidi

Opposite the archaeological site, 8090 **Tel** *22 77 47 05* **Fax** *98 30 08 22* **Rooms** *5*   **Map** *D1*

Tranquil hotel in a lovely Mediterranean villa with a beautiful garden and swimming pool. The charming rooms are simple but tastefully decorated, full of local character, and have en suite bathrooms, air-conditioning and satellite TV, as well as panoramic views from the terraces over the Punic ruins and the turquoise sea. **www.dar-zenaidi.com**

LA GOULETTE Lido

Rue Ali Bach Hamba, 2060 **Tel** *71 73 80 45* **Fax** *71 73 81 60* **Rooms** *44*   **Map** *C1*

Lido is a modern, mid-range hotel with well-kept and bright, spacious rooms decked out with local wrought-iron furniture. Most rooms have en suite bathrooms and balconies overlooking the sea. The hotel is close to the excellent local restaurants and port. **www.hotellido.com.tn**

LA MARSA Pension Predl

7 Rue Salah el-Melki, 2092 **Tel** *71 74 95 29/ 95 03 78 26* **Rooms** *5*   **Map** *C1*

The only bed and breakfast in the region is a simple but good value affair, with just five rather plain but spotless rooms in a private house with a garden and a pleasant terrace. The location is great, right in the centre of La Marsa and near the beach, but the welcome is not always as warm as it could be.

LA MARSA Plaza Corniche

22 Rue du Maroc, 2092 **Tel** *71 74 35 77* **Fax** *71 74 25 54* **Rooms** *12*   **Map** *C1*

Plaza Corniche is a pleasant and well-run small hotel with a lot of atmosphere. The well-appointed rooms are decorated in French country style, with neat bathrooms. The hotel bars, restaurants and nightclub are popular with local residents, and the garden comes to life at night with a variety of fairy lights. **www.plaza-corniche.com.tn**

NABEUL Les Roses

Place Hached, 8000 **Tel** *72 28 55 70* **Rooms** *9*   **Map** *D2*

Friendly but very basic family pension in the middle of the souks. The rooms are spartan and quite clean, but have old-fashioned furnishings and small balconies. As you might expect, rooms on the street side are more noisy, but the welcome is friendly and helpful.

NABEUL Le Fakir

Route Touristique, 8000 **Tel** *72 28 54 77* **Fax** *72 28 76 16* **Rooms** *12*   **Map** *D2*

The home cooking on demand is very good at this pleasant and welcoming family-run hotel, with spacious, airy and colourful rooms, including some family rooms with three, four or five beds. All rooms have bathrooms, and some have great terraces with sea views. The garden is a peaceful place to sit in the shade.

NABEUL Les Oliviers

Rue Abou Elkacem Ecchebbi, 8000 **Tel** *72 28 68 65/ 98 27 48 17* **Fax** *72 28 68 65* **Rooms** *13*   **Map** *D2*

You are assured of an enthusiastic welcome at this totally charming little hotel, where the very friendly Turkiya is always ready to help. The hotel is set in an olive grove, and has immaculate rooms, each with a balcony and a bathroom. Breakfast is served, when possible, under an olive tree. Very peaceful. **pensionlesoliviers@yahoo.fr**

NABEUL Les Jasmins

Rue Abou Elkacem Ecchebbi, 8000 **Tel** *72 28 53 43* **Fax** *72 28 50 73* **Rooms** *23*   **Map** *D2*

Local furnishings add to the charm of Les Jasmins, which is painted in the typical white and blue. The rooms are simple but attractive and well kept. The hotel is set in a tranquil olive and orange grove, has a nice swimming pool and overlooks the beach. Family friendly and with the good Slovenia Restaurant. **www.hotellesjasmins.com**

NABEUL Byzance

Route de la Corniche, 8000 **Tel** *72 27 10 00* **Fax** *72 28 71 64* **Rooms** *70*   **Map** *D2*

This three-star hotel facing the beach particularly welcomes families, with a selection of larger and connected rooms. The traditional white and blue rooms are equipped with good-sized bathrooms, comfortable beds and a large terrace overlooking the sea. **www.hotelbyzance.com**

NABEUL Kheops

Avenue Mohamed V, 8000 **Tel** *72 28 65 55* **Fax** *72 28 60 24* **Rooms** *305*   **Map** *D2*

Very large beach resort, mostly frequented by Eastern European package tourists, with large rooms decorated in a rather tacky style but with all amenities. The pool is gigantic, and there are many sports options as well as several restaurants, including a huge buffet. Rooms with balconies overlook the sea. **www.kheopshotel.com**

SIDI BOU SAID Sidi Bou Fares

15 Rue Sidi Bou Fares, 2026 **Tel** *71 74 00 91* **Fax** *71 72 88 68* **Rooms** *10*   **Map** *C1*

Simple, tiny rooms with colourful tiled walls are arranged around an attractive garden courtyard, where you can read or relax in the shade of a fig tree. The hotel is quiet, if a little spartan, and the friendly staff speak English. This hotel is popular, so it is necessary to book early. **hotel.boufares@gnet.tn**

SIDI BOU SAID Sidi Bou Saïd

On the road to La Marsa, 2026 **Tel** *71 74 04 11* **Fax** *71 74 51 29* **Rooms** *32*   **Map** *C1*

Sample the sweeping views across the bay at this modern hotel just a short distance north of the village of Sidi Bou Saïd, and set high up on the cliff. The architecture is not very attractive but it is a pleasant and tranquil place to stay. The large rooms are luxurious and there is a nice swimming pool in the garden.

SIDI BOU SAID Dar Saïd

Rue Toumi, 2026 **Tel** *71 72 96 66* **Fax** *71 72 95 99* **Rooms** *24*   **Map** *C1*

Many rave about this charming and tranquil boutique hotel, just off Sidi Bou Saïd's main pedestrian street, with lovely, well-equipped rooms set around pretty tiled courtyards filled with jasmine and bougainvillea. Some rooms overlook the Mediterranean, as does the pretty pool and garden. Highly recommended. **www.darsaid.com**

NORTHERN TUNISIA

AIN DRAHAM Beau Séjour

Avenue Habib Bourguiba, 8130 **Tel** *78 65 53 63* **Rooms** *18*   **Map** *B2*

This small hotel, a former hunting lodge, is right in the heart of town and decorated with hunting trophies and memorabilia – it is still very popular with hunters. The rooms all have en suite bathrooms, central heating and balconies. The restaurant has a good reputation and there is a bar serving alcohol.

AIN DRAHAM Les Pins

Main Road, 8130 **Tel** *78 65 62 00* **Fax** *78 65 61 82* **Rooms** *21*   **Map** *B2*

There are 21 cosy and comfortable rooms at this small and welcoming hotel, all with spotless en suite bathrooms, satellite TV, central heating and a balcony overlooking pine trees. It has a pleasant salon and a panoramic terrace with views over the beautiful surroundings. Very good value. **www.lespins-hotel.com**

AIN DRAHAM Nour al-Ain

Tabarka Road, 1 km (0.5 miles) out of town, 8130 **Tel** *78 65 50 00* **Fax** *78 65 51 85* **Rooms** *61*   **Map** *B2*

The hotel stands on top of a hill with great views either over Tabarka and the coast, or over Aïn Draham and the forests. The modern building is uninspiring but the rooms are quite cheerful and comfortable with central heating and an indoor swimming pool. There is a hammam attached to the hotel.

AIN DRAHAM Royal Rihana

Av. Habib Bourguiba, 2 km (1 mile) south of town, 8130 **Tel** *78 65 53 91* **Fax** *78 65 55 78* **Rooms** *65*   **Map** *B2*

Slightly more upmarket hotel, popular with hunters and hikers. The atmosphere is decidedly alpine, but the rooms are cosy and immaculate with great views over the surrounding forests. There is a heated indoor pool, a bar and a good restaurant. The hotel organizes interesting hikes and horse rides. **www.royalrihana-hotel.com**

BIZERTE Africain

Rue Sassi el-Bakri, 7000 **Tel** *72 43 44 12* **Rooms** *15*   **Map** *C1*

Basic budget place right in the market and the centre of town. The rooms are spartan but clean and spacious, with high ceilings and dark-brown furniture. The shared bathrooms on the first floor are clean. The management is friendly and very laid back, and there is a restaurant next door.

BIZERTE Auberge de Jeunesse de Rimmel

On the beach off the road to Tunis, 7000 **Tel** *72 44 08 04* **Fax** *72 44 08 04* **Rooms** *9*   **Map** *C1*

Everybody is welcome in this youth hostel and, as well as the boys/men and girls/women dormitories, there are also large rooms for families. All the rooms are straightforward and basic, but clean, as are the shared bathrooms. The hostel is about 1 km (0.5 miles) north of the centre of town. **madhif.rimel@planet.tn**

BIZERTE Saadi

Rue Salh Ben Ali, 7000 **Tel** *23 73 75 45* **Rooms** *14*   **Map** *C1*

Set in a quiet, residential part of town within easy walking distance of the centre and the old port, the Saadi is popular with backpackers. It is arguably the best of the budget options, offering small but clean rooms with balconies, and spotless shared bathrooms. Friendly, welcoming management.

BIZERTE Hotel de la Plage

34 Avenue Mohamed Rejiba, 7000 **Tel** *72 43 65 10* **Fax** *72 42 01 61* **Rooms** *25*   **Map** *C1*

Standing in the town centre, this hotel has a good range of room sizes. Despite its name, it is not situated on the beach at all but in an alley, just a short walk from the sea. The rooms are simple and clean, but avoid those on the street side as they can be very noisy at night.

BIZERTE Nador

Zone Touristique, 7000 **Tel** *72 44 30 22* **Fax** *72 43 38 17* **Rooms** *106*   **Map** *C1*

Nador occupies a large 1970s-style modern building, set in a huge garden near the beach, about 2.5 km (1.5 miles) from the centre of town. The hotel has some old-fashioned charm. The rooms are clean and comfortable, if a little faded, but there is a great old-style swimming pool in the garden.

BIZERTE Le Petit Mousse

Route de la Corniche, 7000 **Tel** *72 43 21 85* **Fax** *72 44 88 71* **Rooms** *10*   **Map** *C1*

There is a definite Mediterranean feel to this delightful family-run hotel, which has spacious, comfortable and immaculate rooms, all en suite and with balconies overlooking the sea. The excellent restaurant *(see p279)* serves grilled fish on a shady terrace. In summer noise from the road is a problem. **lepetitmousse@hotmail.com**

BIZERTE Sidi Salem

Avenue Hedi Nouria, 7000 **Tel** *72 42 03 65* **Fax** *72 42 03 80* **Rooms** *40*

Map *C1*

Andalusian-style white bungalows are set in a vast garden at this large hotel on the white sandy beach near the port. The peaceful rooms are decorated in local style, and clean. Each is equipped with satellite TV, en suite bathrooms and a mini bar. The hotel has several restaurants and a popular discotheque at weekends. **www.hotel-sidisalem.com**

BIZERTE Bizerta Resort

Route de la Corniche, 7000 **Tel** *72 43 69 66* **Fax** *72 42 29 55* **Rooms** *104*

Map *C1*

This large four-star beach resort is the best hotel in town, situated right on the beach within walking distance of the kasbah and the port. The rooms are spacious and comfortable, and the hotel has all the expected facilities such as an indoor and outdoor swimming pool, a fitness room, a hammam and several restaurants. **www.bizertaresort.com**

BIZERTE L'Hotel Residence Nour

Route de la Corniche, Sidi Salem 7000 **Tel** *72 42 50 03* **Fax** *72 42 53 03* **Rooms** *22*

Map *C1*

The Nour is one of the best accommodation choices in Bizerte. It's modern, with Moorish/Tunisian accents and a mix of rooms and apartments with full cooking facilities. Most rooms have balconies and views of the water, and there's direct beach access too. Relaxed restaurant, bar and guest lounge. **www.hotelresidencenour.com**

HAMMAM BOURGUIBA El-Mouradi

Hammam Bourguiba **Tel** *78 65 40 55* **Fax** *78 65 40 57* **Rooms** *172*

Map *B2*

Four-star luxury hotel renowned for its thermal spa which specializes in rheumatological and dermatological complaints. The comfortable rooms have all the usual amenities, plus balconies overlooking the area. There are several restaurants, indoor and outdoor pools and other sports facilities. **mgt.hb@elmouradi.com**

JENDOUBA Atlas

Rue 1 Juin 1955, 8800 **Tel** *78 60 32 17* **Rooms** *18*

Map *B2*

Atlas is a small pension which is conveniently located near the train station. The rooms are clean, but the furnishings, and particularly the mattresses, have seen better days. However, it will do for a night, and it is a good base if you want to get up early to see the ruins at Bulla Regia in the early morning light.

JENDOUBA Simitthu

Boulevard du 9 Avril 1938, 8800 **Tel** *78 60 40 43* **Fax** *78 60 25 95* **Rooms** *25*

Map *B2*

Within very easy walking distance of the bus and *louage* (shared taxi) station, this is the best hotel in town but that is not saying very much! The modern rooms are clean, and have en suite bathrooms and satellite TV, but the whole place feels a bit abandoned. Breakfast is included.

RAF RAF PLAGE Dalia

RafRaf Plage **Tel** *72 44 16 88/ 630* **Rooms** *10*

Map *C1*

This pleasant hotel is the only one in the village. It has reasonable rooms and is set on a wonderful beach, with some rooms having a view of the sea. In addition, beach huts are available for hire in the summer. There are several simple but lovely fish restaurants near the hotel.

SIDI MECHRIG Auberge de Sidi Mechrig

On the beach, 7010 **Tel** *No telephone* **Rooms** *10*

Map *C1*

There are just 10 rooms overlooking the beach at this small auberge. The rooms are simple but comfortable, with high ceilings, good beds and lovely cool tiled floors. The hotel also has a great restaurant *(see p279)*, equally simple, but serving delicious fresh fish, as well as Tunisian salads and couscous.

TABARKA La Plage

11 Avenue 7 Novembre, 8110 **Tel** *78 67 00 39* **Rooms** *16*

Map *B1*

Delightful and very friendly budget hotel, not on the beach, but not too far off it and right in the centre of town. The small rooms are immaculate and comfortable; some have en suite bathrooms while others share. The brightest and best rooms are in the front and have balconies.

TABARKA Les Aiguilles

18 Avenue Habib Bourguiba, 8110 **Tel** *78 67 37 89* **Fax** *78 67 36 04* **Rooms** *19*

Map *B1*

Les Aiguilles is housed in a charming colonial building and stands close to the beach. The rooms are large and clean, with high ceilings and good-sized en suite bathrooms. The hotel is pretty central – close to the old harbour – and some rooms have views of the sea. Very good value and popular, so book ahead. **hotel.lesaiguilles@wanadoo.tn**

TABARKA Novelty

68 Avenue Habib Bourguiba **Tel** *78 67 01 76* **Fax** *78 67 30 08* **Rooms** *26*

Map *B1*

You'll get a personal welcome and bags of character at this comfortable, family-run two-star hotel in the centre of Tabarka. The bright rooms are spotless and comfortable, with simple but good quality furnishings, and all have en suite bathrooms.

TABARKA Abou Nawas Montazah

Route Touristique, 8110 **Tel** *78 67 35 32* **Fax** *78 67 35 30* **Rooms** *306*

Map *B1*

Large beach resort in Tabarka's Tourist Zone, with well-equipped rooms overlooking the grounds or the sea. All rooms have en suite bathrooms and satellite TV, while the hotel has several dining options, many bars and a wide range of sports facilities, including an olympic-size pool and watersports centre on the beach. **www.abounawas.com.tn**

TABARKA Hotel de France

Avenue Habib Bourguiba, 8110 **Tel** *78 67 06 00* **Fax** *78 67 11 32* **Rooms** *16*   **Map** *B1*

The staff and management are extremely welcoming and there is a popular café terrace at this excellent and affordable three-star hotel, in a good central location. The 16 pleasant rooms have comfortable beds, en suite bathrooms and satellite TV, and some even have small balconies overlooking the sea.

TABARKA Les Mimosas

Road up from Bizerte Road, at entrance of town, 8110 **Tel** *78 67 30 18* **Fax** *78 67 32 76* **Rooms** *75*   **Map** *B1*

This charming hotel is set in a beautiful traditional villa on a hilltop, a short walk from the beach. The garden affords a fantastic view of both the sea and the town, and has a small swimming pool. The rooms have less character, but all are spotless and have en suite bathrooms and great views. Helpful staff. **www.hotel-les-mimosas.com**

TABARKA Dar Ismail

Zone Touristique, 8110 **Tel** *78 67 01 88* **Fax** *78 67 03 43* **Rooms** *180*   **Map** *B1*

There is direct access to a long strip of white sandy beach from this luxury five-star holiday resort. The hotel is set in extensive grounds with pine trees and has several pools, a watersports centre, a nearby golf course and plenty of other activities. The rooms are bright and spacious and offer all five-star amenities. **www.hoteldarismail.com**

TABARKA Mehari

Nouvelle Route Touristique, 8110 **Tel** *78 67 01 84* **Fax** *78 67 39 43* **Rooms** *200*   **Map** *B1*

Large salmon-pink beach resort with very spacious rooms, several restaurants and all the usual holiday entertainment, including swimming pools, children's activities and a watersports centre on the beach. The rooms all have a terrace, en suite bathroom, satellite TV, mini bar and safe. **www.goldenyasmin.com**

THE SAHEL

EL-JEM Julius

Road to Sfax, near the train station **Tel** *73 63 04 19* **Fax** *73 63 05 23* **Rooms** *15*   **Map** *D3*

The only option right in the centre of El-Jem is this small hotel with spacious rooms set around a quiet courtyard. The rooms have seen better days but are pleasant enough for one night – those at the end on the ground floor are definitely much quieter.

EL-JEM Ksar El-Jem

Road to Tunis, 4 km (2 miles) out of town **Tel** *73 63 28 00* **Fax** *73 63 03 90* **Rooms** *16*   **Map** *D3*

All the tastefully furnished rooms have en suite bathrooms at this lovely hotel built in the style of a Roman villa, with lots of large open spaces, a swimming pool, terrace, bar and restaurant. This is a popular place so in summer it is necessary to book well in advance. **hotel.ksareljem@gnet.tn**

GABES Atlantique

Avenue Habib Bourguiba, 6000 **Tel** *75 22 00 34* **Fax** *75 22 13 58* **Rooms** *34*   **Map** *D5*

The Atlantique is a large, attractive colonial building with an ornate façade fronted by palm trees. The rooms are pleasant with attractive furnishings, but sizes vary so it is best to check your room on arrival. The bar-disco on the ground floor can be noisy at weekends.

GABES Rahma

Rue Boulbaba M'Rabet, 6000 **Tel** *75 27 53 85* **Fax** *75 27 57 10* **Rooms** *45*   **Map** *D5*

Modern, and sparkling clean, small hotel which offers excellent value accommodation – definitely the best in this category. The rooms are well kept and equipped with satellite TV and en suite bathrooms, but are quite dark. The hotel has no restaurant but there is a small café where snacks can be ordered.

GABES Chems

Near beach, 6000 **Tel** *75 27 05 47* **Fax** *75 27 44 85* **Rooms** *120*   **Map** *D5*

This large hotel complex consists of chalets set in a large palm tree garden, along the beach at Gabès. There is a large pool in the garden and many of the rooms face the sea. All the rooms are spacious, with en suite bathrooms and TV, and the hotel has several restaurants and bars. **www.hotelchems.com.tn**

KERKENNAH ISLANDS Cercina

Sidi Frej, 3025 **Tel** *74 48 99 53* **Fax** *74 48 98 78* **Rooms** *16*   **Map** *D–E4*

A well-established hotel on the island, the Cercina is right on the edge of the sea. There is a choice of rooms, including some suites, each with a small salon attached. The building is not beautiful, but the reception is welcoming. It's worth taking a sea-view room. **hotel.cercina@point.tn**

KERKENNAH ISLANDS Kastil

Sidi Frej, 3025 **Tel** *74 48 12 12* **Fax** *74 48 04 82* **Rooms** *22*   **Map** *D–E4*

There is direct beach access at this modern, small hotel in large grounds. The choice of rooms includes camping grounds, bungalows, rooms overlooking the courtyard and lovely rooms with en suite bathrooms and terraces overlooking the sea. The hotel also has a good traditional restaurant *(see p281)*. **www.hotel-kastil.com**

KSAR GHILANE Camp Yadis

Opposite the hot springs **Tel** *75 62 18 70* **Fax** *75 62 18 72* **Rooms** *120 beds*   **Map** *C6*

Definitely one of the best of the camps, this is secluded and luxurious. The tents are beautifully decorated and centred around a large swimming pool in the shade of palm trees. All have private bathrooms. The restaurant serves traditional Tunisian cuisine, and is a class above the normal encampment. **www.yadis.com**

KSAR GHILANE Le Paradis

Near the hot springs **Tel** *75 90 05 07* **Fax** *75 47 05 15* **Rooms** *120 beds*   **Map** *C6*

Le Paradis is a large camp site under the palm trees, offering roomy Bedouin tents, with several often reserved for groups, and smaller tents with less comfortable beds for individual travellers. Le Paradis is situated a little way from the spring. It has a simple restaurant and clean bathrooms with hot showers.

MAHDIA El-Medina

Rue de l'Ancienne Port, Medina, 5100 **Tel** *73 69 46 64* **Fax** *73 69 07 03* **Rooms** *10*   **Map** *D3*

An alleyway full of plants leads to the best of the medina hotels in Mahdia, with a tiled courtyard where breakfast is served. El-Medina has character and charm, and a lovely roof terrace with great views over the medina, the port and the sea. Spartan but clean rooms with shared bathrooms. **hotelmedina@yahoo.fr**

MAHDIA La Corniche

Boulevard du 7 Novembre, 5100 **Tel** *73 69 42 01* **Fax** *73 69 42 01* **Rooms** *16*   **Map** *D3*

La Corniche is a very basic beach hotel, but a hotel on the beach all the same, about 2 km (1 mile) northwest of the medina and the town centre. The rooms are simple and plain, some with and others without en suite bathrooms – the communal bathrooms are not as clean. Choose a room with a sea view. Closed mid-Oct–Mar.

MAHDIA Dar Sidi

Marina, Rejicha, 5100 **Tel** *73 68 70 01* **Fax** *73 68 70 03* **Rooms** *10*   **Map** *D3*

This small and quiet "hôtel de charme" *(see p244)* has 10 well-decorated bungalows, all equipped with spotless en suite bathrooms, air-conditioning and satellite TV. The hotel has a pleasant pool and a good restaurant. It is located near the beach and the marina and tourist development. Helpful, articulate staff. Closed Nov–late spring.

MAHDIA El-Mouradi

Nouvelle Zone Touristique, 5011 **Tel** *68 21 11* **Fax** *68 21 20* **Rooms** *394*   **Map** *D3*

Gigantic five-star beach resort spread over large grounds, with a well-kept garden and direct acess to a lovely beach with white sand and turquoise water. The rooms are spacious and comfortable, furnished in the bland style of a four-star hotel, with all modern conveniences. There are several restaurants and pools. **www.elmouradi.com**

MAHDIA Le Phénix

Corner of Av. H. Bourguiba & Av. Bechir Sfar, 5100 **Tel** *73 69 01 01* **Fax** *73 69 01 08* **Rooms** *24*   **Map** *D3*

Wonderful four-star hotel near the beach and the old medina, with contemporary, loft-style architecture. The rooms are spacious, airy and colourful, with floor-to-ceiling windows overlooking the medina or the sea. The bathrooms have luxurious marble floors. The hotel has a good restaurant *(see p281)* and a pool. **phenixmahdia@planet.tn**

MAHDIA Mahdia Palace

Zone Touristique, 5100 **Tel** *73 68 37 77* **Fax** *73 68 38 10* **Rooms** *432*   **Map** *D3*

Magnificent Moorish architecture bedecks this top-range hotel, which has outdoor and indoor swimming pools, a vast garden and large rooms with all five-star amenities. The staff are friendly and the interior is warm and very attractive. The hotel offers many sports activities and has a good thalasso therapy spa. **www.mahdiapalace.com**

MATMATA Marhala

Off the main square, 6070 **Tel** *75 24 00 15* **Fax** *75 24 01 09* **Rooms** *24*   **Map** *D5*

Marhala is definitely the best of the troglodyte or underground hotels in local style. There are 24 small but cosy and comfortable rooms, with comfy beds and spotless shared bathrooms. The hotel's dining room is also in an underground cave and serves good Tunisian food.

MATMATA Ksar Amazigh

On the Douz Road, 6070 **Tel** *75 24 00 88* **Fax** *75 24 01 73* **Rooms** *50*   **Map** *D5*

The Ksar Amazigh is just a short walk out of town, in a traditional underground house, with a pool. The rooms are arranged around a courtyard with whitewashed walls. The place is usually frequented by groups, and can have an abandoned feel to it if you are staying on your own. However, the views are great.

MATMATA Diar El-Barbar

On the Douz Road, 6070 **Tel** *75 24 00 74* **Fax** *75 24 01 44* **Rooms** *165*   **Map** *D5*

This large, luxurious four-star hotel is a short distance out of town, and is inspired by *ksar* architecture, so prevalent in the region. The comfortable rooms are barrel-vaulted, as in the troglodyte dwellings, and set around courtyards. There are great views over the surrounding desert, particularly from the swimming pool. **www.diarelbarbar.com**

MONASTIR Yasmine

Route de la Falaise, 5000 **Tel** *73 50 15 46* **Rooms** *10*   **Map** *D3*

Some rooms have a view over the sea at this rather charming, small family-run hotel. There is a Moorish façade and simple clean rooms, mostly with private bathrooms and little balconies, some with clean shared bathrooms on the landing. There is a good restaurant and bar, which are also open in winter.

MONASTIR Monastir Beach

Route de la Corniche, 5000 **Tel** *73 46 47 66* **Fax** *73 46 35 94* **Rooms** *45*   **Map** *D3*

Monastir Beach is literally on the beach, stretched out under the Corniche, so it can not be seen from the road. The rooms are basic, but fine for this price, more or less clean, with plastic furniture and en suite bathrooms. Air-conditioning and heating require a supplement, but are essential. Bar and restaurant. **monastirbeach@yahoo.com**

MONASTIR Residence Corniche

Place du 3 Août, 5000 **Tel** *73 46 14 51* **Fax** *73 46 14 51* **Rooms** *10*   **Map** *D3*

This hotel is in an attractive, typically Tunisian, building with a large café-terrace on the ground floor. There are rooms and two flats for families with a small salon but no kitchen. The rooms are well kept, with clean, private bathrooms, and some have a balcony. The welcome is quite friendly and the hotel has a restaurant. **hotelcorniche@topnet.tn**

MONASTIR Marina Cap Monastir

Marina, 5000 **Tel** *73 46 23 05* **Fax** *73 46 49 99* **Rooms** *59*   **Map** *D3*

A complex of studios, and two-, three- and four-bedroom apartments, all with a kitchen, bathroom and terrace overlooking the sea or marina. The flats are built in local style, all blue and white, and are close to the ribat and the medina, as well as to the beach. There are plenty of bars and restaurants in the marina. **www.marinamonastir.com**

MONASTIR Amir Palace

Zone Touristique, 5000 **Tel** *73 52 09 00* **Fax** *73 52 18 23* **Rooms** *369*   **Map** *D3*

Situated about 4 km (2 miles) from the centre of town, in the Zone Touristique, this is one of the more upmarket hotels in Monastir. Spacious and elegant, it resembles a palace surrounded by magnificent gardens and it has direct access on to the beach. The hotel has a popular nightclub and a choice of restaurants. **dc.amirpalace@gnet.tn**

MONASTIR Framissima Regency

Marina, 5000 **Tel** *73 46 00 33* **Fax** *73 46 01 17* **Rooms** *200*   **Map** *D3*

French holiday makers fill this large hotel and dutifully join in with all the activities organized throughout the day. The four-star rooms are spacious and light, with colourful furnishings and well-kept bathrooms. The garden is attractive with a great pool, and the hotel has a choice of restaurants. **regency@fram.fr**

PORT EL-KANTAOUI El-Hana Hannibal Palace

Zone Touristique, 4089 **Tel** *73 34 85 77* **Fax** *73 34 83 21* **Rooms** *252*   **Map** *D2*

Five-star hotel very close to the marina in a fading, 1970's-style building that could do with some renovation. The location is great but the service could be better and the fading decor is reflected in the bargain prices paid by package tourists. The rooms, however, are spacious and clean with great sea views. **www.elhanahannibalpalace.com**

PORT EL-KANTAOUI El-Mouradi Palm Marina

Zone Touristique, 4089 **Tel** *73 24 69 00* **Fax** *73 24 65 20* **Rooms** *389*   **Map** *D2*

This all-inclusive five-star luxury beach hotel is one of the five the El-Mouradi chain owns in Port el-Kantaoui alone. The hotel is large and offers all possible sports facilities, including several swimming pools in the garden and a good beach. The rooms have great views over the sea and the grounds, and are well equipped. **www.elmouradi.com**

PORT EL-KANTAOUI Iberostar Diar el-Andalous

Zone Touristique, 4089 **Tel** *73 24 62 00* **Fax** *73 24 63 48* **Rooms** *306*   **Map** *D2*

European sunseekers are well catered for at this gigantic beach resort, set in a 19-hectare park with direct access to the beach. All the rooms offer five-star amenities, and have balconies overlooking the sea and the gardens. The hotel has several restaurants and bars, and a wide choice of entertainment and sports facilities. **www.iberostar.com**

SFAX Ennacer

Rue des Notaires, 3000 **Tel** *74 21 10 37* **Fax** *74 20 01 58* **Rooms** *9*   **Map** *D4*

The best hotel of the budget options in the medina, close to the Bab Jebli gate. The white building has lovely bright blue *moucharaby* latticework windows and simple but immaculate rooms with tiled walls. The best thing is the rooftop terrace with views over the medina.

SFAX Thyna

Place Marbourg, 3000 **Tel** *74 22 53 17* **Fax** *74 22 57 73* **Rooms** *17*   **Map** *D4*

This small, well-run hotel offers excellent value in this price range. Very central and close to Bab Diwan, the main entrance to the medina, the hotel offers spotlessly clean and pleasant rooms each with air-conditioning, a good en suite bathroom, and a balcony overlooking a little square. **www.hotel-thyna.com**

SFAX Les Oliviers Palace

25 Avenue Hedi Chaker, 3000 **Tel** *74 20 19 99* **Fax** *74 20 18 88* **Rooms** *132*   **Map** *D4*

The spectacular neo-Moorish, French colonial-style building has been lovingly restored and is the top luxury hotel in Sfax, awarded five stars. The rooms are beautiful and elegant, decorated with dark wood and fine textiles, and all have a contemporary-style bathroom. The hotel has several good restaurants. **www.goldenyasmin.com**

SFAX Mercure Accor

15 Avenue Habib Bourguiba, 3000 **Tel** *74 22 57 00* **Fax** *74 22 55 21* **Rooms** *130*   **Map** *D4*

The rooms are bright, airy and comfortable in this large four-star hotel in the centre of town, within easy walking distance of the medina and with great views over the city. The hotel has a restaurant, bar, outdoor swimming pool, a conference centre for 800 people and a large shopping arcade. **www.accorhotels.com**

Key to Price Guide *see p248* **Key to Symbols** *see back cover flap*

SOUSSE Claridge

10 Avenue Habib Bourguiba, 4000 **Tel** *73 22 47 59* **Fax** *73 22 72 77* **Rooms** *29* **Map** *D3*

Old-fashioned colonial style hotel on one of the city's main streets, in between the beach and the entrance to the medina. The spacious and airy rooms have faded beyond attractive, but the hotel is inexpensive and full of character. The rooms all have showers and basins, but the toilets are on the landing.

SOUSSE Emira

52 Rue de France, 4000 **Tel** *73 22 63 25* **Fax** *73 22 63 25* **Rooms** *15* **Map** *D3*

The staff are friendly and very efficient at this small budget hotel on one of the main thoroughfares of the old medina, with 15 pleasant and comfortable, if basic, rooms. The rooms have nice tiling, and good clean bathrooms. There is a wonderful roof terrace with magnificent views over the city.

SOUSSE Résidence al-Faracha

Rue al-Farachal Rue des Papillons, 4000 **Tel** *73 22 72 79* **Fax** *73 22 72 70* **Rooms** *15* **Map** *D3*

You'll get good value at this small pension in a quiet side street near the beach and the centre of town, and within walking distance of the train station. The reception is not particularly friendly but the rooms are well kept, with clean en suite bathrooms and telephones. Some rooms have a balcony overlooking the street. **www.hotelfaracha.com**

SOUSSE Abou Nawas Boujaffar

Avenue Habib Bourguiba, 4000 **Tel** *73 22 60 30* **Fax** *73 22 67 76* **Rooms** *246* **Map** *D3*

A five-star beach hotel in the heart of the Ville Nouvelle, close to the port and the medina, as well as shops and restaurants. The hotel offers a choice of comfortable rooms with views over the sea or the city, all with en suite bathrooms. There are also several restaurants and a good-sized swimming pool. **www.abounawas.com.tn**

SOUSSE La Gondole

Avenue Hedi Chaker, 4000 **Tel** *73 21 45 00* **Fax** *73 21 45 10* **Rooms** *65* **Map** *D3*

Although it's huge and ugly, this grey high-rise building has comfortable, bright and well-kept rooms. This is a beach resort, but it is a few streets away from the sea front and has no sea views at all. It's popular with families in the summer and older people who come here for the winter sun. **lagondole@planet.tn**

SOUSSE Sousse Palace

Avenue Habib Bourguiba, 4000 **Tel** *73 21 92 20* **Fax** *73 21 92 21* **Rooms** *178* **Map** *D3*

The Sousse Palace is a typical four-star holiday resort overlooking the beach and the sea. The rooms are pretty standard, with neutral decor, wood furnishings and fresh, patterned textiles. All have balconies overlooking the city or the sea. Facilities include indoor and outdoor swimming pools and a good gym. **www.soussepalacehotel.com**

JERBA AND THE MEDENINE AREA

JERBA Arisha

36 Rue Ghazi Mustapha, Houmt Souk, 4180 **Tel** *75 65 03 84* **Fax** *75 65 39 45* **Rooms** *15* **Map** *D5*

This *fondouk* (inn) has a courtyard filled with bougainvillea and jasmine, and a great roof terrace with views over the old town. The rooms are simple but tastefully decorated in local style and colours, and there is a small pool. The hotel has a good reputation and should be booked in advance in high season.

JERBA Dar Faiza

6 Rue de la République, Houmt Souk, 4180 **Tel** *75 65 00 83* **Fax** *75 65 17 63* **Rooms** *29* **Map** *D5*

The Dar Faiza is an attractive hotel in an old Moorish villa that belonged to a French count until 1959. The neat rooms are simple, but well kept and comfortable, and surrounded by a lovely garden filled with bougainvillea and palm trees. Guests can use the small pool and there is a restaurant-pizzeria. **www.darfaizadarsalem.com**

JERBA El-Machrek

Avenue Habib Bourguiba, Houmt Souk, 4180 **Tel** *75 65 31 55* **Fax** *75 65 31 57* **Rooms** *40* **Map** *D5*

A modern hotel without frills, but perfectly kept, the El-Machrek offers clean and comfortable rooms with en suite bathrooms and air-conditioning. The rooms on the street side are brighter and have a balcony, while the ones above the bar are somewhat noisy. **hotel.elmachrek@planet.tn**

JERBA Erriadh

10 Rue Mohamed el-Ferjani, Houmt Souk, 4180 **Tel** *75 65 07 56* **Fax** *75 65 26 91* **Rooms** *28* **Map** *D5*

Small hotel in a well-preserved old *fondouk* (inn), where the rooms are arranged around a large and picturesque courtyard filled with flowers. The rooms are simple but attractive, with lovely tiles and ceramics, and *moucharaby* wooden windows. The rooms on the first floor are brighter and quieter. **mounir.herbergue@gnet.tn**

JERBA Hotel du Lotos

18 Rue de la République, Houmt Souk, 4180 **Tel** *75 65 00 26* **Rooms** *15* **Map** *D5*

The rooms are simple but large and are decorated in French–Tunisian style – whitewashed walls with blue shutters and doors. Bright and airy, many rooms have spacious terraces overlooking Houmt Souk harbour. There's a good restaurant as well as a bar and pizzeria in the lovely courtyard. **www.lotoshotel.com**

JERBA Sables d'Or

30 Rue Mohamed el-Ferjani, Houmt Souk, 4180 **Tel** *75 65 04 23* **Rooms** 38   **Map** D5

Sables d'Or is a charming budget option in a beautiful old house, tastefully decorated with painted woodwork, old ceramics and *objets trouvés* (found art). The cosy rooms all have basins and showers (though toilets are communal), and are arranged around an internal courtyard which is filled with flower pots. Expect a friendly welcome.

JERBA Djerba Midoun

Rue du 13 Août, Midoun, 4125 **Tel** *75 73 00 06* **Fax** *75 73 00 93* **Rooms** 35   **Map** E5

This modern, mid-range hotel has impeccable rooms which are both cosy and spotless, and each has a large balcony, an en suite bathroom, air-conditioning and satellite TV. The rooms here are arranged around a lovely courtyard with a fountain and colourful tiled walls. Breakfast is served on a delightful terrace.

JERBA Dar Salem

Route Touristique, 4180 **Tel** *75 75 76 67* **Rooms** 22   **Map** D-E5

Light years away from the mostly huge resorts on the beautiful stretch of beach that is Sidi Mehrez, this lovely small hotel is built in Tunisian style, white with bright blue wooden shutters, a colour scheme that is continued in the rooms. The rooms each have en suite bathrooms, a TV and a balcony with sea view. **www.darfaizadarsalem.com**

JERBA Résidence Dar Ali

Route Touristique, 4179 **Tel** *75 75 80 45* **Fax** *75 75 80 45* **Rooms** 15   **Map** D-E5

Small, Tunisian-style hotel in a villa, just a short walk from Sidi Mehrez beach. The villa has a tiny private stretch of beach, a lovely rooftop terrace and a swimming pool in the garden, and is more intimate than the huge hotels in the area, with pleasant, comfortable rooms and en suite bathrooms.

JERBA Abou Nawas

Zone Touristique, 4179 **Tel** *75 75 70 22* **Fax** *75 75 77 00* **Rooms** 498   **Map** D5

This enormous, beautifully designed hotel has spacious rooms and all the usual amenities, including a traditional hammam and a large fitness centre. The garden is magnificent, with several swimming pools. The hotel offers a wide variety of sports facilities, restaurants and bars. **www.abounawas.com.tn**

JERBA Dar el-Bhar

Zone Touristique, Houmt Souk **Tel** *75 12 34 56* **Fax** *75 14 72 58* **Rooms** 10   **Map** D5

Dar Bhar is a lovely boutique hotel with a choice of spacious suites, stylishly decorated in a contemporary style. The rooms are on two floors, in a Cubist white house which is reminiscent of the Greek Islands, with a lovely courtyard. Guests can relax by the pool or on the beach, or use the hotel's wellness centre. **www.darvoyage.com**

JERBA Dar Dhiafa

Erriadh/Hara Seghira, 4146 **Tel** *75 67 11 66* **Fax** *75 67 07 93* **Rooms** 14   **Map** D5

Discreetly tucked away in its own splendid gardens, this luxurious, small boutique hotel is a sort of hideaway. The sumptuous rooms and suites are decorated with the finest local crafts and furnishings. The restaurant has an excellent reputation, and there is a pool and a hammam. English spoken. **www.hoteldardhiafa.com**

JERBA Melia Djerba Menzel

Zone Touristique, 4179 **Tel** *75 75 03 00* **Fax** *75 75 04 90* **Rooms** 635   **Map** D5

The rooms in this hotel are set in small bungalows built like the traditional Djerban *menzels* (houses), arranged in large grounds with several swimming pools and a long stretch of private beach. This is an all-inclusive hotel, with a choice of restaurants, bars and cafés, and every imaginable activity to entertain the guests. **www.elmouradi.com**

JERBA Radisson Blu Resort & Thalasso SAS

Zone Touristique, Houmt Souk, 4179 **Tel** *75 75 76 00* **Fax** *75 75 76 01* **Rooms** 296   **Map** D5

Modern, luxurious five-star beach resort with all the necessary facilities to keep you here for your entire stay. The bright, opulent rooms are beautifully decorated in a pleasant contemporary style, with a terrace overlooking the sea. Large choice of restaurants, bars and entertainment, as well as a thalasso spa. **www.djerba.radissonsas.com**

JERBA Sofitel Palm Beach

Zone Touristique, Houmt Souk, 4179 **Tel** *75 75 77 77* **Fax** *75 75 88 88* **Rooms** 225   **Map** D5

The beach centre offers a wealth of watersports and other activities at this five-star luxurious holiday resort. There is a spa and thalasso therapy centre, several good restaurants, bars, and a popular discotheque. The spacious, elegant rooms all have terraces, en suite bathrooms and all modern amenities. **palmbeach.palace@gnet.tn**

JERBA Villa Azur

Near the Sidi Mehrez Beach, Zone Touristique, 4179 **Tel** *75 75 72 57* **Fax** *75 75 81 29* **Rooms** 16   **Map** D5

Though modern, this family-run hotel takes its inspiration from the traditional Tunisian style. The rooms, decorated in a contemporary style, are well kept and very comfortable, with good mattresses, en suite bathrooms, satellite TV and a balcony or terrace with sea view. The hotel has an American buffet at breakfast. **www.villa-azur-djerba.com**

ZARZIS Zyen

Zone Touristique, 4170 **Tel** *75 70 66 30* **Fax** *75 70 66 29* **Rooms** 15   **Map** E5

Small hotel situated on a hill overlooking the sea and the palmeraie. The rooms are air-conditioned and furnished using local textiles, and each has a clean en suite bathroom. The restaurant is rather elegant and the *café maure* (Arab-style café) is a good place to relax with a cup of mint tea and a *chicha* (water pipe).

Key to Price Guide *see p248* **Key to Symbols** *see back cover flap*

ZARZIS Résidence Sultana

On the seaside, Souihel, 4170 **Tel** *75 70 51 15/ 98 30 24 16* **Fax** *75 70 51 67* **Rooms** *13*   **Map** *E5*

In a great spot for a relaxed beach holiday, this lovely white hotel, built more or less like the traditional local architecture, has five rooms, five suites and three duplexes, all with bathrooms and terraces overlooking the sea. The garden, filled with bougainvillea, palm trees and mimosa, adds to the tranquillity. **www.residence-sultana.com**

ZARZIS Sangho

Zone Touristique, 4170 **Tel** *75 70 51 24* **Fax** *75 70 57 15* **Rooms** *361*   **Map** *E5*

Large, three-star holiday complex in Zarzis's Tourist Zone, which has been attractively designed in a contemporary Tunisian style. The rooms are spacious and airy, with all modern amenities and a terrace overlooking the sea or the beautiful gardens. The hotel has a huge range of activities and entertainment. **www.sangho-zarzis.com**

SOUTHERN TUNISIA

DOUZ El-Medina

Rue el-Hanine, 4260 **Tel** *75 47 00 10* **Fax** *75 47 00 10* **Rooms** *13*   **Map** *C6*

The welcome is friendly at El-Medina, a small, centrally located hotel near the market, which has clean but faded rooms that could do with a splash of paint. The hotel has a lovely cool *café maure* (Arab-style café) and a great terrace for sunset drinks with views over the town, the oasis and the surrounding desert. Some rooms have balconies too.

DOUZ La Tente

Rue el-Hanine, 4260 **Tel** *75 47 04 68* **Fax** *75 47 04 68* **Rooms** *12*   **Map** *C6*

La Tente is a pleasant little budget place with very friendly and welcoming staff. The rooms are basic, as expected for this price, but adequate and very clean. Some have en suite bathrooms, others share, but all are well kept. The rooms on the terrace on the first floor are the best.

DOUZ Résidence du 20-Mars

Rue du 20-Mars, 4260 **Tel** *75 47 02 69* **Fax** *75 47 29 22* **Rooms** *30*   **Map** *C6*

This charming place is in the centre of Douz and handy for exploring the surrounding area. It is very good value and the management are extremely friendly. The rooms, decorated with lovely tiles and immaculately kept, are arranged around a shady courtyard, ideal for a rest from the midday heat. **hotel20mars@planet.tn**

DOUZ Saharien Paradise

Zone Touristique, Palmeraie, 4260 **Tel** *75 47 13 37* **Fax** *75 47 03 39* **Rooms** *160*   **Map** *C6*

A lovely palmeraie is the setting for this large hotel, which was once more sumptuous than today. The chalets are in a garden filled with palm trees and birdsong, and there are several pools and restaurants. The rooms are tiled and decorated in Tunisian style. It's just a shame that everything feels a bit past its best. **www.sdts.tourism.tn**

DOUZ Golden Yasmin Mehari

Zone Touristique, 4260 **Tel** *75 47 10 88* **Fax** *75 47 15 89* **Rooms** *128*   **Map** *C6*

The architecture of this hotel is traditional Tunisian, with some interesting communal areas. The rooms are spacious, with wrought-iron furnishings and all modern amenities. There is a good outdoor pool and a sulphurous hot indoor pool for skin treatments. The gardens are impressive. **www.goldenyasmin.com**

KEBILI Les Dunes

Bechri-Souq al-Had, 4230 **Tel** *75 48 07 11* **Fax** *75 48 06 53* **Rooms** *89*   **Map** *C5*

This hotel is 22 km (14 miles) west of Kebili, near the village of El-Bechri, on the road to Tozeur. The hotel has been renovated, and the Moorish-style complex now has spacious and pleasant rooms. There is an adequate restaurant and a large pool area for sunbathing.

KEBILI L'Oasis Dar Kebili

Route Touristique, on the road to Douz, 4200 **Tel** *75 49 14 36* **Fax** *75 49 11 40* **Rooms** *100*   **Map** *C5*

L'Oasis Dar Kebili is a large, luxury hotel in an attractive location on the edge of town. The rooms are spacious and comfortable, with good views over the grounds and surroundings, and have en suite bathrooms and satellite TV. The hotel offers a wide range of facilities, including a good-sized swimming pool. **l'oasis@gmail.com**

NEFTA Marhala

Zone Touristique, 2240 **Tel** *76 43 00 27* **Fax** *76 43 05 11* **Rooms** *36*   **Map** *A5*

The small, reasonable rooms here have air-conditioning, heating and a shower, though they have little character. It's possible to camp in the garden for a modest fee. The restaurant offers good value Tunisian and international dishes. Usefully, the hotel also organizes desert trips. **marhala@yahoo.fr**

NEFTA Chambres d'Hôtes Dar Houidi

Algma el-Hawaida, Vieille Ville (Old City), 2240 **Tel** *98 57 77 05/ 76 43 25 11* **Rooms** *6*   **Map** *A5*

Take advantage of the unique opportunity to sleep in a real house in the medina. Dar Houidi is a typical 17th-century house that is now part museum and part bed & breakfast, with rooms decorated as a traditional medina with beds made out of palm trees and mattresses stuffed with wool. The food is delicious. **www.darhouidi-tourism.com**

NEFTA Caravanserail

Zone Touristique, 2240 **Tel** *76 43 03 55* **Fax** *76 43 03 44* **Rooms** *134*   **Map** *A5*

Many hotels in Nefta feel a bit tired and worn, but the Caravanserail is probably the best in town – it's a typical large resort hotel centred around a pool, with each spacious room having a small balcony, mini bar, satellite TV and good-sized bathroom. Choose a room on the upper floor for superb views. **hotel.caravanserailnefta@planet.tn**

NEFTA Dar Zargouni

Corbeille, Nefta, 2240 **Tel** *98 62 19 20 / 71 90 80 48* **Rooms** *8*   **Map** *A5*

Gorgeous villa built around two internal courtyards, in the typical Nefta brickwork and with panoramic views over the exotic Corbeille. The entire villa is for rent, or you can rent separate rooms and still use the salons and kitchen. Everything is decorated with local crafts, mostly made of palm tree wood. **www.darzargouni.com**

NEFTA La Rose

Zone Touristique, 2240 **Tel** *76 43 06 96* **Fax** *76 43 03 85* **Rooms** *95*   **Map** *A5*

This is not the most beautiful hotel but the rooms on the upper floor, particularly those with a balcony, command superb views over the oasis and garden. The rooms have all the basic comforts for this category, with bathroom and air-conditioning and heating in winter. The food, however, is quite bland, and service slow.

TAMERZA Les Cascades

Centre of the village, 2212 **Tel** *76 48 53 32* **Fax** *76 48 53 32* **Rooms** *40*   **Map** *A5*

Les Cascades is a popular budget option, with bungalows made from palm trees, and beds and wardrobes made using palm fronds. It's set in the shade of palm trees, along a little wadi in the palmeraie. Most rooms actually have a concrete wall in between them for a little soundproofing. The tiled bathrooms are clean and shared.

TAMERZA Tamerza Palace

Road to Chebika, 2212 **Tel** *76 48 53 44* **Fax** *76 48 53 44* **Rooms** *109*   **Map** *A5*

Enjoy being pampered here, with a whole range of luxurious rooms in this beautiful hotel built against the mountain, and with superb views. The architecture was clearly inspired by the abandoned village opposite the hotel. All rooms are sumptuous, each has a small terrace. The garden is tranquil and has a lovely pool. **www.tamerza-palace.com**

TATAOUINE Mabrouk

Route de Chenini, opp Mémoire de la Terre Museum, 3200 **Tel** *75 86 28 05* **Fax** *75 85 01 00* **Rooms** *25* **Map** *D6*

The spacious rooms here have air-conditioning and heating, with a vaulted ceiling in the style of *ghorfa (see p196)* rooms. Cleanliness is not always a priority, but the manager is friendly and can help to organize trips in the region. Unfortunately, the food is bland and not really recommended. **hotelmabrouk@hotmail.com**

TATAOUINE Résidence Hotel Hamza

Avenue Hedi Chaker, 3200 **Tel** *75 86 35 06* **Fax** *75 86 20 68* **Rooms** *24*   **Map** *D6*

It is best to book in advance at this popular budget option. Some rooms have shared showers and toilets, others have en suite bathrooms. Perhaps avoid the rooms above the bar, as there is little soundproofing. The young manager and staff are very friendly and always ready to help you make the best of your stay.

TATAOUINE Dakyanus

Road to Ghoumrassen, 7 km (4 miles) from Tataouine, 3200 **Tel** *75 83 21 99* **Fax** *75 83 21 98* **Rooms** *100* **Map** *D6*

These small bungalows, vaguely inspired by *ghorfa (see p196)* architecture, are comfortable and spotless with en suite bathrooms, satellite TV and air-conditioning/heating. The hotel has a lovely terrace, a large, well-kept swimming pool right in the desert, and a ranch with horses and camels for desert excursions. **www.hotel-dakyanus.tn**

TATAOUINE Sangho Privilege

On road to Chenini, 2.5 km (1.5 miles) out of town, 3200 **Tel** *75 86 01 24* **Fax** *75 86 21 77* **Rooms** *75* **Map** *D6*

This attractive ochre-coloured hotel blends in perfectly with the landscape, and has bungalows spread over a peaceful and well-kept garden. The good-sized rooms are simply but tastefully decorated, with spotless bathrooms and comfortable beds. The restaurant serves excellent Tunisian dishes, often outside. **www.sangho.fr**

TOZEUR Résidence Karim

Avenue Abou Kacem Chebbi, 2200 **Tel** *76 45 43 74/ 23 34 59 17* **Fax** *76 46 31 63* **Rooms** *27*   **Map** *B5*

Try the cosy, fresh rooms at this charming hotel set around a tranquil courtyard filled with bougainvillea. All rooms have en suite bathrooms and air-conditioning/heating, for which a small supplement is charged. It is possible to eat on the roof terrace, with food coming from the nearby Capitole restaurant *(see p286)*. **www.residencekarim.com**

TOZEUR Résidence Naifer

Place du 7 Novembre, Bab El-Hawa, 2200 **Tel** *76 46 06 10* **Fax** *76 46 19 00* **Rooms** *24*   **Map** *B5*

Spotless and friendly small pension in the centre of town, conveniently located near the bus station. The rooms are large, for two to four people, with clean bed linen and en suite bathrooms. The rooms on the street side are noisier, but some of the quieter rooms are darker, looking out on to the internal corridor. **residence@gmail.com**

TOZEUR Résidence Warda

Avenue Abou Kacem Chebbi, 2200 **Tel** *76 45 25 97* **Fax** *76 45 27 44* **Rooms** *34*   **Map** *B5*

Well located near the centre of town and the palmeraie behind, the Résidence Warda has rooms that are well-kept, and most have en suite bathrooms, while air-conditioning or heating are available for a supplement. All rooms look out over a small garden filled with flowers, and there is a lovely roof terrace. **reservations@residencewarda.com**

Key to Price Guide *see p248* **Key to Symbols** *see back cover flap*

TOZEUR Chambres d'Hôtes Le Minaret/Dar Ennour

A 10-minute walk from Avenue Habib Bourguiba, 2200 **Tel** *23 52 42 03* **Rooms** *2* **Map** *B5*

The French owners of Le Minaret restaurant have opened two rooms in their own home as a bed & breakfast. Both lovely rooms have private terraces and en suite bathrooms, and guests can use the sun terrace and the swimming pool, or enjoy the lush garden. The breakfast is definitely the best in town. **darennour.spm@gnet.tn**

TOZEUR Résidence el-Arish

Avenue Aboulkacem Chebbi, 2200 **Tel** *76 46 03 44/ 76 46 26 44* **Fax** *76 46 15 44* **Rooms** *20* **Map** *B5*

Spotless and welcoming budget option with comfortable rooms and small but clean en suite bathrooms. The front rooms are noisier, while the back rooms overlook the palmeraie. There is a small but pleasant café in the garden for tea and *chicha* (water pipe). Breakfast is served on the roof. **www.elarishtozeur.8m.com**

TOZEUR Yardis Hotel de l'Oasis

Place des Martyrs, 2200 **Tel** *76 45 23 00* **Fax** *76 46 15 22* **Rooms** *114* **Map** *B5*

Lovely hotel in a restored 1920's building, built by the French, close to the old city and the souks. The decor is sober but stylish, incorporating the typical brickwork of the region. The spacious rooms are well equipped and have views over the garden. The large swimming pool overlooks the palmeraie. **www.yardis.com**

TOZEUR Dar Cheraït

Route Touristique, 2200 **Tel** *76 45 48 88* **Fax** *76 45 44 72* **Rooms** *85* **Map** *B5*

Dar Cheraït offers five-star luxury in a modern Oriental palace, sumptuously decorated with taste and attention to detail. The spacious, well-equipped and elegant rooms are all set around tranquil interior courtyards filled with jasmine, birdsong and a small fountain. Some rooms look out over the lush garden. **www.darcherait.com.tn**

TOZEUR Framissima La Palmeraie

Route Touristique, 2200 **Tel** *76 45 45 99* **Fax** *76 45 48 39* **Rooms** *106* **Map** *B5*

Big four-star resort hotel in the Zone Touristique, a short walk from the centre. The rooms are spacious and painted in pastel colours, with good en suite bathrooms, most overlooking the vast palmeraie. The hotel has several restaurants, an indoor swimming pool for winter and a popular discotheque. **lapalmeraie@fram.fr**

TOZEUR Eldorador Ksar Rouge

Route Touristique, 2200 **Tel** *76 45 49 33* **Fax** *76 45 31 63* **Rooms** *112* **Map** *B5*

Don't be put off by the tour groups, as this is one of the most beautiful hotels in town, inspired by the traditional architecture and local brickwork. The spacious rooms offer large, comfortable beds, satellite TV and good bathrooms. There is an indoor and outdoor pool, a hammam and massage parlour, and tennis courts. **www.ksar-rouge.com**

ZAAFRANE Zaafrane

Main road to Douz, 4261 **Tel** *75 45 00 20* **Fax** *75 45 00 33* **Rooms** *40* **Map** *B6*

A slightly faded hotel close to the sand dunes and the departure point for desert trips. The rooms are set in small bungalows, each with bathroom, toilet, air-conditioning and heating in winter. The swimming pool is hard to keep clean as the sand constantly blows in. The hotel also organizes desert trips. **la-mer.desables@gnet.tn**

CENTRAL TUNISIA

GAFSA Khalfallah

44 Avenue Taieb Mehri, 2100 **Tel** *76 22 56 24* **Fax** *76 22 89 00* **Rooms** *15* **Map** *B4*

Small and welcoming hotel with friendly, laid-back staff and good-sized rooms, with showers and basins, but no air-conditioning. The rooms on the street side have more light but are much noisier. Try to get a room with a balcony on the quieter alleyside. The restaurant and bar are mainly frequented by local men.

GAFSA Tunis

Ave 2 Mars, near the bus station, 2100 **Tel** *76 22 77 91* **Rooms** *16* **Map** *B4*

This hotel, conveniently located near the bus station and opposite the little park, is a good budget option offering spartan, reasonably clean rooms. The rooms vary quite a lot in size and brightness – some have no windows, others have a small balcony, so check the room before taking it.

GAFSA Maamoun

Avenue Jamel Abdenaceur Zarrong, 2100 **Tel** *76 22 04 70* **Fax** *76 22 64 40* **Rooms** *69* **Map** *B4*

A well-appointed hotel, Maamoun is one of Gafsa's more upmarket establishments, but it is looking a little worn these days and the nice pool on the rooftop is usually empty. The rooms are large and clean, however, and the hotel does have a very central location, close to Gafsa's market square.

GAFSA Jugurtha Palace

Near Cité Bourguiba, 2100 **Tel** *76 21 12 00* **Fax** *76 21 12 20* **Rooms** *114* **Map** *B4*

With its five stars, this is the most luxurious hotel in town, catering mainly to tour groups and local businessmen. The large rooms are decorated in local style verging on kitsch but the grounds, with a great garden and palmeraie, are beautiful. A wide range of facilities includes opulent dining rooms and pools. **www.jugurthapalace.com**

GAFSA Gafsa Palace

Route de Tunis, km 2, 2100 **Tel** *76 21 76 00* **Fax** *76 21 76 70* **Rooms** *156*   **Map** *B4*

This modern hotel, built in an architectural style inspired by Tunisian traditions, offers spacious, air-conditioned rooms with well-kept bathrooms, satellite TV and mini bars. The rooms have stunning views over the Orbata Park and the surrounding mountains. The hotel also has a swimming pool and a hammam (steam bath). **www.gafsapalace.com**

KAIROUAN Les Aghlabides

Place Bab Tunis, 3100 **Tel** *77 23 08 80* **Rooms** *60*   **Map** *C3*

Though modern, Les Aghlabides is built as a traditional caravanserai, and all the rooms are found on two floors around a large, tranquil courtyard decorated with marble and tiles. The rooms are utterly spartan but clean, some have basins and showers, others make use of shared bathrooms. The hotel is just outside the city walls.

KAIROUAN Sabra

Bab Des Martyrs, 3100 **Tel** *77 23 02 63* **Fax** *77 27 13 55* **Rooms** *30*   **Map** *C3*

This simple hotel, right opposite the main gate into the medina, has basic but well-kept rooms, some with en suite bathrooms. The rooms overlooking the ramparts of the city are particularly pleasant at sunset, if a little noisy in the morning, and the roof terrace has great views over the medina.

KAIROUAN Amina

Avenue des Nations Unies, 3100 **Tel** *77 27 45 55 / 77 23 17 75* **Fax** *77 27 14 11* **Rooms** *42*   **Map** *C3*

Amina is a comfortable three-star hotel popular with European tour groups, and is located a short distance away from the town centre on the road to Tunis. The rooms are decorated with dark wood and well kept, all with en suite bathrooms and air-conditioning. Friendly management. **hotel.amina@topnet.tn**

KAIROUAN Continental

Route de Tunis, 3100 **Tel** *77 23 11 35* **Fax** *77 22 99 00* **Rooms** *160*   **Map** *C3*

Popular with tour groups, this hotel opposite the Aghlabid Basins has very little character on the outside. Although it looks quite drab, the rooms are spacious and comfortable, and furnished in a slightly bizarre way. All rooms have air-conditioning and en suite bathrooms, but the pool is not always functioning.

KAIROUAN Tunisia

Avenue de la République, 3100 **Tel** *77 23 17 75* **Fax** *77 23 15 97* **Rooms** *42*   **Map** *C3*

For a pleasant budget option, try this old-fashioned hotel on one of the town's main streets, near the medina. The rooms are spotless, mostly large with high ceilings, and have either a bath or shower. The rooms in the back are a lot quieter, and some rooms have a balcony. The friendly owner is always happy to tell you about the town.

KAIROUAN Hotel de la Kasbah

Avenue Ibn el-Jazzar, 3100 **Tel** *77 23 73 01* **Fax** *77 23 73 02* **Rooms** *87*   **Map** *C3*

The rooms are centred around the large courtyard with its beautiful swimming pool at this splendid five-star hotel in the restored kasbah. The decor is attractive and tasteful, and rooms are equipped with satellite TV, mini bars and en suite bathrooms with mosaics. There is a good restaurant and a lovely Moorish café. **www.goldenyasmin.com**

KAIROUAN Splendid

Rue du 9 Avril, 3100 **Tel** *77 23 00 41* **Fax** *77 23 08 29*   **Map** *C3*

You'll get very good value at this delightful hotel close to the main entrance of the medina and right in the centre of town, but tucked away on a quiet back street. The rooms are spacious, recently redecorated, and cheerful with white furniture and colourful textiles. All rooms have high ceilings and clean en suite bathrooms.

KASSERINE Hotel de la Paix

Avenue Habib Bourguiba, 1200 **Tel** *77 47 14 65* **Rooms** *12*   **Map** *B3*

Located on the main street, a short way from the town's main square, this hotel is in a busy district. All the rooms are clean and have en suite bathrooms. A hot shower is available on request, as the gas heater needs to be switched on in advance. The hotel has a small restaurant and the management are friendly and helpful.

KASSERINE Amaidra

232 Avenue du 7 Novembre, 1200 **Tel** *77 47 07 50* **Fax** *77 47 73 97* **Rooms** *30*   **Map** *B3*

This is one of the better places to stay in town, though it looks nicer from the outside than the inside. The building and the rooms are not looked after and the opulent-looking hotel seems well worn. The rooms, however, are spacious, with satellite TV and en suite bathrooms. **amaidra@tunet.tn**

KASSERINE Cillium

Near the Cillium ruins, 1200 **Tel** *77 47 46 82* **Fax** *77 47 46 82* **Rooms** *22*   **Map** *B3*

The best place to stay in Kasserine, 4 km (2.5 miles) from the town centre, near the Roman site of Cillium. The hotel is in an interesting building from the 1960s, built as a round structure with an atrium at the centre. The strangely shaped rooms are clean and comfortable, but the staff are unwelcoming.

LE KEF La Source

Rue de la Source **Tel** *78 20 43 97* **Fax** *78 20 43 97* **Rooms** *10*   **Map** *B2*

There is only one room worth staying in in this hotel, which is mainly used by Algerian businessmen, and that is the large family room with four beds under an ornate, vaulted stucco ceiling. The other rooms are unfortunately rather shabby, although those on the street side look slightly brighter.

Key to Price Guide *see p248* **Key to Symbols** *see back cover flap*

LE KEF Ramzi

Rue Hedi Chaker **Tel** *78 20 30 79* **Fax** *78 20 30 79* **Rooms** *18*   **Map** *B2*

This modest but adequate hotel is in the centre of town. The rooms have been redecorated recently, so are still in good condition, neatly arranged and with colourful tiled walls. Some rooms also have en suite bathrooms. The hotel has a convenient restaurant downstairs. A good option for travellers on a tight budget.

LE KEF Les Pins

On the Tunis Road, 7100 **Tel** *78 20 43 00* **Fax** *78 20 24 11* **Rooms** *56*   **Map** *B2*

Under the same management as the Résidence Venus *(see below)*, this hotel is about 1.5 km (1 mile) out of town, on the road to Tunis. It caters mainly for tour groups but individual travellers are welcome. The rooms have good views and tiled bathrooms, and the grounds and swimming pool are pleasant and well kept. **www.hotel-lespins.com**

LE KEF Résidence Venus

Rue Mouldi Khamessi, 7100 **Tel** *78 20 46 95* **Fax** *78 20 46 95* **Rooms** *20*   **Map** *B2*

This hotel has a warm family atmosphere and is in a central location just below the kasbah. The rooms are pleasant, and arranged around a courtyard filled with plants and birdsong. Most rooms are en suite and are heated in winter. Guests can use the pool at the hotel Les Pins *(see above)* on the edge of town. **www.hotel-lespins.com**

LE KEF Sicca Veneria

Place de l'Indépendance, 7100 **Tel** *78 20 23 89* **Fax** *78 20 23 89* **Rooms** *31*   **Map** *B2*

Situated in the town centre, the hotel's eclectic style is a combination of Oriental and European features. Its modest rooms are not particularly tastefully furnished, but are quite spacious. The windows look out on to the busy town square. The bathrooms either have a bath or shower.

LE KEF Dar Chennoufi

7100 **Tel** *71 86 55 28* **Fax** *71 32 06 82* **Rooms** *10*   **Map** *B2*

In a modern villa-farmhouse a short drive outside Le Kef, Dar Chennoufi is the perfect base for those who want to go hiking in the beautiful countryside here, or visit the ancient sites. The rooms are large and comfortable, with en suite bathrooms. Dinner is available on request for guests of the hotel. **www.dar-chennoufi.com**

MAKTHAR Maktharis

Near the archaeological site **Tel** *22 20 49 95* **Rooms** *5*   **Map**

The Maktharis is the only hotel in town, and is conveniently just a short walk from the archaeological site, which is definitely the only reason for staying here. The worn-down rooms have rather uncomfortable beds and extremely spartan bathrooms, but the hotel is good enough for a short stay.

METLAOUI Ennacim

Road to Tozeur, 2100 **Tel** *76 24 19 20* **Rooms** *8*   **Map** *B5*

The hotel is situated on the road to Tozeur, right on the edge of the town, opposite the petrol station. The rooms are spartan but clean and quite pleasant, while the communal rooms are more elaborately decorated with tiles and attractive stuccowork. The young staff are very welcoming.

METLAOUI Seldja

On the Gafsa Road, 2100 **Tel** *76 24 15 70* **Fax** *76 24 14 86* **Rooms** *10*   **Map** *B5*

Outside the town centre, the Seldja is situated on the road to Gafsa. The exterior of the hotel and the lobby are rather dull, but the rooms are clean and have air-conditioning and satellite TV. The bar is mainly frequented by local men, and there is also a reasonable restaurant.

SBEITLA Hotel de la Jeunesse

Place Echouada, 1250 **Tel** *77 46 65 28* **Rooms** *20*   **Map** *B-C3*

This is the cheapest place to stay in town and has cheerful, spotless rooms, mostly with shared bathrooms except for one double room which is en suite. The rooms are arranged around an open courtyard within earshot of the sweet sound of a fountain. Very friendly welcome and the possibility of an evening meal on request.

SBEITLA Bakini

Rue du 2 Mars 1934, 1250 **Tel** *77 46 52 44* **Fax** *77 46 50 48* **Rooms** *41*   **Map**

A clean and comfortable hotel with an attractive façade, in the eastern part of the town near the mosque. The rooms are rather uninspired but have the advantage of reasonably comfortable beds and air-conditioning. Unfortunately, the pool is no longer in use.

SBEITLA Sufetula

On the Kasserine Rd, 1250 **Tel** *77 46 53 11* **Fax** *77 46 55 82* **Rooms** *45*   **Map** *B-C3*

The Sufetula is a surprisingly pleasant three-star hotel, situated on a small hill overlooking the ruins of the Roman town of Sufetula (Sbeïtla). Rooms here are comfortable and cosy, with spotless en suite bathrooms and balconies with good views. Highly recommended.

TEBOURSOUK Thugga

On the main road out of town, 9040 **Tel** *78 46 66 47* **Fax** *78 46 67 21* **Rooms** *33*   **Map** *B2*

The only hotel in town, which is convenient if you want to avoid the tour groups in Dougga by visiting the ruins in the early morning or late afternoon. This two-star hotel offers good-sized rooms with air-conditioning, satellite TV and pleasant clean bathrooms. The hotel restaurant serves regional specialities such as wild boar, and has a bar.

WHERE TO EAT

From upmarket European-style restaurants to streetside vendors, Tunisia can cater for most tastes and budgets. Perhaps the best place to enjoy Tunisian food is in the local cafés. The spicy Tunisian cuisine served in many of these unassuming places often tastes better than in some expensive hotels. There is no need to be afraid of eating in small local eateries as they are almost uniformly clean and

offer good quality. Be aware that most Tunisian stews and sauces in traditional cafés are made with harissa, a fiery condiment that usually appears on the table without anyone asking for it. Alcohol is not generally available and those restaurants that do serve it tend to be pricier. Most major towns have good produce markets where a delicious picnic of baguettes, cheese and fruit can easily be bought.

A display of Tunisian oranges

Café with rugs by the medina wall in Hammamet

TYPES OF RESTAURANT

Simple meals of fish, chicken, meat and vegetables are readily available in *gargottes* (small, inexpensive restaurants), which also serve soup. Bread is served at no extra charge.

Tourist restaurants, so called because they have been inspected and graded by the country's tourist authorities, offer a choice of Tunisian and European cuisine.

Hotels, especially those catering for package groups, offer "international cuisine" as well as tamer versions of Tunisia's spicy stews.

For those who do not wish to spend much time in restaurants, snack bars provide the best answer, offering, among others things, a slice of Tunisian pizza.

WHAT TO EAT

The most popular Tunisian dish is couscous – which is made from semolina and served with chunky stewed vegetables, meat or fish in a hot tomato sauce. Couscous appears in many varieties; the most popular is made with chunks of lamb that have been cooked with vegetables. The couscous is placed above the pot and cooks slowly in a *coucoussier* by absorbing all

Inside the popular Café M'Rabet (p274) in Souk et-Trouk, Tunis

of the steam and flavour from the stew bubbling below.

Another very tasty dish is *kamounia* – an aromatic meat dish made of beef or lamb that is cooked with plenty of cumin and other spices. The most popular dishes in the coastal region are grilled octopus and prawns, and *complet poisson* (a whole fish served with a salad made of tomatoes, lettuce and peppers).

The most common Tunisian snack is the *brik à l'oeuf* (an egg that has been fried inside a thin pastry envelope). For an authentic *brik*, the egg-yolk should be soft and the pastry envelope crescent-shaped. Sprinkled with lemon juice and eaten with the fingers, it makes a delicious lunch. Another very tasty snack is *Swaba Fatimah* (Fatimah's fingers), which are thin rolls of transparent pastry stuffed with meat or egg and then deep-fried. Tunisian pizza is usually made in large trays and often topped with chunks of tuna. Tuna is also

Floating restaurant in Port el-Kantaoui

the main ingredient of *salade tunisienne*, another favourite, which consists of crisp green lettuce, olives, tomatoes, cucumber and slices of hard-boiled egg.

Cheap and filling soups are part of the staple diet in Tunisia. Of all the varieties, *lablabi* is the most common and is made from chickpeas and served with bread and harissa. Sometimes it has a raw egg whisked into it. *Chorba* is a spicier soup. Usually prepared with chicken or lamb stock, it often includes pasta or grains of barley. A spicy fish version is popular in the Sfax region.

Bread is a staple of the Tunisian diet and is served with every meal.

OPENING HOURS

Cafés are usually open from 8 or 9am until about 10pm. In small towns they close a little earlier. Local cafés, where men come to watch TV and smoke *chichas* (hookahs), usually stay open until about midnight. Some cafés remain open 24 hours a day. Restaurants are usually open from 10 or 11am. Lunch is served between noon and 3pm. Restaurants close about 10 or 11pm, though the kitchen normally stops serving an hour earlier.

PRICES

There is a huge difference in the prices charged by hotels and tourist restaurants, and those charged in small establishments frequented by Tunisians. Meals in local restaurants are considerably cheaper. In a local restaurant or café a *brik à l'oeuf* will cost less than 1 TD, while in a tourist-zone restaurant it may cost 3 TD or more. A dish of couscous will cost about 4 TD in a local restaurant, while a hotel may charge 10 TD for virtually the same dish. A main course of grilled meat or a large portion of chicken

Restaurant in a converted medina palace

with chips and salad will cost about 3 TD in a local restaurant and up to 20 TD in an upmarket restaurant aimed exclusively at holidaymakers. A glass of mint tea served with sugar costs about 1 TD. English-style tea is less readily available and may well cost more than this. A puff on a hookah that can be shared by several people costs between 2 and 4 TD.

It is best to buy drinks from a shop. The lowest prices are found in supermarkets; in small shops the cost is normally 10 to 20 per cent more.

A pitta bread vendor in Kairouan

HYGIENE

Tourist restaurants have stringent rules of hygiene. Local cafés and restaurants are also usually clean and tidy, as are the small pavement restaurants. For the first few days of your visit, however, it is best to avoid eating raw fruit and vegetables as these can cause stomach upsets.

RAMADAN

During Ramadan, the ninth month of the Islamic calendar, Tunisians fast from sunrise until sunset. The fast is strictly observed and many local restaurants and cafés remain closed. Some restaurants do remain open but fewer options will be

available. Tunisians do not normally get indignant at the sight of a tourist eating and drinking during Ramadan, but it is good manners not to eat, drink or smoke in public places during the fast. Large towns usually have a few restaurants that cater for tourists.

Once the fast has been broken each evening, it is fairly easy to find a restaurant that serves a Ramadan dinner. Such restaurants stay open for a few hours after sunset and the streets became deserted while the locals sit down to a family meal. After dinner, many families attend concerts and parties. Some of the cafés in the medinas open their doors late in order to serve a final meal before the fast begins again at sunrise.

VEGETARIANS

Tunisians are fond of meat and find it hard to understand people who are willingly vegetarian. In small local restaurants *(gargottes)* and fast-food stands or cafés it would be difficult to get a vegetarian meal. Salads are usually garnished with a piece of tuna fish, while soups are invariably prepared using meat or fish stock. Vegans will have an even harder time. However, vegetarian dishes can usually be ordered in tourist and hotel restaurants.

A restaurant garden in the centre of Sousse medina

The Flavours of Tunisia

Tunisian cuisine is an amalgam of traditional Berber cooking with influences from the many civilizations that ruled the country over the centuries: Phoenician, Roman, Arab, Turkish and French. Bread is a staple, eaten with every meal, from a French baguette to *tabouna*, an unleavened country bread baked in a domed clay oven. A Tunisian saying holds that a husband can tell how much his wife loves him by the amount of chilli pepper she uses in his food – if dinner has no heat, her ardour has also cooled. Tunisians certainly like their food fiery, but they will usually cut back on the spicy seasonings to spare more sensitive palates.

Tub of harissa paste

A date farmer with his harvest at the oasis of Tozeur

THE COAST

Tunisia has a long coastline dotted with fishing ports, so there is always a rich supply of exceptionally fresh fish and seafood, a mainstay of the Tunisian diet. Fish is then usually priced by weight in restaurants (and can be expensive) and cooked to order. Among the most popular varieties are *rouget* (red mullet), *daurade* (sea bream), sole, *loup de mer* (sea bass), *maquereau* (mackerel), sardine, *merou* (grouper), *calamar* (squid), *crevettes* (prawns), *poulpe* (octopus) and *thon* (tuna). Fish is usually simply grilled and served with olive oil and lemon, or baked with lots of *kamoun* (cumin). Squid and cuttlefish are deep fried in batter. *Poisson complet* may be a whole large fish or a selection of smaller ones, fried or grilled, served with fries and *tastira*, a sauce of grilled chillies, tomato, onion and garlic. Sfax and Djerba are famous for their seafood specialities.

THE INTERIOR

Inland, meat is important to the local diet. In the Tunisian home, the main course is

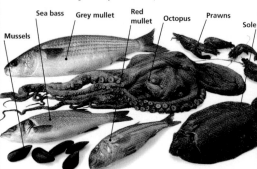

Sea bass   Grey mullet   Red mullet   Octopus   Prawns   Sole   Mussels

Range of seafood found in the clear waters of the Tunisian coast

TUNISIAN DISHES AND SPECIALITIES

Of all Tunisian specialities, undoubtedly the most prominent is couscous. It was originally the food of the native Berbers who called it *k'seksu*. Fine semolina grains are traditionally rolled in flour, then dried in the sun to help preserve them through the winter. When needed, they are steamed in a *couscoussière*, a special two-tiered pan in which the stew cooking below steams the couscous above. Tunisians like a spicy couscous with a hot peppery *marga*, a stew of tomato paste, vegetables, chicken, lamb or beef and especially fish. The couscous is often served with a bowl of harissa on the side.

Fresh figs

Brik a l'oeuf *is a deep-fried parcel of filo pastry filled with potato, shrimps, cheese or mince, and a soft-cooked egg.*

Spices of many colours and aromas in a Tunisian market

Restaurants often serve a mix of traditional Tunisian fare, such as couscous and tajine, and old-fashioned French classics like grilled calf's liver, *boeuf bourguignon* and steak tartare. Others offer a wider range of traditional dishes, such as *koucha*, lamb with potatoes in a tomato sauce. Both the French and the Turks left behind them a legacy of delicious desserts and pastries, and many pastry shops sell a range of European and Eastern sweets.

usually a spicy meat stew with couscous, buckwheat, pasta or beans. In local restaurants it is more often grilled meat, such as beef steak, lamb chops or *brochettes* (kebabs). In the north, during the hunting season, it is not unusual to find *sanglier* (wild boar) on the menu for visitors, though Muslims do not eat it. In the south, particularly in Tozeur, you may be served camel meat, which can be delicious.

Fertile plains are the source of excellent vegetables, and fruit such as figs, dates, pomegranates and citrus.

CITY CUISINE

The main cities, Tunis in particular, are where the melting pot of Tunisian culinary history comes to the fore. The French influence is

particularly strong. A popular snack is the *casse-croûte*, a French baguette with harissa (the ubiquitous hot, spicy chilli sauce), vegetables, olives, oil and a chunk of tuna, as is *fricassée*, fried bread with a similar filling.

Piles of sweet, sticky baklava on display in a city pastry shop

TUNISIAN SWEETS

Baklava A Turkish sweet. Filo pastry layered with chopped nuts, sugar and butter, baked and soaked in honey syrup.

Bouza A rich, sticky sorghum cream, served in Ramadan.

Kâk Less sweet than other pastries. A delicate almond paste wrapped in filo.

Makroud A fried semolina pastry stuffed with date paste. A speciality of Kairouan.

Mhalbya A rice, nut and geranium-water cake.

Mille feuille French-inspired. Baked filo pastry layered with custard cream and then iced.

Samsa Filo filled with ground roast almonds and sesame seeds in rosewater syrup.

Yoyo A doughnut made with orange juice, deep-fried and then dipped in honey syrup.

Couscous au poisson, *a Tunisian favourite, is topped with grilled fish – red or grey mullet are preferred.*

Salade mechouia, *char-grilled chillies, tomatoes and onions, is served with tuna and hard-boiled egg.*

Tajine, *in Tunisia, is similar to frittata with meat and vegetables, quite different from a Moroccan tagine.*

What to Drink

The most popular Tunisian beverage is coffee, which is drunk often and everywhere. Meals are usually accompanied by tap or mineral water as well as all kinds of fizzy drinks (known as *gazouz*), including the big-name brands as well as local products. Although a Muslim country, Tunisia produces good wines, both red and white, an interesting liqueur and one brand of home-brewed beer called Celtia. Brightly-coloured fruit syrups, diluted with water, are also available. Fruit juices are sold in many resorts in the summer.

A decorative coffee brewing set

TEA

A waiter pouring mint tea from a height to produce a froth

Mint tea is popular in Tunisia. Granulated black or green tea is stewed slowly, with a large amount of sugar and fresh mint (honey may be used in place of sugar), until it produces a dark infusion. This is poured from a pot into small glasses, from a height, so as to create a froth. Fresh mint leaves, pine nuts, almonds or pistachios are sometimes added to this. Tunisian tea is strong and aromatic and is not to everyone's taste, though it is thought by Tunisians to assist the digestion. Tea is not often served with milk, apart from in the larger hotels or tourist centres and even these may use UHT in place of fresh milk.

A glass of mint tea

A packet of green tea

COFFEE

Strong, black coffee

Tunisians are dedicated coffee drinkers and can spend a long time over a small cup of coffee as they contemplate the world passing by. Every small café and even the most humble local bars can serve an excellent espresso. It is often served with small shortbread or date biscuits. The coffee is strong, but is not always offered with water, as it is in many countries. Coffee in Tunisia is normally served in small glasses. Anyone wanting a larger cup of slightly weaker coffee can order a *café direct* or *café crème* (similar to a cappuccino) or a *café au lait* (a filter coffee with milk). Other popular types include coffee with condensed milk (*Capucin nouveau*) and Turkish coffee (*qahwa arbi*). This strong, sweet brew is made by boiling the coffee and is served with the fine grounds which settle to the bottom.

Coffee with milk

MINERAL WATER

Unlike many African countries, tap water is clean in Tunisia and can be safely drunk anywhere in larger towns. Its taste, however, leaves a lot to be desired and many people prefer to drink bottled water, which is cheap and readily available. The most popular mineral water – Safia – is produced in plain and sparkling versions (the latter is usually sold in glass bottles). They both taste good and should be considered indispensable when travelling around the country. In summer, a bottle of mineral water should always be taken on sightseeing tours of archaeological sites and open-air museums to avoid the risk of dehydration.

Water in large bottles

Safia bottled water

BEER

Tunisia has only one brand of home-brewed beer – Celtia – which is produced on licence from Stella Artois and Lowenbrau. It is slightly less potent than European beers, but it tastes good nevertheless. It is usually only available in major supermarkets, and is sold in botles or in red and white cans. Some restaurants serve beer in bottles but prices tend to be higher than restaurants that do not serve alcohol. The more expensive restaurants and hotels offer foreign beers to their guests, but even here the choice is limited. The most easily available are the popular brands of German, Danish and Dutch beer.

Celtia in a bottle

Celtia in a can

Red wine

Rosé wine

White wine

WINE

Tunisia has been producing wine for 2,000 years. New varieties of grape were introduced in the 1990s and in 2002 an even wider range of wines was launched, including the Château Saint Augustin. Wine is produced in several regions. These include Cap Bon in the north, especially around Grombalia and Mornag, and in the vicinity of Jendouba in the west. Red wines includes Château Feriani, Coteaux d'Utique, Château Defleur and Lambolt. Note-worthy among rosé varieties are Tyna, Koudiat and Château Saint Augustin Princess Elissa. The white Coteaux de Carthage is also very good.

VODKAS AND LIQUEURS

The only strong alcoholic beverage produced in Tunisia is *boukha* – a clear spirit made from figs. It contains 40 per cent alcohol and resembles a dry fruit-flavoured vodka. It is often served with fizzy cola. *Laghmi* is a palm wine that is fermented for 24 hours. It is not sold in shops, but it can be obtained from one of the oases during the palm season. Another alternative is Thibarine, a liqueur derived from dates and herbs that is produced in the village of Thibar (near Dougga) according to a secret recipe handed down by French monks. Cedratine, a liqueur made from lemons, is also popular.

Boukha, made from figs

Thibarine, made from dates

Cedratine, made from lemons

Sparkling Boga

Sweet dark Boga

LOCAL BEVERAGES

The Tunisians produce their own kinds of fizzy drink which are sold alongside brand names such as Coca-Cola and Pepsi. The most popular of these is Boga, which comes in several varieties, including citrus-flavoured Boga Lim and Boga Cidre, which is cola-coloured and has a distinctive carob flavour. Also popular are syrups that must be diluted with water. Flavours include pomegranate and rose essence. Fresh fruit juices are available in resorts.

Fresh orange juice

Choosing a Restaurant

The following restaurants have been chosen for their fine food, as well as for the quality of their decor and location. Establishments are listed by region starting with Tunis, and alphabetically within price categories. Some restaurants do not accept credit cards. Map references refer to the road map on the back inside cover.

PRICE CATEGORIES
For a three-course meal for one person, including cover charge and service but not alcohol.

ⓣⓓ Under 10 TD
ⓣⓓⓣⓓ 10–15 TD
ⓣⓓⓣⓓⓣⓓ 15–20 TD
ⓣⓓⓣⓓⓣⓓⓣⓓ 20–25 TD
ⓣⓓⓣⓓⓣⓓⓣⓓⓣⓓ Over 25 TD

TUNIS

Abid

98 Rue de Yougoslavie, 1000 **Tel** *71 25 70 52*   **Map** *C1*

You are assured of a warm welcome and good service at this wonderful and inexpensive restaurant in the heart of the city centre, which is open from 11am until midnight every day. The food is typically Tunisian, so expect hot and spicy couscous, *chorba* (soup) and tagine dishes.

Café Chaouachin

Grand Souk des Chechias, 1008 **Tel** *No telephone*   **Map** *C1*

The oldest café in the medina is hidden in a corner of the old *chechia*, or felt hat, makers, which is now slowly being taken over by souvenir shops. Men, and a few women, sit on benches and chairs around painted tables to smoke a *chicha* (water pipe) and drink coffee or mint tea, while exchanging gossip. Open late. Closed Sun.

Grand Café du Théâtre de l'Étoile du Nord

Avenue Habib Bourguiba, 1001 **Tel** *71 25 40 66*   **Map** *C1*

Adjacent to the theatre, with a large terrace on Avenue Habib Bourguiba, this is the meeting place for many arts and theatre people in the country. Unlike most places in town, women can come here on their own or in a group and feel at ease. There is no alcohol, but soft drinks, snacks, pastries and ice creams all feature. Smoky atmosphere.

La Brasserie

Hotel Africa, 50 Avenue Habib Bourguiba, 1001 **Tel** *71 34 74 77*   **Map** *C1*

The Brasserie is a large open room – and an even bigger terrace – which is one of the most popular meeting places in town. Breakfast, sweets and sandwiches are served along with a large drinks menu, including cold beer on tap and cocktails. It's much frequented by groups of young Tunisian women, so is a good place for lone women to come.

Latino

38 Rue Gandhi, 1001 **Tel** *71 33 17 45*   **Map** *C1*

Pleasant and slightly trendy *salon de thé* and lunchtime restaurant serving good pastas, pizzas and sandwiches as well as a daily menu, plus sweets, hot drinks and fresh juices in the evening. The decor and music attract a younger crowd, with futuristic white cocoon furniture, cow hides, cactuses and small kiosks made from bamboo.

Panorama Kedidi

41 Avenue Habib Bourguiba, 1001 **Tel** *No telephone*   **Map** *C1*

This huge outdoor terrace mainly serves drinks but also offers excellent Tunisian-style sandwiches (mention you don't want spicy *harissa* sauce spread on yours if necessary), great crusty pizzas sold by weight and delicious French pastries. These can be consumed on the premises or as a take-away. Delicious fresh juices are also on offer.

Salem

Rue de Yougoslavie, 1000 **Tel** *No telephone*   **Map** *C1*

Salem is the locals' favourite ice cream parlour. The home-made ices come in many flavours and are truly scrumptious. Locals come also for the house speciality "cannelloni" – a thin, crispy pancake filled with a mixture of ricotta and cream, and partly covered in pistachios. There is another popular Salem outlet in La Marsa near the TGM station.

Carcassonne

8 Avenue de Carthage, 1000 **Tel** *71 24 07 02*   **Map** *C1*

This long-established restaurant has reasonable prices and good, efficient service, and is mainly frequented by Tunisians. On the menu are solid Tunisian dishes such as *brochettes* (kebabs), *kemia* (various dishes) and couscous, as well as pasta, pizzas and some typical French dishes. This is a good place for a quick and simple, but delicious, meal.

Chez Abid

4 Rue du Caire, 1001 **Tel** *71 99 63 41*   **Map** *C1*

Simple but excellent eatery which attracts both locals and budget tourists with its traditional Sfaxienne cuisine focussing on fish and seafood dishes. The service is swift and friendly and the decor traditionally Tunisian, with white paper tablecloths, lots of mirrors and tiled walls. The fish soup and couscous with fish are particularly recommended.

Key to Symbols *see back cover flap*

Le Bleuet

23 Rue de Marseille, 1000 **Tel** *71 34 92 80*

Map *C1*

This is a typical Tunisian restaurant, with an attractive Art Deco façade and old-fashioned dining rooms. The atmosphere is very much "men only"; they come here for the good value beers and good wine list. The food, Tunisian salads and grills, is fine, but regarded very much as an accompaniment to the drinks. Can be noisy.

Le Ciel de Tunis

Tunisia Palace, 13 Avenue de France, 1001 **Tel** *71 34 54 78*

Map *C1*

Elegant bar, *salon de thé* and pizzeria on the 5th floor of the stylish Tunisia Palace hotel *(see p250)*, with a large outdoor terrace overlooking most of Tunis centre. Already popular with well-heeled Tunisians, the terrace is definitely the place for afternoon tea, a pre-dinner drink or a light but good Italian dinner of pasta, pizza or salad.

Le Neptune

3 Rue du Caire, 1000 **Tel** *71 25 48 20*

Map *C1*

The service is fast and the staff are welcoming at this friendly neighbourhood restaurant. At lunchtime it is popular with employees from the surrounding offices. At night it is mainly men who come here to have dinner while watching TV. The Tunisian food – grilled meats, couscous with lamb and seafood pasta – is good, and portions are generous.

Mahdaoui

Rue Jemaa Zitouna, 1008 **Tel** *No telephone*

Map *C1*

A straightforward cheap eatery right on the main drag in the souks and opposite the Great Mosque. The food is simple but good, and some swear by the couscous with meat. The atmosphere is busy – possibly too busy for some – with lots of passers-by. Definitely not the place for a long lunch, but it is great fun. Open Mon–Sat noon–4pm.

Las Margaritas

Hotel La Maison Dorée, 6 Rue de Hollande, 1000 **Tel** *71 24 06 32*

Map *C1*

Popular with locals and ex-pats, this small and pleasant restaurant is in the centre of town, on the ground floor of the old French hotel La Maison Dorée *(see p249)*. It's furnished with lots of dark wood, and serves mainly French cuisine to regulars, who come for the excellent and good value *plat du jour*. The service is friendly and very efficient.

Andalous

13 Rue de Marseille, 1001 **Tel** *71 24 17 50*

Map *C1*

Enjoy the excellent food at this dimly lit, typical downtown restaurant. There are plenty of grilled fish and meats on the menu as well as French and Tunisian specialities, including a great couscous with fish. It's probably best to come here for dinner, as it gets very crowded at lunchtime – its popularity owes much to the friendliness of its waiters.

Chez Nous

5 Rue de Marseille, 1001 **Tel** *71 25 40 43*

Map *C1*

Chez Nous serves good French cuisine – nothing too complicated – such as grilled fish and steaks, as well as the classic Tunisian dishes, including couscous with fish, and *brik a l'œuf (see p268)*. The good value lunch menu makes it a very popular place at midday, particularly with Tunisians who work in offices nearby. Brisk service.

Hong-Kong

85 Avenue Taieb Mehiri, 1002 **Tel** *71 78 79 57*

Map *C1*

A small Asian-style garden and tropical fish aquarium front this old-fashioned Chinese restaurant. The decor is plain and simple but not unpleasant, and the kitchen offers a wide variety of well-prepared, if not entirely authentic, classic Chinese dishes, including tasty crispy duck and sweet and sour beef.

La Mamma

11 bis Rue de Marseille, 1001 **Tel** *71 33 23 88/ 71 24 01 09*

Map *C1*

This recently refurbished cosy restaurant serves very good grilled steaks with a selection of sauces, as well as fish and seafood, but it is especially popular with locals for its authentic Italian pastas and pizzas, and delicious desserts. It is particularly busy at lunchtime, but you can always get a table as the service is professional.

Le Carthage

10 Rue Ali Bach Hamba, 1000 **Tel** *71 25 56 14*

Map *C1*

Don't be put off by the decor – fake Roman statues and other kitsch – at this Tunisian interpretation of an Italian restaurant. The food is much more attractive, with Tunisian, French and Italian dishes on the menu, and a wide choice of excellent desserts. The house speciality is the award-winning couscous. Very friendly service.

Le Paradiso

16 Avenue des États-Unis d'Amérique, 1002 **Tel** *71 78 68 63*

Map *C1*

Popular with diplomats from the neighbouring embassies and bank employees, the bright and cheerful Le Paradiso offers well-prepared Mediterranean dishes: a good selection of pastas, fish and seafood in particular. Service is friendly and swift, and the dish of the day is particularly recommended. Closed Sun.

L'Orient

7 Rue Ali Bach Hamba, 1001 **Tel** *71 25 20 61*

Map *C1*

A discreet wooden entrance door leads to L'Orient's dark but cosy Moorish-style interior. On the menu are French and Tunisian specialities, including Tunisian salads, grilled meats and excellent fresh fish and seafood. The wine list is good and the service efficient but friendly.

Le Bolero

6 Passage el-Guettar, 1000 **Tel** 71 25 59 28

Map C1

This old fashioned restaurant from the 1960s has a mixed menu of French and Tunisian dishes. The restaurant hasn't changed much since its beginnings, and although the decor is Andalusian-Moorish, the service is efficiently French and friendly. Favour the Tunisian rather than the French dishes. Can be noisy in the evenings.

Le Maalouf

108 Rue de Yougoslavie, 1000 **Tel** 71 25 42 46

Map C1

The elegant dining room of this lovely downtown restaurant is decorated with large paintings; there are also some outside tables in the pleasant courtyard. The menu features a few Tunisian specialities, but this predominantly Italian restaurant mainly serves good Italian cuisine. There is live guitar music on Thursday, Friday and Saturday nights.

M'Rabet

27 Rue Souk el-Trouk, 1008 **Tel** 71 56 17 29

Map C1

The M'Rabet has a splendid *café maure* (Arab café) on the ground floor, close to the Great Mosque. It's a great place to relax away from the bustle of the souks. The restaurant on the first floor has marvellous decor and good food but is a popular stop for tour groups – individuals sometimes get forgotten in the crowd.

Bayrouth Café

6-7 Rue du Lac Windermere, 1053 **Tel** 71 96 02 44

Map C1

The Bayrouth Café is a Lebanese café-restaurant popular with Tunis's well-heeled crowd, who come with friends or family to eat a table full of *mezzeh* (appetizers) while watching a show of Lebanese musicians and singers. The Lebanese food makes for a pleasant change, as there is much more variety and it is milder than Tunisian cuisine.

Chez Slah

14 bis Rue Pierre de Coubertin, 1001 **Tel** 71 25 85 88

Map C1

You'll need to reserve a table at Chez Slah, Tunis's leading fish restaurant, as it is not overly large. Housed in a villa in a street which is just off Avenue Bourguiba, the delicious food makes this a popular lunchtime destination for local bank and financial services staff. Alcohol is served. Closed Mon.

Dar Bel Hadj

17 Rue des Tamis, Medina, 1008 **Tel** 71 20 08 94

Map C1

You must ring the bell to get into this upmarket medina restaurant in an opulent small palace with an impressive courtyard. The food is expertly prepared and served either in the courtyard or, more intimately, in the smaller rooms leading off it. Some specialities need to be ordered in advance, and alcohol is served. Closed Sun.

Dar El-Jeld

5 Rue Dar el-Jeld, 1008 **Tel** 71 56 09 16

Map C1

This is undoubtedly one of the top restaurants in the country, with an amazing menu of Tunisian specialities. The restaurant, set in a well-restored mansion, is much frequented by politicians from the nearby government offices and diplomats introducing their foreign guests to the best of Tunisian cuisine. A band plays soothing Moorish tunes.

Dar Hammouda Pacha

56 Rue Sidi Ben Arous, 1008 **Tel** 71 56 17 46

Map C1

All the classic Tunisian dishes are offered at this upmarket restaurant inside a beautiful 17th-century mansion in the heart of the medina. The delicious food is served in one of the sumptuous salons or in the tiled covered courtyard. Some labour-intensive dishes need to be ordered 24 hours in advance. Also open for afternoon tea. Closed Sun.

Essaraya

6 Rue Ben Mahmoud, Souk Essakajine, Bab Menam, 1008 **Tel** 71 56 03 10 / 71 56 30 91

Map C1

Eleborate Tunisian cuisine, including a *tajine* (see p269) with pistachios and lamb *mosly* (roast lamb with saffron potatoes), is served in a grand medina palace with lots of original tiles and stuccowork. The complex includes an art gallery and a lovely *café maure* (Arab café) where you can have tea with Tunisian sweets or smoke a water pipe.

Le Boeuf sur le Toit

3 Avenue Fatouma Bourguiba, La Soukra, 2036 **Tel** 71 76 48 07

Map C1

A wealthy young crowd comes to this trendy hangout in the upcoming suburb of La Soukra for the ambience and the music. The international cuisine is also good, if not very inspired. There are regular live gigs, with jazz blues on Thursday night, rock on Friday night and international DJs on Saturday. Contemporary decor.

Le Diwan Dar El-Jeld

10 Rue Dar el-Jeld la Medina 1006 **Tel** 71 56 09 16

Map C1

This is the sister restaurant to Dar El-Jeld close by, with a large shop selling excellent crafts, a good art gallery featuring Tunisian artists and the same delicious Tunisian food. The restaurant has great tile and stuccowork, painted ceilings and marble stairways. Le Diwan is also open for tea and sweets, and can be booked out for groups.

Le Dôme

Tunisia Palace, 13 Avenue de France, 1001 **Tel** 71 24 27 00

Map C1

Elegant gourmet restaurant in the most beautiful dining room in town, under a grand dome with *Belle Epoque* stained-glass windows. The menu is inventive Mediterranean with some Tunisian specialities, and a strong emphasis on fish and seafood. The wine list is impressive for Tunis. Keep some space for the delicious desserts.

Key to Price Guide see p272 **Key to Symbols** see back cover flap

Le Pacha

Rue Jemaa Zitouna, Porte de France, 1001 **Tel** *71 32 03 75*

Map *C1*

In an old house on the edge of the medina, Le Pacha has breezy grand rooms, traditionally decorated with colourful tiles, elaborately painted ceilings and cool marble floors. The terrace overlooking the square and Avenue de France is particularly attractive. The food is typically Tunisian with salads, couscous, grills and stews. Dinner for groups only.

GREATER TUNIS AND CAP BON PENINSULA

CARTHAGE Le Neptune

1 Rue ibn Chablat, 2016 **Tel** *71 73 13 28*

Map *C1*

Neptune is an archetypal Mediterranean restaurant – all white and blue, elegant but laid back and simple – and with a large terrace overlooking the sea and the ruins of Carthage. The perfect setting to enjoy a dish of perfectly cooked fish or squid served with a good Tunisian salad and a cold glass of wine, while contemplating a little history.

CARTHAGE Restô

Villa Didon, Rue Mendès France, Byrsa Hill, 2016 **Tel** *71 73 34 33*

Map *C1*

Stunning restaurant decorated in the same contemporary style as the hotel Villa Didon *(see p251)*, with lots of Philippe Starck and Ron Arad furniture, and with the same floor-to-ceiling views. The food – inventive Mediterranean cuisine – is very good, with great pasta, seafood risotto and *carpaccio* on offer as well as Tunisian dishes with a twist.

EL-HAOUARIA La Daurade

Close to the Roman caves, 8045 **Tel** *72 26 90 80*

Map *D1*

This highly regarded seafood restaurant affords a magnificent view of Cap Bon and has an incredible setting on several shaded terraces. This is a perfect place for a lunch of grilled fish with olive oil and lemon served with fresh salads. The menu also includes a delicious couscous and freshly caught lobster. Evening shows are staged in summer.

EL-HAOUARIA L'Épervier

3 Avenue Habib Bourguiba, 8045 **Tel** *72 29 70 17*

Map *D1*

An excellent restaurant, part of the hotel with the same name *(see p251)*, specializing in fish and seafood. The set menu is very good value and uses fresh produce in season, and fish freshly caught that day. It's all served either in a pleasant dining room or a tranquil interior courtyard under the shade of trees.

GAMMARTH Le Grand Bleu

Avenue Taieb M'Hiri, 1057 **Tel** *71 91 39 00*

Map *C1*

Built on the highest part of the corniche, this smart (you are expected to dress up) and luxurious restaurant has amazing views over the sea from several terraces. The service is very attentive and the food is excellent, focusing on fish and seafood, with specialities of lobster, sea bass and fish-filled paella. Book ahead.

GAMMARTH Les Dunes

130 Avenue Taieb M'Hiri, 1057 **Tel** *71 72 99 40*

Map *C1*

Wonderfully set on several terraces, one on top of the other and all facing the sea, this smart Italian restaurant offers pasta and other Italian dishes, but particularly focuses on fish and seafood. One indoor room is rustically elegant, with a fireplace, another is contemporary and bright. The food is excellent and the service swift and efficient.

HAMMAMET Sidi Bou Hdid

Near the medina, 8050 **Tel** *No telephone*

Map *D2*

Lovely terrace at the foot of the old medina city walls, facing the sea. This is the perfect place (albeit a little crowded) to watch the sun set over the sea while having a freshly squeezed fruit juice, a mint tea or smoking a *chicha* (water pipe). The café gets very lively at night too, and serves ice creams and snacks. No alcohol.

HAMMAMET La Brise

2 Avenue de la République, 8050 **Tel** *72 27 89 10*

Map *D2*

One of the best cheap eateries in the centre of town, with modern decor and bright yellow and blue tiling. It is perhaps not huge on atmosphere, but the food is very good, particularly the *couscous maison* (couscous of the house) which comes in generous portions. Also recommended are the warm salads, which are perfect for lunch.

HAMMAMET Resto Vert

Avenue de la République, 8050 **Tel** *72 27 82 00*

Map *D2*

Open late and popular with young people from Hammamet as well as tourists, this small bistro offers a Tunisian and international snack menu, including great and filling salads, *briks (see p268)*, *crêpes*, and good pastas. The small first-floor room is more intimate and decorated with Italian film posters.

HAMMAMET Chez Achour

Rue Ali Belhouane, 8050 **Tel** *72 28 01 40*

Map *D2*

Chez Achour is a very pleasant Moorish-style restaurant with tables set in an attractive garden. The terrace is a splendid place to dine, as are the rustic indoor rooms. The speciality is fish and seafood, chosen from a counter and prepared as you wish. Also recommended is the lamb on a spit, but this needs to be ordered in advance.

HAMMAMET La Scala

🍴 📋 🚗 Ⓥ 🍷 ⓉⓉⓉⓉⓉ

On the Corniche, 8050 **Tel** *77 28 07 68*   **Map** *D2*

La Scala was the disgraced Italian Prime Minister Bettino Craxi's favourite restaurant and there is a little shrine to him in one corner. It serves the best Italian food in town, with excellent main course pastas and fish specialities. The restaurant is elegant and also has a few tables in a lovely small garden.

HAMMAMET Le Voiliers

🍴 📋 🚗 🍷 ⓉⓉⓉⓉ

Marina, Yasmine Hammamet, 8050 **Tel** *72 28 01 22*   **Map** *D2*

The decor of Le Voilier evokes the interior of one of the many luxury yachts moored outside the restaurant in the marina of Yasmine Hammamet. This sumptuous restaurant serves excellent fish and seafood, and specializes in lobster as well as excellent steaks, all perfectly prepared. An upmarket place for well-dressed customers.

HAMMAMET Les Trois Moutons

📋 Ⓥ 🍷 ⓉⓉⓉⓉⓉ

Centre Commercial, 8050 **Tel** *72 28 09 81*   **Map** *D2*

The best restaurant in town is on the first floor of the Centre Commercial, with views over the bay and the town. The restaurant specializes in fish and seafood, and also serves an excellent *brik à l'oeuf (see p268)* and Tunisian salads. Another speciality worth trying is the grouper in a peppery sauce. Very attentive service.

HAMMAMET Pomo d'Oro

🍴 📋 Ⓥ 🍷 ⓉⓉⓉⓉⓉ

6 Avenue Habib Bourguiba, 8050 **Tel** *72 28 12 54*   **Map** *D2*

This small restaurant is situated between the harbour and the kasbah. The excellent menu features Tunisian as well as international cuisine, with the chef promoting his daily specials. The food is well prepared and includes a delicious couscous with fish, as well as several perfectly grilled fish dishes. At night there is usually live music.

KELIBIA Anis

📋 ♿ 🍷 ⓉⓉⓉ

Avenue du Dr Mongi ben Hunida, 8090 **Tel** *72 29 57 77*   **Map** *D1*

The Pension Anis's restaurant serves tasty fish dishes and has a good value menu with a wide choice of Tunisian and French cuisine. The couscous of the house comes, of course, with fish, and is excellent. The old-fashioned ground floor dining room with wooden latticework is simple but pleasant.

KELIBIA El-Mansourah

🍴 🖼 📋 🚗 🍷 ⓉⓉⓉ

Kelibia plage, on the southern part of the Mansourah beach, 8090 **Tel** *72 29 51 69*   **Map** *D1*

Situated on the rocks on a headland by Mansourah beach, this breezy café-restaurant enjoys some magnificent views from the round room with big windows and from the lovely terrace facing the sea. Excellent fish and seafood dominate the menu, but you should also try the local Muscat de Kelibia wine. Note that in summer it can get very busy.

KELIBIA Le Goeland

📋 🚗 🍷 ⓉⓉⓉⓉ

Port de Peche, 8090 **Tel** *72 27 30 74*   **Map** *D1*

From the airy terraces on two floors here there are excellent views over the sea and the lovely port. The food is unpretentious and served simply, but it is very well prepared. On the menu are Tunisian specialities, with an emphasis on fish and seafood, but there are also some good pizzas, which perhaps make for a welcome change at lunchtime.

LA GOULETTE Café Vert

🍴 📋 ♿ 🚗 Ⓥ 🍷 ⓉⓉⓉⓉ

68 Avenue Roosevelt, 2060 **Tel** *71 73 61 56*   **Map** *C1*

Café Vert is the town's favourite fish restaurant. In summer there are outdoor tables, but the road nearby gets fairly busy at night. Choose your fish straight from the counter – you are charged by the weight. Definitely the place to eat fish, seafood or the excellent fish soup – the meat dishes in comparison are mediocre.

LA GOULETTE Le Monte Carlo

🍴 🖼 🍷 ⓉⓉⓉ

4 Avenue Roosevelt, 2060 **Tel** *71 73 53 38*   **Map** *C1*

One of the less expensive eateries in the row of fish restaurants on Avenue Roosevelt, with simple decor, clean white tablecloths and pictures of fruit on the wall. The fish is perfectly grilled, having been collected ultra-fresh from the fish market that morning. The restaurant has a deservedly good reputation.

LA GOULETTE Lucullus

🍴 🖼 📋 ♿ 🎵 Ⓥ 🍷 ⓉⓉⓉⓉ

1 Avenue Habib Bourguiba, 2060 **Tel** *71 73 73 10*   **Map** *C1*

This elegant, upmarket restaurant specializes in excellent fish and shellfish, although their meat dishes are also really good. The restaurant has a pleasant indoor dining room and a large terrace in summer, which is filled with plants and shaded by majestic palm trees. The service is friendly, fast and very efficient. Recommended.

LA GOULETTE La Victoire

🍴 🖼 📋 🚗 Ⓥ 🍷 ⓉⓉⓉⓉⓉ

1 Avenue Roosevelt, 2060 **Tel** *71 73 53 98*   **Map** *C1*

La Victoire has a non air-conditioned dining room on the ground floor, with a more elegant, formal air-conditioned room on the first floor with views over the town. The restaurant specializes in perfectly cooked fresh fish and seafood. The tourist set menu offers great value, but the *à la carte* fish dishes are more interesting.

LA GOULETTE Mamie Lily

🍴 🖼 Ⓥ 🍷 ⓉⓉⓉⓉⓉ

14 Avenue Pasteur, 2060 **Tel** *71 73 76 33*   **Map** *C1*

There are only six tables, with a few more in the garden in summer, at this charming and unusual restaurant serving Jewish-Tunisian cuisine, so it's best to book in advance. Mamie Lily and her son prepare the food, which includes specialities such as couscous with meatballs. The desserts are very good too. Closed Fri dinner and Sat lunch.

Key to Price Guide *see p272* **Key to Symbols** *see back cover flap*

LA MARSA Café Safsaf

Place de la Mosquée, 2092 **Tel** *No telephone* **Map** *C1*

Large outdoor café and inexpensive restaurant with specialities such as *fricassée* (a fried bread with hot *harissa*, tuna, vegetables and olives), *casse-croûte* (the same filling in a French baguette), *brik (see p268)* or grilled kebabs. A place where families gather at long tables, or where you can come and smoke a *chicha* (water pipe). Very lively at night.

LA MARSA Au Bon Vieux Temps

Rue Abou Elkacem Echchebbi, 2092 **Tel** *71 77 43 22* **Map** *C1*

Just a little way from the TGM station, this well-established restaurant offers sophisticated dishes, excellent Mediterranean cuisine and good Tunisian specialities, as well as a large selection of wines. It is expensive, but good value considering the quality. The dining room is charming and there is a pleasant tree-shaded terrace. Book ahead.

LA MARSA La Falaise

Corniche in Sidi Dhrif, 2078 **Tel** *71 74 78 06* **Map** *C1*

La Falaise has an amazing setting on a terrace teetering on a cliff at the edge of the sea. The views are magnificent and the atmosphere elegant and relaxed. The specialities are fish and seafood, expertly prepared and very fresh. The restaurant is popular with the well-heeled crowd of La Marsa and is best booked in advance.

NABEUL Café Errachidia

Avenue Habib Thameur, 8000 **Tel** *No telephone* **Map** *D2*

This rather pretty *café maure* (Arab-style café) has low tables and Moorish benches, and attracts both locals and throngs of tourists. Errachidia specializes in good mint tea served with excellent pastries, as well as *chichas* (water pipes) with a small range of different aromatic tobaccos. No alcohol is served.

NABEUL Sidi El-Maharsi

Road to Hammamet, 5 km (3.5 miles) from Nabeul centre, 8000 **Tel** *No telephone* **Map** *D2*

The views, both during the day and at night, are stunning at this blissful café overlooking one of the most beautiful beaches in the area. Very tranquil and peaceful, this is the perfect place to drink a mint tea, Turkish coffee or *bsissa* – a traditional spicy drink based on malt flour. Open from early afternoon until late at night, but only in summer.

NABEUL Al-Bahja

38 Avenue Habib Thameur, 8000 **Tel** *No telephone* **Map** *D2*

There are just a few tables at this tiny restaurant occupying the ground floor and a mezzanine. The decor is simple, and so is the food, but the restaurant is very popular with locals and budget travellers. The Tunisian food is well prepared and comes in generous portions. The Algerian owner is always very welcoming and likes a little chat.

NABEUL Les Arcades

56 Avenue Habib Bourguiba, 8000 **Tel** *No telephone* **Map** *D2*

Near the Archaeological Museum, the breezy terrace of Les Arcades is the perfect place to sit back and watch the world go by, although it tends to be quite noisy. The food is served swiftly and comes in large servings at good value prices. Specialities of the house include *couscous royale*, seafood spaghetti and *crêpes* for dessert.

NABEUL Le Bon Kif

Rue Marbella, 8000 **Tel** *72 22 27 83* **Map** *D2*

You can eat some of the best fish and seafood in the region at Le Bon Kif, a sophisticated and elegant restaurant which is also one of the more expensive places in town. The service is totally professional but can be a bit too fast at times, leaving hardly any time to recover between the excellent courses. Open both for lunch and dinner.

NABEUL L'Olivier

Avenue Hedi Chaker, 8000 **Tel** *72 28 66 13* **Map** *D2*

This beautiful and elegant restaurant, one of Nabeul's best, serves refined Tunisian-French cuisine with an emphasis on fresh fish and seafood, although the meat is equally good. This is an intimate place that comes complete with classical music in the background, a flotilla of discreet waiters and dimmed lights – perfect for a romantic night out.

NABEUL Slovenia

Rue Abou Kacem Chebbi, 8000 **Tel** *72 28 53 43* **Map** *D2*

The Slovenia, next to Hotel Les Jasmins *(see p253)*, is run by one of Tunisia's best chefs, Rafik Tlati, who serves an innovative Tunisian cuisine with Spanish, Indonesian and Slovenian influences. The food is light, using only the freshest ingredients in season, and makes for a nice change from the routine menus at other Tunisian restaurants.

SIDI BOU SAID Café des Nattes

Main square, 2026 **Tel** *71 74 96 61* **Map** *C1*

A delightful café on the main square, this was once the favourite haunt of painters Paul Klee and Auguste Macke, who lived for a while in the village. All the seats are on the terraces, although many people like sitting either on the steps or on rugs, which add to the Oriental atmosphere. Mint tea and water pipes are the house speciality.

SIDI BOU SAID Café Sidi Chaabane

Rue Sidi Chaabane **Tel** *No telephone* **Map** *C1*

Several terraces, all on different levels, make this picturesque Tunisian café very popular at sunset and later in the evening, as there are marvellous views over the little marina and the entire bay. The speciality of the house is mint tea with pine nuts, and water pipes, but coffee, sweets and cold drinks are also available.

SIDI BOU SAID La Petite Suède

Place du 7 Novembre, 2026 **Tel** *71 74 18 43*

Map *C1*

Why not try this very unusual place – a small and incredibly popular (mainly with Tunisians) *salon de thé*, which is owned and run by a Swedish woman. The comforting, home-baked cakes are superb, and perfect for a different afternoon break, while enjoying the pictures of Sweden on the wall. A rare non-smoking area is available.

SIDI BOU SAID Le Chargui

39 Rue Habib Thameur, 2026 **Tel** *71 74 05 91*

Map *C1*

One of the town's less expensive restaurants, occupying several roof-covered terraces, though only the large white and blue one affords a sweeping view of the sea. It's a pleasant environment in which to eat Tunisian specialities such as couscous with lamb or a selection of salads. The food is reasonable – the begging cats can be annoying though.

SIDI BOU SAID Dar Zarrouk

Rue Hedi Zarrouk, 2026 **Tel** *71 74 05 91*

Map *C1*

This lovely courtyard restaurant belongs to the upmarket Dar Saïd hotel *(see p254)* just above it. The restaurant has wonderful views over the entire bay, and becomes even more magical at night when lit by lanterns. The mouth-watering menu includes both Tunisian and Mediterranean dishes, with a strong emphasis on fish and seafood.

SIDI BOU SAID TamTam

7 Avenue du 7 Novembre, 2026 **Tel** *71 72 85 35*

Map *C1*

There's definitely a contemporary beat at this lively restaurant, popular with trendy locals. It is one of the few restaurants that serves something like a fusion menu, with good Mediterranean and Asian specialities including pastas, pizzas and Asian curries. The dining room is very colourful but stylish and the welcome is friendly. No alcohol.

SIDI BOU SAID Au Bon Vieux Temps (Ayyem Zaman)

56 Rue Hedi Zarrouk, 2026 **Tel** *71 744 733*

Map *C1*

The beautiful Au Bon Vieux Temps has a romantic terrace overlooking the bay, while the elegant indoor dining room is decorated with contemporary Tunisian art and old photographs. The delicious food is Tunisian-Mediterranean; try the couscous with fish or the tagliatelle with seafood. Excellent Tunisian wines.

SIDI BOU SAID Le Pirate

Blvd de l'Environnement, Port de Plaisance, 2026 **Tel** *71 74 82 66*

Map *C1*

Le Pirate offers the perfect setting for a great evening, treating diners to a fine view of the yacht marina and providing a great place for alfresco dining in summer. The house speciality is fish and seafood. The *à la carte* menu is definitely recommended, being far more interesting than the set menu. The restaurant has a great wine list too.

NORTHERN TUNISIA

AIN DRAHAM L'Escale

Main road near the roundabout, 8130 **Tel** *No telephone*

Map *B2*

During the day this small eatery serves simple but delicious rotisserie chicken, in quarters or halves, with a spicy sauce, plus salads, French fries and sandwiches. At night there are a few slightly more elaborate Tunisian dishes on offer. Worth seeking out among a row of other budget places and street stalls.

BIZERTE Café Patisserie Bellahouel

Avenue Habib Bourguiba, on the corner with Rue de Tunis, 7000 **Tel** *No telephone*

Map *C1*

With views over the old port from the terrace tables, this is the perfect place for breakfast or afternoon tea. Delicious pastries are baked throughout the day – the *mille feuille* of filo pastry interspersed with custard cream is particularly recommended, and the coffee is very good. A lovely place to watch the locals going about their business.

BIZERTE Chez Jendoubi

Corner of Rue du 1 Mai and Rue d'Algérie, 7000 **Tel** *No telephone*

Map *C1*

Chez Jendoubi is a truly local restaurant with a menu in Arabic only, which the friendly owner is all too happy to translate. The place is small but the tables spill over on to the pavement. The couscous with fish or with lamb is excellent, and is the speciality of the house. Customers often go to the patisserie across the road for a dessert.

BIZERTE La Cuisine Tunisienne

7 Rue du 2 Mars 1934, 7000 **Tel** *No telephone*

Map *C1*

This is a reliable budget eatery where you often have to share a table with locals. The food is nothing special – just good, well-prepared Tunisian fare, including all the standard dishes like *brik (see p268)*, couscous and *ojja* (poached eggs in tomato sauce), at a low price. A small and friendly place with cheerful and welcoming staff.

BIZERTE Le Grand Bleu da Ciccio

Rue Ahmed Tlili, 7000 **Tel** *72 42 35 84*

Map *C1*

Downstairs at Le Grand Bleu there's a bright and cheerful pizzeria serving authentic Italian pizzas as well as sandwiches and *shawarma*. Upstairs is a more upmarket Italian restaurant with an Italian chef, which offers a wide choice of well-prepared pastas and meat dishes. The decor is kitsch Italianate but the food is good.

BIZERTE Du Bonheur

31 Rue Thaalbi, 7000 **Tel** *72 43 10 47* **Map** *C1*

This smart restaurant has a wide selection of Tunisian and international dishes on the menu, including a tasty couscous which is a house speciality. The dining room is decorated in a typical North African style, with lots of private niches and *moucharaby* latticework screens. A good selection of wines is offered, including a rosé from Bizerte.

BIZERTE La Mammina

1 Rue d'Espagne, 7000 **Tel** *No telephone* **Map** *C1*

Popular with the younger crowd, this pleasant and inexpensive Italian restaurant-pizzeria is small – just a few tables in a room brightened by colourful wall paintings. The menu features a large choice of pastas, omelettes, salads, tasty meat and fish dishes, plus good pizzas in the evening. No alcohol. Closed during Ramadan.

BIZERTE Le Petit Mousse

Route de la Corniche, 7000 **Tel** *72 43 21 85* **Map** *C1*

Attached to a comfortable hotel *(see p254)* overlooking the sea, this restaurant has a lovely Mediterranean-style white and blue terrace. The food is delicious, with an emphasis on perfectly grilled fish, which is chosen from the counter and weighed. There are equally good meat dishes and a fine selection of wines and delicious desserts.

BIZERTE Le Phénicien

Old Port, 7000 **Tel** *72 42 44 80* **Map** *C1*

This is actually a pirate ship moored in the town's old port. Decor aside, the food is actually rather good, with a wide range of fish and seafood dishes, Tunisian salads and other standard fare, all very fresh and well prepared. The top deck has a pleasant bar with great views over the port.

BIZERTE Le Sport Nautique

Quai Tarek ibn Ziyad, 7000 **Tel** *72 43 22 62* **Map** *C1*

People come from as far away as Tunis to eat fish and seafood at this highly regarded restaurant, which was founded in 1928 for the French colonels living in Bizerte. There is a huge range of fish on offer, including oysters which are rarely found on a Tunisian menu. The superb fish couscous and paella need ordering in advance. Book ahead.

BIZERTE L'Eden

Route de la Corniche, 4 km (1.5 miles) from Bizerte, 7000 **Tel** *72 43 9023* **Map** *C1*

The Eden is popular with Tunisians, and unlike most other eating options in Bizerte, it focuses on European cuisine with a choice of meat dishes, including a delicious chateaubriand steak with a pepper sauce. The food is good, the service swift and friendly, and the decor smart, but prices have remained reasonable. Belly dancer at weekends.

JENDOUBA Hotel Atlas

Rue 1 Juin, 8800 **Tel** *78 60 32 17* **Map** *B2*

Attached to the Atlas Hotel *(see p255)*, this is just about the only place in Jendouba to eat. The interior of the restaurant is rather uninspiring but the set menu (often the only option) is fine, if nothing special. In the hunting season there may be wild boar on the menu. You can also have a cool beer or a glass of wine with your meal.

SIDI ALI EL-MEKKI Cap Farina

On the beach, 7033 **Tel** *98 44 28 51* **Map** *C1*

This idyllic restaurant lies on the most beautiful stretch of beach. It's open every day from May to mid-October, but only at weekends for the rest of the year. There isn't a very large menu – mainly very fresh salads and fish barbecued on a fire with pine cones. Check that it's open and book ahead before setting out. No alcohol. Closed Ramadan.

SIDI MECHRIG Auberge de Sidi Mechrig

On the beach, 7010 **Tel** *No telephone* **Map** *C1*

The restaurant next to the Auberge *(see p255)* overlooks the beach. The food is simple but delicious – the small menu includes mainly grilled fresh fish and a small selection of Tunisian dishes, including a very good couscous. At the end of the day there is nothing like sampling a cool beer here while watching the sunset.

TABARKA Café Andalous

Rue Hedi Chaker, 8110 **Tel** *No telephone* **Map** *B1*

Try this old-fashioned *café maure* (Arab-style café), with lovely tiled walls, and wooden hand-puppets of Ottoman Turks hanging from the ceiling. It's a trendy meeting place, perfect for a tea stop with mint tea, a game of cards perhaps, and the chance to try a *chicha*, or water pipe. Live performances during the Tabarka jazz festival.

TABARKA Les Etoiles

Rue du Peuple, 8110 **Tel** *No telephone* **Map** *B1*

Les Etoiles is a popular local restaurant, very much frequented by Tunisians. It is the best in a row of similar places and serves straightforward Tunisian staples and fresh grilled fish. The few tables on the pavement are good for people-watching too.

TABARKA Corail

70 Avenue Habib Bourguiba, 8110 **Tel** *No telephone* **Map** *B1*

Rub shoulders here with the locals, who come to this small and clean eatery for a fast bite to eat. The friendly staff serve a good value traditional set menu, consisting of a Tunisian salad, grilled fish and fruit for dessert. Sit in the simple inside dining room or outside at one of the few tables on the pavement.

TABARKA Khemir

!◎! 🗐 🖼 🍴   ⓜⓜⓜ

Avenue Habib Bourguiba, 8110 **Tel** *78 67 15 86*   **Map** *B1*

Khemir is a small, authentic Tunisian restaurant with two dining rooms, one of which is mainly a bar where locals seem to drink huge amounts of beer. On the menu are the usual Tunisian standards, but well prepared and without any frills. Fish is chosen from the counter and priced by weight, before being grilled and served with fries and salad.

TABARKA Le Pescadou

!◎! 🗐 🖼 🍴   ⓜⓜⓜ

Place Fréjus, 8110 **Tel** *78 67 15 86*   **Map** *B1*

Delicious fresh crayfish and tasty fish dishes are the highlights of this restaurant's menu, as is the hearty *bouillabaisse* (fish soup), made with a selection of fish. The restaurant has a pleasant outdoor terrace with views over the boats in the marina. The service is professional and attentive and there is a good wine list.

TABARKA Les Aiguilles

!◎! 🗐 🖼 🍴   ⓜⓜⓜ

18 Avenue Habib Bourguiba, 8110 **Tel** *78 67 37 89*   **Map** *B1*

Some fine seafood and fresh fish, as well as a varied selection of Tunisian specialities, can be enjoyed on the pleasant terrace of this hotel-restaurant. The restaurant offers excellent value, with the possible exception of the lobster, which is pricey but freshly caught from the coral sea. The good wine list incorporates plenty of local wines.

TABARKA Les Mimosas

!◎! 🗐 🖼 🍴   ⓜⓜⓜ

Road up from the Bizerte Road, at the entrance of town, 8110 **Tel** *78 67 30 28*   **Map** *B1*

Situated on a hilltop, the restaurant commands panoramic views over the town and the sea. Some fine fish courses are on offer, as well as a variety of Tunisian staples. The wild boar from Aïn Draham and the crayfish are particularly recommended. The food is very well prepared and served with attention to detail. A excellent address.

TABARKA Touta

!◎! 🗐 🖼 Ⓥ 🍴   ⓜⓜⓜⓜⓜ

Near the marina, 8110 **Tel** *78 67 10 18*   **Map** *B1*

From the pleasant, shaded and breezy terrace at Touta there are great views over the boats and the kasbah. The restaurant definitely ranks as one of the best in town, with excellent seafood and crayfish on the menu. Particularly recommended is the *brik (see p268)* with seafood. In summer the terrace fills up quickly, so book ahead.

THE SAHEL

EL-JEM Le Bonheur

!◎! 🗐 🖼   ⓜⓜ

Road to Sfax, 5160 **Tel** *73 63 23 84*   **Map** *D3*

Le Bonheur is a family-run restaurant, slightly out of the centre but with a very friendly atmosphere. Straightforward Tunisian dishes predominate, including some spicy stews, a good couscous, and salads and sandwiches for those in a hurry. The restaurant has just two rooms and a noisy street-side terrace.

GABES Patisserie Linoise

🗐 🖹   ⓜ

Avenue Farhat Hached, 6000 **Tel** *No telephone*   **Map** *D5*

The best patisserie in town is perfect for a snack at any time of day: breakfast *pâtés* (pastries), savoury pastries with spinach, meat or cheese for lunch, and delicious sweet pastries in the afternoon. At night families descend upon Lina for an ice cream, pastry or freshly-squeezed orange juice. Only a few counters and high chairs to sit down on.

GABES Restaurant El Pino

🗐 🖹 Ⓥ   ⓜ

144 Avenue Habib Bourguiba, 6000 **Tel** *75 27 20 10*   **Map** *D5*

This modern, cosy restaurant is decorated in orange hues and plays contemporary music. There is a wide range of excellent pizzas as well as a small choice of Tunisian staples such as *ojja* (egg dish) and *brochettes* (lamb kebabs). Pino's is filled with students from the nearby university at lunchtime, while local families come for dinner.

GABES Le Petit Dauphin

🗐 🖼   ⓜⓜ

Avenue Farhat Hached, 6000 **Tel** *No telephone*   **Map** *D5*

Near the bus and *louage* station in Gabès, Le Petit Dauphin is open from breakfast until about 9:30pm. This is a friendly, family restaurant which serves gigantic portions of couscous, chicken or beef stew, and fresh salads, which are probably a better option if you are planning a long journey afterwards. The owner is friendly and welcoming.

GABES L'Oasis

!◎! 🖹 🖼 🍴   ⓜⓜⓜ

15-17 Avenue Farhat Hached, 6000 **Tel** *75 27 00 98*   **Map** *D5*

L'Oasis has been a Gabès institution since it was founded in 1949, under the name of Franco-Arabe. One of the city's top establishments, it provides a successful combination of French and Tunisian cuisine. You can be sure of a good meal here. The speciality is fish with giant prawns, but the meat – especially the leg of lamb – is equally delicious.

GABES Restaurant du Port

🖼   ⓜⓜⓜ

Avenue Farhat Hached, 6000 **Tel** *No telephone*   **Map** *D5*

The only restaurant within the port, this eatery is small but very popular with local families for its ultra-fresh fish. The specialities of the house are grilled fish or prawns, and a very fine spaghetti with octopus. There is no sign outside but everyone in town knows the place. Friendly atmosphere, and a good place for lunch.

Key to Price Guide *see p272* **Key to Symbols** *see back cover flap*

KERKENNAH ISLANDS Le Régal

El-Attaya, 3025 **Tel** *74 48 41 00 / 98 29 12 35*　　　　　　　　　　　　　　　　　*Map D–E4*

Chef Najet cooks, and often serves too, at this highly recommended small café-restaurant, one of only a very few in this tiny village of fishermen. The menu is centred on a simple island cuisine, based on fresh fish and seafood, and Najet has won several awards for her tasty seafood dishes, like the octopus stew. Friendly staff.

KERKENNAH ISLANDS Cercina

Sidi Frej, 3025 **Tel** *74 48 99 53*　　　　　　　　　　　　　　　　　　　　　　*Map D–E4*

A lovely family restaurant at Hotel Cercina *(see p256)* with a large, breezy terrace overlooking the sea and boats. On the menu are the specialities of the island, with great emphasis on fish and seafood. Particularly recommended are grilled fish, octopus salad and squid eggs. The hotel also has a snack bar in summer with cheaper dishes and sandwiches.

KERKENNAH ISLANDS Kastil

Sidi Frej, 3025 **Tel** *74 48 98 84*　　　　　　　　　　　　　　　　　　　　　　*Map D–E4*

The restaurant at Hotel Kastil *(see p256)* serves a very local cuisine *kerkennaise*, which inevitably means a lot of fish and fresh seafood, as well as some typically French dishes such as onion soup, mainly because the owner lives in Paris for half the year. The terrace is a pleasant place to hang out.

KERKENNAH ISLANDS La Sirène

Remla, 3025 **Tel** *74 48 11 18*　　　　　　　　　　　　　　　　　　　　　　　*Map D–E4*

The best restaurant on the island, La Sirène is situated right on the beach in Remla and has a pleasantly shaded terrace as well as a lovely dining room. The seafood is superb, particularly the octopus stew and the spaghetti with seafood. Don't confuse this with another La Sirène restaurant found on the road leading to the beach.

MAHDIA Café El-Medina

Place de la Grande Mosquée, 5100 **Tel** *No telephone*　　　　　　　　　　　　　*Map D3*

A very lovely café with a picturesque interior and waiters dressed up in the local, traditional costume. The terrace is shaded by trees, and is a great place to have breakfast while watching the world go by. Fresh fruit juices and a selection of teas and pastries are served all day. As popular with locals as with visitors.

MAHDIA El-Moez

Near the Skifa and entrance gate to the museum, 5100 **Tel** *No telephone*　　　*Map D3*

El-Moez, also known as Chez Kacem, is a tiny restaurant in an alleyway between the museum and the port. It is mainly frequented by Tunisians, but individual travellers also receive a friendly welcome from the boss. There might not always be a menu but staff will let you know about the daily specials, usually including grilled fish and couscous.

MAHDIA Sidi Salem

Rue du Borj, 5100 **Tel** *No telephone*　　　　　　　　　　　　　　　　　　　*Map D3*

A great café on the south side of the medina, built on several terraces overlooking the sea. This is a place where local families like to come at night, but at any time it is a tranquil and peaceful place to recover from the heat of the beach or sightseeing in the medina. On offer are mint tea, a *chicha* (water pipe) and reasonably priced sandwiches.

MAHDIA Le Lido

Avenue Farhat Hached, 5100 **Tel** *71 68 13 39*　　　　　　　　　　　　　　　　*Map D3*

One of the best of the restaurants with terraces overlooking the port, Le Lido has a loyal local clientele but welcomes visitors too. There is a wide range of fresh fish and seafood dishes on offer, as well as Tunisian staples, including a *méchouia* salad (roast peppers, onion and tomatoes, served with boiled egg and a chunk of tuna), and *ojja* (egg dish).

MAHDIA Le Neptune

Blvd du 7 Novembre, 5100 **Tel** *73 68 19 27*　　　　　　　　　　　　　　　　　*Map D3*

This old-fashioned fish restaurant is decorated with fish nets, shells and kitsch paintings. The menu features a range of grilled meats, fish dishes and seafood, but the octopus salad, couscous with seafood and grilled cuttlefish are particularly recommended. On the first floor is a terrace overlooking the sea and the white medina.

MAHDIA Le Phénix

Corner of Av. H. Bourguiba & Av. Bechir Sfar, 5100 **Tel** *73 69 01 01*　　　　　*Map D3*

One of the most elegant and classy venues in town, located in the upmarket Le Phénix hotel *(see p257)*, this restaurant has an elaborate, Moorish-style decor. Sometimes a buffet is served, and *à la carte* dishes are also available, with good and well-presented Tunisian food including a choice of couscous. A small wine list.

MATMATA Ben Khalifa

Avenue Habib Bourguiba, 6070 **Tel** *No telephone*　　　　　　　　　　　　　　*Map D5*

The food tends to be rather hot and spicy (but you can ask for less chilli) at this simple cafeteria serving honest, no-frills southern Tunisian cuisine. It caters mainly for locals, so there are no innovative dishes on the menu, just the usual tasty staples of omelettes, *brochettes* (kebabs), soup and couscous.

MATMATA Chez Abdoul

Just north of the main square, 6070 **Tel** *75 24 01 89*　　　　　　　　　　　　*Map D5*

In the heart of the town of Matmata, Chez Abdoul is a welcome small and simple restaurant amid the rather bland hotel restaurants of the area that cater mostly for tour groups. It has a good selection of simple southern Tunisian dishes, and is also popular with the locals of Matmata. Friendly atmosphere.

MATMATA Sidi Driss

Centre of Matmata, 6070 **Tel** *75 23 00 05* — **Map** *D5*

This hotel restaurant caters mainly for tour groups and serves good value three-course meals, with international and Tunisian options. Fans of the film *Star Wars* will recognize the courtyard where Luke Skywalker sat down to eat with his aunt and uncle. The hotel also has a bar with cool beers and a range of Tunisian wines.

MONASTIR Café Bir Andalous

Medina, 5000 **Tel** *No telephone* — **Map** *D3*

Very pleasant café with a lovely garden in the heart of the medina, behind the government craft shop and opposite the Bourguiba Mosque. It's a tranquil place to recover from shopping in the crowded souks, with excellent fresh fruit juices and cocktails, mint tea, Turkish coffee and, for those who like it, a *chicha* (water pipe).

MONASTIR Café Sidi Massoud

Avenue Habib Bourguiba, 5000 **Tel** *No telephone* — **Map** *D3*

There is a superbly tiled terrace at this traditional café in a 19th-century *zaouia* (a complex around the tomb of a holy man). No alcohol is served here, but it's a perfect spot to relax in at any time of day, enjoying a mint tea or a fresh fruit juice while watching the locals go about their business. Very popular with Tunisians too.

MONASTIR Ali Baba, Hotel Amir Palace

Route Touristique, 5000 **Tel** *73 52 09 00* — **Map** *D3*

The owners are very welcoming at this delightful Tunisian restaurant in a bougainvillea-shaded square in the medina. There is always couscous on the menu, and if you order it earlier in the day they will make you the most wonderful home-cooked couscous with fish for dinner. Good value and highly recommended.

MONASTIR Alhambra

Rue Sidi el-Mezri, side street off Avenue Habib Bourguiba, 5000 **Tel** *73 46 53 58* — **Map** *D3*

One of Monastir's better restaurants, Alhambra has a welcoming atmosphere and an elegant indoor dining room, as well as cosy courtyard seating. The food is mainly Mediterranean, with generous portions of very well-prepared pasta dishes, grilled steaks and pizzas as well as fish and seafood and a few Tunisian staples. Very attentive service.

MONASTIR Dar Chakra

Avenue de l'Indépendance, 5000 **Tel** *73 46 05 28* — **Map** *D3*

In a beautifully restored house near the tourist office is this attractive restaurant with several small dining rooms and a lovely courtyard, all decorated with original tiles. The menu features the usual Tunisian staples, but it pays to order the much recommended house specials in advance, such as the *couscous au cherkaw* (tiny fish from Monastir).

MONASTIR Grottes del Corsario

Old port, 5000 **Tel** *73 42 55 00* — **Map** *D3*

This restaurant is an excellent option for dinner rather than lunch, as it is set in a dimly lit pirate den with a terrace overlooking the old port. It sounds tacky but the food is excellent, following almost the same formula as Le Pirate (*see below*): soup, *mezzeh* (platters) of seafood, grilled fish, lemon sorbet, fruit and mint tea to digest it all.

MONASTIR Le Chandelier

Cap Marina Monastir, 5000 **Tel** *73 46 22 32* — **Map** *D3*

Eat outside on the large terrace here, looking out at the boats and marina. The restaurant has a highly recommended menu of Tunisian and Mediterranean specialities, and a good selection of wines. The grilled fish, the *brik* (see p268) with seafood and the couscous with fish are particularly good. Very pleasant atmosphere.

MONASTIR Le Pirate

Porte de Peche, El Ghdir, 5000 **Tel** *73 46 81 26* — **Map** *D3*

This restaurant is a 20-minute walk along the beach, or you can take the little tourist train. It is recognizable by the large skull and anchor above the entrance, but inside you'll find wealthy families from Monastir who know the place for its excellent food – with a winning formula of soup, seafood appetizers, grilled fish, lemon sorbet and mint tea.

PORT EL-KANTAOUI La Daurade

Marina, 4089 **Tel** *73 34 88 93* — **Map** *D2*

A top-class fish restaurant overlooking this large marina, with a very good reputation locally. The long and varied menu includes excellent fish and seafood dishes, cooked in Tunisian or Mediterranean style. The seafood bisque is superb, as is the grilled red mullet, and all dishes are beautifully presented. Music and belly dancing at weekends.

PORT EL-KANTAOUI Le Méditérranée

Marina, 4089 **Tel** *73 34 87 88* — **Map** *D2*

Situated just by the harbourmaster's office, this is the best fish restaurant in the area. The splendid first-floor dining room has a pleasant decor, with windows offering a lovely view over the marina. The restaurant's tasty fish soup and spicy prawns are well worth a try, but all dishes are excellent and so is the service. Closed Tue.

SFAX Café Maure Le Diwan

Inside Bab Diwan, Medina, 3000 **Tel** *No telephone* — **Map** *D4*

Very pleasant Moorish-style café on several floors, set in a courtyard within the old city walls. There's a lively atmosphere at night when families and courting couples come to relax, drink mint tea and smoke a *chicha* (water pipe). It's a tranquil place and a refuge from shopping in the warren of the medina or from the hubbub of the Ville Nouvelle.

Key to Price Guide *see p272* **Key to Symbols** *see back cover flap*

SFAX Patisserie Masmoudi

Rue Docteur Ahmed Sikeli, 3000 **Tel** *74 40 53 30*

Map *D4*

This is the best patisserie in town, which was once in the *Guiness Book of World Records* for producing the largest *baklava (see p269)* in the world. It is renowned for its large choice of some of the best Tunisian pastries in the country, though prices have remained very reasonable despite the high quality of the product. A must!

SFAX La Renaissance

77 Avenue Hedi Chaker, 3000 **Tel** *74 22 04 39*

Map *D4*

La Renaissance is an old-time French restaurant with a colonial-style, faded but nicely-kept interior and formal, slightly surly waiters. It's popular with wealthy locals, who come for the comfort food and cold beers. The food is mostly French but includes Tunisian staples such as grilled fish, *salade mechouia (see p269)* and couscous.

SFAX Le Bagdad

63 Avenue Farhat Hached, 3000 **Tel** *74 29 91 73*

Map *D4*

Close to the medina, this small restaurant has a big reputation, and is very well known among the locals for its reliably excellent Sfaxian specialities. There is a good selection of regional dishes on the menu, including octopus salad and Sfaxian soup. Most dishes are reasonably priced for the quality on offer. Pleasant decor.

SFAX Le Corail

39 Rue Habib Maazoun, 3000 **Tel** *74 22 73 01*

Map *D4*

This modern, sophisticated restaurant, right next door to Hotel Thyna *(see p258)*, is arguably Sfax's leading restaurant and attracts well-off locals. It has a delicious *à la carte* menu with inventive local specialities based on fish and seafood, including *ojja* (egg dish) with large prawns and a delightful fish stew *(marmite du chef)*. Attentive service. Closed Sun.

SFAX Le Petit Navire

127 Rue de Haffouz, 3000 **Tel** *74 21 28 90*

Map *D4*

The seafood and fish are prepared according to traditional recipes but given an inventive twist at this attractive and very smart Moorish-style restaurant situated right next to the old port. The menu focuses on regional cuisine, and in addition there is a choice of sophisticated French dishes such as salad of foie gras.

SOUSSE Caracas

Rue Ali Behouane, 4000 **Tel** *No telephone*

Map *D3*

Caracas is a young and trendy contemporary restaurant with a Latin American feel to the decor and large screens showing Arabic pop music videos. The menu is large, with Tunisian, American and European dishes, and the food is good. It also comes well presented and in generous amounts. Very popular with the hip crowd.

SOUSSE Restaurant du Peuple

Rue du Rempart du Nord, Medina, 4000 **Tel** *No telephone*

Map *D3*

A tiny but very popular restaurant with a small menu of a few Tunisian starters, followed by beef stew, couscous or grilled fish as a main course. The owner offers fruit and mint tea to finish. The food is lovingly prepared, very much like home-cooked, and customers are given a warm welcome. A good and very friendly place.

SOUSSE Dodo

Rue el-Hajra, Medina, 4000 **Tel** *73 21 23 26*

Map *D3*

The attractive decor of this most modern of the medina restaurants offers a pleasant haven away from the hubbub of the souks. The wide-ranging menu includes simple Tunisian and international dishes, such as generous plates of pasta, tasty meat dishes and fish. Friendly service.

SOUSSE L'Escargot

87 Boulevard de la Corniche, 4000 **Tel** *73 22 47 79*

Map *D3*

In this slightly more upmarket beach-area restaurant, diners can enjoy their food to the accompaniment of piano-bar music. A large *à la carte* menu incorporates French and Tunisian dishes, but particularly recommended are the *salade mechouia* (roasted vegetables with tuna and hard-boiled egg), roast duck and the French *pâté*.

SOUSSE Marmite

8 Rue Remada, 4000 **Tel** *73 22 67 28*

Map *D3*

This venue is reminiscent of an old fishermen's tavern, although a bit more upmarket. Among the local specialities are some fairly spicy stews which are flavoured with orange blossom to produce a very interesting taste. Fish and seafood specialities are offered here too. The wine list is fairly extensive, and the atmosphere is jovial and relaxed.

JERBA AND THE MEDENINE

JERBA Carthage

Avenue Mohammed Badra, Houmt Souk, 4180 **Tel** *No telephone*

Map *D5*

The big, working bread oven is the only interior decoration at this small restaurant in the centre of Houmt Souk, opposite Place du 7 Novembre. The menu offers no surprises, but the Tunisian staples are well prepared, and so are the tasty pizzas and grilled meat on skewers. This a good place for a quick no-frills bite.

JERBA La Fontaine

Rue 2 Mars, 4180 **Tel** *75 25 42 05*

Map *D5*

La Fontaine has several rooms decorated in various styles – from Swiss-Chalet to Tunisian tiled-courtyard. The menu is just as eclectic, with a large choice of international dishes and snacks as well as Tunisian favourites. An international set menu is available from late afternoon onwards. Very touristy but good for a quick bite.

JERBA Restaurant du Sportif

147 Avenue Habib Bourguiba, Houmt Souk, 4180 **Tel** *No telephone*

Map *D5*

This venue is cheap and cheerful and serves good meaty, rather than fishy, Tunisian cuisine from a short menu. A simple restaurant away from the tourist hubbub, it is frequented by locals. The tables under the arcades are a good place to watch passers-by on this busy street.

JERBA Pizzeria Zitouna

4 Rue Sidi Sherif, 4125 **Tel** *No telephone*

Map *D5*

There is a large, no-frills dining room at this simple but bright and cheerful restaurant on the little square of the Syndicat d'Initiative, as well as a little terrace overlooking the goings on in the square. The menu offers hearty Tunisian dishes such as couscous, *ojja* (egg dish), pizzas and delicious grilled fish.

JERBA La Grande Jarre

Near the Museum of Guellala, 4180 **Tel** *22 18 83 12*

Map *D5*

This lovely little restaurant is perfect for a lunch stop if you are driving around the island. Some specialities need to be ordered in advance, such as roast lamb or lamb cooked in terracotta *(gargoulette)*, but most Tunisian classic dishes are available on the menu, and expertly cooked. Very good value for this quality.

JERBA La Mamma

Rue Habib Bougatfa, 4180 **Tel** *No telephone*

Map *D5*

A simple, popular eatery, La Mamma offers unfussy and wholesome Tunisian and Mediterranean dishes with a home-cooked taste. The hearty soups and generous pasta dishes are particularly worth trying. This is a friendly and welcoming place, convenient for either a drink or a quick meal.

JERBA Le Lotophage

Avenue du 7 Novembre, Midoun, 4125 **Tel** *No telephone*

Map *D–E5*

You can order sandwiches or spicy local specialities such as *ojja* (egg dish), *merguez* (spicy lamb sausages) and pizzas. at this large, kitsch cafeteria/tea salon. On the first floor there is a beautiful *café maure* (Moorish-style café), where you can drink tea or smoke a *chicha* (water pipe), and try the excellent house pastries. Very popular with young locals.

JERBA Le Moulin

Zone Touristique, 4180 **Tel** *75 75 83 36*

Map *D5*

Le Moulin has an excellent reputation both for good food and friendly service. The restaurant is a calm haven away from the noisy tourist zone, and serves daily specials based on what's available at the market. Try the delicious *brik* with prawns *(see p268)*, the superb couscous with fish or the octopus salad. The dining room is bright and colourful.

JERBA Pierre Marina

Marina, Houmt Souk, 4180 **Tel** *No telephone*

Map *D5*

French-run pizzeria in the little port, serving good pastas and pizzas as well as standard Tunisian dishes. All the food is beautifully presented and the service is very friendly. The restaurant bakes its own bread, too, which is delicious, as are the authentic *crêpes* with a choice of fillings. The terrace with parasols is a pleasant place to stop for lunch.

JERBA Ar-Rachid

Rue Habib Thameur, Houmt Souk, 4180 **Tel** *No telephone*

Map *D5*

The clean ground-floor dining room here is pleasant enough, but most customers head for the pergola-shaded roof terrace at Ar-Rachid, an enjoyable restaurant in a small street that runs off Place Farhat Hached, going towards the fish market. On the menu are good Tunisian staples, both fish and meat, served with saffron rice, salad and chips.

JERBA El-Guestile

Rue Marsa et-Touffa, Midoun, 4125 **Tel** *75 65 77 24*

Map *D–E5*

El-Guestile, just off the market square, is famous for its excellent Tunisian food, particularly the seafood and the fish dishes. On the first floor there are two pleasant rooms decorated with *objets d'art*, and a little terrace, while on the ground floor there is a small, jasmine-festooned courtyard. Mint tea is complimentary at the end of the meal.

JERBA Papagallo

Avenue Habib Bourguiba, Houmt Souk, 4180 **Tel** *21 41 62 16*

Map *D5*

Run by an Italian lady and her Tunisian husband, this restaurant is a cut above the rest in the centre of Houmt Souk. The food reflects their partnership – partly Tunisian and partly Italian – and all the dishes are well prepared. The atmosphere is relaxed and the place doesn't get too crowded, as it's slightly off the beaten track. Excellent fresh lasagna.

JERBA Restaurant de L'Île

Place Hedi Chaker, Houmt Souk, 4180 **Tel** *75 65 06 51*

Map *D5*

One of several restaurants in Place Hedi Chaker, Restaurant de L'Île has some excellent fish and seafood dishes, as well as good starters such as *ojja*, which here consists of a small vegetable stew with scrambled eggs in it. Head straight for the terrace on the first floor – it commands great views over the animated square below.

Key to Price Guide *see p272* **Key to Symbols** *see back cover flap*

JERBA Hôtel du Lotos

18 Rue de la République, Le Port, Houmt Souk, 4180 **Tel** *75 65 00 26*

Map *D5*

This atmospheric restaurant serves excellent fish and seafood in French–Tunisian style. In summer, the courtyard is the perfect spot for an aperitif and a leisurely dinner. Part of a small hotel, the restaurant is an easy walk from the town centre and is directly opposite the Hournt Souk harbour.

JERBA Princesse d'Haroun

At entrance to the port, Houmt Souk, 4180 **Tel** *75 65 04 88*

Map *D5*

The food is excellent here, with the emphasis on the freshest fish and seafood available. Reputedly the best restaurant in town, with a large, attractive dining room decked in fake amphoras and rusty fishing nets. This room and the summer terrace both command views over the port. Popular with Tunisian families, so book ahead.

MEDENINE Montazah El-Meria

Avenue du 7 Novembre, 4100 **Tel** *No telephone*

Map *D5–6*

Montazah El-Meria is a pleasant, simple restaurant – the nicest in town – serving great Tunisian food as well as sandwiches and extremely tasty, if not totally authentic, pizzas. The indoor dining room is nice enough but the garden is special – lovely and peaceful, and the real attraction of the place. Just north of Medenine's *ksar*.

METAMEUR Le Café Metameur

On Gabès-Medenine Road, 4110 **Tel** *75 64 02 94*

Map *D5*

A café set in the atmospheric, restored *ghorfas* (rooms) of a 17th-century *ksar*. There are mainly drinks – mint tea, juices and sodas – on the menu, but also sandwiches and snacks. The venue is popular with tour groups visiting the area, who stop for a drink or to have the set menu lunch, but individual travellers are also welcome.

ZARZIS Le Pirate

Route des Hotels, Souihel, 4170 **Tel** *75 70 62 52*

Map *E5*

This is an enjoyable family restaurant on two floors, with a small terrace overlooking the rather noisy street. The menu includes a large choice of Tunisian classic dishes, plus fish and seafood. The decor is attractive and the service welcoming and attentive. Snacks and sandwiches are available throughout the day too.

ZARZIS Le Typique

Souihel, 4170 **Tel** *75 70 57 88*

Map *E5*

Opposite the Sangho hotel *(see p261)*, Le Typique is a tourist-oriented restaurant with very few surprises on the menu. The food, however, is reliably good, and includes the usual couscous with fish, good meaty dishes and the typical fish specialities of this part of the country. Good atmosphere and friendly service.

SOUTHERN TUNISIA

DOUZ Ali Baba

Avenue Habib Bourguiba, 4260 **Tel** *75 47 24 98*

Map *C6*

This charming little restaurant has a shaded, sandy courtyard at the back where it is possible to dine in a lovely Bedouin-style tent. It is inexpensive and very clean, and the chef's couscous with lamb is delicious. The restaurant is a short distance from the roundabout, on the road to Kebili. Very enjoyable atmosphere.

DOUZ Bel Habib

Avenue du 7 Novembre, 4260 **Tel** *No telephone*

Map *C6*

This simple eatery on the ground floor of the Bel Habib hotel caters for tourists and a few Tunisians. There are no surprises on the menu, with *brochettes* (lamb skewers), salads, couscous with lamb and vegetables, and a good roast chicken. The room is plain, with little decoration, but the service is friendly.

DOUZ La Rosa

Place 7 Novembre 1987, 4260 **Tel** *75 47 16 60*

Map *C6*

A small and enjoyable family-run restaurant, La Rosa has an indoor dining room and some tables out on the terrace. On offer are a large selection of inexpensive but well-prepared Tunisian dishes, including some good vegetable dishes such as okra. Opposite is La Rosa Café, which belongs to the same family.

DOUZ Le Rendez-Vous

Avenue Taieb Mehiri, 4260 **Tel** *75 47 08 02*

Map *C6*

The large dining room here has little character, but the roof terraces are lovely and have good views. There is also a small terrace on the street side. The food is standard Tunisian fare with a selection of salads, couscous and hearty stews. It is worth noting that there are very few desserts on the menu.

DOUZ Tej El-Khayem

Zone Touristique, 4260 **Tel** *75 47 24 46*

Map *C6*

This is a tourist experience, but a rather pleasant one at that. You can either dine in a Berber tent or out on the sand, but the food is surprisingly good and if you order in advance you can eat lamb *koucha*, lamb cooked in a terracotta jar under the desert sand. If there is a group a good folklore show will be laid on.

NEFTA Ferdaous/Zembretta

Route de la Corbeille, 2240 **Tel** *No telephone* **Map** A5

It's worth seeking out this restaurant situated in a palm grove a short way into Nefta, on the left if coming on the road from Tozeur. It offers a modest selection of Tunisian salads and main courses, as well as sandwiches, but all the food is good and the venue's location is very beautiful and tranquil. A perfect place to go for a stroll in the palmeraie.

NEFTA Jamel

Avenue Habib Bourguiba, 2240 **Tel** *No telephone* **Map** A5

Next door and very similar to Les Sources restaurant, Jamel is a useful, inexpensive and cheerful budget option. Although it is definitely nothing fancy, the atmosphere is undoubtedly friendly and enjoyable. The restaurant is highly recommended for its excellent couscous.

NEFTA Les Sources

Avenue Habib Bourguiba, 2240 **Tel** *No telephone* **Map** A5

The pleasant dining room spills over on to a small terrace at this tiny restaurant with a typical brickwork façade next to the Syndicat d'Initiative on the main road. There is an equally tiny menu, with typical southern Tunisian dishes, which are simply but well prepared, including *tajine (see p269)*, salads and couscous.

NEFTA Dar Houidi

Medina, 2240 **Tel** *76 43 25 11/ 76 43 16 95* **Map** A5

This 17th-century house incorporates a bed & breakfast, a museum and a restaurant. Delicious home-cooked three-course meals, such as couscous with spinach, stuffed pigeon or spinach stew are available, but need to be ordered in advance. Dinner with a folklore show can be organized. Very beautiful terrace and indoor room in Tozeur brickwork.

TAMERZA Les Palmiers

Near the waterfall, 2212 **Tel** *No telephone* **Map** A5

A small café near the little waterfall with a café-terrace on the rocks, which offers a superb view over the *oued* (river bed), the palmeraie and the magnificent canyon. The café is at the back of a complex of souvenir shops, but worth finding just for the views. It's a perfect place for a drink, and meals can be prepared if ordered in advance.

TAMERZA Le Soleil

Near the mosque, 2212 **Tel** *No telephone* **Map** A5

This charming restaurant, in a beautifully-restored old house, is on the left near the mosque, if coming on the road from Chebika. The restaurant is spread over several rooms and terraces and there is a lovely atmosphere. The food is simple but also excellent, the menu often listing slightly different Tunisian dishes not usually served in restaurants.

TATAOUINE Essindabad

Rue du Premier Juin 1955, 3200 **Tel** *75 85 23 67* **Map** D6

Reputedly the best cheap eatery in town, serving rotisserie chicken, *brochettes* (meat kebabs), *merguez* (spicy lamb sausages) and good tuna sandwiches with spicy sauce. The chef also prepares a few daily specials. The dining room is pleasant if nothing special, and it's conveniently located near the bus station. Closed during Ramadan.

TATAOUINE La Medina

Rue H. Mestaoui, 3200 **Tel** *75 86 09 99* **Map** D6

Situated in a hotel of the same name, this restaurant prides itself on its cleanliness. It has a confortable, if slightly dark, interior and friendly service. The menu offers simple, well-prepared Tunisian dishes – nothing more and nothing less – for a modest price.

TATAOUINE La Gazelle

Avenue Hedi Chaker, 3200 **Tel** *75 86 00 09* **Map** D6

Part of a hotel of the same name, this restaurant offers a more authentic dining experience than most others in the town, with white tablecloths and a formal waiter service. The food, however, is fairly similar to that available elsewhere, except that there is a wine list – or you can have a cool beer to wash it all down if you prefer.

TATAOUINE Le Borj

On the Remada Road, 3200 **Tel** *75 85 15 39* **Map** D6

Slightly away from the centre, this restaurant is worth the walk for its beautiful surroundings and amazing views. After the roundabout with the globe, just before the little bridge, take a left towards the mosque – the venue is then signposted. Set in a lovely garden, with a tower for the views, this is a charming place with reasonable food.

TOZEUR Al-Qods

Avenue Habib Bourguiba, 2200 **Tel** *No telephone* **Map** B5

Open for breakfast and throughout the day until 10pm, this wonderful patisserie serves the best pastries in town. Specialities of the house include *makhrouds* (sweets stuffed with date paste), and *cornes de gazelle* (almond paste in a thin dough). At lunchtime there are sandwiches and small pizzas. Not much seating and popular with the locals.

TOZEUR Capitole

152 Avenue Abou Elkacem Echchebbi, 2200 **Tel** *76 46 26 31* **Map** B5

This convivial restaurant is popular with Tunisian families, who come to eat the southern Tunisian specialities. Most of these are pretty time consuming to prepare and need to be ordered in advance, such as *gargoulette* (lamb cooked in a terracotta jar). Worth trying is the *metabgha* or Berber pizza, or the grilled camel steak.

Key to Price Guide *see p272* **Key to Symbols** *see back cover flap*

TOZEUR Le Soleil

58 Avenue Abou Elkacem Echchebbi, 2200 **Tel** *76 46 12 48*

Map *B5*

One of very few places in the south which has vegetarian dishes on its menu, so it comes recommended for that. The atmosphere is friendly and the interior quite cosy, while the menu also has a wide choice of options for meat-eaters – including dromedary (camel) stew and a tender dromedary steak – as well as for couscous lovers.

TOZEUR Azzurra

Opposite the Museum of Dar Cheraït, 2200 **Tel** *76 46 30 82/ 97 34 65 00*

Map *B5*

Popular with tourists from the surrounding hotels in the tourist zone, this small but busy hotel offers very good pizzas as well as Tunisian staples such as couscous and *brochettes* (meat on skewers) and good, fresh salads. The small terrace overlooking the crossroads is a great place for lunch or to have a drink. No alcohol.

TOZEUR La Medina

Avenue Farhat Hached, 2200 **Tel** *No telephone*

Map *B5*

A simple neighbourhood eatery, mostly frequented by Tunisians who come for an inexpensive and quick meal. On the menu are sandwiches (with spicy *harissa* unless you ask otherwise), *tajine* (see p269), salads, pasta and, of course, couscous. No-frills interior with a TV, cheap paintings, and a few tables outside. Small and friendly restaurant.

TOZEUR La République

108 Avenue Habib Bourguiba, 2200 **Tel** *76 45 23 54*

Map *B5*

Tucked away in a shopping arcade near the El-Ferdous mosque, this small, family-run restaurant has a dimly lit indoor dining room in Moorish style, and a small terrace in a courtyard with a fountain, away from the busy main street. The menu has plenty of classic Tunisian dishes, including a good range of salads and a delicious couscous.

TOZEUR Le Minaret

Avenue Habib Bourguiba, 2200 **Tel** *23 52 42 03*

Map *B5*

As a newcomer on the scene, this restaurant is a breath of fresh air. It's set in the tranquil patio of a modern house, with Tunisian-style sofas and low tables under a palm tree. There's an equally charming indoor room, and the food is excellent Tunisian, both traditional and with a twist – such as camel *carpaccio*, which is delicious. Recommended.

TOZEUR Tozorous

Avenue Habib Bourguiba, 2200 **Tel** *No telephone*

Map *B5*

Tozorous serves great food at reasonable prices. The pizza is not particularly authentic but tastes good, and there are several tasty meat and chicken dishes as well as a choice of salads on the menu. The dining room is built using Tozeur brick, and an interior fountain adds to the tranquillity.

TOZEUR Le Petit Prince

Rue el-Berka, 2200 **Tel** *76 45 25 18*

Map *B5*

A once upmarket but now slightly faded restaurant, Le Petit Prince sits beautifully in a palm grove off Avenue Abou Elkacem Echchebbi. The chef here specializes in southern Tunisian cuisine and is justly famous for his roast leg of lamb as well as a wide variety of couscous dishes. One of the few places outside the hotels that serves alcohol.

TOZEUR Dar Cheraït

Route Touristique, 2200 **Tel** *76 45 48 88*

Map *B5*

This luxury hotel *(see p263)* has three different restaurants, which are popular with tourists and locals for the quality of the food and the opulent decor. The restaurants serve both international-Mediterranean and Tunisian specialities, although the latter are a lot less spicy than authentic Tunisian food.

TOZEUR Planet Oasis Tozeur

Palmeraie, 2200 **Tel** *76 46 03 10*

Map *B5*

One large and several smaller Berber tents purport to offer an authentic Berber meal in the middle of Tozeur's beautiful palmeraie. Unfortunately, busloads of tourists are dropped off for buffet meals, camel rides, a folklore show and a sound-and-light show, though individuals are welcome too. The food is well presented if a little unexciting.

CENTRAL TUNISIA

GAFSA Abid

Rue Laadoub, 2100 **Tel** *No telephone*

Map *B4*

This is one of a handful of inexpensive restaurants near the bus station. In fact, it is two restaurants, Abid I and II, both offering similarly tasty Tunisian fare. The menu includes a choice of simple Tunisian dishes but the *kamounia* (meat stew with cumin) and the *tajine* (see p269) are particularly recommended.

GAFSA Tony Pizzeria

Rue Abou Elkacem Echchebbi, 2100 **Tel** *No telephone*

Map *B4*

A good range of large pizzas as well as good, freshly-prepared salads, both international and Tunisian, are on offer at Tony Pizzeria. The food is not really authentic but there are no pretensions to that either. You should bear in mind when ordering that one pizza is usually enough for two people.

GAFSA Pizzeria Tomato
Rue Abou Elkacem Echchebbi, 2100 **Tel** *No telephone*   **Map** *B4*

This Western-style pizzeria, with a modern black-and-white decor, serves really good pizzas as well as a range of sandwiches – all at modest prices. Take-away food is available too. As you might expect, all this makes Pizzeria Tomato very popular with young locals from Gafsa.

GAFSA Errachid
Rue Jamel Abd Ennaceur, 2100 **Tel** *76 22 44 41*   **Map** *B4*

Convenient for its central location, this restaurant is part of the Maamoun hotel *(see p263)* and one of the few real sit-down restaurants in town. The food is well presented and reasonably priced – although there are no surprises on the menu. Starters include *briks (see p268)* and salads, followed by couscous dishes and grills, with fruit for dessert.

GAFSA Les Ambassadeurs
Rue Ahmed Senoussi, 2100 **Tel** *76 22 40 00*   **Map** *B4*

Les Ambassadeurs serves a fairly sophisticated French and Tunisian menu with some success. Specialities include grilled calf's liver, steak *au poivre* (peppery steak) and *koucha* (a spicy, slow-cooked lamb stew) for at least four people. The large, elegant dining room is on the second floor. A wine list is available.

KAIROUAN Barouta
Rue 7 Novembre, 3100 **Tel** *24 13 37 75*   **Map** *C3*

This small medina restaurant has existed on the same site for over 50 years and claims to be the oldest restaurant here. It specializes in Berber cuisine, offering lamb *tagine (see p269)*, couscous and *ojja* (egg dish) at really good prices. There are a few tables outside overlooking the small square, with a small, tiled interior dining room as well.

KAIROUAN Ben Sokrana
Rue R'Dat el-Hadid, 3100 **Tel** *No telephone*   **Map** *C3*

Kairouan is famous for its *makhroud* (pastries made using dates or figs), and this well-established patisserie is the place in Kairouan to taste them – the excellent recipe has been in the same family for generations. To get there from Place des Martyrs, follow Avenue Ali Belhouane past Hotel Sabra, then take the second small street on the left.

KAIROUAN Café Maure au Kasbah
Hotel La Kasbah, Avenue ibn Jazzar, 3100 **Tel** *77 23 73 01*   **Map** *C3*

A beautifully-restored room in the kasbah, with high vaults and arches, and stone benches with cushions. This romantic Moorish café is where local lovers meet, or where friends get together to smoke a *chicha* (water pipe) and drink mint tea with almonds. There is a pleasant outdoor terrace looking out at the kasbah walls.

KAIROUAN Karawan
Rue Soukaina bint el-Houceine, 3100 **Tel** *77 23 25 56*   **Map** *C3*

Karawan is a simple, family-run restaurant which is extremely clean, friendly and pleasant. The menu offers a few well-prepared, although not very spicy, local specialities, including fresh salads, good lamb *tagine (see p269)* and a tasty couscous. The room upstairs is quiet, airy and bright, and women on their own will feel quite comfortable here.

KAIROUAN Le Splendid
Avenue du 9 Avril, 3100 **Tel** *77 22 75 22*   **Map** *C3*

This restaurant, attached to the hotel of the same name *(see p264)*, caters mainly for tour groups at lunch but also has a room for individual travellers. It serves a set menu with three choices for each course, including both Tunisian and international cuisine. The food is fine if rather bland, but tastes better when served with a cool Celtia beer.

KAIROUAN Piccolomondo
Avenue ibn el-Jazzar, 3100 **Tel** *No telephone*   **Map** *C3*

There is a lively atmosphere at this small restaurant, which is very popular with young locals who come for the contemporary decor and excellent pizzas. The service is friendly but efficient, and the menu also includes pastas and other European dishes, as well as Tunisian salads, *tagines (see p269)* and a delicious couscous dish. Good value.

KAIROUAN Restaurant de la Jeunesse
Rue 7 Novembre, 3100 **Tel** *77 22 61 07*   **Map** *C3*

Don't let the plastic flowers and brash metal chairs put you off trying this friendly medina restaurant, which serves good value Tunisian dishes, grilled chicken and lamb chops. The food is well prepared and has an authentic spiciness, while the mint tea afterwards is delicious. This is the perfect place to watch the comings and goings in the souk.

KAIROUAN Sabra
Avenue de la République, 3100 **Tel** *77 23 50 95*   **Map** *C3*

Sabra is a pleasant restaurant – part of the Sabra hotel and also convenient for the hotel Tunisia *(see p264)* just next door. The menu offers some good value Tunisian fare, including all the classic Tunisian dishes such as couscous with lamb, *couscous royale* and *kamounia* (stew liberally spiced with cumin).

KAIROUAN Marhaba
Rue 7 Novembre, 3100 **Tel** *77 23 60 61/ 22 44 50 06*   **Map** *C3*

The dining room of this simple restaurant is decorated with Berber symbols and flowery plastic tablecloths; there are also a few outdoor tables in a quiet alley just off the main thoroughfare of the souk. This is a good place to come for tea and to sample Kairouan *makhroud* (date cakes), or for a lunch of couscous – the house speciality.

Key to Price Guide *see p272* **Key to Symbols** *see back cover flap*

KASSERINE Ben Yabbala

Rue Ahmed Taieb Mehiri, 1200 **Tel** *No telephone*

Map *B3*

You'll often see people queueing up outside this small pizzeria, as the venue is a great success with the locals. It's tucked behind the Banque du Sud building, with a sign in Arabic only – just ask as everyone will know where it is. Only a small seating area, but most people eat standing up. Great sandwiches, pizzas, pastries and fresh orange juice.

KASSERINE El Amir es-Saghir

Avenue Habib Bourguiba, 1200 **Tel** *98 27 69 27*

Map *B3*

El Amir es-Saghir is Arabic for "The Little Prince" – it's a modern joint which is hugely popular with Kasserine's youngsters. The menu is international and lists good pizzas, hamburgers, sandwiches and *crêpes* with a variety of fillings. The decor is brash and contemporary, with bright red banquette seats. Friendly service.

LE KEF Andalous

Rue Hedi Chaker, 7100 **Tel** *No telephone*

Map *B2*

Andalous is the best in a row of cheap restaurants and is open all day. It is particularly popular at lunchtime, when locals queue up for the daily specials, which usually include delicious and generous servings of couscous, excellent roast chicken with spices, and *lablabi* (chickpea soup). In the evening this is more of a fast-food joint.

LE KEF La Kheffoise

Avenue Habib Bourguiba, 7100 **Tel** *78 20 38 87*

Map *B2*

This small and unpretentious little bakery-pizzeria is in the centre of town and convenient for a quick bite at any time of day. There is only one small seating area, but most customers are happy to eat the good pizzas and substantial sandwiches standing up or on the go. Perfect for satisfying your hunger in a hurry.

LE KEF Ramzi

Rue Hedi Chaker, 7100 **Tel** *78 20 30 79*

Map *B2*

The restaurant of the Ramzi hotel sees a few passing tourists but is mainly frequented by local men. The dining room is pleasant enough and is decorated with an exotic-looking mural. The menu features all the usual Tunisian fare – stick to the more obvious dishes, such as *brik a l'oeuf (see p268)* with egg, and couscous, which are done well.

LE KEF Bou Maklouf

Rue Hedi Chaker, 7100 **Tel** *98 28 52 11*

Map *B2*

Little more than a small, inexpensive café, this unassuming but incredibly busy place is deservedly popular. It offers good food with some fairly spicy dishes, including hearty soups and delicious servings of couscous. The limited menu is in Arabic only, but the owner is happy to translate. The seats are very close together.

LE KEF Chez Venus

Rue Farhat Hached, 7100 **Tel** *78 20 03 55*

Map *B2*

One of the best restaurants in Le Kef (though the competition is quite slim!), and one of the few places that sells alcohol. Its popularity relies on a good selection of Tunisian and European cuisine, including a tasty couscous and *grillades* (grilled meats) and some interesting salads which are particularly worth trying.

METLAOUI Ellafi

Main road in the centre of town, 2100 **Tel** *No telephone*

Map *B5*

Try to get a table on the small terrace outside under the arcade at this enjoyable roadside restaurant, which welcomes many returning customers and locals. There is a small menu as well as daily specials – all tasty Tunisian dishes, simply yet well prepared. Check the prices before ordering, particularly for the daily specials.

SBEITLA Carthage

On the edge of city, on the road to Kasserine, 1250 **Tel** *77 46 77 22*

Map *B–C3*

On the road out of Sbeïtla leading towards the Roman ruins, you can identify the entrance to this restaurant by the kitsch statuary. The Carthage specializes in Tunisian cuisine, offering several set meals as well as an *à la carte* menu, with well-prepared Tunisian fare, including soups, salads and couscous.

SBEITLA Relais El-Ridha

Rue Essaloum, 1250 **Tel** *77 46 75 00*

Map *B–C3*

This popular restaurant-cafeteria has sparkling, bright decor in the typical Tunisian colours of blue and white. The good value fare includes sandwiches and snacks as well as more substantial meat and fish dishes. Leave some space for dessert, as the cakes and sweets are good. Very friendly service.

SBEITLA Ambassadeur

Rue Farhat Hached, 1250 **Tel** *No telephone*

Map *B–C3*

Ambassadeur is a rather grand name for a small and unassuming restaurant near the market. A restricted but interesting menu is available – Tunisian dishes such as couscous with lamb, hot and spicy *salade mechouia (see p269)*, *salade tunisienne* (tomato, cucumber and onion) and *brik* with egg or meat *(see p268)*.

TEBOURSOUK Thugga

On the main road leading out of town, 9040 **Tel** *78 46 66 47*

Map *B2*

If you are here in the hunting season (from November until April) try the regional speciality of *marcassin*, a hearty, rich stew of wild boar. This popular restaurant is often busy with tour groups, but you get better food as an individual traveller. The menu offers a wide range of Tunisian and international dishes. Wine list available.

SHOPPING IN TUNISIA

Throughout Tunisia there are colourful markets crammed with all sorts of Tunisian-made goods including rugs and carpets, ceramics, jewellery and perfumes. Tunisia also has large shopping centres, which have about as much charm as their European counterparts and often sell imported goods. Shops selling souvenirs can be found all over the country. Those aimed at tourists in the big medinas often charge high prices and are stocked with poor quality goods. For this reason, it is worth stepping into the smaller craft shops. These will give some idea of the prices of the most popular souvenirs. They may also help to spot poor quality items that are sold as souvenirs of Tunisia but may well have been made elsewhere.

Cuddly stuffed camel

WHERE TO BUY

The most interesting places to shop in Tunisia are the souks, which can be found in most medinas of Tunisia's cities and towns. Prices charged at these market shops are not fixed in stone and are always open to haggling *(see box)*. As well as the markets, visitors can also shop in large, state-owned department stores. These have fixed prices and opening hours. Small hotel shops usually sell high-quality goods, but charge top prices for them. In duty-free shops, often found at border crossings, goods must be paid for in convertible currencies and prices charged for Tunisian products are far higher than those paid in state-owned shops in souks.

The Bardo Museum *(see pp88–9)* sells good quality books on the art and history of Tunisia and North Africa, as well as in-depth guides to museums and archaeological sites all over the country.

Weekly market by the beach in Tabarka

OPENING HOURS

Most Tunisian shops close for lunch; some may also be closed on Sunday while other shops close on Friday afternoons. Hairdressers close on Monday. Normally, the shops that sell food and household products are open from 8am until 12:30pm and 2:30pm to 6pm, Monday to Friday. However, supermarkets open early in the morning and may stay open until 10pm in summer. Throughout the summer season office hours are 7:30am to 1:30pm. In tourist resorts souvenir shops stay open until late at night, and sometimes until the last shopper leaves.

During Ramadan, many shops open between 8 and 9am and close at about 1pm. They open again in the evening and often remain open until late at night.

HOW TO PAY

The national currency is the Tunisian dinar (TD). In privately owned shops, especially those that sell carpets, payment can often be made in US dollars or euros. When shopping for small items in souks, it is useful to have some one-dinar coins. In the state-owned department stores as well as in larger shops, shopping centres, ONAT shops and duty-free shops, credit cards are accepted. Credit cards are also accepted by some upmarket restaurants and hotels, from three-star upwards.

When settling a bill in a restaurant or a café it is customary to leave a tip. In cafés this need be no more than some small change. Waiters in more upmarket restaurants will expect about 10 per cent of the total bill.

Always be prepared to haggle in a souk. Haggling is an accepted part of the process and it is often possible to purchase an item for half the price that was originally quoted by the vendor.

A souvenir from Tunisia – colourful desert sands

Carpet and fabric shop in Tunis medina

SHOPPING CENTRES

There are shopping centres in most of Tunisia's larger towns. They are very popular with the locals, particularly with the younger generation. Their boutiques stock many foreign-made goods and imported craft items, but prices are high and the quality can sometimes leave a lot to be desired. Department stores and souks are a better bet for visitors.

A very popular shopping centre is the Palmarium, in Avenue Habib Bourguiba in Tunis. Tunis City is a vast complex a short cab ride from the city centre. The large and popular Zephyr shopping centre can be found in La Marsa. This is not only a favourite shopping venue, but also a popular meeting place for young Tunisians. On the ground floor are restaurants and stalls selling delicious ice creams. This is one of few places in Tunisia where low-fat ice cream can be obtained.

MARKETS

Markets were once the economic centre of Tunisian towns and were often given special privileges. Today, they still play an important economic role. Various parts of a market

One of the few supermarkets to be found in Sousse

wake up at different times. The first to open are the souks that sell meat and vegetables; the rest start trading a little later. Stalls and shops usually stay open until about 6 or 7pm, but the main tourist alleys, such as Rue Jamaa Zitouna in Tunis's main souk, remain open much later.

Tunisia's markets are often covered with roofs that provide shelter from the sun. A few of the expensive shops, such as those selling carpets and gold, are air-conditioned.

Medinas also contain many small restaurants and cafés where it is a good plan to stop for a glass of tea and a sit down. One of the most charming and atmospheric of these is Café M. Rabet in the Souk et-Trouk, in Tunis medina (see p274). When planning a trip to one of Tunisia's markets, if looking for something specific, begin by finding out the location of the appropriate souk, as they are governed by a hierarchy (see pp294-5).

It is often worth venturing further than the main souks. In the souk situated near Tunis's Zaouia Sidi Mehrez (see p81), for instance, there are cheap, good quality ceramics, while in the Souk el-Grana it is easy to become caught up in crowds of women searching for bargains.

ADVICE ON HAGGLING

Although prices are not fixed in stone, haggling follows certain general rules. First of all, allow plenty of time and know roughly the value of the article required. Do not hurry. The conversation starts with general topics, later on an interest may be shown in some other object. Only after a while should one approach the article that is desired. Never mention a price before the vendor does. A rule of thumb is to begin negotiations from one third of the initial price. The seller puts on a show of indignation, but will lower the price. Smile and continue with the negotiations, saying that in this case you will have to think about it. Walking off will usually bring about a further reduction in price. However, stick to the rules of fair play and continue to haggle only if you really want to buy the product. If a compromise is not reached it is only necessary to smile and bid the vendor a pleasant goodbye. When buying several items at once, haggle over each of them separately, and then in the end ask for an overall discount. It can sometimes help to be the first or the last customer of the day.

Vegetable souk

CRAFT SHOPS IN TUNISIA

State-run craft shops have now been streamlined and craft villages created, notably at Denden, in the Tunis suburb of Manouba, and at the privately funded Ken Craft Village near Bou Ficha in the Sahel. These villages regroup workshops and craftsmen from a variety of specializations. Cooperative craft workshops, often run by women, have also started to develop, mainly in rural areas.

Tunisian arts and crafts do, however, face competition from imported goods, and it is worth checking the origins of products before buying, particularly in the main tourist areas. A number of retail outlets which were formerly state-run have retained the practice of fixed prices for those visitors who prefer not to haggle.

Some craft shops, notably the Office National de L'Artisanat in Sousse, are vast, and spread over several floors. As there is so much to see, allow plenty of time when shopping for souvenirs in these stores. The assistants at genuine Tunisian craft shops are usually helpful and knowledgeable, and will take great care when wrapping up your goods to ensure they will not be damaged during the journey home. Most will also accept credit cards.

Some craft shops can also provide information on carpets and tapestries, their patterns and weaving methods,

Traditional craft shop selling the highest quality products

but it is best to ask about them at the Kairouan Carpet Museum *(see p237)*. El Jem has a number of mosaic workshops, Sfax's medina has a few remaining coopers who produce delightful miniature barrels, and Nabeul mats *(basira)* are still made from rushes.

ART GALLERIES

Art galleries in Tunisia that deal only in paintings are few and far between and most establishments sell a range of artworks, from graphics and ceramics to books and sculpture. The influence of the École de Tunis *(see p18)* is evident in most of the contemporary paintings found in Tunisia's galleries. In the 1940s its pioneers introduced modern art to Tunisia and began to combine new trends such as Futurism with everyday scenes such as weddings, markets, and hammams (steam baths). Alongside these, there are more traditional paintings, executed in watercolours or oils, which attempt to capture the light and colour of Tunisian architecture and landscape. Also, traditional Islamic art, including calligraphy and arabesques, are combined with more modern techniques of abstract and figurative painting.

As well as paintings of this type, many galleries sell a variety of antiques and contemporary artifacts. These are not cheap, but every now and then a gallery has good quality works by less well-known Tunisian artists going

for very reasonable prices. One such shop is the gallery in Souk al-Caid, in Sousse. It sells attractive art works as well as beautiful fabrics. The Negrat gallery in Rue Sidi ben Arous, in Tunis, sells good quality lamps. Galleries selling contemporary Tunisian art, as well as work by foreign artists, can also be found in Sidi Bou Saïd and Port el-Kantaoui.

Antiques and old junk for sale in a souk in Houmt Souk

ANTIQUES

There is a ban on exporting certain kinds of antiques from Tunisia. It is nevertheless worth looking at the shops that sell them, even if only to admire the beauty of the objects. Items such as old carpets, tapestries, fabrics, ceramics, traditional wedding costumes, antique mirrors and everyday items are not subject to an export ban. However, always make sure by asking the vendor if there are likely to be any problems with taking an item abroad.

One good Tunis antique shop is Ed-Dar, in Rue Sidi ben Arous; another can be found at No.7 in the Souk

One of the many art galleries in Sidi Bou Saïd

et-Trouk. The small shops in Rue des Glacières are excellent places for buying old bric-a-brac. With their shelves piled high with items, these shops can resemble the mythical cave discovered by Ali Baba. If seriously contemplating buying anything in an antique shop, allow at least one hour. The conversation usually starts with a glass of mint tea!

JEWELLERY

Gold and silver jewellery is popular in Arab countries. Common motifs include crescent pendants and the hand of Fatima, known as "the Hamsa" meaning "five", which is used in many different forms from earrings to necklaces.

Another frequent motif used in jewellery is the fish, which is a popular good luck charm against the "evil eye".

Golden pendant

Other popular items, beside pendants, include chunky bracelets. Coral and amber jewellery is popular in the Tabarka region. Items of jewellery sold in Houmt Souk, on Jerba, are produced by Jewish designers. This has long been a jewellery centre and is still a good place to purchase gold and silver.

Gold and silver hallmarks should be stamped on every item. This practice is regulated by the Standards Office. A scorpion means that the item is made of nine-carat gold, a goat stands for 14-carat gold

while a horse's head, the Carthaginian symbol for money, denotes 18-carat gold.

Silver hallmarks include a bunch of grapes with the figure 1 (90 per cent silver) and an African head (80 per cent silver or less). Gold and silver items that do not bear hallmarks are of dubious quality but visitors may wish to buy them solely for their attractive designs. Berber jewellery is also worth seeking out. Though Berber jewellery is usually made of low-grade silver it is nevertheless sought-after for the uniqueness of its ancient designs.

OTHER SOUVENIRS

The *khoffa* is the traditional straw basket used by Tunisians to carry their food purchases from the market. Colours and designs vary from region to region, and the baskets also come in a range of sizes. Beautiful handmade examples are priced from around 2 TD. Look in the local markets and roadside stalls for them.

Honey produced in Tunisia is from free range bees, meaning that the bees are not artificially fed and the honey will not contain added chemicals and preservatives. A deep golden colour, Tunisian honey is one of the staples of the Tunisian kitchen. Some of the best honey is sold from roadside stalls on the way to Tabarka, which is a well known and

Pottery displayed in front of a shop in Nabeul

extensive honey-producing area. A large jar containing around 1 kg (2.2 lb) of honey should cost around 10 TD. Be sure to wash the outside of the jar and wrap it in bubble wrap before you pack it in your suitcase.

DIRECTORY

CRAFT SHOPS

Aïn Draham

Tapis de Khroumirie,
8130 Abul Qasim Shabbi.
Tel (78) 655 226.

Bardo

Sopro Femmes
47 Avenue H. Bourguiba
Tel (71) 223 300.

Bou Ficha

Ken Craft Village.
4010 Sidi Khelifa.
Tel (73) 252 110.

El Hamma de Gabes

Société des Tapis d'Oudref.
Tel (75) 365 012.

UTAIM (Union Tunisienne d'Aide aux Insuffisants Mentaux).
Tel (75) 330 366.

Sousse

Office National de L'Artisanat.
Tel (73) 224 008.

Jewellery shop in the centre of Sousse's medina

Souks

Tunisia's markets, which on the surface appear to be chaotic, are in reality well-ordered spaces. Every craft and every trade has its own allocated position and place in a hierarchy. The closer to the main mosque, the more numerous are the "noble" souks – those selling gold, scents, carpets and traditional Tunisian *chechias* (hats) worn by men. Away from the centre, the souks become less prestigious, producing and selling wrought-iron products, as well as trading in meat and vegetables.

Visitors *can watch workmen decorating copper plates. This is supposed to guarantee its authenticity. For the best quality, try to find where the Tunisians buy such items.*

A Tunisian souk *is not only a place to shop and trade. For the Tunisians it is also a place of fun and recreation. Meetings with friends in a café to play a game of backgammon is a common sight in souks.*

Perfume and jewellery *can be bought in the most elegant souks, situated near the main mosque. They are easy to find as the intense fragrance of perfumes leads the way. Colourful and vibrant, these souks attract the most visitors.*

COVERED BAZAARS

Since the 10th century the main streets and markets of towns were illuminated with lamps mounted on the walls of houses or on the roofs covering the streets. In the 11th century the main streets that run across the souks began to branch into smaller ones that form the present tangle of narrow alleyways. This labyrinth was ventilated by a system of roof openings.

Perfume-making and the production of essences have for years been traditional Tunisian crafts. Rose and jasmine oils are particularly highly valued.

The centre *of the medina (old quarter) is the site of the most important souks, which remain open from morning until night with a break in the afternoon. It is busy at any time of day but gets particularly crowded during the summer, when the local shoppers are joined by visitors.*

Weavers' workshops, *as with the workshops that produce leather or wooden articles for sale, are often to be found in the souks, directly behind the shops that sell these goods.*

The stone-paved street of a souk

Ventilation and illumination holes in the vault of a covered souk

Tunisians like to shop *in souks where they can also buy clothes and household goods. The shopping ritual includes haggling and a thorough inspection of the goods.*

Fruit and vegetable markets *were often situated close to town gates to make trade easier for market gardeners. They give a glimpse of present-day Tunisian life.*

What to Buy in Tunisia

There is a wide range of products on sale in Tunisia. Much of what is available has been produced by local craftsmen and it pays to seek out items that have been made locally such as coral jewellery from Tabarka or a sea sponge from the Gulf of Gabès. Kairouan is famous for its carpets and leatherware; Nabeul and Jerba for their ceramics; Sidi Bou Saïd for its intricately made bird cages; Douz and Tozeur for footwear. If travelling in the south of the country it is worth looking out for Berber products including tapestries, beautiful ceramics and silver jewellery.

Ceramic vessel, Nabeul

Ceramics
The inhabitants of Guellala on Jerba have long been associated with pottery and employ Berber motifs in brown and beige. Nabeul craftsmen favour bright colourings dominated by blue and green. Berber ceramics from Sejnane are also famous (see p134).

Woollen tapestry

Carpets
The best places to buy carpets are in Tunis, Kairouan, Tozeur and Jerba. There are two basic types. Woven (Mergoum) carpets predate Islam and have Berber origins. They are distinguished by geometric patterns and sharply contrasting colours. Alloucha carpets are knotted and feature natural tones. These can be bought in Aïn Draham in northern Tunisia (see p129).

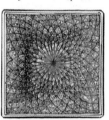
A cobalt-decorated plate

Bracelets
Tunisian jewellery is mostly made of silver or gold. The hedeyed is a wide bracelet that is worn on the wrist. Bracelets for the ankles are known as kholkal and are a symbol of fidelity. The largest jewellery centres are in Tunis, Sfax and Jerba.

Typical silver bracelet, with a fish motif

A richly embroidered waistcoat

A headdress made of golden leaves

Shoes
Leather shoes come in a wide variety of designs. It is worth looking out for the traditional balgha, which are worn mainly in the south of the country. In the north a more highly decorated version that is worn by women can be seen.

Perfumes
When visiting a souk that specializes in perfume look out for jasmine oil, as well as oil produced from the damask rose. White musk is also of a good quality. A small bottle costs about 5 TD.

Necklace made of silver and precious stones

Traditional shoes

Glass perfume bottle

Mosaics

Many of the products on sale in Tunisia stem from a variety of cultures and influences. Mosaics are a prime example of this, and most museums and souvenir shops sell ceramic tiles reminiscent of the mosaics from Carthage, Dougga and El-Jem.

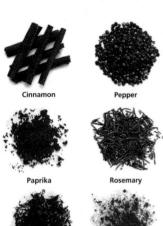

Cinnamon

Pepper

Paprika

Rosemary

Saffron

Turmeric

Chichas

Water pipes used for smoking tobacco, can be bought anywhere in Tunisia, but the best ones are produced in Tunis. Check that all the parts fit together and that the air flow is not obstructed. The tobacco mixture is readily available. Most Tunisians smoke an aromatic tobacco, flavoured with such things as apple or cherry.

Chicha from Tunis

Food and Drink

Tunisia produces good-quality wines and strong liqueurs such as boukha *(a clear spirit made from figs). When exploring a souk look out for spices and homemade* harissa *(a spicy sauce).*

Tunisian white wine

Wooden Articles

The best wooden items are made of olive wood. Mostly produced in Sfax, these make good souvenirs, especially salad bowls and mortars.

Wooden mortar and pestle

A traditional ornamental teapot

A brass plate

Other Souvenirs

Probably the most typical Tunisian souvenir is a stuffed camel. Every souvenir shop has a large variety of them. Other popular souvenirs include woven mats, baskets, fans and the ubiquitous leather pouffes.

Metalwork

Very popular traditional copper and brass items for sale include trays, bowls, vases and jugs with distinctive narrow necks. Trays can be bought in several sizes, up to 65 cm (26 inches) in diameter, and in two types of finishes – shiny or matt.

A decorative brass plaque

A pouffe seat

Leather pouffe

ENTERTAINMENT IN TUNISIA

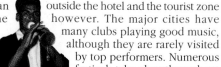

Tunisia has more to offer than beautiful beaches, and the lively programme of entertainment available to visitors is both rich and varied. Many of the most interesting events take place during the peak season. The big hotels provide their own nighly entertainment in the form of discos and performances of traditional dance. It is always worth venturing

A fife-playing musician

outside the hotel and the tourist zone however. The major cities have many clubs playing good music, although they are rarely visited by top performers. Numerous festivals take place throughout the year and these are also worth seeking out (see pp38–42). These colourful events provide the best display of Tunisian culture and also a chance to meet some of the locals.

Evening performance of a jug-balancing act in a hotel

INFORMATION

Information about major cultural events and festivals can be found in French language newspapers, particularly La Presse which, although it does not have listings pages, has a good cultural section. The ONTT (Organization Nationale de Tourisme Tunisien), with its main office in Tunis, publishes a number of brochures containing information on annual festivals, which can be picked up in advance of a trip. The programme for the prestigious Carthage International Festival can be found in the local press or on the Internet. In June it is also available from ONTT information desks. The programme of the Medina Festival, held annually in Tunis during Ramadan, is published about three weeks in advance and is also available from the ONTT.

TRADITIONAL SHOWS

A variety of traditional performances can be seen in many places throughout Tunisia. Belly dancing is extremely popular, as are the Berber shows and dances. A good show can be seen in the M. Rabet café in Tunis medina (see p274), which consists of a lively mix of traditional folk music, Berber dances and belly dancing. The show is an additional cost on top of the meal.

A novel alternative to belly dancing is a traditional dance with jugs (left), which might be encountered on the island of Jerba.

MUSIC

Sidi Bou Saïd's **Centre of Arab and Mediterranean Music** puts on wonderful traditional concerts, which are held in the former palace of Baron d'Erlanger (see p97). The varied programme

includes not only classical Arab music, but frequent guest appearances of world-class artists performing various types of music – from flamenco to Chopin's mazurkas or modern music.

Any local festivals held in towns and villages are usually accompanied by music.

FESTIVALS

Horse riding display, the Sahara Festival

Tunisia boasts a vast number of festivals, which are celebrated throughout the year (see pp38–42). The reasons for celebrations range from marking the end of the harvests to events of religious or cultural importance. Many festivals are of a local character. Most concerts and shows are staged during July, August and Ramadan.

The big event of the summer is the Carthage International Festival. Its programme is exceptionally

Evening concert in the El-Jem amphitheatre

rich, and includes top performances of symphony music, classical Arab music and pop music. In addition, the festival has theatre, ballet, musicals, operas, cinema and exhibitions. The main venue for the events is the Roman amphitheatre in Carthage *(see pp102–6)*. Another very interesting event is the Symphony Music Festival in El-Jem *(see p163)*. In the evenings the amphitheatre becomes a magnificent concert hall under the stars. Hammamet's Arab Music Festival, held in July and August, and the Jazz Festival held each year at the end of June in Tabarka are both very popular events, as is Testour's International Malouf Music Festival, which takes place in June.

CINEMA

Going to the movies is a popular Tunisian activity, with cinemas in Tunis, Bizerta, Sousse and Sfax. Tunis has the best selection, including the **ABC** and **Le Palace**. The programme, however, is aimed mostly at young cinemagoers and consists mainly of action films shown in Arabic language versions. American and European blockbusters are usually dubbed into French. Information on programmes can be found in the cultural section of *La Presse*. Ticket prices start at around 3 TD for a seat in the stalls.

THEATRE

Tunisia has only a handful of full-time theatre companies. The best-known and the most prestigious of the few that do exist is in Tunis, and performs in the **Théâtre Municipal** *(see p82)*. Its programme is dominated by plays of European playwrights, but it also puts on some Arab (mainly Egyptian) works. The splendid theatre building is also a frequent venue for concerts of both classical and Arabic music.

Casino in the Sousse tourist zone

NIGHTLIFE

The big hotels usually run their own entertainment programmes which include nightly shows of belly dancing and performances of *malouf* (folk) music. Along with all this, many hotels have their own nightclubs, such as **The Blue Moon** attached to the Hôtel Hasdrubal in Yasmine Hammamet and Hôtel Topkapi's **Le Pacha Club** in Mahdia. These put on shows by artists from various Arab countries. Such places can be expensive and are frequented mainly by visitors.

Many of Tunisia's clubs are in the northern suburbs of Tunis, the most central being **Romeo**. Out in the suburbs,

A live performance in a Tunisian club

Ornate Théâtre Municipal in Tunis

venues such as **Les Jasmins**, the **Cotton Club**, **Queen** and **Plaza** play more up-to-date dance music, and at greater volume. Outside of Tunis, clubs tend to be attached to major hotels such as **Abou Nawas Montazah** in Tabarka and **Club Le Rameau** in Sfax.

Similar to European clubs in music style and decor, Tunisia's clubs are popular with young Tunisians who can sometimes experience problems when trying to get in, either because they are under-age or do not meet with the door-staff's approval. Many clubs in Tunisia close at about 1am.

CASINOS

Casinos in Tunisia are found only in large towns and tourist zones. They operate during the peak summer season and are open only to foreigners, though the staff consists entirely of Tunisians.

Two of the biggest are the **Cleopatra** in Hammamet and **Casino Caraibe** in Sousse. Both are glitzy affairs with a floor-full of blackjack, poker and roulette tables, bars, restaurants and live entertainment. An option in the south is the **Casino de Jerba**.

In order to be allowed to play, visitors must show their passports or ID cards. Only convertible currencies are accepted. Men visiting casinos are expected to dress smartly in a suit and tie.

CHILDREN'S ACTIVITIES

Exploring ancient remains such as those at Dougga is fascinating but not to every child's taste. Fortunately, most hotels in the tourist zones have beach play areas for children. These are well organized and have trained supervisors to keep young guests entertained. Activities in these children's play areas range from beach volleyball and rounders to closely supervised paragliding taster sessions. Lessons in tennis and windsurfing for children can also usually be arranged.

If staying in the south of the country children will enjoy a visit to Tozeur's Dar Cheraït museum (see below).

The north of the country has several funfairs. The best-known of these is **Parc des Loisirs Dah Dah** situated on the outskirts of Tunis, which has rides, merry-go-rounds and other amusements. **Parc des Loisirs Bah Bah** on Jerba is a more modest affair with a small fairground and bumper cars.

Park Friguia crocodiles

Another popular place for family outings is **Belvedere Park** in Tunis. This is Tunis's largest park and has plenty of room for children to let off steam. There is a small zoo in its southern section, and also a small but informative exhibition on the plants and wildlife of Tunisia (see p87).

Many children may enjoy a trip to the **Oceanographic Museum** at Carthage where life beneath the waves can be discovered thanks to the numerous aquariums, scale models, educational boards and interactive displays.

Visitors exploring the ancient ruins in Dougga

AMUSEMENT PARKS

Situated close to the town of Bou Ficha, 35 km (22 miles) from Hammamet and 58 km (36 miles) from Sousse is **Park Friguia**. This is a large recreation area, which combines a small, but well-run zoo with an amusement park. It is run by the Tunisian forestry commission and has a collection of African animals including crocodiles, giraffes and elephants. As well as the amusement area, which has all the usual rides, the park also includes a number of restaurants and a venue for performances of *malouf* (folk) music.

Tozeur has a private ethnography museum, **Dar Cheraït**, whose formula vastly exceeds that of a mere museum. It is devoted to the history and everyday life of southern Tunisia. One section carries visitors to the world of the *Thousand and One Nights*, where they will meet, amongst others, Ali Baba and the 40 Thieves, Sinbad the Sailor and Scheherazade. This display is deservedly popular with children and includes secret labyrinths, ghosts, fire-eaters and a hall of mirrors. The fairytale stories are accompanied by accounts of everyday life in Arabic countries. The museum is best visited in the evening when it is festooned with fairy-lights.

Planet Oasis can be found in the palm groves close to Tozeur. This vast cultural complex consists of a huge air-conditioned tent (used for concerts, occasional receptions and Ramadan dinners), a row of fountains and an amphitheatre seating 2,000 spectators. The stage is built on the Saharan sand, with the natural backdrop of palm trees. It makes the most of state-of-the-art laser effects to stage spectacular concerts and open-air events. Planet Oasis also has regular displays of handicrafts such as glass blowing, painting, leather-work and pottery.

Tunisia's largest water park is undoubtedly **Acqua Palace** at Port el-Kantaoui. With water chutes, slides, drops, tunnels, whirlpools and every other kind of splashy fun, Acqua Palace provides an enjoyable way for children both big and small to find some cooling relief from the hot Tunisian sun.

The beach – a favourite place for children and adults alike

DIRECTORY

MUSIC

Centre of Arab and Mediterranean Music
Rue 2 Mars 8, Sidi Bou Saïd.
Tel (71) 740 102.

CINEMAS

ABC
Rue ibn Khaldoun, Tunis.
Tel (71) 336 360.

Alhambra
Marsa Plage, Tunis.
Tel (71) 980 966.

Colisée
Av. H. Bourguiba, Tunis.
Tel (71) 331 875.

Le Palace
Av. Habib Bourguiba, Tunis.
Tel (71) 256 989.

THEATRES

El-Hamra
Rue el-Jazira 28, Tunis.
Tel (71) 320 734.
www.theatrelhamra.com

El-Teatro
El-Omrane, Tunis.
Tel (71) 894 313.

Etoile du Nord
Av. Farhat Hached, Tunis.
Tel (71) 254 066.

Théâtre Municipal
Rue de Grèce 2, Tunis.
Tel (71) 259 499.

NIGHTLIFE

Abou Nawas Montazah
Tabarka.
Tel (78) 673 532.

Adonis
Hôtel Yadis Thalasso Golf, Midoun.
Tel (75) 747 410.

Ben's
Av. Moncef Bey, Hammamet.
Tel (72) 227 053.

Calypso
Av.-Moncef Bey, 8050 Hammamet.
Tel (72) 226 803.

Club Le Rameau
Av. H. Bourguiba, Hôtel Mercure, Sfax.
Tel (74) 225 700.

Club Pin's
Hotel Mehari, Tabarka.
Tel (78) 670 440.

Cotton Club
Hôtel Nova Park, Gammarth.
Tel (71) 913 766.

Disco Marina Yasmine
Hôtel Marina Palace, Hammamet.
Tel (72) 248 653.

El-Barka
Hôtel Penelope, Houmt Souk.
Tel (75) 731 456.

Guitoun
Av. Moncef Bey, Hammamet.
Tel (72) 248 820.

Hotel Morjene Dar Tabarka
Tabarka.
Tel (78) 673 411.

Hotel Sfax Centre
Sfax.
Tel (74) 225 700.

La Baleine
Tourist zone, Hôtel Golf Beach, Tabarka.
Tel (78) 673 002.

La Bamba
Hôtel Alhambra, Port el-Kantaoui.
Tel (73) 246 477.

Las Vegas
Route Touristique Nord, Hôtel Nahrawess, Hammamet.
Tel (72) 266 555.

Le boeuf sur le toit
Av. Fatouma, La Soukra, Tunis.
Tel (71) 764 807.

Le Crocodile
Route Touristique Nord, Hôtel le Président, Hammamet.
Tel (72) 280 211.

Le Pacha
Hôtel Riu Royal Garden, Midoun.
Tel (75) 745 777.

Le Pacha Club
Route Corniche, Hôtel Topkapi, Mahdia.
Tel (73) 671 261.

Les Jasmins
La Goulette.
Tel (71) 736 016.

Nirvana
Tourist zone, Hammamet.
Tel (72) 278 408.

Plaza Hotel
Marsa, Tunis.
Tel (71) 743 577.

Queen
Hôtel Karim, Gammarth.

Rancho Club
Av. Moncef Bey, Hammamet.
Tel (72) 226 462.

Romeo
Hôtel el-Mechtel, Tunis.
Tel (71) 783 200.

Sahara Club
Route Touristique, Hôtel Sahara Beach, Monastir.
Tel (73) 521 088.

Sirocco
Monastir.
Tel (73) 462 305.

The Blue Moon
Hasdrubal Thalassa, Yasmine Hammamet.
Tel (72) 248 800

Tropicana
Route Touristique, Hammamet.
Tel (72) 227 200.

Turquoise
Hôtel Abou Nawas Jerba, Sidi Mahares.
Tel (75) 757 022.

Yamama
Corniche, Hôtel Abou Nawas Nejma, Sousse.
Tel (73) 226 811.

CASINOS

Casino Caraibe
Av. 7 Novembre, Sousse.
Tel (73) 252 723.
Fax (73) 211 798.

Cleopatra
Hotel Occidental, Hammamet.
Tel (72) 244 999.
Fax (72) 226 315.

Casino Hammamet
Yasmine, Hammamet Sud.
Tel (72) 241 051.

Casino de Jerba
Tourist zone, Sidi Mahares.
Tel (75) 757 537.

CHILDREN'S ACTIVITIES

Belvedere Park
Tel (71) 890 386.
@ ami.belvedere@planet.tn

Park de Loisirs Bah Bah
Rue 20 Mars, Houmt Souk, Jerba.

Park de Loisirs Dah Dah
Berges de Lac, Tunis.
Tel (71) 860 888.

Oceanograpic Museum
Rue 2 Mars 1934 28, Carthage.
Tel (71) 730 420.

AMUSEMENT PARKS

Acqua Palace
Rue des Palmiers, Port el-Kantaoui.
Tel (73) 348 855.
@ acquapalace@planet.tn

Centre d'Animation Touristique les Grottes
Route des Grottes, El-Haouaria.
Tel (72) 297 296.
Fax (72) 269 070.

Dar Cheraït
Route Touristique, Tozeur.
Tel (76) 454 888.
Fax (76) 454 472.
www.darcherait.com.tn

Park Friguia
On route GP1 between Enfida and Bou Ficha.
Tel (73) 252 723.
www.friguiapark.com.tn

Planet Oasis
Tozeur.
Tel (76) 460 310.
www.planet-oasis.com

SPORT IN TUNISIA

Football is Tunisia's favourite sport and men often gather in large groups to watch matches live on TV. Another popular sport is the Dakar Rally, which from time to time passes through the Tunisian desert on its route from Europe to Senegal. Since the late 1960s, Tunisian athletes have often

A four-wheel-drive car in the Dakar Rally

done well in athletics and also in sports such as handball and volley-ball, achieving world-class results. Tunisian swimmers have also been successful. Most notably, at the Olympic Games in Beijing in 2008 Oussama Mellouli won a gold medal in the men's 1500 metres freestyle event.

Tunisia's national football team in action

FOOTBALL

As elsewhere in Africa, football is a passion in Tunisia and it's not hard to find a game on television. Watching football matches is almost a ritual in many traditional Tunisian cafés. Viewers react with great passion during live transmissions and the outcome of a game is a matter of some importance to many Tunisian football fans. Demand for tickets is high, so anyone wishing to see a game should arrive at the ground well before kick-off.

Tunisia's national team ranks as one of the best on the African continent and won the African Nations Cup in 2004 when they beat Morocco 2–1. Tunisian league teams are also successful and usually reach the later stages of continental club competitions. Two particularly outstanding teams are Etoile Sportive du Sahel from Sousse and Tunis's Espérance Sportive, which plays at the El-Menzah ground at the Cité Olympique. Other teams that are also successful are Club Africain (which is also from Tunis and shares its ground

with Espérance Sportive), and Club Sfaxien, based in Sfax.

As in other countries, the Tunisian League championship is fiercely contested each year by the major clubs.

Tunisia's National Cup is held each year and provides the lower league clubs with an opportunity to play some of the top teams.

A local celebrity in Tunisian football is "the golden boy" Ali Zitouni, the talented forward formerly of Espérance Sportive who now plays for Turkish team Antalyaspor and competed with the national team at the 2004 Olympics.

Tunisia have reached the finals of the World Cup four times (1978, 1998, 2002 and 2006) and have been ranked as highly as 21st in the world

by FIFA. Currently, the coach of the Tunisian national team is Bertrand Marchand.

Tunisia's match season starts in early October and finishes at the end of March. Most games are played on Saturdays and Sundays, with a 3pm kick-off. Up-to-date information about matches can be found in the local press or via the Tunisian Football Federation's website at www.ftf.org.tn

HOT-AIR BALLOONING

Tunisia provides favourable conditions for hot-air ballooning. The areas on the outskirts of the Sahara Desert are especially popular and are used as locations for many of the competitions that attract entries from all over the world. Hot-air balloons taking-off from this region can sometimes travel hundreds of kilometres.

Hot-air balloons over the Sahara Desert

Rally car navigating northern Tunisia's rough terrain

RALLIES

The first Paris–Dakar Rally began on 26 November 1978, with 170 entrants. Now the event is known as the Dakar Rally and traditionally starts on 1 January, in France. Each year the route of the rally, split into several sections, is changed, but it always leads through rough terrain and across the Saharan sands. The last time the rally passed through Tunisia was in 2003 when two of the legs took in Tunis, Tozeur and El-Borma. Vehicles participating in this punishing race include lorries, cross-country cars and motorcycles. Also of interest is the vintage car rally which takes place in Belvedere Park, Tunis *(see p87)*, usually in late autumn.

ATHLETICS

Tunisia has many talented athletes. In 2001 the country was proud to host the Mediterranean Games.

The most famous runner in Tunisia is Mohammed Gammoudi. Born in 1938, he became a national celebrity after winning medals in three consecutive Olympic Games. In 1964 he won a silver medal in Tokyo in the 10,000-m race. At the Olympic Games in Mexico City four years later, he picked up a gold medal for the 5,000 m, and then took a silver at the 1972 Munich Olympics for the same distance. Tunisian runners have also achieved numerous successes in world championships and excel in medium- and long-distance running.

HANDBALL

Handball is a game played on a court similar to that used in squash. It is very popular in Tunisia and receives plenty of TV and press coverage.

The men's team has participated several times in world championships and also at the Olympic Games, and the Tunisian squad continually ranks among the world's leading teams.

Tunisian runner at the Mexico City Olympics

SAILING

Tunisia is a sailor's paradise, with its 1200-km (746-mile) long coastline, countless bays and coves, and an average air temperature of 18° C (64° F). Costs for sailing in Tunisia are very attractive, and lower than in other parts of the Mediterranean. The country has five large marinas. Port el-Kantaoui has 320 spaces for yachts. Sidi Bou Saïd's harbour can accommodate 380 vessels. Monastir's marina has space for 386 boats.

The most important sailing events include an annual race from Malta (Valletta) to Port el-Kantaoui and another from Marseille to Tabarka.

OTHER SPORTS

In 2001, during the Judo World Championships held in Korea, Anisa Lounife became the first Muslim woman to win a gold medal at judo. Swimming has really surged in popularity in Tunisia since Oussama Mellouli became the first African male swimmer to win an Olympic gold medal in an individual event, at the Beijing Olympics in 2008. He went on to win five gold medals at the Mediterranean Games and one at the World Aquatic Championships in 2009.

The Tunisian basketball team is one of the best in Africa. In 2009 the team came third in Africa's Basketball Championship. In 2010, Tunisia defeated Egypt to win the African Cup. Though the Tunisian team does not have many tall players (the tallest is just over 2 m (6 ft 6 in), Tunisian players have a world reputation and have competed in the Czech Republic and Poland.

Windsurfing is another sport that is becoming increasingly popular in Tunisia and the country was represented in the Athens Olympics for this event.

Volleyball has many followers and is particularly popular with Tunisian women. The high popularity of this sport is due to several spectacular victories, such as in the African Championships held in Lagos in 1997, when the Tunisian team defeated Cameroon 3–0.

Tunisian judo competitors at the Korean Olympics

ACTIVITIES FOR VISITORS

Tunisia's climate makes the country an exceptional place for all types of outdoor activity. Visitors naturally favour watersports, including diving and sailing. Tourist zones have excellent golf courses – the best ones are in Port el-Kantaoui, while the most scenic ones are located around Tabarka. More exotic sports,

Holidaymakers learning to windsurf

such as paragliding, surfing on the dunes and sand-yachting on the salt flats of Chott el-Jerid are specialities of the southern region. Horse riding on the beaches of Jerba and Zarzis is a popular activity, as is camel trekking across the desert. Tunisia's national parks and the mountains around Aïn Draham offer visitors plenty of opportunities for hiking.

Catamarans off the beach at Jerba

DIVING

Some of the Mediterranean's best diving and snorkelling can be enjoyed in Tunisia. One of the most beautiful places to go is the coral reef off Tabarka where the clear, warm waters, coral and seawater beds are ideal for underwater exploration. Ten minutes by boat are enough to get to rocks surrounded by red coral. A little bit further on are magnificent tunnels, grottoes, underwater caves and caverns.

The warm sea and a vigorous and sustained programme of conservation mean that the reef is teeming with fish and other marine life. There are as many as six sites open to divers; each looks different and requires a different level of ability.

The yacht club in Tabarka and the International Diving Centre organize excursions to the reef for more experienced divers. The most popular site is Roche Merou – the Miller's Thumb Rock – where divers can swim amid rainbow-

coloured fish. La Tunelle, or Tunnels Reef, is less than 20 minutes from Tabarka and comprises a complex of tunnels, caves and caverns some 18 m (60 ft) below sea level. Club de Plongée, which is by the yacht jetty in Tabarka, also organizes taster excursions for total beginners as well as a 7-day course for less experienced divers. They also rent out boats and diving

equipment. Tabarka is not the only place where it it possible to go diving, however. The International Diving Centre in Port el-Kantaoui is open all year round and provides facilities for more experienced divers as well as running courses for beginners. Ideal conditions for exploring the beauty of the underwater world can also be found in Hergla, 15 km (9 miles) north of Port el-Kantaoui. Most diving clubs insist that divers are over 14 years old.

OTHER WATER SPORTS

Tunisia is a great place for windsurfing, which can be enjoyed all year round, although between December and April it is advisable to wear a wetsuit because the sea is so cool. One of the best windsurfing schools is situated in Sidi Bou Saïd. Favourable conditions for the sport are also found in Hammamet, Sousse and on Jerba. Seaside tourist resorts offer water skis for hire.

PARAGLIDING

Another popular sport in Tunisia is paragliding and lessons from qualified instructors can usually be arranged. Having the right equipment for this activity is essential and you should make sure this is supplied by the club or instructor when booking.

Paragliding, a popular activity

HIKING

Tunisia's national parks are splendid hiking grounds. An ideal place for this type of activity is Ichkeul National Park – one of the largest wintering sites for birds in the whole of the Mediterranean basin *(see pp136–7)*. Jebel Ichkeul, on the lake's south side, has a number of sandy footpaths leading through hills overgrown with wild olive trees. In the spring it can be carpeted with wild flowers.

Another great place is the Boukornine National Park. Situated near Tunis, it is full of Persian cyclamens that flower in the spring. Excellent conditions can also be found in the Khroumirie Mountains *(see p130)*, near Aïn Draham, where it is possible to climb to the top of Jebel Bir (1,041 m/ 3,415 ft) and the Col des Ruines overlooking the village.

Wild boar hunting around Aïn Draham

HUNTING

The forests around Aïn Draham are popular with hunters in search of wild boar. The season lasts from October until February. Hunting also takes place around El-Haouaria, Sbeïtla and Zaghouan. Special licences are required and can only be obtained by people who are part of an organized tour.

CAMEL TREKKING

Those dreaming of a real desert adventure should try a several day-, or several week-long trek across the sands of the Great Eastern Erg on a camel. The most popular

Caravan with tourists leaving Zaafrane

journey is a five-day trek from Douz to Ksar Ghilane. Shorter rides are also available and for a few dinars it is possible to enjoy an hour-long camel ride which, for some people, is quite enough.

The price per day (which includes all the necessary equipment and meals) is usually about 30–35 TD. An hour-long ride costs far less.

When embarking on a camel trek take a down-filled sleeping bag (nights are cold in the desert), a rolled-up sleeping mat, a pair of loose trousers and a large cotton scarf to protect the head and neck from the sun and wind. A flask containing water is, of course, indispensable. A tasty snack for the camel may also come in handy.

Another very important item when travelling in the desert is a well-stocked first-aid kit. As well as pain-killers, it is also advisable to carry a general antibiotic, a snake-bite serum, antihistamine and a remedy for gastric conditions. Also don't forget sunglasses, eye-drops, sun-block lip cream and large quantities of sun-cream.

Ideal months for such a trip are April, October and November as the temperature is then cooler. In December and January, however, night temperatures can drop to freezing. March brings sandstorms, while July and August are far too hot.

CYCLING AND MOTORBIKE TRIPS

All hotels offer bicycles for hire and tourist resorts also often run bike-hire services. Always check the condition of the hired bicycle before accepting it (usually it is far from perfect). Jerba and the coast of Sahel are ideal areas for cycling. If cycling around the country, take a set of spare parts such as inner tubes as there are practically no service and repair facilities outside the main towns.

A motorbike is an ideal vehicle for exploring the country. However, there is only one rental firm in Tunisia – Holiday Bikes on Jerba. Anyone wishing to hire a motorbike must be at least 21 years of age and hold a valid motorbike driving licence.

Driving a jeep across the desert – a taste of the Dakar Rally

Riders on a beach in Jerba

HORSE RIDING

Horse riding is available in many seaside resorts in Tunisia as well as in the areas close to the hotels that run their own riding stables.

The most popular place for horse riding is Jerba. The island also has the greatest number of riding stables. Here, it is possible to gallop for hours along virtually deserted beaches. Horse riding at sunrise or sunset can be an unforgettable experience.

GOLF

Although Tunisia does not have many golf courses, its climate is exceptionally favourable for the sport. Tunisia is firmly established on the international golf circuit and many people come to the country with the sole purpose of playing golf. There are a handful of top quality golf courses available. All of these offer a good range of facilities, including equipment hire, bars and restaurants. Friendly instructors are ready to assist those new to the sport.

Many hotels can arrange transfers to and from courses and also pre-set teeing-off times. Few of the clubs have stringent membership requirements though some of the larger ones may ask for a valid handicap certificate before they will allow a new player on the course. Failing that, a letter of introduction from a home club will often be sufficient.

The top golf course in Tunisia is the **El-Kantaoui**.

This 36-hole, professional course has a championship layout that winds through the olive groves opposite the marina. Twenty minutes from Tunis is the 18-hole **Carthage Golf Course**, which was founded in 1927. Two top-quality 18-hole courses are

Golfer on a course near Port el-Kantaoui

located in Monastir and Hammamet, while in Bir Bou Regba, near Hammamet, there is a 9-hole course. Jerba also has a golf club, which comprises three 9-hole courses. Tabarka's golf course is in the tourist zone and is set in a picturesque landscape of eucalyptus and olive trees overlooking the coast. The club features an 18-hole, 72-par course and a 9-hole practice course for less experienced players.

THALASSOTHERAPY

Tunisia is second only to France in terms of its thalassotherapy facilities. This treatment uses hot seawater combined with seaweed or mud in order to alleviate such common ailments as stress, rheumatism and arthritis. Many people enjoy it for its own sake, however, and thalassotherapy centres tend to be attached to hotels that also run life-enhancing programmes such as quitting smoking. They usually also promote healthy eating in their restaurants. Three of the best are the **Abou Nawas**, Sousse, the **Residence Hotel**, Carthage and the **Hasdrubal Thalassa**, Hammamet.

OTHER ACTIVITIES

There are relatively few facilities for extreme sports in Tunisia. Nevertheless, there are some unusual attractions on offer for those who seek high-octane thrills. Most of them are associated with the southern regions of the country and with the Sahara Desert.

Thrill-seekers should certainly try sand-skiing and sand-yachting. The latter is carried out on the dunes around Kelibia and Douz, while sand-skiing is practised in the El-Faour oasis, 30 km (19 miles) from Douz. The hard bottom of the dry Chott el-Jerid salt flat is perfect for the use of sand-yachts.

Any kind of flying is also very popular in Tunisia. The Sahara Desert offers good conditions for flying light aircraft. This sport is, however, rather expensive and depends very much on the weather.

A microlight aircraft preparing for a flight over the Sahara

DIRECTORY

DIVING

HAMMAMET

Nabil Jegham
Tel (98) 345 960.
Fax (95) 110 111.
@ nabil.jegham@
planet.tn

HERGLA

Hergla Scuba Dive Centre
Tel (73) 251 387.
Fax (73) 251 388.

JERBA

Gold Beach Jerba
Tel (75) 750 750.
Fax (75) 733 079.

MONASTIR

Club de Plongée Subway
Tel (73) 696 492.

Plongée et Loisirs
Cap Marina Monastir.
Tel (73) 462 509.
Fax (73) 462 509.

TABARKA

Aquamarin
Tel (78) 673 408.
Fax (78) 761 866.

Loisirs de Tabarka
Tel (78) 670 664.
Fax (78) 673 801.
@ diving.tunisie
@planet.tn

Mehari Diving Center "Le Merdu"
Tel (78) 673 136.
Fax (78) 673 868.

Valtur Tabarka
Tel (78) 670 333.
Fax (78) 671 770

YACHT MARINAS

HAMMAMET
Marina Yasmine Sud
Rue Jaafar el-Barmaki 3.
Tel (72) 241 111.
Fax (72) 241 212.
www.yasmine.com.tn

MONASTIR
Marina Cap Monastir
Tel (73) 462 305.
Fax (73) 464 999.

TABARKA
Montazah Tabarka
Tel (78) 670 599.
Fax (78) 673 595.

BOAT CHARTER

PORT EL-KANTAOUI

Tunisie Sailing
Quai Amilcar.
Tel (73) 246 588.
Fax (73) 348 490.

MOTOR RALLIES

Touring Club de Tunisie
Rue d'Allemagne 15, Tunis.
Tel (71) 323 114.
Fax (71) 324 834.
@ touringclub@
planet.tn

BICYCLE HIRE

All tourist hotels have bicycles for hire.

HORSE RIDING

JERBA

Hôtel Riu Royal Garden Palace
Tel (75) 745 777.
www.riu.com

Hôtel Coralia Club Palm Beach
Tel (75) 757 404.

Royal Carriage Club
Route Touristique.
Tel (75) 759 084.
Fax (75) 759 084.
www.royalcarriageclub.
com

MAHDIA

Hôtel Cap Mahdia
Tel (73) 680 300.

Hôtel Thapsus
Tel (73) 683 538.
Fax (73) 694 476.

TUNIS

Club Hippique de la Soukra
Tel (71) 765 619.

Hippodrome de Ksar Said
Tel (71) 653 938.
Fax (71) 653 297.
@ stedecoursesdetunis
@email.ati.tn

GOLF

HAMMAMET

Golf Yasmine
B.P.61. *Tel (72) 227 001.*

JERBA
Jerba Golf Club,
Tourist zone, Midoun.
Tel (75) 745 055.
Fax (75) 745 051.

MONASTIR
Flamingo Golf
B.P.168, Rte Ouerdanine.
Tel (73) 500 284.

PORT EL-KANTAOUI
El-Kantaoui Golf
Tel (73) 348 756.
Fax (73) 348 755.

TABARKA
Tabarka Golf
Route touristique,
El-Morjane.
Tel (78) 670 038.
Fax (78) 671 026.

TUNIS
Golf de Carthage
Choutrana 2, La Soukra.
Tel (71) 765 700.

THALASSOTHERAPY

CARTHAGE
The Residence
B.P. 697, Les Côtes de
Carthage.
Tel (71) 910 101.
Fax (71) 910 144.

HAMMAMET
Hasdrubal Thalassa
Yasmine Hammamet.
Tel (72) 248 800.
Fax (72) 248 923.

JERBA
Hasdrubal
Tel (75) 730 650.

SOUSSE
Abou Nawas
Avenue Habib Bourguiba.
Tel (73) 226 030.
Fax (73) 226 595.

TRIPS TO THE SAHARA

Au Coeur du Désert
Rue Abou Kassem
el-Chabbi, Tozeur.
Tel (76) 453 570.
Fax (76) 453 515.
www.tunisiedesert.com

Calypso Voyages
Avenue H. Bourgiba 69,
Houmt Souk.
Tel (75) 620 561.
Fax (75) 620 558.
@ calypso.voyages
@planet.tn

Centrale de Voyages (La)
Av Mohamed Badra,
Jerba.*Tel (75) 652 815.*
Fax (75) 623 704.

Comptoir de la Tunisie
BP 162, Houmt Souk.
Tel (75) 653 3000.
Fax (75) 652 931.
www.cdd-tn.com

Desert Explorer
24 Avenue Chebbi, Tozeur.
Tel (76) 461 950.
www.choosedex.com

Dream Travel
Route de l'Aéroport,
Houmt Souk.
Tel (75) 673 451.
Fax (75) 673 504.
www.dreamtravel-tunisie.
com

Douz Voyages
Place de l'Indépendance,
Douz.
Tel (75) 470 178.
Fax (75) 470 315.
www.douzvoyages.chez.
com

Hafsi Travel
Route de Nefta, Tozeur.
Tel (76) 452 611.
Fax (76) 452 455.

Houria Voyages
Zone Touristique, Tozeur.
Tel (76) 461 022.
Fax (76) 462 029.

Jerba Voyages
Rue ibn Khaldun 2, Tunis.
Tel (71) 240 105.
Fax (71) 337 212.

Sable d'Or Voyages
Avenue d'Afrique
26–Menzah, Tunis.
Tel (71) 237 303.
Fax (71) 237 505.

Sud Tourisme
Residence Habib, Tunis.
Tel (71) 724 184.

SURVIVAL
GUIDE

PRACTICAL INFORMATION

Tunisia is a visitor-friendly place and, in its outlook, is probably one of the most "Western" of all Islamic countries. Within resorts and hotels visitors may behave as they would at home. When venturing further afield, however, it is important to be aware of local attitudes and

A street name written in Arabic and French

customs. For instance, exposed shoulders and the wearing of miniskirts by women are considered inappropriate. Mosques, particularly prayer halls, are not open to non-Muslims. Although Tunisia is a Muslim country, it follows the European calendar and has adopted Sunday as its day of rest.

Visitors resting on the steps of the Great Mosque, Tunis

WHEN TO VISIT

Holidays can be taken in Tunisia at any time of the year. The hot summer season lasts from May until early October, although the heat is moderated by the sea breezes on the coast. Summer is the best time for sunbathing on the beach and swimming. If venturing inland or to the south of the country, however, then it can get unbearably hot during the summer months; the heat is particularly intense in the mountain valleys.

In autumn, cold currents coming from the northwest Atlantic can bring wind and rain. Then, the temperature drops to 20–24° C (68–74° F), though the sea remains warm. The most rainfall can be expected in the north.

During winter the days are warm and mostly sunny, with temperatures between 16 and 24° C (61 and 75° F), but be prepared for weather changes

as some of the most unpredictable weather occurs at this time. The daytime temperature may be 25° C (75° F) one day, and suddenly drop to just a few degrees above freezing the next. On windy days the cold can feel acute, particularly on the Cap Bon peninsula and in the northern regions of the country. These cold spells never last long, however.

In the main, the best seasons for visiting Tunisia are spring and autumn when sightseeing can be combined with sea-bathing. The best time to visit the south is from early September until May, but trips to the desert should ideally be undertaken in September, October or March, when the daytime temperature is 25–28° C (77–82° F). The main festival period is in summer. During Ramadan the shops stay open until late. Concerts and poetry evenings are held at numerous venues in the medinas of Tunis and Kairouan. On Jerba, the holiday season lasts most of the year, though the sea cools off towards the end of October.

PASSPORTS AND VISAS

Citizens of the European Union and nationals of the United States and Canada, Australia and New Zealand require a valid passport to visit Tunisia. It should be valid for at least six months after the date of arrival, and will allow visits of up to three months without a visa for citizens of the EU, USA and Canada. Australians may purchase a 30-day visa on arrival at Tunis airport. New Zealanders should apply for a visa in advance of their trip. For stays exceeding three months, most visitors will need to obtain a visa. If in doubt, contact the Tunisian Embassy, or seek advice from a travel agent.

CUSTOMS REGULATIONS

The limits on what can be taken in and out of the country are stated in detail in customs regulations. Duty-free allowances include 1 litre of spirits, 2 litres of wine, 400 cigarettes, 250 ml of perfume, two cameras, 20 rolls of film

Transport for holidaymakers in Sousse

◁ **Avenue Habib Thameur – the main street of Nabeul**

Tourist information office in Houmt Souk on Jerba

and one video camera. There are no limits on the amount of foreign currency visitors may bring in. Tunisia has certain rules on the value of items brought into the country and it is advisable to declare items such as expensive cameras on arrival to save confusion when leaving.

Various products in duty-free shops can be purchased, using any convertible currency. Note that Tunisian duty-free shops do not take dinars. The prices of products bought in Tunisia's duty-free shops may be slightly higher than those in town.

LANGUAGE

Arabic is the official language of Tunisia. French is also in common use and most educated Tunisians are bilingual. The staff working in tourist zones will usually also speak English but with a dialect that varies from region to region. Outside tourist zones English

is virtually unknown, apart from a handful of basic phrases. In the main markets almost all languages can be heard. This is especially the case with shopkeepers, who encourage tourists to buy in as many languages as they can think of. Tunisia's Berber population has kept its own language, though they also usually speak Arabic. Tunisian children are generally able to speak French, as this is taught in school from primary level.

Road sign to the Dar Jellouli Museum in Sfax

TOURIST INFORMATION

ONTT Tourist Information Bureaux (Organization Nationale de Tourisme Tunisien) can be found at all the major airports, as well as

in larger towns. Small information desks are also in some selected museums. Some of them hand out free pamphlets and detailed road maps, but there is not likely to be much detailed information from these small ONTT offices regarding sightseeing, transport or obtaining hotel accommodation. The ONTT also has an office in London, however, which can provide information on all aspects of Tunisia *(see p247)*.

FACILITIES FOR THE DISABLED

There are not many facilities for wheelchair users in Tunisia. Wheelchair ramps are rarely seen and many of the major sights are inaccessible to wheelchair users for this reason. The Association Générale des Insuffisant Moteurs de Tunis can provide information for wheelchair users visiting Tunisia *(see p247)*.

STUDENTS

Students up to 32 years of age holding a valid International Student Identity Card (ISIC) may be entitled to concessions in museums, historic buildings and archaeological sites. They may also be entitled to reduced travel fares within the country. Tunisia also has a network of youth hostels that admits YHA card holders.

DIRECTORY

EMBASSIES

Tunisian Embassy
29 Prince's Gate,
London, SW7 1QG.
Tel *(020) 7584 8117.*

British Embassy
Rue du Lac Windermere,
Les Berges du Lac,
1053 Tunis.
Tel *(71) 108 700.*

Canadian Embassy
Rue du Sénégal 3, Place
d'Afrique, Belvedere,
P.O. Box 31, 1002, Tunis.
Tel *(71) 104 000.*
Fax *(71) 104 090.*

US Embassy
Les Berges du Lac, Tunis.
Tel *(71) 107 000.*
Fax *(71) 963 263.*

*Note: Australians should
contact the Canadian
Embassy; New Zealanders
the British Embassy.*

INFORMATION

ONTT Main Office
Avenue Mohamed V 1,
Tunis.
Tel *(71) 350 997.*
Fax *(71) 341 997.*
www.tourismtunisia.com

**REGIONAL
ONTT OFFICES**

Bizerte
Rue de Constantinople 1.
Tel *(72) 432 897.*
@ crtb.ontt.ontt@email.ati.tn

Jerba
Blvd. de l'Environnement,
Houmt Souk.
Tel *(75) 650 016.*
Fax *(75) 650 586.*
@ crtd.ontt@email.ati.tn

Mahdia
Rue el Moez.
Tel *(73) 681 098.*
Fax *(73) 680 662.*

Monastir
Opposite airport, Monastir.
Tel *(73) 461 960.*
@ crtmo.ontt@email.ati.tn

Nabeul
Avenue Taieb Mehiri.
Tel *(72) 286 737.*
@ crtn.ontt@email.ati.tn

Sousse
Av. Habib Bourguiba 1.
Tel *(73) 225 157.*
@ crts.ontt@email.ati.tn

Tabarka
Av. Habib Bourguiba 32,
Tabarka.
Tel *(78) 671 491.*
@ crtt.ontt@email.ati.tn

Customs and Etiquette

Although open to new ideas, Tunisians cherish their traditions, observing the Ramadan fast and celebrating Muslim feasts with great ceremony and devotion. Many Tunisian men enjoy spending their time in cafés, playing games and smoking *chichas* (hookahs). Women spend much time within their own family circles. Visits to hammams (steam baths) are popular. Pre-wedding customs including a "henna night" are also widespread.

MEALS

Breakfast tends to be a light meal in Tunisia, consisting of coffee, baguette with perhaps honey or olive oil, or cakes. The resort hotels, however, usually offer a large selection of dishes for breakfast. Lunch may also be light, and is taken between noon and 3pm. It may consist of *brik à l'oeuf* (egg inside an envelope of pastry) or a main course with salad.

Many restaurants have special lunch menus; these are usually offered at reduced prices. Dinner is eaten in the evening, around 8pm. There is no need for any misgivings about eating in small cafés and restaurants – in fact, dining in such humble places can be preferable to eating in upmarket restaurants or hotels as the food is likely to be more authentic. The food served in the big tourist hotels is often more adapted to European tastes, with a wider menu and lighter use of spices. Bread is served with

meals free of charge. Sometimes harissa (a spicy sauce) with olive oil appears on the table. This is eaten with bread, or may be added to any other dish.

Tunisia's national dish is couscous. It comes in several varieties; the most popular of them are made with lamb, chicken, fish or vegetables.

Sweet cakes on sale in a market in Kairouan

HOSPITALITY

As a nation, Tunisians are family-orientated and welcoming. It happens frequently that Tunisians will invite foreign visitors to their homes or ask them to participate in their meal. There is no need to be afraid to accept such an invitation, but try to assess whether it is not purely a gesture of politeness. The first expression of Tunisian hospitality is to offer the guest a glass of mint tea. Accepting tea in a shop does not oblige the customer to purchase anything. Offering tea is, of course, part of the sales technique, but it also arises out of Arab traditions of hospitality.

Berber woman in her doorway

Tunisian man dressed in traditional white attire

CLOTHES

Many Tunisian women wear European clothes, particularly in cities. Typical office dress consists of a skirt and a jacket. Young people dress in styles similar to those found in European countries. The official dress for a man is a suit.

Traditional Tunisian attire, including the veil, is worn mainly by older women and is more common in the provinces. Berber women living in Chenini wear red-and-white checked veils.

The red *chechia* hat is often worn by men to complement a traditional garb consisting of a loose robe opened at the chest and covered with a arge wrap. Sometimes a *chechia* is worn with a Western suit. Often, traditional clothes are reserved for religious ceremonies, and are more commonly worn by persons associated with religious organizations.

Although many Tunisians have adopted Western dress, visitors should avoid short skirts, shorts, anything transparent and clothes that leave the shoulders or chest exposed. To help avoid unwanted attention, women should dress modestly. In tourist zones visitors are freer to wear what they like, but if exploring the countryside be aware that exposure of the body is frowned upon by many Muslims.

CAFES

Traditional cafés are an important part of Tunisian life and are frequented mainly by men, who come to relax. The menfolk gather to watch TV, talk about sport and politics, play cards and smoke their *chichas* (hookahs). The latter are generally smoked at noon, in the afternoons and in the evenings. Smoking a pipe is accompanied by sips of strong tea served with fresh mint leaf. The *chicha* is usually supplied free of charge, the men paying only for the tobacco. Mild mixtures of tobacco with dried apples or mint soaked in honey are available. If the pipe goes out, a waiter will usually bring a few glowing lumps of charcoal to reignite it.

Alongside these cafés, Tunisia has an increasing number of European-style ones. These are popular meeting places for Tunisian women and younger people.

Man smoking a hookah

ALCOHOL AND OTHER BEVERAGES

Although drinking is discouraged by Islam, alcohol and beer drinking are permitted in Tunisia, but these drinks are sold only in specially-licensed shops and bars. The latter tend to be very much smoke-filled, male refuges. Many supermarkets sell alcohol, though it may be harder to purchase on Fridays. If buying alcohol from a supermarket be discreet and carry it in a closed bag. Drinking alcohol openly in the street is likely to cause offence. Beer and spirits are generally served only in more

Removing shoes before entering a mosque

expensive restaurants. During Ramadan alcohol sales cease everywhere.

RELIGION

Islam is the state religion of Tunisia, but *sharia* (Islamic) law is not part of the state legislation. Muslims profess faith in one God, Allah, and recognize a number of holy scriptures including the Torah and the Gospels. A number of biblical figures are common to Christianity and Islam including Adam, Moses, Abraham and Jesus. Mohammed is considered the greatest of the Muslim prophets in that he was the final prophet to whom was revealed the direct word of God, which is written down in the Islamic holy book, the Koran.

Islam plays an important part in Tunisian's cultural life. Prayers are said when a baby is first born and a few days later there is a ceremony which involves shaving the baby's head. Circumcision for boys is carried out at any time from seven days after birth to the age of eight or nine. Islamic weddings popularly take place in the summer. The marriage ceremony is short but celebrations are often lengthy. When a Muslim dies a simple ceremony is held in the mosque. The body of the deceased is buried with the feet facing towards Mecca.

When visiting mosques, note that only the courtyard areas are open to tourists.

PHOTOGRAPHY

There is no problem with taking a camera to Tunisia. Some Tunisians, however, may object to having their picture taken so always ask for permission first. This applies especially to Tunisian women and when taking pictures of people in rural areas. Be aware, too, that taking pictures (inadvertently or not) of airfields, military installations, police stations or other government buildings may lead to arrest.

Men playing a game of cards in a traditional café

Health and Security

**Tunisian
Police badge**

Most visitors to Tunisia will experience no serious problems with crime. The streets and hotels are discreetly patrolled by security guards and plain-clothes policemen. This high level of safety is due to untiring official vigilance, especially in the tourist zones. Crimes such as groping against women do happen, but are rare. Alcohol-fuelled crime is not uncommon, and measures against drink-driving are limited, so be vigilant especially at night and weekends. The greatest danger is from the sun; ignoring basic safety precautions may lead to severe burns and sunstroke.

**Policemen talking to young people
on the street in Sfax**

POLICE

When staying in Tunisia, even on a brief visit, visitors soon become aware of the large numbers of police. The National Guard are responsible for national security and its officers wear military khaki uniforms. The Sûreté, or state police, wear light and dark blue uniforms and mainly operate in the towns. Crimes and thefts should be reported to the state police. Police personnel speak French, but very few are likely to speak much English. The National Guard have responsibility for rural areas and the country's borders. They may set up road blocks, stop cars, check documents and the contents of the car. Tourist cars and coaches are usually not checked, but a hired car may be stopped. Visitors must then present their documents and explain the purpose of their journey. Although this may seem excessive, it has to

be remembered that Tunisia shares borders with Algeria and Libya. The police are mainly on the lookout for smugglers, arms dealers and terrorists.

With tourists' safety in mind, police stations have been built in virtually every tourist zone. If visitors are a victim of a crime, they should request a police certificate (a copy of the police report) in order to claim compensation from their insurance company.

PERSONAL PROPERTY

It is recommended that any valuables be stored in a safe or locked securely in your suitcase, or at least kept out of sight. Every hotel employs security staff; the porter not only opens the doors, but also stops any stranger from entering the premises. Beaches are patrolled around the clock to make sure that no unauthorized persons use this means to enter the hotel compound.

A lost or stolen passport should be reported to the Sûreté. In markets, trams and other crowded places be especially vigilant about pickpockets. In some of the larger resorts, such as Sousse, Jerba and Hammamet, it also pays to keep personal property out of sight. In places such as the narrow, crowded alleys of the medinas (old quarters) avoid carrying valuables in a handbag or backpack. It is better to keep wallets or purses under a shirt. The

safest method is to use an inside pocket in a shirt or jacket that is fastened with a separate button or zip. Be aware, also, when on the beach – sleeping tourists can sometimes fall victim to pickpockets or bag-snatchers.

HEALTH AND HYGIENE

Tunisia is a country where restaurants maintain high standards of hygiene. This applies not only to the big hotel restaurants, but every small café that offers a quick meal will have a washbasin. Tunisians wash their hands before and after eating. Food poisoning is rare.

Despite this, visitors may experience stomach problems a few days after arriving in Tunisia. The usual symptoms are fever, shivering, general weakness, and diarrhoea. Usually this is not a case of food poisoning, but the body's reaction to the sun and the different diet and climate. This type of problem may be avoided by keeping out of the sun and reducing the consumption of raw vegetables and salads, particularly during the first few days of a visit. Prior to leaving home be sure to provide yourself with remedies for diarrhoea. The most important thing when suffering from an upset of this kind is to replace the fluid that is lost. In the course of such an illness drink plenty of bottled water.

There are not many public toilets in Tunisia, and most are usually to be found at petrol stations. In an emergency look for a restaurant or a hotel. It is worth carrying a roll of toilet paper for such an eventuality.

The greatest health hazard in Tunisia is the sun. In summer always keep the head cov-

**Sign of a private ambulance
service in Jendouba**

Patrol car of the Gendarmerie

A fire engine from Bizerte

An ambulance from a hospital in Tunis

Their staff are well trained and likely to speak fluent French, although they may not be able to speak more than a few words of English. They will be able to offer simple medical advice and prescribe a wider range of drugs than are available without prescription in Europe. Most towns will have a pharmacy that remains open all night – a list of pharmacies open round the clock is printed in the French language newspapers such as *La Presse* or *Le Temps*. The symbol for a pharmacy in Tunisia is a serpent on a green background.

FIRE BRIGADE

If a fire breaks out within the hotel compound, contact the reception or call the number of the fire brigade *(Protection Civile)*. The operator will speak French, but only rarely be able to communicate in English. The fire engines in Tunisia are painted red.

The fire service is also called out during heavy rainfall, to pump water out of flooded cellars and apartments and to unblock the main drainage systems.

ered and avoid long exposure. Another danger is heatstroke, which is particularly likely in the desert, and in the mountain valleys. Among the signs of heatstroke are disorientation, headaches and a high body temperature without the other signs of fever. When out in the sun, drink plenty of water. In larger towns the tap water is fit for drinking.

During desert trips wear ankle-length boots to protect against scorpion bites. Also be aware that in older buildings in urban areas tarantulas may appear after heavy rain.

Neon sign of a pharmacy in Tunis

MEDICAL CARE

Every hotel has a list of doctors who will come at any time of day or night, when called by the reception. Medical advice is not expensive in Tunisia; doctors charge about

25–30 TD for a visit. Nevertheless, it is worth taking out insurance.

Tunisian hospitals have well-trained medical staff and good quality equipment; they also have their own ambulances. Dental services are also of a high standard. If there is a minor medical problem ask for advice in a pharmacy *(see below)*. In more remote and sparsely populated areas (particularly in southern Tunisia) emergency treatment and transport are provided by the police and army. Many of the big tourist hotels have doctors and nurses on call round the clock.

PHARMACIES

Tunisian pharmacies are clean, well stocked and can be found in many small towns and some villages.

Banking and Currency

The national currency is the Tunisian Dinar (TD). The exchange rate is fixed on a daily basis and can be looked up online or in the local paper. The TD cannot be traded, like the US dollar or UK pound, and it is illegal to either import or export it, so Tunisian currency cannot be purchased before arriving. All of Tunisia's larger towns, provincial capitals and tourist resorts have banks, bureaux de change and ATMs, and most hotels above three-stars will also change currency.

Cash dispensers can be found in large towns and tourist zones

BANKS

The country's main bank is the Central Bank of Tunisia – Banque Centrale de Tunisie. There are also a number of state-owned banks. The first private bank – Amen Bank – was established in 1995. Branches of Tunisian banks can be found all over the country. There are a number of foreign banks, which also offer a full range of services.

Banks are usually open Monday to Thursday, from 8 to 11:30am and from 2 to 5pm; between July and August they are open from 8 to 11am. Opening times are shorter during Ramadan. In larger towns, during Ramadan the longest opening hours are offered by small branches of the Amen Bank – some even stay open until 4pm. Banks remain closed during Muslim holidays as well as during state and national holidays. In the tourist areas banks are often open longer for visitors to exchange money.

EXCHANGING MONEY

Banks and most large hotels in Tunisia can exchange the main world currencies, including sterling, euros and US dollars, into Tunisian dinars (TD). The exchange rate is determined on a daily basis by the Central Bank of Tunisia. Differences in the exchange rate between banks are negligible, and involve only the commission. Hotels can give favourable rates, but even here, the difference is never very large.

In addition to banks there is also a network of bureaux de change, which are usually more convenient than a bank. They can be found in many parts of the main towns and tourist zones and are often open longer than banks. There are a number of automatic exchange machines (though these are still few and far between) which change foreign currencies into dinars.

Money can also be changed at some post offices. If venturing away from the main tourist areas, however, it can be harder to find facilities for exchanging money, especially in rural areas.

Distinctive automatic currency exchange machine

It is illegal to take Tunisian currency out of the country, or to bring it in. Visitors who have not used all their dinars by the time they are ready to leave may change back 30 per cent of the total sum, but not more than 100 TD, on presenting the original proof of exchange. It is therefore worth changing only small sums of money at one time and keeping all the exchange receipts, including the ones issued by ATMs. Foreign currencies in excess of 500 TD should be declared on arrival. Duty free shops at the airports accept only foreign credit cards and currency.

Even luxury hotels that quote their prices in euros or US dollars on their websites or in brochures can only accept cash payments in Tunisian dinars.

Readily identifiable sign of an ATM in Tunisia

CREDIT CARDS, ATMS AND TRAVELLER'S CHEQUES

Besides cash, most large shops, hotels and tourist-orientated restaurants will accept payment by major credit cards including Visa and MasterCard. Some of the more upmarket restaurants also accept Diners Club cards. Cards are not accepted at petrol stations, however. Credit cards are often required when checking in at some of the more upmarket hotels. ATMs can be found in tourist resorts and they accept most major cards. To ensure you are able to withdraw cash while you're away, inform your bank of your travel plans prior to departure.

Traveller's cheques are no longer widely used, but are still accepted at some banks and hotels. If traveller's cheques are lost or stolen this should be reported to the issuing company's Tunisian office. Most companies should be able to replace lost traveller's cheques within 24 hours.

CURRENCY

The Tunisian dinar is divided into 1,000 millimes. Banknotes are issued in denominations of 1, 5, 10, 20, 30 (gradually being phased out) and 50 TD; the face values of coins are 0.5 TD (called the ½ dinar), 1 TD, 5 TD, and 5, 10, 20, 50 and 100 millimes. Prices are sometimes quoted in millimes, which can be confusing – if a sign says 1,800 it means 1 dinar, 800 millimes. 1-, 2- and 5-millime coins are no longer issued by the Central Bank but are still in circulation and it is worth having some low denomination coins to hand, particularly when shopping in the medinas.

When leaving Tunisia remember that at airports dinars are accepted only up to the border crossing point. In duty-free zones visitors must pay in convertible currencies.

CASH DISPENSERS

Cash dispensers (ATMs) can be found on the main streets of big towns and in the larger medinas. They are also in all the major holiday resorts. Only those displaying the sign of Visa, MasterCard, Cirrus or Maestro will dispense money on cards issued by foreign banks. Cash dispensers display instructions in Arabic, French and English.

Banknotes
Banknotes differ in colour and (slightly) in size. The highest denomination – 50 TD – is a distinctive green colour. Banknotes bear images of prominent figures from Tunisia's history, as well as Arabic and French lettering.

5 dinars

10 dinars

20 dinars

50 dinars

5 dinars

1 dinar

1/2 dinar

100 millimes

50 millimes

Coins
Coins in circulation come in denominations of ½, 1 and 5 dinars, as well as 5, 10, 20, 50 and 100 millimes. Coins from 10 to 100 millimes are golden in colour, and are worth very little. Half-dinar and one-dinar coins are silver in colour.

20 millimes

10 millimes

5 millimes

Communications and Media

Post offices in Tunisia offer the whole range of postal services and can also be used to send a fax or make a telephone call. More convenient, however, is the system of public phones, known as taxiphones, which can be found all over the country – these can be used to phone abroad.

Tunisia's public phone sign

Foreign newspapers and magazines are sold in Tunis, Tabarka and Bizerte, as well as tourist areas of the Sahel. The French language version of *La Presse*, the national daily paper, is available everywhere.

The most frequently-seen type of coin-operated telephone

TELEPHONE

Making a local call is fairly straightforward in Tunisia as only the subscriber's number need be dialled. When making a long-distance call within the country, precede the number with 7, followed by the appropriate area code, e.g. 1 for Tunis, 2 for Bizerte. When calling a Tunis number from Bizerte, for example, dial 71, followed by the number. Telephone boxes can usually be found near post offices. Some shops have public phones (identifiable by their blue signs). Calls made from hotels are expensive (this applies to both telephones installed in guest rooms and reception areas).

A telephone call made from a post office is cheaper than one made from a hotel, which charges a higher rate for the first three minutes.

The most practical solution is provided by taxiphones. These are small telephone exchanges found in almost every town and village. Identifiable by their yellow signs, there are several booths and attendants who can supply change. They can be used to make a call (from a coin-operated phone) or to send a fax. Taxiphones are very popular and have an extensive network. Calls made from taxiphones are much cheaper than ones made from hotels. Most Tunisian public telephones are coin-operated. Telephone calls are cheaper between 8pm and 6am.

Making an international call from Tunisia is also fairly straightforward, although it can be costly. To dial abroad from most public phones, first dial the international code 00, followed by the country code, then the local code and finally the number. The country code to dial Tunisia from abroad is 216.

Mobile phones can be used in most of Tunisia apart from the desert areas. Visitors may need to notify their provider before going abroad in order to have their international access switched on. Alternatively, simply purchase a local SIM card to use for the duration of your stay. These may be obtained from Orange, Tunisiana, Tunisie Telecom or Elissa.

INTERNET

Internet access is widespread in Tunisia, provided by the state-owned Publinet company. You will also find a growing network of private internet cafés in towns and cities throughout the country. In Tunis a popular private internet café is located close to the railway station at Rue de Grèce 4, near Place Barcelone. Publinet branches, as well as private internet cafés, are generally open from 8am until late into the evening.

One hour of internet access costs approximately 1 TD, with students sometimes offered a discount for frequent use. Most private internet cafés also provide webcams for VOIP calls, although their use may be restricted to certain times.

Wi-Fi is available in some hotels in Tunis city, parts of the north and the coastal tourist zones, and is progressively being introduced throughout Tunisia. Some cafés also offer Wi-Fi facilities.

Telephone booths inside a taxiphone exchange

Post office in Monastir

RADIO AND TV

Tunisia has four national TV channels, Tunis 7, Tunisie 21, Hannibal and Tunisie Television. All transmit in Tunisian dialect, and there are also some programmes in French. There are a number of entertaining local productions, including game shows, soap operas, cultural shows and sporting programmes.

It is also worth watching the frequent transmissions of contemporary music concerts, recorded at the Carthage Festival of the Medina, for instance, or live studio performances of *malouf* (folk) music. These broadcasts provide good quality Arab music, and also demonstrate how deeply such music is rooted in Tunisian culture.

Rai Uno and France 2 are two additional TV channels received throughout much of Tunisia.

The majority of homes in Tunisia have satellite dishes, which provide access to a huge number of international channels. Tourist zone hotels normally offer a number of international TV channels via satellite. News channels generally include BBC, CNN, Euro News and Al-Jazeera (in Arabic). Eurosport is also generally available in English. A sample of Tunisian TV can be seen before visiting on the internet at www.tunisiatv.com.

There are several radio stations catering to foreign listeners. A French-language radio station (broadcasting on about 98 FM) regularly transmits in other European languages for short periods: in English from 2–3pm; in German from 3–4pm and in Italian from 4–5pm. Radio Tunis is a French language station that is good for music and is available at 93.1 FM. In addition, a number of European stations are available, including Voice of America and the BBC's World Service, which can be picked up at 15,070 and 12,095 MHz, or from 4–9am and 2–8pm at either 9,410, 6,195, 12,095 or 15,485 kHz, depending on the time of day.

Sign displaying post office logo

THE PRESS

European magazines and newspapers are readily available in Tunis from large hotels and at various newsagents throughout the city centre. They usually arrive one day late. There are three French-language newspapers published in Tunisia (*La Presse*, *Le Renouveau* and *Le Temps*) and one weekly English-language magazine, *Tunisia News*. *La Presse*, in particular, is a valuable source of information. Its weekend edition has a large cultural section, which contains the programmes of cinemas, shows and other current cultural events. Alongside these, it also publishes reviews and announcements for all major forthcoming attractions. *Le Temps* puts more of an emphasis on international events; *La Presse* is good for coverage of sporting events.

POSTAL SERVICES IN TUNISIA

Tunisian post offices are easy to recognize by their yellow boards inscribed with the letters PTT. Postboxes are usually yellow too. There are post offices in all sizeable towns. Stamps can be bought from them and letters, parcels, telegrams or cash can be sent abroad. Overseas telephone calls can also be made from a Tunisian post office.

The Tunisian postal system is reliable. Letters to Europe take seven to 10 days, while letters to the USA and Australia take about two weeks. Post offices also provide an express mail delivery service (*Rapide Poste*).

Some hotels have a system whereby they collect their guests' mail in decorative cages situated in the reception areas. Hotel staff then take them to the post office.

Stamps can be obtained from newspaper kiosks and from the larger souvenir shops. Stamps are also often available from taxiphone offices. During the summer, post offices are open Monday to Saturday, from 7:30am until 1pm. Throughout the rest of the year they are open from 8am until noon, and again from 3 to 6pm. On Saturdays post offices are only open from 8am until noon. During Ramadan, post offices are open from 8am to 3pm, though these opening hours can be subject to change.

Light yellow postbox, as seen everywhere in Tunisia

TRAVEL INFORMATION

The most convenient way of getting to Tunisia is by air; there are frequent scheduled services year-round from the UK, France and other European countries. Tour operator services, often using charter flights, and usually including accommodation and airport transfers, are competitively

Tunisair's logo

priced and can represent excellent value when compared with scheduled airfares. If planning to take a car, travelling by ferry from France or Italy, book tickets well in advance as ferries can be busy, especially in summer. Overland travel via Algeria or Libya is difficult, as visas for Algeria are only available for residents of Tunisia.

Road sign to an airport

AIR TRAVEL

Flights to Tunisia from the UK take about three hours. Tunisia's national airline is **Tunisair**, which operates direct scheduled flights from London Heathrow to Tunis four times a week. **British Airways** also has at least five services a week, from London Gatwick Airport. Alternatively, it is possible to fly indirectly via major European hubs, with connections from several UK regional airports. Tunisair has connecting flights from Tunis to Monastir, Sfax, Jerba and Tozeur. There is also a direct service, weekly on Sundays, operated by **Nouvelair** between London Gatwick and Monastir. There are no direct services between the Republic of Ireland and Tunisia; therefore it is best to travel via London or Paris. Direct flights are available from North America and

there are also flights from Australasia via the UAE.

Apart from scheduled flights, a wide range of charter flights is offered by tour operators direct to Monastir from London and selected UK regional airports. These include Luton, Birmingham, Manchester, Newcastle and Glasgow.

Prices vary according to season and are highest in July and August. Short-notice spring and autumn bookings can prove excellent value, and it is possible to save money by booking online via an airline or one of the discount travel websites. On all airlines weekend flights usually cost more.

INTERNATIONAL AIRPORTS

Tunisia has a number of international airports. The four main ones are: Tunis Carthage Airport (6 km/4 miles from Tunis); Enfida International Airport (at Herghla at the heart of the coastal resorts); Monastir Habib Bourguiba

Airport (12 km/7 miles from Monastir, Sousse and Port el-Kantaoui); and Jerba (9 km/6 miles from the island's capital Houmt Souk). All are able to handle large numbers of flights and passengers. Tunisia's other airports are at Sfax, 112 km (70 miles) south of Monastir; Tabarka, on the coast close to the border with Algeria; and Tozeur, in Tunisia's western desert region.

Sign for a taxi rank at one of Tunisia's airports

TRAVELLING FROM THE AIRPORT

Tunis Carthage Airport is a short drive from the centre of Tunis. A taxi ride to Avenue Habib Bourguiba should take about 15 minutes (depending on the traffic) and cost not more than 5 TD. Taxis are plentiful and the competition is fierce. An overpass under construction between Tunis and the airport will ease traffic and shorten the journey time. The price of a taxi ride is likely to go up at night or during the rush hour. Negotiate the cost before getting into the taxi. Alternatively, the No. 35 bus for Tunis leaves from the airport twice an hour. It takes about 30 minutes and terminates at Tunis Marine station on Avenue Habib Bourguiba. The bus

Tunisair aircraft at Tunis airport

also makes drop-off stops at Avenue Habib Thameur and Place Palestine. It costs about 1 TD. Tunis airport also has a direct bus link with Bizerte, Sousse and Monastir.

Just a short walk from the air terminal is a train that

Road sign for La Goulette harbour

connects Monastir's airport to Monastir, Mahdia and Sousse. From Jerba's airport take a taxi (about 5 TD), although many hotels on Jerba are happy to arrange transport for their guests.

TOUR OPERATORS

Over 60 tour operators offer packages to Tunisia from the UK and Ireland; many are specialists while others offer only flight and beachside hotel packages. In addition to hotel, apartment and self-catering accommodation, tour operators can arrange car rental, golf packages and private transfers. Holiday durations can vary from weekend breaks to month-long vacations. Special interest holidays range from golf, hiking, deep-sea diving and desert adventures on a camel to archaeology, gastronomy and thalassotherapy.

For those interested in a particular activity, booking through a specialist operator can work out cheaper than organizing something once in the country. The Tunisian Tourist Office in London can provide a comprehensive list of tour operators (see p247).

FERRIES

Another way of getting to Tunisia is by ferry. Between July and the end of September there is a regular car ferry service from Marseille to La Goulette – Tunisia's main passenger port. Two companies, **CTN** and **SNCM**, handle most of the crossings. In July there is also a weekly service to Bizerte. Throughout the rest of the year there are two to three services a week. The journey from Marseille takes 24 hours. It is also possible to sail to La Goulette from Italy. The ferries sail from Trápani (Sicily), and also from Genoa, Naples and La Spezia. The weekly service from La Spezia (100 km/62 miles southeast of Genoa) to La Goulette is much cheaper than sailing from either Genoa or Naples.

OVERLAND TRAVEL

Tunisian residents may travel to Tunisia overland, from Algeria or Libya. Foreign travellers will probably find this difficult due to visa restrictions.

There is a daily bus service from Tripoli to Tunis that takes about 16 hours. A daily bus service from Tripoli to Sfax takes about 10 hours. There is also a *louage* (shared taxi) that runs from Annaba in Algeria to Tunis's medina.

Although people do travel to Tunisia via Libya or Algeria, the border regions of these two countries can be dangerous. Furthermore, since the outbreak of the civil war in 1993 Algeria has been practically out of bounds to tourists.

A small ferry sailing to Jerba

DIRECTORY

AIRLINES

British Airways
Tel (71) 963 120 (Tunis).
Tel (71) 285 766 (airport).
www.britishairways.com

Nouvelair
Tel (01276) 600 100 (UK).
Tel (73) 520 600 (Tunis).
www.nouvelair.com.tn

Tunisair
24 Sackville St, London, W1S 3DS.
Tel (020) 7734 7644.
Tel (71) 336 500 (Tunis).
www.tunisair.com.tn

AIRPORTS

Tunis Carthage
Tel (71) 754 000 or 755 000.

Enfida Zine-el Abidine
Tel (73) 524 524.

Monastir Habib Bourguiba
Tel (73) 520 000.

UK TOUR OPERATORS

Aspects of Tunisia
Tel (020) 7836 4999.
www.aspectsoftunisia.co.uk

Cadogan Holidays
Tel (0845) 615 4390.
www.cadoganholidays.com

First Choice Holidays
Tel (0871) 200 7799.
www.firstchoice.co.uk

Sunway Holidays
Tel (01231) 1888.
www.sunway.ie

FERRY COMPANIES

Compagnie Tunisienne de Navigation (CTN)
Rue Dag Hammarskjöld 5, Tunis.
Tel (71) 341 777.
Fax (71) 345 736.
www.ctn.com.tn

SNCM
Tel (+33) 0891 701 801, (+33) 825 888 088.
www.sncm.fr

Tirrenia Navigazione
Tel (+39) 022 630 2803.
www.tirrenia.it

Travelling Around Tunisia

Tunisia has a well-developed road network. Air-conditioned buses provide transport links between most major towns. A more convenient way of travelling is by *louage* (shared taxi). These travel between many of the small towns and villages and operate more frequently than buses. On shorter routes to villages, visitors will need to take a taxi (only yellow ones). Much of the rail network (SNCFT) is devoted to freight. The passenger trains that do run, however, are comfortable and punctual. The main routes run south from Tunis to Sfax and Gabès. Tunisia has a number of internal flights, run by Sevenair. The most popular routes are those that connect Tunis with the south of the country.

Train crossing the main square in Sousse

TRAVELLING BY TRAIN

The Société Nationale des Chemins de Fer Tunisiens (SNCFT) has over 2,000 km (1,250 miles) of track, and was built by the French during the colonial period. The main routes run from Tunis: north to Bizerte (about 2 hours); west towards the Algerian border (about 6 hours); southwest to the Tell region (about 6 hours), and south to Sfax and Gabès, via Hammamet and Sousse. The most popular line is the one that links Tunis with Sfax and Gabès (via Sousse). There are six trains a day to Sfax and three to Gabès. The journey time is 5 hours and costs about 14 TD. One train a day runs to Metlaoui and Gafsa. About eight services a day run to Sousse; the journey takes 2 hours and the ticket costs about 6 TD. A journey to Hammamet takes one hour and costs about 4 TD.

There is a narrow gauge train that runs between Nabeul and Hammamet and stops in several places within the tourist zone. A ticket from Hammamet to Nabeul costs

Sfax railway station

about 400 millimes. Metro Sahel is another convenient service and runs between Sousse, Monastir and Mahdia.

A local service, called the TGM, runs from Tunis to many of its suburbs including Carthage, La Goulette and Sidi Bou Saïd.

Most Tunisian trains have two classes. First class is about 40 per cent more expensive than second class and is air-conditioned. Second class is usually very crowded and in order to be sure of a seat it is best to board the train at the first stop. Even the suburban trains include first class carriages, which are generally less crowded and have soft, padded seats.

Long-distance trains usually have an additional *Grand Confort* class. This is more expensive than first class and offers travellers slightly more exclusive compartments.

Long distance trains usually include a restaurant car, where a hot meal, sandwiches and drinks are available. When planning several train journeys, consider buying the Blue Card that gives unlimited travel within the country. These are valid for one, two or three weeks and can represent good value. The card is valid on all local and long-distance journeys on SNCFT trains. Costs are: one week – 30 TD (second class), 42 TD (first class); two weeks – 60 TD (second class), 84 TD (first class); three weeks – 90 TD (second class), 120 TD (first class). The blue card is sold at all main stations, plus some large hotels and travel agencies.

Timetable details are available in the daily press, although it is always best to check at the station in advance. It is essential to reserve a seat on mainline trains at holiday periods otherwise passengers may end up standing. There may be a small charge for making reservations in first class.

Sousse bus station

Colourful "Intercity" bus run by the SNTRI company

DIRECTORY

RAILWAY STATIONS

BIZERTE
Avenue Habib Bourguiba.
Tel (72) 431 071.

MONASTIR
Avenue Habib Bourguiba.
Tel (73) 460 755.

NABEUL
Avenue Habib Bourguiba.
Tel (72) 285 054.

SOUSSE
Blvd. Hassouna Ayach.
Tel (73 224 955.
Fax (73) 226 955.

TUNIS
Place Barcelone, Tunis
SNCFT 67 Avenue Farhat Hachet.
Tel (71) 259 977 or 254 427.

BUS STATIONS

TUNIS

**North Bus Station
Bab Saadoun**
Rue Nord de Bab Saadoun, Tunis.
Tel (71) 562 562 532.

**South Bus Station
Bab Alleoua**
Rue Sud de Bab el-Fellah, Tunis.
Tel (71) 399 391.

BUSES

The Société Nationale de Transport Rural et Interurbain (SNTRI) is the state-owned bus company, and runs services between most of Tunisia's towns. Services to the smaller towns run once a day. There are about 10 daily services from Tunis to Sousse, Hammamet and Sfax. The price of a bus ticket is comparable to a second-class train ticket. In the summer, due to the hot weather, long-distance buses sometimes travel at night. Buses are more comfortable than *louages* and offer plenty of space for passengers and their luggage. They are also air-conditioned. In addition to SNTRI, there are also a number of suburban carriers, serving various local villages and small towns. There are quite a number of these smaller companies and it can be difficult to obtain information about their schedules. Quite often one town is served by a number of carriers and the staff of one will not always know about the timetable of another carrier, even if they operate from the same bus station.

Tunis has two main bus stations. Bab Saadoun serves the north of the country and is at the bottom of Rue Sidi el-Bechir and Avenue 9 Avril. Bab Alleoua, sometimes also referred to as Bab el-Fellah, connects Tunis to the centre and south of the country and is just south of Place Barcelone. A transport link between the two stations is provided by the Nos. 50, 72 and 74 buses.

AIR TRAVEL

There are airports in Tunis, Enfida, Monastir, Sfax, Tozeur, Gabès, Gafsa, Tabarka and Jerba. The most popular routes are between Tunis and Jerba (several flights a day), Tunis and Sfax and Tunis and Tozeur. In the summer there are also flights to Gabès and Gafsa. A one-way ticket costs about 50 TD. There is also an air-taxi service, Tunisavia. This is often used by VIPs and businessmen and lands not only at the major airports, but also at a number of small regional ones.

LOUAGES

Shared taxis are a popular form of transport in Tunisia. *Louages* do not run to any particular schedule and depart only when they have a full complement of passengers (in practice one never need wait long). Though they are less comfortable than buses, they offer greater convenience. The price of a ride is only fractionally higher than that of a bus ticket. *Louage* stops are usually near bus and railway stations. There are two types of *louage* – those with a red stripe are allowed to travel all over Tunisia; the ones with blue stripes are permitted to travel only on local routes.

Tunis has three main *louage* stops. *Louages* departing from the square in front of the south station (Bab Alleoua) go to Cap Bon; the ones leaving from the stop at the east end of Rue Aid el-Jebbari travel south. From Place Sidi Bou Mendil yellow Algerian taxis marked with a white stripe go to Algeria. *Louages* with a yellow stripe are Libyan and those with a red stripe Tunisian.

Louage with a red stripe, licensed to travel anywhere in the country

Travelling by Car in Tunisia

Tunisia's road network is excellent, with clear signs and well-maintained surfaces for most of the country. The traffic regulations are almost the same as in Europe. The standard of driving is not always satisfactory, however, so you will need to be vigilant. There are numerous police patrols on the roads, and the introduction of radar surveillance has helped to reduce speeds. Generally the police do not stop tourists, but visitors should still carry their passports and driving licence with them. Hiring a rental car is an excellent way of exploring Tunisia, though it can be expensive.

Winding narrow roads around Toujane

A frequently-seen sign in Tunisia – Warning! Camels!

HIGHWAY CODE

Tunisia's highway code does not differ significantly from mainland Europe. Vehicles drive on the right, and overtake on the left. The road signs are clear and mostly bilingual (French and Arabic). The speed limit is 90 km/h (55 mph) on open roads; 50 km/h (30 mph) in towns and built-up areas. The speed limit on motorways is 110 km/h (70 mph). Seatbelts are supposed to be worn at all times in Tunisia. Frequent patrols and

heavy fines ensure that Tunisians rarely exceed speed limits, although drink-driving is not uncommon. Many inter-city roads are patrolled by radar detectors and highway patrol cars. The other main hazards on the roads come from straying animals, motorcycles and pedestrians.

ROAD SIGNS

In addition to the commonly seen road signs, there are warning signs with a picture of a camel, which are seen mostly in the south where camels may stray on to roads. Take heed, too, of the signs warning about the danger of wet surfaces during or after a period of heavy rainfall. Signs may be few and far between on minor roads.

ROADS

Most of the country's roads are well surfaced and reasonably straight. There are three motorways: from Tunis to Sfax, from Tunis to Bizerte and from Tunis to Beja.

Warning sign – Stop!

A-roads are known as *Routes Nationales* (RN), and B-roads are referred to as *Routes Regionales* (RR). Surface damage on RN roads is rare. Even on the RR roads, potholes are few and far between. Outside the summer season, however, some of the roads may become impassable due to rainfall. Roads in the south are not so good, but are still passable.

Driving on desert roads requires a four-wheel-drive vehicle. Whilst driving in the desert, always travel in a group of at least two cars (to assist each other in case of breakdown). Also bear in mind that desert roads can suddenly disappear if they get buried in the sand. When this happens it can be difficult to see in which direction to drive. Because of the dangers, trips to the desert are best undertaken with a Tunisian driver who knows the area.

TOWN DRIVING

Although Tunisian drivers are generally careful, pay particular attention to motorcycles and pedestrians when driving in towns. This is especially true during the rush hours, between 5 and 8pm and at night. Pedestrians can be disconcerting in towns, giving the impression that they have not seen oncoming vehicles. Drivers should use their horn if in doubt as to whether other road users are aware of their presence.

The crowded centre of Sousse

The situation can be worse when there is heavy rainfall. At these times it can be better to resort to walking instead.

MAPS

Road maps can be purchased from hotel shops and bookstores. Generally, however, the maps published by the ONTT (Tunisian Tourist Bureau) are clear and, for the most part, accurate and include additional information in English and French relating to historic sites. The range published by the ONTT includes maps of Carthage and Tunis's medina. The ONTT offices can also provide street maps of a number of the other most popular towns. When travelling by car around Tunisia purchase a more detailed road map before leaving. Michelin produces a good one (No. 956), as do Freytag and Berndt. Both are on a scale of 1:800,000 and provide information on Tunisia's major and minor roads.

BUYING PETROL

The price of fuel in Tunisia is cheap by European standards – though prices do fluctuate. One litre of super (high octane) fuel costs about 1200 millimes; lead-free petrol costs approximately 1350 millimes and is available throughout Tunisia; diesel is 950 millimes a litre. Generally, there are no problems with finding some-where to fill up in Tunisia, even on Sunday or at night.

Information on parking in the centre of Tunis

CAR RENTAL

Car hire firms are in all of the major towns and tourist resorts. Their services are rather expensive, but hiring a car enables you to visit many interesting and less accessible parts of the country.

There should be no problem with finding a major rental firm; Avis, Azur, Europcar and Hertz all have offices in Tunis and elsewhere. The best option, however, is provided by local firms – these are cheaper and are often more willing to strike a deal. Prices start from about 50 TD per day for a small car, plus 250 millimes for each kilometre travelled. Though it may mean having to pay a higher daily rate, it can work out far cheaper to hire a car from a company that does not charge extra for the distance travelled, especially if intending to use the car for long journeys.

Rental companies will require that the driver be over 21 years old and hold a licence that has been valid for at least a year.

When hiring a car it is imperative to check that the vehicle documents include an accident report form. In case

of an accident both parties are required to complete such a report. Visitors who do not fill out the form may be liable for the costs, even if the accident was not their fault.

BREAKDOWNS AND ACCIDENTS

Tunisia has no roadside telephones or road emergency services. In case of a breakdown ask another driver for a tow to the nearest town or village where there is a garage able to repair the car. Alternatively, it may be necessary to wait for a passing police patrol. Repair services are cheap in Tunisia, but parts can be expensive.

In the case of a serious accident, such as one involving injury to a pedestrian, the driver should endeavour to contact the police. The driver may be detained and should contact his or her Embassy in Tunis as soon as possible.

Libyan petrol on sale in southern Tunisia

Getting Around Tunis

Transport within Tunis includes a variety of options. The furthest corners of the city should be accessible without any problem, if not by public transport, then by taking a taxi, which is cheap by European standards. Tunis's medina is partly pedestrianized and can easily be explored on foot. Travelling to seaside resorts close to the capital is also quite easy. The best way of getting to them is by using the fast TGM train that stops near the town centre.

A tram – one of the best means of getting about in Tunis

TRAMS

Trams are probably the most convenient way of moving around Tunis. This network, known as *métro leger*, runs down the middle of the street and has green paintwork with distinctive white and blue stripes. The city's trams are efficient and not particularly expensive, though they can be crowded, especially at peak times.

Five main lines run to various parts of Tunis. All except No. 5 pass through the centre. Since many streets in central Tunis are one-way, the tram often returns by a different route (usually along a parallel street). Tickets must be purchased before boarding the tram and are available from the kiosks at the entrance to each station. The standard fare is 380 millimes.

Line No. 1 runs from Tunis, Marine via Place Barcelone, to Bab Alleoua, at the south end of the town. Bab Alleoua is the best stop for the southern bus station.

Line No. 2 runs from Place de la République and heads north towards Ariana.

Line No. 3 runs from Place Barcelone, via Place de la République, to Ibn Khaldoun.

Line No. 4 starts by Tunis Marine and runs westwards, through Place de la République. This line is particularly convenient for the Bardo Museum (Bardo) and the north station – Saadoun; alight at Bouchoucha.

Line No. 5 is an extension of line No. 3, and runs from Ibn Khaldoun to El-Intilaka.

BUSES

Although Tunis's buses are modern and in better condition than those in other major towns of the country, travelling by them is not a particularly pleasurable experience, particularly since they are often even more crowded than the trams.

The bus number and the direction in which it is heading are usually written in Arabic and placed at the rear of the bus by the entry door. The Latin alphabet is used only on those buses serving the most popular tourist destinations, such as the Bardo Museum or the airport. On these buses the Latin number is displayed at the front.

There are three main stops in Tunis. These are Tunis Marine, situated close to the TGM train stop at the end of Avenue Habib Bourguiba; the stop at Place Barcelone near the railway station and the stop in Jardin Thameur, near the Passage. Bus No. 3 begins at Tunis Marine and runs to the Bardo Museum. Transport to the airport is provided by the No. 35 bus, which also departs from the Tunis Marine stop.

Tickets are fairly cheap, costing about 380 millimes and are purchased on the bus. Alternatively, a book of tickets is available from Tunis Marine bus station.

TAXIS

Tunis's yellow taxis are a cheap and efficient means of getting about. Many locals use them and it can sometimes be hard to find a free cab for this reason. All taxis are fitted with meters. In general, the drivers stick to the meter, apart from journeys to the airport that start from bus stations or the railway station. A trip from the town centre to the airport will cost about 5 TD; a taxi to the Bardo Museum will cost about 3 TD. At night (from 9pm–5am) the prices can be slightly more. Always check that the meter has been activated, though it is rare that a taxi driver will attempt to swindle his customer.

Taxis can be hailed from the side of the road, just as they can in other major cities. It is worth paying attention to the condition of the car, however. Some of Tunis's taxis are old and rather dilapidated. Most, however, are new and well maintained. It is worthwhile holding out for a new model, particularly if intending to travel a bit further, to Sidi Bou Saïd or Carthage for instance.

"Collective Urban Taxis" (called *Nakel Jamai*) are now found on the streets of Tunis. They are yellow with a distinctive blue stripe. Popular with locals, they may also be used by visitors.

A typical Tunisian yellow taxi

ما عدا المسلمين
SAUF MUSULMANS
NUR MOSLEM
ONLY MUSLEMS

A sign prohibiting entry to a mosque for non-Muslims

DRIVING

Driving in Tunis is not a good idea. Unless there is no alternative, don't even consider it. Despite being wide, all the main streets of town get congested. Tunis's drivers show little respect for marked traffic lanes and it often happens that a three-lane road suddenly becomes an impromptu five-lane one. Police help or understanding cannot be counted on either. Policemen only try to ease the traffic flow at the most congested junctions. If stuck in traffic, pay particular attention to motorcycles and pedestrians that often weave in and out of the stationary cars with little apparent concern for their own safety.

Although Tunis's drivers undoubtedly break many regulations, it is very rare for them to break the speed limit. If attempting to drive in town, remember that many streets are one-way, and getting to a destination may not be as simple as it appears from the map. There may also be serious problems when parking. Pay close attention to the paid parking zones, as there are severe fines for not paying the required amount.

WALKING

The centre of Tunis, like most towns in Tunisia, is fairly compact. At its heart is the medina, much of which is closed to traffic. A stroll around the medina can be a real pleasure and enables visitors to soak up the ancient atmosphere at a leisurely pace. In parts of the medina where the streets are relatively wide, visitors should be on the alert for scooters or delivery vans, which can arrive at speed. Tunis's Ville Nouvelle is also suitable for exploring on foot. The only problem with this area is the heat in summer. To avoid heat exhaustion, walk on the shady side of the street and carry a bottle of mineral water. Anyone who feels tired should sit down in a café and have a drink.

Outside Tunis, there is no sense in walking the large distances that separate many of the towns from the tourist zones, unless it is to walk along the seashore.

موزع تذاكر
HORODATEUR

"Pay Here" sign for a public car park

GUIDES

The quality of service provided by Tunisian guides varies tremendously. When somebody offers to act as a guide for free, it is practically certain that the person works for a carpet shop or a store selling some other kind of merchandise. The trip will therefore end very quickly in one of the medina's markets. However, employing guides who work at archaeological sites, such as Dougga or Bulla Regis, can be particularly useful if the details of the site and its history are of particular interest.

TGM TRAINS

An excellent way of exploring Tunis's environs and the coast of Carthage is by taking the TGM train that links the centre of Tunis with Carthage, Sidi Bou Saïd and the main beaches. The train leaves from the end of Avenue Bourguiba (Tunis Marine station). The journey to the final station (La Marsa) takes about 35 minutes. The first station after crossing the causeway is Le Bac. Confusingly, Aeroport, the sixth stop, has nothing to do with the airport as TGM trains do not run there. Salammbô has a nice beach, while Carthage Byrsa is the main stop for Carthage's Museum and Byrsa Hill. Sidi Bou Saïd (*see pp96–7*) is an excellent stopping-off point, as is La Marsa, which has the best beach in the vicinity of Tunis.

The ticket costs about 600–800 millimes. Many people opt for the first-class ticket, which is only slightly more expensive. The first train on a weekday leaves before 4am, and the last runs about half past midnight (slightly later at weekends). The departure times of the last trains should, however, be checked at the station – in Tunis, Sidi Bou Saïd or La Marsa.

Station on the suburban TGM line

General Index

Acknowledgments

Dorling Kindersley would like to thank the following people whose contribution and assistance have made the preparation of this book possible.

Publisher
Douglas Amrine
Publishing Manager
Kate Poole
Managing Editor
Vicki Ingle
Senior Editor
Jacky Jackson
Cartography
Uma Battacharya, Mohammad Hassan, Jasneet Kaur, Casper Morris
DTP
Vinod Harish, Vincent Kurien, Azeem Siddiqui, Conrad Van Dyk
Consultant
Mike Gerrard
Factchecker
David Bond
Proofreader
Stewart Wild
Indexer
Helen Peters
Additional Contributors
Sylvie Franquet, Mike Gerrard
Additional Photography
Ian O'Leary
Additional Picture Research
Rachel Barber, Ellen Root
Design and Editorial Assistance
Nadia Bonomally, Simon Davis, Nicola Erdpresser, Camilla Gersh, Claire Jones, Carly Madden, Lesley Mendoza, Helen Partington, Conrad van Dyk

Special Assistance
Wiedza and Życie would like to thank the following persons and organizations for their help in the preparation of this guide:
Faical Aouni; Zbigniew Dybowski, Biuro Podróży Kredytowa 2, Warszawa; Abdelfettach Gaida, Raouf Ghazzai, Odyssée Resort, Zarzis; Pawel Kulesza, ONTT in Warsaw; Joanna Nowowiejska-Moskal, ONTT in Warsaw; Startours, Hammam-Sousse; Katarzyna Wierzba, ONTT in Warsaw.

The Publisher would also like to thank all persons and organizations for their permission to reproduce photographs of their property and for allowing the use of photographs from their archives.
Bijouterie Bel Hadj Younes Frères, Midoun; Bijouterie du Musée el-Kobba, Sousse; Corbis/Agencja Free in Warsaw (Maciej Sztyk, Łukasz Wyrzykowski, Aleksandra Żymełka); Centre Culturel d'Animation Touristique Dar Houidi, Nefta; La Grotte, Souk Erebaa, Sousse; Military Museum of the Mareth Line, Mareth; Musée Dar Essid, Sousse; Musée Guellala, Jerba; Ocean-Photos (Carlos Minguell); Scoop Organisation (Mourad Mathari); Tunisair in Warsaw; ZOOM s.c.

Picture Credits
t=top; tl=top left; tc=top centre; tr=top right; c=centre; cl=centre left; cr=centre right; cb=centre below; ca=centre above; clb=centre left below; crb=centre right below; cla=centre left above; cra=centre right above; b=bottom; bl=bottom left; br=bottom right; bla=bottom left above; bra=bottom right above; blb=bottom left below; bcb=bottom centre below; brb=bottom right below; bcl=bottom centre left; bcr=bottom centre right; ra=right above; la=left above.

4Corners Images: Bildagentur Huber/R. Schmid 11tr; Alamy Images: Blaine Harrington III front end paper Rbc, 174, Greg Balfour Evans 158-159, Simon Horswell 268cla, IMAGEiN 269tl, Yadid Levy 10cla; Corbis: 28-29, 34c, 35t, 39ca, 39cr, 39cb, 46t, 47t, 48t, 49dp, 50cla, 53t, 53c, 55t, 55c, 55b, 56t, 53c, 56cb, 56bl, 56br, 57c, 57b, 58t, 58c, 59ca, 81c, 102b, 106bl, 143br, 173t, 173b, 199bl, 209c, 220b, 303c, 303b; Shean Adey 137cb; Theo Allofs 137ca; Philip de Bay 29br; Nial Benvie 135clb; Yann Arthus-Bertrand 12, 13t, 13b, 196t, 204-205, 229t; Michael de Boys 39b; Margareth Courtney-Clarke 32t, 32b, 33b; Nigel J. Dennis 135cla, 135clb; Bernard and Catherine Desjeux 42t, 114-115, 219b; Rick Ergenbright 38c, 40b, 270; D. Robert Franz 135bl, 137t, 227b; Stephen Frink 127bl; Lowell Georgia 20b; Richard Hamilton Smith 60-61; Klaus Honal 23ca; Erick Hosking 135br; Peter Johnson 136cb; Wolfgang Kaehler 181c; Steve Kaufman 227t; 227clb; Douglas Kirkland 35b; David Lees 46c; Michael S. Lewis 199cr; Peter Lillie 227clb; Araldo de Luca 44; Francoise de Mulder 39t; Christine Osborne 110t; photocuisine/Roulier/Turiot/ 269c; Fulvio Roiter 33ca; Hans Georg Roth 28b, 41b, 173clb, 173crb, 221t; Kevin Schafer 22c; Michael T. Sedman 306t; Jonathan Selkowitz 95b; Michael Setboun 183cla, 183clb, 183cr, 183br; Sean Sexton 56ca; Monika Smith 26lw; William Thompson 199ca; Roger Tidman 136ca, 227cra; Ruggero Vanni 11br, 27c; Tim De Waele 302c; Patrick Ward 32c, 32-33; John Watkins 135cra, 136t; Kurt-Michael Westermann 173cra; Nik Wheeler 149b, 183bl; Martin B. Withers 135t; Roger Wood 15t, 29bl, 33t, 46b, 54cl, 220c, 231c; Inge Yspeert 38b, 191, 203br; Hemispheres Images: Stéphane Frances 11cl, Franck Guiziou 10br; Piotr Kiedrowski: 77b, 97c, 266b; Andrzej Lisowski: 29tr, 35c, 41t, 42b, 78b, 98cra, 98br, 142t, 143t, 143ca, 203bl, 209b, 292c, 298ca, 298cb; Grzegorz Micuła: 5cl, 16c, 19c, 22cl, 148br, 179b, 193, 198b, 199t, 206b, 247t, 270cla, 324ca; Carlos Minguell: 127tl, 127tr, 127cl, 127cr, 127br; Izabella Mościcka: 93b, 115c, 154t, 154cb, 244t, 304b, 318c, 319t, 320cb, 323t; Robert D. Pasieczny: 19b; Socopa: 299b; Photolibrary: Photononstop/ Sébastien Boisse 10tc; Tunisair: 320b.

Jacket: Front: Corbis: Hemis/Paule Seux. Back: Alamy Images: Harry Lands 0lb; AWL Images: Peter Adams cla; FAN Travel Stock tl; Travel Pix Collection bl. Spine: Corbis: Hemis/Paule Seux t.
All other images Dorling Kindersley
For further information see: www.dkimages.com

SPECIAL EDITIONS OF DK TRAVEL GUIDES

DK Travel Guides can be purchased in bulk quantities at discounted prices for use in promotions or as premiums. We are also able to offer special editions and personalized jackets, corporate imprints, and excerpts from all of our books, tailored specifically to meet your own needs.

To find out more, please contact:
(in the United States) **SpecialSales@dk.com**
(in the UK) **travelspecialsales@uk.dk.com**
(in Canada) DK Special Sales at **general@tourmaline.ca**
(in Australia) **business.development@pearson.com.au**

Glossary

Abbasids: Rulers of the Arab Empire from AD 749–1258.

Aghlabids: Ninth-century Arab dynasty that ruled Tunisia from Kairouan.

Aisha: the third and favourite wife of the Prophet Mohammed, who unsuccessfully opposed the fourth caliph, Ali.

Al-Hasan and Al-Husayn: sons of Ali, revered as Shia martyrs.

Ali: Ali ibn Abi Talib, the fourth orthodox caliph, cousin and son-in-law of the Prophet Mohammed, husband of his daughter Fatima. He originated the greatest split in the history of Islam – into Sunni and Shia Muslims. According to the Shia tradition he was endowed with spiritual gifts and the power to perform miracles. To Shias he is virtually god incarnate.

Allah: the highest and the only god in the Muslim religion, the creator of the world and its people. He is believed to be omnipotent, omnipresent and merciful. He has 99 names by which he may be addressed.

alloucha: carpets produced in beige and brown, or black and white colours with a medallion pattern in a shape of a stylized octagon with floral design.

Almoravids: Berber dynasty from Morocco that invaded Tunisia in the 12th century.

Baal Hammon: the most important god in the Phoenician (later Punic) pantheon, often identified with Saturn.

bab: gate.

balgha: traditional slippers with flattened toe-ends.

baraka: divine blessing passed down from parent to child; the power to work miracles, may be obtained by pilgrimage.

barnoose: wide, spacious cloak worn by men in Arab countries.

basilica: Roman administration building, early Christian church.

Berbers: non-Arab, indigenous inhabitants of Tunisia with their own distinctive language, culture and customs.

bey: title of a provincial governor in the Ottoman Empire. During the Ottoman era it was used by the Tunisian rulers.

bir: well.

bismillah: a popular Muslim expression – "Bismi Allah ar-rahmani ar-rahim" (In the name of Allah the Beneficient,

the Merciful). Every *sura* or chapter of the Koran begins with it. Uttered by Muslims prior to any activity such as meals or travel. It is also a popular ornamental motif on ceramics and in architecture, etc.

borj: turret or tower that is set in the walls of fortified houses and castles.

boukha: a clear alcoholic spirit made from figs.

brik: Tunisian snack, a kind of pastry.

burnous: hooded cloak made of thick wool, worn by Arab men.

caliph: Muslim chief, title designating Mohammed's successor.

capitol: Roman town's principal temple.

caravanserai: see *fondouk*.

chamsa: hand of Fatima – a talisman that symbolizes five pillars of faith, five daily prayers, five holy nights, etc.

chechia: red cap with silk tassle.

chicha: hookah or hubble-bubble pipe used for smoking tobacco.

chorba: delicious soup with noodles, normally made of chicken stock.

chott: salt lake or marshland.

corsairs: pirates, active on the North African coast from the 16th to the 19th century.

couscous: a dish made of steamed semolina that is served as the main course with boiled mutton, vegetables and spices.

dar: house, palace or residence.

dawwar: a circle of tents with which tribesmen surrounded their chieftain's abode, creating a mini-state. It was sovereign and autonomous.

deglet ennour: a variety of dates.

diwan: sultan's privy council in the former Turkish state, alternatively spelled divan.

djellaba: long, loose garment worn by Tunisian women.

driba: an outer entrance room in a *dar*, used for receiving callers.

emir: governor or military leader.

erg: expanse of desert sand.

Fatima: Mohammed's only daughter and the wife of Ali. In the Muslim tradition she originated the Fatimid dynasty. Fatima is the subject of many legends which have led to a belief in her protective powers.

Fatimids: Muslim dynasty founded by Fatima that replaced the Aghlabids and ruled Tunisia from AD 909 to 1171.

fondouk: a type of inn, also known as a *caravanserai*, that was used as a hotel by journeying merchant caravans.

fouta: cotton towel provided in a hammam.

fula: a triangular tattoo placed on a Berber woman's chin.

gargotte: small, inexpensive restaurant serving basic food.

ghorfa: originally a *ksar*'s granary. The cells, built cylindrically around a courtyard, later began to serve as dwellings.

guetiffa: thick-pile carpets used by Berber tribes.

hadith: tale of deeds and teachings of the Prophet Mohammed as reported by his companions; source of religious knowledge for Muslims.

hadj: pilgrimage to Mecca, one of the five pillars of Islam.

hamada: rocky desert.

hammam: public steam bath.

Hanefite: one of four schools of orthodox Sunni Islam.

harissa: spicy sauce made of dried red chillies, garlic, spices, olive oil and salt.

henna: a dye obtained from privet leaves which is used by the Berbers for marking the skin.

hijab: veil or headscarf worn by Muslim women in the presence of strangers.

hijra: emigration of Mohammed and his early followers from Mecca to Medina in AD 622. It is also the name of the Muslim calendar.

houch: courtyard of a troglodyte house carved in soft rock.

Husaynids: dynasty that ruled Tunisia from 1705 to 1957.

Ibadites: Offshoot of Kharajite sect found on Jerba and also in parts of Algeria.

Ifriqiyya: term used to describe Africa by the Romans.

imam: a learned Muslim cleric, prophet and religious leader of the Shia, caliph, spiritual and lay leader of Islam.

Isa: Islamic name for Jesus Christ, who is regarded by Muslims as a noble and honourable messenger sent to reveal the coming of the Prophet Mohammed.

Jamaa mosque: from the Arabic "jam", meaning to "gather things". Usually the Great Mosque, it was initially the only mosque with a *minbar*.

jirak: a strong tobacco mix smoked in a *chicha*.

kamounia: an aromatic meat stew.

kasbah: castle, fortress.

Khadija: the first wife of the Prophet Mohammed.

Kharijites: early sect of Islam which won Berber support.

khlela: a Berber pin made of silver; often believed to have magic properties.

khutba: traditional sermon preached on Fridays by the *imam*.

Koran: the holy book of Islam.

koubba: a dome that often covers the tomb of a marabout.

ksar: fortified Berber village.

louage: shared taxi.

Maghreb: term used to describe northwestern section of Africa that includes Morocco, Algeria and Tunisia.

mahari: camelback expedition to the desert lasting several days. Those taking part often sleep in Bedouin tents or *ghorfas*.

mahdi: in the Arab tradition "the One who is led by God" – a spiritual leader endowed with power to bring about religious revival, and restore order.

Malekite: sect of orthodox Sunni Islam founded in the 8th century.

malouf: Tunisian folk music.

marabout: Islamic holy man and also his place of burial.

mashrabiyya: wooden latticework panel used in the windows of mosques and houses.

medersa: residential Islamic school. A type of Muslim college that is often built around a courtyard and attached to a mosque.

medina: traditional Arab town or a town's oldest part.

Medina: also known as Madinat an-Nabi (Town of the Prophet), or Madinat el-Munawwara (City of Light). It is situated 300 km (186 miles) north of Mecca. The Prophet and his followers found refuge there after fleeing Mecca.

melya: an attire worn by Berber women, consisting of a draped length of cloth held by a belt and fastened at the shoulder.

menzel: a traditional fortified farm compound.

mergoum: lightweight carpets of Berber origin with vivid colours and geometric patterns.

mihrab: niche found in a mosque that points in the direction of Mecca, and therefore prayer.

minaret: tower of a mosque from which the muezzin calls the faithful to prayer.

minbar: pulpit in a mosque, from which the *imam* delivers his homily during Friday prayers.

Mohammed: (*c*.570–632), the messenger of Islam and creator of the Arab state. He experienced his first revelations at the age of about 40 (AD 610). These are collected together in the Koran.

mosque: Arab place of worship and a house of prayer. It usually consists of a courtyard, a minaret and a prayer-hall.

muedhim (muezzin): person who calls the faithful to prayer from the minaret. In the early days of Islam the calls were made from the roofs of mosques.

mukarnas: a distinctive ornamental element of the interior design in Muslim architecture (in the shape of a stalactite).

mullah: a Muslim theologian and scholar. Also a teacher, and an interpreter of religious law and Islamic doctrines.

Muradids: hereditary line of beys that ruled Tunisia during the 17th century.

Musa: The Arabic name for Moses. The Koran presents him as one of many predecessors of Mohammed.

oued: river that is often dry.

Phoenicians: seafaring and trading nation that dominated the Mediterranean in the 1st century BC; the founders of Carthage.

Protectorate: period of French control over Tunisia from 1881–1956.

Punic: Phoenician culture.

qibla: the direction (towards the Al-Kaaba temple in Mecca) in which Muslims turn when saying their prayers; in mosques it is usually indicated by the *mihrab*.

Ramadan: the ninth month of the Muslim lunar calendar (numbering 354 days and eight hours). Also a period of fasting.

reg: stony desert.

ribat: fortified Muslim monastery that is surrounded by defensive walls including watchtowers. Inside is the prayer hall (and sometimes a mosque).

salat: obligatory prayer said five times a day. It is one of the five pillars of Islam.

sa'alik: knight errant of the desert, an exile expelled by the tribes.

They congregated into groups in order to survive.

sawm: fast during Ramadan, one of the five pillars of Islam.

sebkha: salt flat.

serir: stony desert.

shahada: a proclamation of faith, one of the five pillars of Islam.

shheelee: warm or hot sirocco wind.

Shia: the smaller branch of Islam. Its followers regard Ali as the true *imam*.

sidi: Muslim leader, sir. This title is accorded to a Muslim of noble birth or outstanding merits.

sirat: in Arab literature a knightly episode recounting historic events, fantasy or legendary tales and romances.

souk: market place or covered bazaar that is organized into areas according to the goods on sale.

Sufi: ascetic sect of Islam which places an emphasis on spiritual development rather than on a study of the Koran.

Suleyman: in Muslim tradition Suleyman is endowed with magic powers; he knows the language of birds, is able to control the wind, and rules over the earth and air spirits.

Sunni: the main branch of Islam, created by followers of the Ummayyad caliphate.

sura: verse of the Koran.

Tanit: goddess in the Punic pantheon associated with the cult of Baal Hammon. She is also the patron of Carthage.

tesserae: small pieces of brick, glass or marble smoothed round the edges and used for laying mosaics.

tourbet: mausoleum.

washm: the first tattoo given to a child soon after birth. It is usually placed on the cheeks or on the forehead.

wikala: a stately *caravanserai* for wealthy merchants.

zakat: the giving of alms to the poor, one of the five pillars of Islam.

zarbia: knotted carpets with geometric patterns, produced in a mixture of red, green and blue colours.

zaouia: a tomb for a good man or building – a dwelling place of people who devote their lives to spiritual practices, a sanctuary of Sufi mystics.

Phrase Book

In Emergency

Help!	Au secours!	oh se**koor**
Stop!	Arrêtez!	aret-**ay**
Call a	Appelez un	apuh-**lay** uñ
doctor!	médecin!	medsañ
Call an	Appelez une	apuh-**lay** oon
ambulance!	ambulance!	oñboo-**loñs**
Call the	Appelez la	apuh-**lay** lah
police!	police!	poh-**lees**
Call the fire	Appelez les	apuh-**lay** leh
department!	pompiers!	poñ-**peeyay**
Where is the	Où est le téléphone	oo ay luh tehleh**fon**
nearest telephone?	le plus proche?	luh ploo **prosh**
Where is the	Où est l'hôpital	oo ay l'**opee**tal luh
nearest hospital?	le plus proche?	ploo **prosh**

Communication Essentials

Yes	Oui	wee
No	Non	noñ
Please	S'il vous plaît	seel voo **play**
Thank you	Merci	mer-**see**
Excuse me	Excusez-moi	exkoo-**zay** mwah
Hello	Bonjour	boñzhoor
Goodbye	Au revoir	oh ruh-**vwar**
Good night	Bonsoir	boñ-**swar**
Morning	Le matin	matañ
Afternoon	L'après-midi	l'apreh-**meedee**
Evening	Le soir	swar
Yesterday	Hier	eeyehr
Today	Aujourd'hui	oh-zhoor-**dwee**
Tomorrow	Demain	duhmañ
Here	Ici	ee-see
There	Là	lah
What?	Quel, quelle?	kel, kel
When?	Quand?	koñ
Why?	Pourquoi?	poor-**kwah**
Where?	Où?	oo

Useful Phrases

How are you?	Comment allez-vous?	kom-moñ ta**lay voo**
Very well,	Très bien,	treh byañ,
thank you.	merci.	mer-**see**
Pleased to	Enchanté de faire	oñshoñ-**tay** duh fehr
meet you.	votre connaissance.	votr kon-ay-**sans**
See you soon.	À bientôt.	byañ-**toh**
That's fine	Voilà qui est parfait	vwalah kee ay par**fay**
Where is/are...?	Où est/sont...?	oo ay/soñ
How far	Combien de	kom-**byañ** duh keelo-
is it to...?	kilomètres d'ici à...?	metr d'ee-see ah
Which	Quelle est la	kel ay lah **deer**-
way to...?	direction pour...?	ek-**syoñ** poor
Do you speak	Parlez-vous	par-lay voo
English?	anglais?	oñg-**lay**
I don't	Je ne	zhuh nuh kom-
understand.	comprends pas.	**proñ** pah
Could you	Pouvez-vous parler	poo-**vay** voo par-**lay**
speak slowly	moins vite s'il	mwañ veet seel
please?	vous plaît.	voo play
I'm sorry.	Excusez-moi.	exkoo-**zay** mwah

Useful Words

big	grand	groñ
small	petit	puh-**tee**
hot	chaud	show
cold	froid	frwah
good	bon	boñ
bad	mauvais	moh-**veh**
enough	assez	assay
well	bien	byañ
open	ouvert	oo-**ver**
closed	fermé	fer-**meh**
left	gauche	gohsh
right	droit	drwah
straight ahead	tout droit	too drwah
near	près	preh
far	loin	lwañ
up	en haut	oñ **oh**
down	en bas	oñ **bah**
early	de bonne heure	duh bon **urr**
late	en retard	oñ ruh-**tar**
entrance	l'entrée	l'on-**tray**
exit	la sortie	sor-**tee**
toilet	les toilettes, les WC	twah-let, vay-**see**
free, unoccupied	libre	leebr
free, no charge	gratuit	grah-**twee**

Making a Telephone Call

I'd like to place a	Je voudrais faire	zhuh voo-dreh fehr
long-distance call.	un interurbain.	uñ añter-oorbañ
I'll try again	Je rappelerai	zhuh rapel-
later.	plus tard.	eray ploo tar
Can I leave a	Est-ce que je peux	es-keh zhuh puh
message?	laisser un message?	leh-**say** uñ mehsazh
Hold on.	Ne quittez pas,	nuh kee-**tay** pah
	s'il vous plaît.	seel voo play
Could you speak	Pouvez-vous parler	poo-**vay** voo par-
up a little please?	un peu plus fort?	lay uñ puh ploo for
local call	la communication	komoonikah-
	locale	**syoñ** low-**kal**

Shopping

How much	C'est combien	say kom-**byañ**
does this cost?	s'il vous plaît?	seel voo play
I would like ...	je voudrais...	zhuh voo-**dray**
Do you have?	Est-ce que vous avez?	es-**kuh** voo zavay
I'm just	Je regarde	zhuh ruh**gar**
looking.	seulement.	suhl**moñ**
Do you take	Est-ce que vous	es-**kuh** voo
credit cards?	acceptez les cartes	zaksept-**ay** leh kart
	de crédit?	duh kreh-**dee**
Do you take	Est-ce que vous	es-**kuh** voo
travellers'	acceptez les	zaksept-**ay** leh
checks?	chèques de voyage?	shek duh vwa**yazh**
What time do	À quelle heure vous	ah kel urr voo
you open/close?	êtes ouvert/fermé?	zet oo-**ver**/fer-**may**
This one.	Celui-ci.	suhl-wee-**see**
That one.	Celui-là.	suhl-wee-**lah**
expensive	cher	shehr
cheap	pas cher,	pah shehr,
	bon marché	boñ mar-**shay**
size, clothes	la taille	tye

Types of Shops

bakery	la boulangerie	booloñ-**zhuree**
bank	la banque	boñk
chemist	la pharmacie	farmah-**see**
grocery	l'alimentation	alee-moñta-**syoñ**
hairdresser	le coiffeur	kwa**fuhr**
market	le marché	marsh-**ay**
newsstand	le magasin de	maga-**zañ** duh
	journaux	zhoor-**no**
post office	la poste	pohst
supermarket	le supermarché	soo pehr-**marshay**
tobacconist	le tabac	tabah

Sightseeing

bus station	la gare routière	gahr roo-tee-**yehr**
library	la bibliothèque	beeb**leeo**-tek
museum	le musée	moo-**zay**
tourist	les renseignements	roñsayn-**moñ** too-
information	touristiques, le	rees-**teek**, sandee-
office	syndicat d'initiative	ka d'eenee-sya**teev**
train station	la gare (SNCF)	gahr (es-en-say-**ef**)
public holiday	jour férié	zhoor fehree-**ay**

Staying in a Hotel

Do you have a	Est-ce que vous	es-**kuh** voo-**zavay**
vacant room?	avez une chambre?	oon shambr
double room,	la chambre à deux	shambr ah duh
with double bed	personnes, avec	pehr-**son** avek un
	un grand lit	gronñ lee
twin room	la chambre à	shambr ah
	deux lits	duh lee
single room	la chambre à	shambr ah
	une personne	oon pehr-**son**
room with a	la chambre avec	shambr avek
bath, shower	salle de bains,	sal duh bañ,
	une douche	oon doosh
I have a	J'ai fait une	zhay fay oon
reservation.	réservation.	rayzehrva-**syoñ**

Eating Out

Have you	Avez-vous une	avay-**voo** oon
got a table?	table libre?	tahbl leebr
I want to	Je voudrais	zhuh voo-**dray**
reserve a table.	réserver une table.	rayzehr-**vay** oon
		tahbl
The bill	L'addition s'il	l'adee-**syoñ** seel
please.	vous plaît.	voo **play**

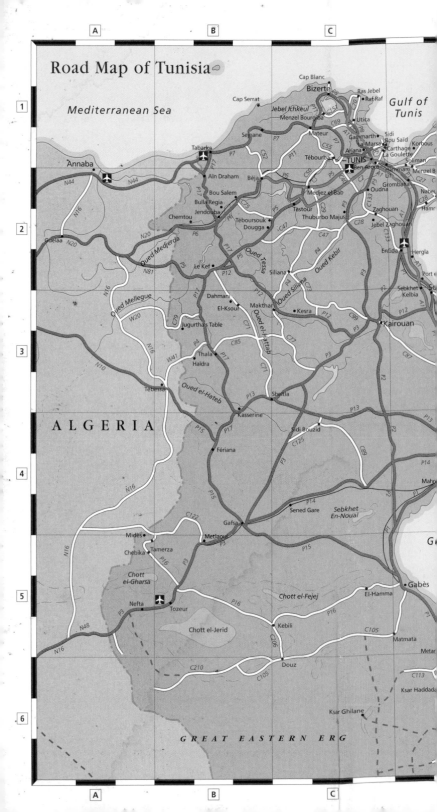

Road Map of Tunisia

Mediterranean Sea

Gulf of Tunis

Cap Blanc
Bizerte
Ras Jebel
Raf Raf
Cap Serrat
Jebel Ichkeul
Menzel Bourgiba
Mateur
Gammarth
Sidi
Bou Saïd
Korbous
Selnane
Utica
Ariana
Carthage
La Goulette
Soliman
Menzel B
Tabarka
Téboursba
TUNIS
Ben Arous
Hammam
Ain Draham
Béja
Medjez el-Bab
Oudna
Grombalia
Nabel
Bou Salem
Testour
Zaghouan
Hamr
Bulla Regia
Jendouba
Thuburbo Majus
Jebel Zaghouan
Chemtou
Téboursouk
Dougga
Enfida
Hergla
Guelaa
Port
Oued Medjerda
Le Kef
Siliana
Sebkhet
Kelbia
So
Oued Mellegue
Dahmani
Makthar
Kesra
Kairouan
El-Ksour
Jugurtha's Table
Thala
Haidra
Sbeitla
Tébessa
Oued el-Hateb
Kasserine
Sidi Bouzid
ALGERIA
Fériana
Sened Gare
Sebkhet
En-Noual
Mahr
Gafsa
G
Mides
Metlaoui
Chebika
Tamerza
Chott
el-Gharsa
Chott el-Fejej
El-Hamma
Gabès
Nefta
Tozeur
Kebili
Matmata
Chott el-Jerid
Douz
Metar
Ksar Haddada
Ksar Ghilane
GREAT EASTERN ERG

Annaba